DATE DUE

BIBLIOGRAPHY OF EARLY AMERICAN ARCHITECTURE

University of Illinois Press   Urbana · Chicago · London   1968

Bibliography
of Early American
Architecture

Writings on Architecture Constructed Before 1860
in Eastern and Central United States

by Frank J. Roos, Jr.

Preface

Although this new edition is published, as was the original book, in a time
of great unrest, it is our hope that it may contribute to a sense of continuity.
It is intended to furnish a further research tool for another generation of
students of Early American architecture, working to preserve something of
our heritage.

The original termination date of 1860 has been adhered to for the listings,
and when there is a difference in dates in titles of some of the structures, the
author's dates have been used. The architects listed in the back of the book
are those mentioned in this volume; no attempt has been made to list Early
American architects.

Some changes in emphasis should be noted. The Historic American Buildings Survey has a renewed activity in the field, although architectural magazines have fewer articles on historic architecture. An interest in Gothic and
other revival buildings has been on the increase, and auxiliary structures,
such as barns, lighthouses, and covered bridges, have been subjects of other
contemporary study.

My gratitude goes to the many people who have helped in the preparation
of the book, to the Graduate Research Board of the University of Illinois, and
to the University of Illinois Press, especially Donald Jackson. Without the
help and devotion of my husband's assistant, Mrs. Sharon Villenes Albert,
this revision could not have been completed, and to her go my sincere thanks.

Beatrice Adams Roos
Champaign-Urbana, Illinois
1968

Preface to the First Edition

Although published at a time when the world is in flames and many of us have anxiously turned firemen, this book is a product of, and a hopeful preparation for, a time of peace. It started ten years ago as a small bibliographic index for the use of students of early American architecture at Ohio University. The need for such a list of titles was very real since there was available no comprehensive geographic bibliography of the subject. Constantly expanding, it proved so useful a tool to students that we were encouraged to see it through to completion. It is hoped that it will not only prove valuable to those who have projects under way in this field, but also point the way to further subjects that need investigation, perhaps for those who have not previously worked on this subject.

While the list was in leisurely process of preparation, interest in the subject was constantly increasing, with a significant rise in the quality as well as the quantity of articles and books. More well-trained observers have become interested in it than ever before, a phenomenon due in part at least to the increased interest in nationalism, evident earlier in other countries than in America. Indeed, it may be that the greater interest in America and in things American is the defensive result of the central European trend toward a supernationalism. Also, our institutions of higher education have been turning out more and more students, equipped not only with training to do scientific research on non-scientific subjects, but also with the tools to make such studies more effective, such as cameras with which to document buildings on the spot. Many of them were interested in European subjects until, finding that continent closed by war, they looked around for subjects nearer home. Some turned hopefully to Latin America while others discovered fruitful material on their own doorsteps.

As scholarship on American architecture matured and expanded, the need for research tools became more and more evident. This book is an attempt to supply one of them — that means of "searching the literature" so necessary before sound work on historical subjects can be attempted. It could not, of course, have been done without the pioneering of others. Richard Bach between 1915 and 1928, and A. Lawrence Kocher in the 1920's, admirably paved the way, while more recently Dean Rexford Newcomb, Professor Henry-Russell Hitchcock, and Mr. Charles E. Peterson have continued the necessary drudgery — for which this writer for one has been thankful (see titles 60, 4324–4326, 4353, 4359, 4367). It seems logical to publish this list now, since no effort has been made to find titles published after January, 1941, when Miss Ruth Cook's excellent list of current titles was started in the *Journal of the American Society of Architectural Historians* (see 4337). We have attempted to fill in the gaps left by the earlier bibliographers, to arrange the titles in a more useful manner, to include notes and cross references where such seemed indicated, and thus to make easier the "preliminary searching" on titles published before the appearance of the lists in the journal just mentioned.

Such a list as this could hardly be the work of one person. The staff of the Library of The Ohio State University was prodigal of its time. The writer is particularly grateful to Mr. Earl N. Manchester, the Librarian, to Miss Bertha Schneider, Catalogue Librarian, who among other things suggested the form of the entries, to Miss Margaret Oldfather and Miss Maude E. Avery of the same staff, as well as to my wife, Beatrice Adams Roos, and Mrs. Robert MacKellar who also gave much of their time. We are grateful, too, for the encouragement given us by Dean Rexford Newcomb, Dr. Fiske Kimball, and Mr. Talbot Hamlin.

Some of the typing and preliminary searching was done by students working under the National Youth Administration. A generous grant through Dean Alpheus W. Smith from The Ohio State University Graduate School funds made possible the final and detailed checking of the titles as well as the publication of the list. It is a pleasure also to thank Professor William R. Parker of this University for his many helpful suggestions, the numerous graduate students who called our attention to obscure titles and, finally, Professor William Charvat of New York University for his help in making possible the inclusion of some titles from the *Index to Early American Periodical Literature, 1728–1870*, a Works Progress Administration project at New York University.

F. J. R., Jr.
Columbus, Ohio
May, 1943

Contents

Introduction

Scope of the List of Writings
on Early American Architecture

Included are titles of books and articles on architecture of the United States, from the East Coast to the western edge of the Mississippi Valley. Not included are titles concerned with architecture constructed later than the Civil War, and architecture in the Far West or the Southwest. It is hoped that someone may subsequently make a similar list for the latter areas.

TYPES OF TITLES INCLUDED

1. Books and articles on American architecture in which the subject is considered historically.

2. Non-architectural titles that include important architectural sections, e.g., the *Federal Writers' Project Guides*, each of which locates the more important examples and includes an essay on the architectural history of the region covered.

3. Purely historical titles containing architectural material not elsewhere available.

4. Titles concerned with such minor arts as are normally attached to buildings, e.g., wrought and cast iron, and wallpaper.

5. References to descriptions and discussion in some early American magazines, many of which were contributed by the periodical index at New York University, mentioned in the Preface. This group is far from complete and is included here because of its usefulness and because it is not elsewhere available in print. Many other references to magazines and newspaper articles can of course be found in the better documented historical titles included in this list.

6. Some titles that could not, perhaps, be printed today because of their unscholarly nature. They are sometimes included, even though their facts are open to question, when they contain the only information on the subject or when they suggest leads for further investigation.

7. A few titles concerning American Indian structures, since there is evidence that the pioneer was sometimes influenced by the forms he found in the newly settled regions.

8. Some types of structures not normally considered in histories of architecture, such as lighthouses, windmills, and shot towers.

TYPES OF TITLES NOT INCLUDED

1. Histories of towns, counties, and states. Although often a rich source of information they are much too numerous to warrant inclusion.

2. Purely historical titles about places and buildings, except for a few included when they were found to contain pertinent material.

3. Many titles of a purely romantic and antiquarian nature, including those in the picture-book class, even though containing some discussion of architecture. Wallace Nutting's *States Beautiful Series* was omitted, but Samuel Chamberlain's many recent titles were included because of their excellent illustrations and factual accuracy.

4. Handbooks for the use of architects and builders, since this group is well covered in Hitchcock's *American Architectural Books . . . published in America before 1895* (see 4353).

5. With few exceptions, no newspaper articles, even though they are often the only source of information on some subjects.

6. No attempt has been made to include all the editions of popular titles.

METHOD OF CLASSIFICATION OF TITLES

As nearly as possible all titles are located under specific place names, e.g., if possible under city or county, or failing that, under state or region. Some titles are so geographically inclusive as to necessitate classification by style.

Brief descriptive notes are often included when a title is not adequately descriptive. Included are the dates ascribed to the buildings by the author of the publication.

Parentheses in notes are used to indicate dates derived from sources other than the titles in question.

Multiple title numbers are used for multiple entries. It is intended that the titles be numbered in the order in which they are listed (e.g., 414–421).

The smallest geographical division here used is the town or city. Nearby buildings are normally included under the name of the nearest urban unit. In Virginia, however, most titles are classified by counties, since this has long been the primary geographic unit used there.

FURTHER SUGGESTIONS TO THE USER OF THIS LIST

The reader is uged to remember that if he fails to find a title for a specific building under the town or county in which it is located, it may be included in a more general title classified under state, region, or style. If the building sought still does not appear, it must not be assumed that there has been no discussion in print. This basic list obviously is not exhaustive; indeed, no such first list could be. A student familiar with any part of the general subject should know of more titles on that part than are here included. Later perhaps, a list of additions and corrections can be collected and made available. It is hoped that the user will be lenient if and when errors are found. The writer takes all responsibility for such and would gladly correct them if he knew where they were. Finally, let the reader beware of the confusion of terminology common in the writings listed here. Such terms as Colonial, Post-Colonial, Georgian, Federal, Early Republican, Classic Revival, and Romantic Revival have had different meanings for different writers. For the benefit of the user of this list, the following classification was before the writer when it was being organized. Not all students of the subject will agree with it, but it will have served its purpose if it leads to further discussion which may bring about a more authoritative classification.

SOME TERMS AND THEIR MEANINGS

Early American Architectural Styles — Eastern Half of the United States, to 1860

I. COLONIAL (1611—*ca.* 1800)
  A. ENGLISH COLONIES
    1. Jacobean (to *ca.* 1725). Seventeenth-century type. Sometimes called First Period or Early Colonial
    2. Georgian (*ca.* 1725—*ca.* 1800). Primarily Palladian influence through England. Sometimes called Second Period
  B. OTHER COLONIES
    1. Dutch influence. Primarily Hudson Valley and Long Island. Usually called Dutch Colonial
    2. German influence. Primarily Pennsylvania
    3. Spanish and French influence (before 1819). Primarily Florida, Georgia, and Louisiana
II. EARLY REPUBLICAN (*ca.* 1780—*ca.* 1860). Sometimes called Federal
  A. CLASSIC REVIVALS OR INSPIRATION (1799—*ca.* 1860)
    1. Roman Revival
      a) *Adam type* (*ca.* 1790—*ca.* 1840). Primarily New England; e.g., Samuel McIntire and some Bulfinch work. Sometimes called Post-Colonial, Late Georgian, Third Period, or Federal
      b) *Jeffersonian type* (1785—*ca.* 1840). Some Palladian with more direct Roman and French influence. Primarily middle Atlantic and southern states. Sometimes called Republican
    2. Greek Revival (1799—*ca.* 1850). E.g., Benjamin Latrobe and his followers: Robert Mills, William Strickland, and T. U. Walter. National in scope. Modified by Asher Benjamin
    3. Renaissance Revivals
      a) *French type* (*ca.* 1803—*ca.* 1850). E.g., Pierre L'Enfant, Joseph Mangin, and John McComb. Some Bulfinch work
      b) *English type.* James Hoban and James Gibbs influence on church spires. The latter a continuation in part of Georgian. Sometimes called Post-Colonial
    4. Egyptian Revival (from 1815). Scattered examples by many architects
  B. ROMANTIC REVIVALS OR INSPIRATION
    1. Gothic Revival (1800—after 1860). E.g., Maximilian Godefroy, A. J. Davis, Richard Upjohn, and James Renwick
    2. Romanesque Revival (*ca.* 1850). E.g., Robert Dale Owen and Renwick. Later popularized by Richardson

3. Battle of the styles (after *ca.* 1840). Italian villas, Swiss chalets, Victorian Gothic, French Second Empire, Downing cottages, jig-saw work, etc.
C. ORIGINAL OR UNUSUAL FORMS. E.g., block houses, dog trot cabins and other log forms, cobblestone houses, decorative wrought and cast iron, Orson Squire Fowler's octagonal houses, and simplified Classic Revival of the Middle West

SCHOLARSHIP ON EARLY AMERICAN ARCHITECTURE

In building such a list as we are here presenting, one gets a perspective on the scholarship in the field such as could not easily be achieved in any other way. One becomes conscious not only of the men and the areas of study that have been important in the past, but also of the areas and types of subjects that deserve some attention in the future.

Totals of Titles on Architecture Listed, by Two-Year Periods *

1900–01	21	1920–21	126
1902–03	51	1922–23	138
1904–05	36	1924–25	170
1906–07	65	1926–27	168
1908–09	54	1928–29	160
1910–11	62	1930–31	138
1912–13	80	1932–33	137
1914–15	102	1934–35	146
1916–17	137	1936–37	154
1918–19	105	1938–39	202

PRODUCTION, 1900-1940

As the preceding table shows, interest in early American architecture has been increasing since 1900, but it has not had a steady rise, since from time to time world events have diverted study of this as well as other subjects. We can conjecture at the reasons for some of the hills and valleys in the curve that might be made from this table. The long and fairly steady rise in the number of titles from 1900 to 1918 may be seen, on examination of the titles themselves, to be for the most part the result of the interest of antiquarians and romanticists, sometimes indistinguishable, with a sprinkling of a few architectural historians. The subject matter was primarily architecture in the "Colonial style," used then in a very loose sense, in New England and a few southern states.

In the number of titles, the First World War brought an inevitable decline which, however, was comparatively short lived, since a new and higher peak was in the making. It may be significant that the totals began to slacken even before the stock market crash of 1929, which produced another depression in

* Only titles considering architecture historically were counted.

our curve. But the new peak of 1938–40 rose higher than ever, partly because of the great number of titles about the Williamsburg restoration. A breakdown of these figures by regions shows that the South in 1935 had twice as many titles as the totals on New England and the middle Atlantic states combined. Although this list does not attempt to include titles published after 1941, future listings will probably show a decline in the totals beginning in 1940.

THE ANTIQUARIANS AND THE COLONIAL STYLE

As might be expected, most of the early writers were interested in the subject because of the age of the buildings or their historical associations, rather than in the architecture as such. They tended to ignore contemporary styles and anything, for that matter, newer than the Revolution. As Hitchcock has pointed out (4353), the first separate publication on Colonial architecture was probably by Nathan Henry Chamberlain, published in 1858 (500). Eleven years later, when the American Institute of Architects was three years old, we find Richard Upjohn, its founder and first president, discussing the Colonial architecture of New York and New England (352). Not until after his death, however, do we find any official expression of the need for study of the Colonial style on the part of that organization (338). The bulk of the early writings was by untrained observers, writing under such titles in the 1870's and '80's as *Nooks and Corners of the New England Coast* (371) and *The Homes of Our Forefathers* (588, 589).

By 1877 R. S. Peabody had added the term Georgian to Colonial in an illustrated article in the new *American Architect and Building News* (581). Between that year and 1891 Glenn Brown and others discussed the Colonial works in Virginia and Maryland (2492, 2495). The next year Joseph Chandler wrote on Maryland, Pennsylvania, and Virginia (308), and Corner and Soderholtz published their first study on the South (2498), to be followed three years later by Crane and Soderholtz' work on Charleston and Savannah (2499). Although the subject was well under way in the South in the 1890's, the bulk of titles was still concerned with New England. There again Corner and Soderholtz were pioneers, with a parallel to their southern work in the same year (560). Not until 1895, however, does there seem to be enough material available for Montgomery Schuyler to attempt what was probably the first history of Colonial architecture (349), preceded by his more general *American Architecture* in 1892 (66).

By the late 1890's the subject had been so well covered that critical articles began to appear, with such titles as the *So-called Colonial Architecture of the United States* (307), *Good and Bad Colonial Architecture* (299), and *The Case for Colonial* (354). In the meantime the romanticists and the antiquarians were adding scores of articles and books which, although they were and are useful, reflected in their titles the authors' primary impulse for writing. Typical are *Some Colonial Homesteads and Their Stories* (380), *Stately Homes in America* (192), *The Romance of Old New England Rooftrees* (563), and *Among Old New England Inns* (594). Even as late as the 1920's such titles continue, with *The Mystery of Early American Doorways* (382) and *Ye Old Picture Wall-papers* (363). Most of the titles of this type appeared in the house and home magazine group, however, and seldom in the architectural journals. Some of the antiquarians were inclined to make sweeping statements that remind one of the recent attempt to find the oldest house in Massachusetts, proving anew the danger in trying to identify "firsts" (3049). These earlier writers, romanticist or antiquarian, contributed much that must be commended, however, for in their writings is considerable material that can still be found nowhere else. And they did describe and illustrate many buildings that have since been destroyed.

SCHOLARSHIP

We have already mentioned a number of pioneer historians such as Chandler, Schuyler, and Upjohn. The first of them all is, of course, William Dunlap, who seems to have made fewer errors than his prototype Vasari (18). His monumental work in 1834 is still the only source of some material — a fact the more noteworthy because he received little cooperation from some of his contemporaries. The 1860's saw the beginning of formal architectural teaching in the United States, even though Europe was still the primary training ground for architects and historians. The Massachusetts Institute of Technology started a course in architecture in 1865, with William Robert Ware as director, and by 1868 the subject appeared in the University of Illinois catalogue, and soon after was taught at Cornell. William Rotch Ware, just back from the Ecole des Beaux Arts in 1876, was the first editor of *The American Architect*, our first architectural magazine. We have already mentioned the publication of an article there on Georgian architecture in 1877 (581). In 1898 Ware started publication in his own magazine of his important series of measured drawings on the Georgian period, which were to appear later in folio form (356). Montgomery Schuyler broke the spell of the Colonial by pausing to look at our college architecture, starting in 1909 (1045), and at our Greek Revival in 1910 (471). He had been preceded in his study of the latter style, however, by W. H. Goodyear in 1892 (457). At this time, too, a number of photographer-writers were working on the documentation of buildings. One of them, Frank Cousins, deserves special mention because of the quantity and quality of his work. The prints produced by these men of the horse and buggy days, with cameras and plates that we would call clumsy and inadequate, deserve all the praise we can give them. One wonders if those of us who photograph architecture today, with our automobiles, good roads, high speed films and lenses, could have done as well in their day, with their equipment. But some of our contemporaries use light and shade and composition in a manner that the earlier men would not have thought possible. Kenneth Clark, Arthur C. Haskell, Samuel Chamberlain, and Frances Benjamin Johnston are a few of the many whom we could name here.

In 1915 appeared Volume One, Number One, of that invaluable *White Pine Series of Architectural Monographs* that continued until recently, through its descendant the "Monograph Series" in *Pencil Points*. Russell F. Whitehead, its editor from the beginning, and the editors of *Pencil Points* are to be congratulated for having continued such a useful source of material. One regrets only that the series did not include more material from the South and from states west of the Atlantic seaboard. We cannot proceed without mentioning the measured drawings of early buildings that have appeared regularly in this and the other architectural publications. They were a true labor of love, and the architects who did them deserve the thanks of all later students of the subject.

In the previous year appeared the first of a series of articles, no less monumental, by that indefatigable worker, Fiske Kimball. His research on Jefferson (e.g., 3539, 4235–4238) has done much to establish the latter's reputation in this field. Another important contributor to the general study of the subject is Talbot F. Hamlin, whose *American Spirit in Architecture* in 1926 filled a long standing need for illustrations (28). From the 1920's on, the list of students of early American architecture grows continuously, with useful contributions from Frank Chouteau Brown, Aymar Embury, I. T. Frary, Rexford Newcomb, and William Rusk, to name but a few. That the field had become of interest to university art departments is evidenced by the appearance in 1938 of four doctoral dissertations devoted to the subject (423, 478, 479, 4034).

Nineteen forty-one saw the first volume of the *Journal of the American Society of Architectural Historians* under the energetic editorship of Turpin Bannister. Some of the society's members, with the inspiration of Kenneth Conant, are devoting such time as they now have to the subject.

SOME SUGGESTIONS

All past studies in this field may be said to fall into one of the following general classifications: (1) studies of one structure; (2) studies of one geographic unit, such as town, county, state, or region; (3) studies of a style, type, or detail from one or more geographic units or in a given period of time; (4) studies of architects and their work; (5) studies of source materials; (6)

collecting for archives; (7) studies concerning restoration and preservation; and (8) studies of a sociological, critical, or developmental nature.

None of these headings has been exhausted by any means. We shall attempt to identify early studies in each classification as well as point out some of the needs in the following pages.

STUDIES OF ONE STRUCTURE

This type of study is normally the easiest and the earliest attempted. It often may take the form of a simple description of a new building or one that is very old. As far back as the 1790's one finds separate descriptions of newly erected structures, mostly of a public type (414–421). Through the first half of the nineteenth century occur numerous contemporary descriptions of buildings, since destroyed or altered, which should prove a profitable source of information to the architectural historian (e.g., 2306, 2328). By 1830 we have what is probably the first separate publication on a building — the recently completed Tremont House in Boston (964). Only four years later comes what may be the first guidebook to a building — by Robert Mills on the Capitol at Washington (2702). By the 1880's building guides were quite common, those of David Scattergood being typical (2450, 2451).

Almost any city or town still has much to offer in the way of studies of individual buildings, even such as Boston, New York, Baltimore, and Philadelphia, to say nothing of the smaller towns. The Early Republican and the Romantic Revival styles offer more profit than the Colonial in most regions. The tendency has been to write about the largest, best preserved, or most historical structures, ignoring other examples that are sometimes as good or even better architecturally. Future historians who will further codify our architectural past will be grateful to the student who furnishes them with many illustrations of details as well as the usual photograph of the structure as a whole. The Historic American Buildings Survey has done good work along this line. Particularly important is the availability of these records. (4372).

GEOGRAPHIC STUDIES

A geographic arrangement of titles such as we offer here immediately shows up the areas that have apparently not been touched at all or that have not been worked on recently by competent observers. Any student may find these areas for himself by scrutiny of the list.

Virginia might be said to have had a head start in this type of title, since as early as 1853 we find an article concerning the progress of architecture there (3310). In 1877 appeared Westcott's *Historic Mansions and Buildings of Philadelphia,* probably the first of the long list of town studies (2346). The older cities of the Atlantic seaboard have been fairly well covered, although, as we said before, there is still much to do in all of them. A particular tendency may be noted, to write about the architecture of the cities or parts of cities that time has left comparatively intact, such as Charleston, Portsmouth, Salem, and the Vieux Carré in New Orleans. These groups have been of interest alike to the antiquarian, the descendants of the old families, and the historian.

Once in a while one finds an area that was worked on very early and has remained almost untouched since. The Genesee Valley is such a region. Claude Bragdon did some excellent measured drawings there in 1894 which he published in the *American Architect* (1838), and in 1923 a paper by him was published on the same subject. This and other parts of central New York are less well covered than the Hudson Valley or Long Island. It is true, of course, that older structures adjacent to large cities are likely to be covered early.

Much work should be done on the Dutch architecture of the Middle Atlantic states and more is still possible on the work of the Pennsylvania Germans. New Jersey, too, has much unrecorded material and there is more in Florida than this list would lead one to suppose. Although there have been numerous articles on Natchez since 1930, Mississippi can stand more attention, as can the western counties of Virginia, and West Virginia as a whole.

The Midwest has much untouched material. Our knowledge of the Classic Revival there has increased since Fiske Kimball first wrote about it in Michigan in 1922. Illinois, Indiana, Iowa, Kansas, Michigan, Minnesota, Missouri, and Wisconsin all have material enough for books on the subject. Although Ohio is the best covered of the states of this region, there are still many unphotographed and unstudied buildings there. In it and the other states mentioned above exist also many local styles, variations of European prototypes built by the immigrant groups, that are not mentioned anywhere but in the *Federal Writers' Project State Guides*. For this region, as for the nation as a whole, we need a geography of architecture as well as a geography of antiques.

STUDIES OF STYLES, TYPES, AND DETAILS

As we have said before, of the chronological styles, the Colonial has been best covered. The Greek and Roman Revivals still need considerable codification, especially west of the Atlantic states where the examples are numerous and often very good. It is hoped that Talbot Hamlin's work on the Greek Revival will soon appear in print. The next chronological style or group of styles, the Romantic Revivals, are practically untouched, although the groundwork has been laid in a few books and articles (475, 478, 479, 491). We can no more afford to ignore this period than an American Wing could afford to leave out the horsehair sofa, the rosewood chair, or the whatnot. If architecture, like the other arts, is the visible index of a cultural period, then we are doubly bound to study this one if we are to understand ourselves and our past. The approach to the works of the Romanticists must be different, psychologically speaking, from the approach to the preceding styles, but the results can be as profitable as in any other period.

Grouping by type as well as by style has, of course, also been common. We find religious and public structures written about briefly in 1859 (286), but it is rather surprising to find as long ago as 1865 a large volume on the early churches of even so important a city as New York (2030). Aymar Embury's work on churches in 1911 and 1912 is still standard. Public buildings were discussed as early as 1884 (273) but they are still comparatively neglected as a group. We have already mentioned Montgomery Schuyler's pioneer work on college architecture, starting in the *Architectural Record* in 1909, but he was not the first to consider it. The *Yale Literary Magazine* carried a brief note on it in 1853 (427).

Of the other types, military architecture could stand more attention although there have been a number of good localized articles on blockhouses, forts, and garrison houses (e.g., 554, 1420, 1894, 2272, 3312). Although Henry Chapman Mercer (222) and Harold Shurtleff have both concerned themselves with log cabins, the subject warrants further investigation. There are many types from the Atlantic to the Mississippi still unrecorded. This is a particularly profitable group to study, since in the log cabin form we can see native ingenuity at work, often uninfluenced by training. Further study of the examples surviving will tell us something about the development of functionalism and, in the mutations of their types, something about the development of style when unhampered by aesthetic considerations. Little has been done except locally, with such infrequent and minor forms as windmills, lighthouses, and shot towers.

We need, too, a closer study and codification of original details of existing buildings, such as bricks, bonds, molding profiles, muntin details, hardware, heating and sanitation systems, and internal construction generally. We have been too much in the habit of looking at the stylistic proportions of the exteriors and interiors and not seeing the buildings as the builders themselves seem to have seen their handiwork — as a series of details put together to make a whole. One of the useful indirect results of such studies would be better restorations.

George Francis Dow in 1926 did some work on hardware (312) and Henry Chapman Mercer's study of old carpenters' tools is very useful (160). We need more knowledge of wrought and cast iron, the foundries and their molds. Thomas T. Waterman and others have done some good work in this field (2540). When more facts are gathered about such details it will be possible to have more articles like those written by Mercer in 1923 and 1924 on the dating of old houses (219, 220). All these studies will be furthered by more photographs, especially of details, with a measuring stick somewhere in the picture.

Color as an architectual factor was practically ignored by the writers until about 1928, when A. Lawrence Kocher wrote about it in the *Architectural Record* (336 and 132). Much more knowledge has come out of the Williamsburg researches, but additional work in this field is needed.

The reader of Giedion's *Space, Time and Architecture* (433) will become aware of a large body of material that Giedion only scratched, and his approach to the study of architecture is itself well worth studying.

STUDIES OF ARCHITECTS AND THEIR WORK

Although the listed writings on architects show much good work done by numerous authors, it also shows that many good architects have been comparatively neglected. The list does not show, of course, those architects who have been completely ignored. Perhaps we should not refer to them all as architects, since many of our early builders were something less than well trained. These builders and architects generally fall into one of five groups.

The *carpenters* were for the most part anonymous and drew upon their memories or the handbooks for their designs. These sometimes excellent craftsmen have been almost completely ignored. Research in the future will probably reveal a few of them to have been better trained and more influential than we now think. The *carpenter-designers* were a step above the carpenters in both training and ability. Some of them achieved considerable originality in practice or print while keeping within the bounds of contemporary "good taste" and proportion. One might mention Samuel Rhoads of Philadelphia and William Buckland of Annapolis. Asher Benjamin is also in this group, with the distinction of being the author of the first original book on architecture published in America, in 1797 (4353). The wide distribution of this and Benjamin's subsequent handbooks made him one of the most influential builders in the first half of the century. A detailed study of his and Minard Lafever's handbooks will tell us more than we now know of the psychology and methods of our early builders. A large collection of telephoto pictures of details of buildings will show, when compared with the plates of these and earlier handbooks, such as those by William Pain, Batty Langley, and William Halfpenny, the great use to which these volumes were put. We feel that these books can be shown to account not only for some of the changes in style and for the wide geographic spread of certain styles, but also for the excellent design of many of the buildings, especially in the Early Republican period. The carpenter, as long as he sought his inspiration from one book or from plates in one style, could hardly go far wrong stylistically. They not only gave him his elementary mathematics for laying out stairs, trusses, arches, or moldings, but some of them adapted the complicated popular styles to his materials, tools, and abilities. It is significant that these books seldom give full plans and elevations. If the elevations are given, they are often in terms of proportions only, with alternate choice of details given elsewhere. In the arrangement of these details lay the carpenters' opportunity for freedom of choice and originality. Any person concerned with restoration would do well to consult these handbooks, too, since in many cases they make it possible accurately to restore the building as it might have been, if it cannot be done as it was.

Montgomery Schuyler sensed their importance as early as 1906 (348), but he knew of only a few, and as late as 1924 Alexander Wall listed only 21 published before 1830 (4377). We will be surprised if many are found in the future that are not already listed in the cooperative list compiled by Hitchcock (4353). It is a pleasure to observe that many architectural libraries are now collecting them. There should be more reprinting, like Aymar Embury's reproduction of some of Asher Benjamin's plates in 1917 (4180).

Thomas Jefferson is the outstanding name in the third group, which we may call *gentlemen-designers*. Although professionally untrained, Jefferson had considerable influence, partly no doubt because he had a reputation in other fields. In this group might also be included Andrew Hamilton and Dr. John Kearsley of Philadelphia, as well as such men as Maximilian Godefroy, who have not been adequately covered.

Some of the *early professional architects*, such as Charles Bulfinch, our first professional, have been given considerable attention in print. Even he has not been studied much since 1925, although Samuel McIntire has attracted discussion of late. Samuel Blodget, George Hadfield, Stephen Hallet, Peter Harrison, David Hoadley, James Hoban, and others, with varying degrees of experience and training, have been comparatively neglected. Some of them and their followers, the *later professional architects*, were discussed by Rexford Newcomb in a series of articles in *The Architect* between 1926 and 1929. Because of their excellence, one wishes that they had appeared in a publication allowing footnote documentation and that Newcomb had continued the series. Of the men in this group, Mills, Town, and Davis have been well covered since 1935, and Thornton, Latrobe, Walter, and Upjohn have had some attention, although some of them are still not as completely covered as they should be. In several instances, work on them cannot be completed until the necessary source materials become available. Latrobe particularly deserves a large volume, not only because of his work but also because of his influence on other architects. He started both the Greek and Gothic Revivals here. His versatility is evidenced by the fact that he seems to have built the first railway, put the first sheet iron roof on a building when fireproofing was a new subject, and apparently utilized for the first time a steam engine to pump water (4261).

Henry Austin, James Bogardus, A. J. Downing, John Haviland, Minard Lafever, John McComb, James Renwick, Isaiah Rogers, and Martin Thompson invite more thorough study. William Strickland, who practically invented a substitute for the dome by using the "Lanthorn of Demosthenes," and who contributed to progress by using illuminating gas in 1809, should soon appear in print. We are glad to be able to say that some of these men are being given attention by competent students. Lastly, such men as Samuel Sloan, whose influence, although later, was not unlike that of Benjamin, should receive more attention, and although Orson Squire Fowler could hardly be called an architect, his influence cannot be ignored if one will check his book against the numerous and widely scattered octagonal houses. Some of the architects who worked in the Midwest and the South, such as Francis Costigan, John Francis Rague, and James Gallier, deserve more attention than they have had. Rexford Newcomb has given us some material on Gideon Shryock of Kentucky (4289) and both I. T. Frary and this writer have brought some of the early Ohio carpenter-designers to light (4014, 4034).

We have named only a few of the men who seem to merit attention, but there are many more, some of whose names we do not yet know. Every so often some good architect is suddenly brought to light. Some of them have had their reputations established for posterity by one title, such as Philip Hooker (4227). We confess that we were not familiar with Thomas Tefft before Barbara Wriston's articles on him appeared a few years ago (4299, 4300).

STUDIES OF SOURCE MATERIALS

Well-trained students habitually gravitate to such source materials as contemporary accounts and manuscripts. Antiquarians have recorded for sentimental reasons much that is useful, but we now need students to sort this mass of information and organize it both for themselves and others. The printed records of such historical societies as those in Cambridge, the District of Columbia, the Essex Institute in Salem, the Society for the Preservation of New England Antiquities, the Maryland Historical Society, the Daughters of the American Revolution, and the art museum bulletins all offer gold for the digger. We need from such records more itemized bills and contracts for building, for example, although George Francis Dow and others have published some from time to time (e.g., 848, 867, 1078, 1126, 1164, 1263, 1994, 2991, 3012). Manuscript collections in libraries and museums are also full of these documents, which can be checked against the lists of time to be spent on house details by the carpenter, as published in some of the builders' handbooks. Through such studies we can learn more about the builder and his work, his economic life, and his day.

Newspapers are obviously profitable. Dow and Rusk have done some good work with them (510, 900, 2959). The inventories catalogued by the Works Progress Administration and such projects as the New York University periodical index will become increasingly useful as they become better known. Much important material, too, is still hidden away in such publications as the old *New Yorker*, the *Portfolio*, and even in such remote places as the *Coast Artillery Journal* (3312), and architectural historians would be thankful for more titles like Stokes' *Iconography of Manhattan Island* (1947).

More states and cities should collect manuscript histories of houses, as Connecticut has done (657) and Michigan is doing, although the recent accounts must be quoted with some caution, unless double checked or otherwise documented. A typical instance of the usefulness of manuscripts that at first glance would not seem pertinent occurred recently when we found one in the collections of the Ohio Archaeological and Historical Society by Dr. S. S. Walker entitled *Journal of a Voyage to New England Performed in the Year 1844*. In it he wrote, "It [Bunker Hill Monument] is kept by a man who for a quarter will take you to the top in a steam car, or for a shilling you may have the privilege of walking up a never ending spiral staircase. The ascent by the car is pleasant. You step into a bird cage big enough for six persons to stand at once, and in three minutes you open the door of the cage and walk out upon a floor . . . at the height of 225 feet." This is obviously the same stone hoist which Wheilden mentions as having been used for a year to carry visitors to the top (4316, p. 246). A minor matter to be sure, but it double checks Wheilden and gives more information than he did, such as the size and rate of climb. And apparently it puts the date of the first mechanically powered elevator used for passengers some nine years earlier than James Bogardus' first proposal, cited by Giedion (433, p. 142).

ARCHIVES

The last decade has seen a number of attempts at gathering together in a few places factual material about early American architecture for the use of students, architects, or restorers. Collections of this sort will be particularly useful to the future historians who try to codify further this area of American production and culture. It is interesting to note that the opportunity for beginning two of these came as a result of the Depression in the early 1930's. One of them was started in 1933 by the Civil Works Administration which, with the cooperation of seventy chapters of the American Institute of Architects, used unemployed architects and draftsmen to survey and document some of the extant buildings (4372). This project eventually developed into the more permanent and invaluable Historic American Buildings Survey, whose records are deposited in the Library of Congress under Leicester B. Holland, Chief of the Division of Fine Arts, who had earlier started to collect negatives and photographs of good examples. Since many students now do their own photographing of buildings, it is to be hoped that more of them will leave their negatives to this Library of Congress collection.

Another product of the Depression was the series of state and city guides done by the Federal Writers' Project. They are invaluable in leading one directly to the structure one wishes to see. Many of us remember the difficulty, before their appearance, of finding the buildings we had heard or read about. Although the information about the individual buildings in these guides is sometimes based on hearsay, the architectural essay in each state volume was written by or after consultation with local historians. These and the mass of material from which they were condensed, as well as the other Works Progress Administration inventories, should offer many leads to work undone and much information to the student who has his problem under way (see Historical Records Survey, etc.).

RESTORATION AND PRESERVATION

Many organizations such as the Society for the Preservation of New England Antiquities, the Daughters of the American Revolution, and the members of the American Association of Museums, to name only a few, have long been concerned with the restoration and preservation of historic and architecturally distinguished houses (e.g., 85, 90, 190, 202). The Williamsburg project is, of course, the most ambitious and best known, and it has received the greatest amount of scholarly attention of all the efforts in this field. But preservationism, which in Europe had almost developed into a science, has had but scattered attention here until recently. It is now receiving concerted attention from new quarters, as the 1941 numbers of the *Journal of the American Society of Architectural Historians* show. It is to be hoped that as time, interest, and funds become available the suggestions for organized preservation, architectural museums, and research centers can be further implemented (e.g., 111, 3993).

STUDIES OF A SOCIOLOGICAL, CRITICAL, OR DEVELOPMENTAL NATURE

Architectural styles or forms do not spring full fledged into being, nor do they develop in a predetermined manner, completely independent of outside influences. Some of us have been too prone to think and write as if they did. Not only do we need more studies of individual examples and groups of examples, but there is an even greater need for studies that relate these examples to each other and to the numerous sociological and physical factors that influenced their form. John Coolidge's *Mill and Mansion* and John Kienitz' dissertation are two recent titles in this direction that should be followed by more (1147, 479). Van Wyck Brooks's popular *The Flowering of New England* offers the student of architecture much profitable material of a similar sort.

It is time now to study further some of the many factors that influenced plans and elevations, such as religious and national habits and backgrounds, laws, geographic distribution of materials, and climate.

Someone could profitably do an analysis of the factors that constituted excellence of design in each period. The Palladian emphasis on minute differences in proportion so varies from our concept of goodness today that two buildings which look much alike to us were considerably different according to contemporary critics. To our eyes almost all the production in the Romantic Revival styles seems bad. And yet these eclectics, too, had their standards which made some buildings aesthetically better than others. We could find profit also in more studies of the background of our city planning, the relation of the town plan to architecture, and of early attempts at cooperative housing.

Studies could profitably be made, too, of early evidences of factors common in architecture today, such as functionalism, or American ingenuity. Modern American architecture is no more completely a borrowing from Europe than is the contemporary American culture which it expresses. We have had many functionalists in our architectural history, even before the Civil War. Horatio Greenough, our first trained sculptor, in the 1850's had nothing less than a twentieth-century attitude toward clipper ships and architecture, and Thomas Jefferson's well-known idea for a serpentine brick wall would do credit to a contemporary of ours. We think today that "the most exquisite ornaments lose all their value, if they load, alter or confuse the form they are designed to enrich and adorn." But this is no contemporary of ours talking. It is Asher Benjamin in 1814 in his *Rudiments of Architecture*. His ingenuity in adapting designs from such sources as Stuart and Revett's *Antiquities of Athens* so that they could be used by carpenters was a step in what we today would call the right direction. Benjamin was not only being a functionalist of sorts, but he was also expressing an originality that would more readily be accepted in this country than abroad in his own day. Perhaps we can call it part of the American Idea.

The man who thought of floating houses from Pennsylvania to Mississippi in 1836 was probably as far from Palladian and Periclean thinking as most of our architects today (445). Was the amazing Orson Squire Fowler (4353) a forerunner of Louis Sullivan, Frank Lloyd Wright, or Buckminster Fuller? They have much in common with him, although separated from him by almost a century.

It may have been only boredom with classic forms that prompted Latrobe, apparently at Jefferson's suggestion, to experiment with indigenous plants such as corn, tobacco, and cotton in place of the non-American acanthus in his capitals. He did not create an American Order of course, but he was not alone in his thinking about this anomaly in our Classic Revival, since he was congratulated from many sides for his originality — by the members of Congress, by Robert Dale Owen (2642, p. 9), by James Fennell (*An Apology for the Life of James Fennell,* 2736, p. 415) — and even the ubiquitous Mrs. Trollope was impressed. Alexander J. Davis tried out wheat and corn together at Chapel Hill, and corn and morning glories appear around the middle of the century on a cast iron fence at 915 Royal St., in New Orleans. Later, Henry Ives Cobb essayed capitals of fish, eels, frogs, cattails, and other aquatic flora and fauna on the east colonnade of the Fisheries Building in 1893 at Chicago, and most of us are familiar with Bertram Goodhue's combination of corn and wheat with some suspiciously Persepolis-like bulls in the north vestibule of the Nebraska capitol. These are scattered examples to be sure, but they seem like the murmurings of a new culture and an ingenuity that in our day has already given us mass production and produced hundreds of new synthetic materials for architecture and the other arts, that will give us architectural forms as true to and typical of ourselves as the Colonial and Early Republican examples were true to and typical of their day.

General References

1 ADAMS, JAMES TRUSLOW (ed.). Album of American history. N. Y., Charles Scribner's Sons, 1944–60. 5v., index. illus.

2 ADAMS, RICHARD PERRILL. Architecture and the romantic tradition: Coleridge to Wright. American Quarterly, 9:46–62, Spring 1957.
1818———. Philosophical discussion.

3 ALLESON, DONALD MAHANEY. A study of the architecture of the United States with particular reference to certain characteristic tendencies in American architecture. Master's Thesis, University of Illinois, 1920.

4 ANDREWS, FAITH, AND ANDREWS, EDWARD DEMING. Sheeler and the Shakers. Art in America, 53:90–95, Feb. 1965.
Paintings by Charles Sheeler of Shaker buildings.

5 ANDREWS, WAYNE. Architectural photographs. No. 1———, 194—.
A corpus of excellent photographs, mainly of American architecture, issued by the author. Prime source.

6 ———. Architecture, ambition, and Americans; a history of American architecture, from the beginning to the present, telling the story of the outstanding buildings, the men who designed them, and the people for whom they were built. N. Y., Harper, [1955]. 315p. illus.
1636–1955.

7 ———. Architecture in America; a photographic history from the Colonial period to the present. N. Y., Atheneum Publishers, 1960. 179p. illus.

8 BANNISTER, TURPIN C. Architectural development of the northeastern states. Architectural Record, 89:61–80, June 1941. illus.

9 ———. What's happened in architectural history? American Institute of Architects. Journal, 32:52–57, Nov. 1959.
Primarily on progress in scholarly publications.

10 BOWERS, DAVID FREDERICK (ed.). Foreign influences in American life; essays and critical bibliographies. Princeton, N. J., Princeton University Press, 1944. 254p. illus.
Princeton Studies in American Civilizations.

11 BRAGDON, CLAUDE FAYETTE. Architecture in the United States. Architectural Record, 25:426–33; 26:38–45, 1909. illus.

12 BURCHARD, JOHN ELY, AND BUSH-BROWN, ALBERT. The architecture of America; a social and cultural history. Boston, Little, Brown and Co., 1961. 595p. illus.

13 BUSH-BROWN, ALBERT. Image of a university: a study of architecture as an expression of education at colleges and universities in the United States between 1800 and 1900. Doctoral Dissertation, Princeton University, 1959. 519p.

14 CAHILL, HOLGER, AND BARR, ALFRED H., JR. Art in America in modern times. N. Y., Reynal and Hitchcock, 1934. 162p. illus.

   Chapter 3 by Henry-Russell Hitchcock, Jr., is a brief history of American architecture before the Civil War.

15 CHURCHILL, HENRY STERN. The city is the people. 2nd ed. N. Y., W. W. Norton and Co., 1962. 204p. illus.

16 CONDIT, CARL W. American building art: the nineteenth century. N. Y., Oxford University Press, 1960. 371p. illus.

   Structural forms and techniques used in bridges, dams, and buildings.

17 CREIGHTON, THOMAS HAWK. American architecture. Washington, D. C., Robert B. Luce, 1964. 85p. illus.

   America Today Series, 1.

18 DUNLAP, WILLIAM. History of the rise and progress of the arts and design in the United States. Edited by Alexander Wyckoff with notes and additions by Frank W. Bayley and Charles Goodspeed. N. Y., Benjamin Blom, 1965. 3v. 1302p. illus.

   First edition: N. Y., G. P. Scott and Co., 1834; second edition: Boston, C. E. Goodspeed and Co., 1918. An invaluable source book.

19 FARIS, JOHN THOMASON. Historic shrines of America. N. Y., George H. Doran Co., 1918. 421p. illus.

20 FEDERAL WRITERS' PROJECT. Catalogue of the American guide series. Washington, D. C., Government Printing Office, 1938. 31p. illus.

21 ———. The ocean highway; New Brunswick, New Jersey to Jacksonville, Florida. N. Y., Modern Age Books, 1938. 244p. illus.

22 ———. U. S. One, Maine to Florida. N. Y., Modern Age Books, 1938. 344p. illus.

23 FEISS, CARL. The heritage of our planned communities. American Society of Architectural Historians. Journal, 1:27–30, July–Oct. 1941. illus.

24 FITCH, JAMES M., JR. American building; the forces that shape it. Boston, Houghton Mifflin Co., 1948. 382p. illus.

25 GOWANS, ALAN. Images of American living; four centuries of architecture and furniture as cultural expression. Philadelphia, J. B. Lippincott Co., 1964. 498p. illus.

26 GUTHEIM, FREDERICK ALBERT. 1857–1957: one hundred years of architecture in America, celebrating the centennial of the American Institute of Architects. N. Y., Reinhold Publishing Corp., [1957]. 96p. illus.

27 HALL, LOUISE. Artificer to architect in America. Doctoral Dissertation, Radcliffe College, 1954.

28 HAMLIN, TALBOT FAULKNER. The American spirit in architecture. New Haven, Conn., Yale University Press, 1926. 353p. illus.

V. 13 of the *Pageant of America*; a pictorial history of the United States. A general history of American architecture, well illustrated.

29 ———. Roots of modern architecture. House and Garden, 88:84–87, 148, 150, 152, 156, Sept. 1945. illus.

Modern Design Series, 1. From 1683 through the nineteenth century.

30 HINTON, JOHN HOWARD. History and topography of the United States of North America, brought down from the earliest period. London, 1830–32. 2v. illus.

Several editions; fourth edition: London Printing and Publishing Co., 1850.

31 HITCHCOCK, HENRY-RUSSELL. Architecture, nineteenth and twentieth centuries. Baltimore, Penguin Books, 1958. 498p. illus.

Pelican History of Art Series.

32 ———. Art of the United States: Architecture: a. the 17th and 18th centuries; b. Romantic classicism. in: Americas: Art since Columbus, Encyclopedia of World Art 1959 ed. v. 1, col. 246–55. illus.

[*Holiday Magazine* features well-illustrated descriptions of early towns and buildings at irregular intervals.]

33 KETCHUM, RICHARD M. The American Heritage book of great historic places. N. Y., American Heritage Publishing Co., 1957. 376p. illus.

34 KIMBALL, SIDNEY FISKE. American architecture. Indianapolis, Bobbs-Merrill Co., 1928. 262p. illus.

A general discussion; includes bibliography.

35 ———. Architecture in the history of the Colonies and of the Republic. American Historical Review, 27:45–57, Oct. 1921.

36 ———. The development of American architecture. Architectural Forum, 28:1–5, 81–86, Jan.–Mar. 1918; 29:21–25, July 1918. illus.

37 ———. The history and monuments of our national art. Art and Archaeology, 4:161–68, Sept. 1916. illus.

38 ———. Three centuries of American architecture. Architectural Record, 57:560–64, June 1925.

39 KOCHER, A. LAWRENCE. Early building with brick, tradition and practice in America. Antiques, 72:47–48, July 1957. illus.

40 KOUWENHOVEN, JOHN ATLEE. Made in America; the arts in modern civilization. Garden City, N. Y., Doubleday and Co., 1948. 303p. illus.

Originally a dissertation, Columbia University. Paperback: Doubleday and Co., 1962.

41 ———. What is American in American architecture and design? Art in America, 46:40–47, Fall 1958. illus.

42 LANCASTER, CLAY. Architectural follies in America; or, hammer, saw tooth and nail. Rutland, Vt., C. E. Tuttle Co., 1960. 243p. illus.

43 ———. Fads in nineteenth-century American architecture. Antiques, 68:144–47, Aug. 1955. illus.

44 ———. Floating palaces aground. Art News, 49, no. 5:26–29, Sept. 1950. illus.
About the influence of steamboats on architecture, 1840–1905.

45 LARKIN, OLIVER W. Art and life in America. N. Y., Holt, Rinehart and Winston, 1960. 559p. illus.
Original edition, 1949.

46 LEWIS, WINTHROP. Our architecture, yesterday, today and tomorrow. Country Life in America, 39:40–42, Apr. 1921.

47 LOCKWOOD, ALICE G. B. (ed.). Gardens of Colony and State: gardens and gardeners of the American Colonies and of the Republic before 1840. N. Y., Charles Scribner's Sons, 1931–34. 2v. illus.
Includes many illustrations of buildings.

48 LORANT, STEFAN (ed.). The new world; the first pictures of America, made by John White and Jacques Le Moyne and engraved by Theodore De Bry, with contemporary narratives of the Huguenot Settlement in Florida, 1562–1565, and the Virginia Colony, 1585–1590. N. Y., Duell, Swan, and Pearce, 1946. 292p. illus.

49 McCAUSLAND, ELIZABETH. The Shaker legacy. Magazine of Art, 37:287ff., Dec. 1944.
From Maine to Kentucky.

50 MAGINNIS, CHARLES D. History and the new architecture. American Institute of Architects. Journal, 11:174–79, Apr. 1949.
Philosophical comparison of old and new building materials.

51 Makers of tradition: Palladio, and the eighteenth century. Interiors, 108:106–11, Mar. 1949. illus.

52 Man made America: a special number. Architectural Review, 108:338–416, Dec. 1950. illus.
Discussion: 109:398, June 1951; 110:217–20, Oct. 1951. Abstract: *Architectural Forum*, 94:158–59, Apr. 1951. Philosophical approach.

53 MERCER, HENRY CHAPMAN. Indian habitation in the eastern United States. American Naturalist, 30:430–33, 1896.
Some early reactions to Indians.

54 METZGER, CHARLES REID. Whitman on architecture. Society of Architectural Historians. Journal, 16:25–27. Mar. 1957.

55 MOFFATT, MAURICE P., AND RICH, STEPHEN G. Buildings as mirrors of change. Journal of Educational Sociology, 28:329–42, Apr. 1955.

56 MOHOLY-NAGY, DOROTHEA PAULINE. Native genius in anonymous architecture. N. Y., Horizon Press, 1957. 223p. illus.
Some examples from other countries.

57 MUMFORD, LEWIS. American architecture. Freeman, 8:344–46, 394–96, 418–20, 538–40, 584–86, Dec. 19, 1923, Jan. 2, 9, Feb. 13, 27, 1924.
Covers 1620–1890.

58 ———. Sticks and stones: a study of American architecture and civilization. N. Y., Dover Publications, 1955. 238p. illus.

1620———. First edition, 1924.

59 NATIONAL PARK SERVICE. Historical Handbook Series, no. 1, 1949———. illus.

Each number deals with a particular site. Primarily historical information and factual data.

60 NEWCOMB, REXFORD. Outlines of the history of architecture. Part 4, Modern architecture with particular reference to the United States. N. Y., John Wiley and Sons, 1939. 319p.

Lists buildings with dates. Bibliography.

61 PEARSON, R. M. Dark age of American architecture. Design, 52:14–15ff., Apr. 1951. illus.

Discussion of stylistic imitation.

62 PIERSON, WILLIAM HARVEY, AND DAVIDSON, MARTHA (eds.). Arts of the United States; a pictorial survey. N. Y., McGraw-Hill Book Co., 1960. 452p. illus.

63 RAPOPORT, AMOS, AND SANOFF, HENRY. Our unpretentious past. American Institute of Architects. Journal, 44:37–40, Nov. 1965. illus.

Anonymous barn architecture.

64 REPS, JOHN WILLIAM. The making of urban America; a history of city planning in the United States. Princeton, N. J., Princeton University Press, 1965. 574p. illus.

65 ROOS, FRANK J., JR. Research in American architecture. College Art Journal, 4:186–90, May 1945.

66 SCHUYLER, MONTGOMERY. American architecture. N. Y., Harper and Bros., 1892. 211p. illus.

67 SHAFFER, ROBERT B. Emerson and his circle: advocates of functionalism. Society of Architectural Historians. Journal, 7:17–20, July 1948.

68 SINGLETON, ESTHER (ed.). Historic buildings in America. N. Y., Dodd, Mead and Co., 1906. 341p. illus.

As seen and described by famous writers.

69 SLOANE, ERIC. An age of barns. N. Y., Funk and Wagnalls Co., 1966. 96p. illus.

70 SMITH, G. E. K. Tragedy of American architecture. Magazine of Art, 38:255–60ff., Nov. 1945. illus.

Philosophical discussion.

71 STURGIS, R. C. Voice from the past. American Institute of Architects. Journal, 16:23–28, July 1951.

Philosophical comparison of early and late nineteenth century design.

72 TALLMADGE, THOMAS EDDY. The story of architecture in America. N. Y., W. W. Norton and Co., 1936. 324p. illus.

73 THUM, F. C. Balanced simplicity, and a glance at the Quakers. American Institute of Architects. Journal, 19:195–200, May 1953.

Quaker architectural philosophy.

74 TUNNARD, CHRISTOPHER. The city of man. N. Y., Charles Scribner's Sons, 1953. 424p. illus.

Urban development, 1791——.

75 ——. The romantic suburb in America. Magazine of Art, 40:184ff., May 1947.

From 1850's on.

76 TUNNARD, CHRISTOPHER, AND REED, HENRY HOPE. American skyline: the growth and form of our cities and towns. Boston, Houghton Mifflin Co., 1955. 302p. illus.

On the design, materials, and distribution of buildings, 1607——.

77 VANDERBILT, CORNELIUS. The living past of America; a pictorial treasury of our historic houses and villages that have been preserved and restored. N. Y., Crown Publishers, 1955. 234p. illus.

78 WALKER, RALPH THOMAS. The fly in the amber. N. Y., n.p., 1957. 169p. illus.

Comments on building, 1830–1956.

79 WATERMAN, THOMAS TILESTON. French influence on early American architecture. Gazette des Beaux Arts, s.6 28:87–112, Aug. 1945. illus.

80 Where to find our historic houses. Old-Time New England, 55:110–16, Apr. 1965. illus.

81 WILSON, EVERETT BROOMALL. America east: its architecture and decoration. N. Y., A. S. Barnes, 1965. 322p.

82 ——. Fifty early American towns. N. Y., A. S. Barnes, 1966. 353p. illus.

Built before 1820.

PRESERVATION AND RESTORATION

Many titles on these subjects are listed by geographic location.

83 Architecture worth saving. Architectural Forum, 108:93–100, June 1958. illus.

Examples from all over the country.

84 BANNISTER, TURPIN C. AIA's national preservation program. American Institute of Architects. Journal, 20:284–89, Dec. 1953.

Reply: Steese, E. 21:180–81, Apr. 1954.

85 BARRINGTON, LEWIS. Historic restorations of the Daughters of the Revolution. N. Y., Richard R. Smith, 1941. illus.

86 BURTON, E. MILBY. Historic house restoration. Yearbook, Park and Recreation Service, Department of the Interior, National Park Service, 1941. pp. 60–65. illus.

Discussion of historic house museums and illustrations of Tempe Wicke house, near Morristown, N. J.

87 CLOUGH, PHILIP, AND CLOUGH, BETSY (eds.). Guide to covered bridges in the United States. Arlington, Mass., National Society for the Preservation of Covered Bridges, 1956. 89p. illus.

88 ——. World guide to covered bridges. Arlington, Mass., National Society for the Preservation of Covered Bridges, 1959.

Revised edition: Harold F. Eastman (ed.), 1965. A checklist for standing bridges.

89 CODMAN, JOHN. Preservation of historic districts by architectural control. Chicago, American Society of Planning Officials, 1956. 35p. illus.

90 COLEMAN, LAURENCE VAIL. The museum in America. Washington, D. C., American Association of Museums, 1939. 3v.
List of buildings preserved.

91 CONGDON, HERBERT WHEATON. Early American homes for today; a treasury of decorative details and restoration procedures. Rutland, Vt., C. E. Tuttle Co., 1963. 236p. illus.

92 CUMMINGS, ABBOTT L. (ed.). Restoration villages; with checklist. Art in America, 43:12–76, May 1955. illus.

93 DRURY, NEWTON B. The National Park Service and the preservation of historic sites and buildings. American Society of Architectural Historians. Journal, 1:18–19, July–Oct. 1941.

94 FRIEDLANDER, L. Historic buildings — landmarks and monuments. American Institute of Architects. Journal, 27:102–5, 152–55, Mar.–Apr. 1957.
Plea for planning and preservation.

95 GRIGG, M. L. Preserving historical church buildings. American Institute of Architects. Journal, 13:180–85, Mar. 1950.

96 Historic house keeping. Antiques, 70:1–88, July 1956. illus.
Special issue on all aspects of preservation.

97 Historic preservation. Magazine of the National Trust for Historic Preservation, v. 4, 1952——.
Short, good articles on restored buildings and preservation projects.

98 Historic preservation. Antiques, 75:309–404, Apr. 1959. illus.

99 HOSMER, CHARLES BRIDGHAM, JR. Presence of the past, a history of the preservation movement in the United States before Williamsburg. N. Y., G. P. Putnam's Sons, 1965. 386p.
1796–1925.

[Houses, historically considered and in terms of preservation and restoration.] Much material may be found in the publications of the various state and county historical societies. Some titles from these sources are included here. County atlases of the late nineteenth century contain lithographed illustrations of individual houses. *See also* American Scenic and Historical Preservation Society; *Annual Reports*, 1896–1928, *Bulletin*, 1929——; *Museum News*, 1924——.

100 HOVDE, EVELYN DOOHEN. Historic preservationism of architecture in the United States. Master's Thesis, University of Illinois, 1961. 187 leaves. illus.

101 HOWLAND, R. H. Architecture worth saving. American Institute of Architects. Journal, 31:29–31, May 1959. illus.
Mostly public buildings.

102 HUTH, HANS. Observations concerning the conservation of monuments in Europe and America. Washington, D. C., Department of the Interior, National Park Service, 1941. 64p. Mimeographed.

103 KIMBALL, SIDNEY FISKE. The preservation movement in America. American Society of Architectural Historians. Journal, 1:15–17, July–Oct. 1941.
Considered historically.

104 KINGSBURY, F. D. Town planning methods applied to preservation. Old-Time New England, 41:92–95, Apr. 1951.
Also: *Landscape Architecture*, 42:18–20, Oct. 1951.

105 KOCHER, A. LAWRENCE. Restoration of old buildings. Architectural Record, 67:174–75, Feb. 1930. illus.

106 LITTLE, NINA FLETCHER. Finding the records of an old house. Old-Time New England, 40:145–48, Oct. 1949.
Types of sources available and their usual location: deeds, probate records, wills, etc.

107 LOCKWOOD, ALICE G. B. Problems and responsibilities of restoration. Old-Time New England, 28:49–59, Oct. 1937. illus.

108 National Trust for Historic Preservation. A report on principles and guidelines for historic preservation in the United States. Washington, D. C., 1964. 23p.
Preservation Leaflet Series.

109 National Trust for Historic Preservation and Colonial Williamsburg. Historic preservation today. Charlottesville, University of Virginia Press, 1966. 265p.
Papers from the seminar on preservation and restoration, Williamsburg, Va., Sept. 1963.

110 PETERSON, CHARLES E. American notes. Society of Architectural Historians. Journal, v. 9, Oct. 1950——. illus.
Regular articles, primarily concerning restoration and preservation.

111 ——. A museum of American architecture. The Octagon, Nov. 1936. 5p.
Concerning a proposed museum in connection with the Jefferson National Expansion Memorial in St. Louis.

112 ——. Our national archives of historic architecture. The Octagon, July 1936. 4p.
Origin in 1933 of Historic American Buildings Survey.

113 POWYS, A. R. Repair of ancient buildings. N. Y., E. P. Dutton and Co., 1929. 208p. illus.

114 Preservation notes. Antiques, v. 72, no. 6, June 1957. illus.
Notes on restorations proposed, in progress and completed.

115 [Preservation of historic buildings.] American Society of Architectural Historians. Journal, Apr.–Oct. 1941.

116 Restoration villages east of the Mississippi; guide. Art in America, 46:83–84, Summer 1958.

[Restored buildings.] For notices of individual buildings restored, see various numbers of the *Museum News* and *New York Times* index.

117 RUSK, WILLIAM SENER. What price progress? Art and Archaeology, 33:195–205, 1932.
Covers destruction of old buildings in Boston, New York, and Philadelphia.

118 SNOW, B. Preservation portfolio, 1958. Antiques, 73:360–65, Apr. 1958. illus.

Projects proposed, planned, and completed in Massachusetts, Rhode Island, Connecticut, North Carolina, and Missouri.

119 A symposium on principles of historic restoration: and a portfolio of restorations. Antiques, 58:29–49, July 1950. illus.

Significant statements of principles involved and survey of the major restorations in the U. S.

120 UDALL, STEWART LEE, AND OWINGS, NATHANIEL ALEXANDER. Two looks at preservation. American Institute of Architects. Journal, 37:30–37, Feb. 1962. illus.

Arguments for.

121 U. S. Conference of Mayors. Special committee on historic preservation. With heritage so rich. N. Y., Random House, 1966.

122 WEINBERG, ROBERT CHARLES. Pitfalls and plausibilities of landmarks preservation. American Institute of Architects. Journal, 44:50–57, July 1965. illus.

DETAILS AND MISCELLANEOUS

123 BANNISTER, TURPIN. Iron and architecture: a study in building and invention from ancient times to 1700. Doctoral Dissertation, Harvard University, 1945.

124 BISHOP, JAMES LEANDER. History of American manufacture, from 1608–1860. Philadelphia, Edward Young and Co., 1864. 2v. illus.

125 Brick precedent in American architecture: views and details of early American brickwork. American Architect, 149:59–66, July 1936. illus.

126 BROWN, FRANK CHOUTEAU. Examples of interior doors and doorways from the eighteenth and early nineteenth centuries. Pencil Points, 21:245–60, Apr. 1940. Monograph Series, 26:113–28. illus.

Ca. 1725—*ca.* 1820.

127 ———. Some examples of period windows with details of their interior treatment. Pencil Points, 20:793–808, Dec. 1939. Monograph Series, 25:81–96. illus.

Covers 1668–1820.

128 BUGBEE, BURTON ASHFORD. On fireplaces. Antiques, 20:349–53, Dec. 1931. illus.

Colonial and Classic Revival.

129 CAYE, ROGER. Decorative wood-carving in Colonial and Post-Colonial America. Arts and Decoration, 11:178–79, Aug. 1919. illus.

130 CHRISTENSON, ERWIN O. The index of American design. N. Y., Macmillan Co., 1950. 229p. illus.

Includes architectural details.

131 CORNELIUS, CHARLES OVER. American metalwork and fixed decorations. Architectural Record, 51:88–92, Jan. 1922. illus.

132 Decoration of early American interiors. Dutch Boy Painter, pp. 115–18, July 1926. illus.

Includes some color formulas.

133 Detailed charts of architectural styles in America. House Beautiful, 77:62–63, Oct.; 52–53, Nov.; 62–63, Dec. 1935.
Covers 1700–1850.

134 DYER, WALTER ALDEN. Creators of decorative styles. Garden City, N. Y., Doubleday, Page and Co., 1917. 177p. illus.
Sources of early American styles.

135 ———. Comparative study of a group of early American doorways, part 2, porches. White Pine Series of Architectural Monographs, v. 7, no. 5, Oct. 1921. 16p. illus.
Covers 1790–1830.

136 ———. Comparative study of a group of early American windows. Monograph Series, 16:197–224, 1930. illus.

137 ———. Roofs, the varieties commonly used in the architecture of the American colonies and the early Republic. Pencil Points, 13:249–64, Apr. 1932. Monograph Series, 18:166–80. illus.

[Early American details.] Many isolated photographs and measured drawings have appeared from time to time in various numbers of *Architectural Forum*, *Architectural Record*, *Brickbuilder*, *Pencil Points*, etc.

138 EBERLEIN, HAROLD DONALDSON. The best use of brickwork. House and Garden, 19:85–87, 118–19, Feb. 1911. illus.
Discussion of bond types.

139 EMERICK, R. H. Heating historic structures. Progressive Architecture, 38:152–56, Aug. 1957.

140 FRARY, IHNA THAYER. Early American doorways. Richmond, Va., Garrett and Massie, 1937. 193p. illus.

141 FRASER, ESTHER STEVENS. Some Colonial and early American decorative floors. Antiques, 19:296–301, Apr. 1931. illus.

142 FOWLER, ROBERT LUDLOW. Historic houses and revolutionary letters. Magazine of American History, 24:81–100, Aug. 1890. illus.

143 GLOAG, JOHN, AND BRIDGWATER, DEREK. History of cast iron in architecture. London, G. Allen and Unwin, 1948. 395p. illus.

144 GUILD, LURELLE VAN ARSDALE. Geography of American antiques. Garden City, N. Y., Doubleday, Page and Co., 1927. 283p. illus.
Includes some material on builders.

145 GUTH, ALEXANDER CARL. Pencil Points, 15:271–72, June 1934.
Experiences of the architects working for the Historic American Buildings Survey.

146 HALSEY, RICHARD TOWNLEY HAINES, AND CORNELIUS, CHARLES OVER. The American Wing. Metropolitan Museum of Art. Bulletin, 19:251–65, Nov. 1924. illus.

147 ———. Handbook of the American Wing. N. Y., Metropolitan Museum of Art, 1938. 295p. illus.
First edition, 1924.

148 HERSEY, G. L. Godey's choice. Society of Architectural Historians. Journal, 18:104–11, Oct. 1959. illus.
1846–92.

149 HITCHCOCK, HENRY-RUSSELL. Early cast iron façades. Architectural Review, 109:113–16, Feb. 1951. illus.
Brief mention of American cast iron.

150 HOLLOWAY, EDWARD STRATTON. The practical book of American furniture and decoration — Colonial and Federal. Philadelphia, J. B. Lippincott Co., 1928. 191p. illus.
New edition, 1937.

151 HUNT, VIRGINIA LIVINGSTON. Franco-American memorials. American Society Legion of Honor Magazine, 26:251–61, Autumn 1955.
On buildings, sculpture, and tablets in France and the United States, 1692——.

152 HUXTABLE, A. L. The balloon frame, ca. 1833. Progressive Architecture, 38:145–46, May 1957.

153 ———. Concrete technology in U. S. A. Progressive Architecture, 41:143–204, Oct. 1960. illus.
Historical survey.

[Inventories of Federal, state, county, and city archives, church records, manuscript collections.] See Historical Records Survey, Works Progress Administration, for each state.

154 JOHNSTONE, KATHLEEN YERGER. Iron as ornament. Antiques, 45:308–10, June 1944. illus.

155 KAUFFMAN, HENRY J. Early American ironware: cast and wrought. N. Y., C. E. Tuttle Co., 1965. 166p. illus.

156 LANCASTER, CLAY. Some secret spaces and private places in Early American architecture. Antiques, 50:324–27, Nov. 1946. illus.
Hidden, built-in passages and compartments. Examples from New England to New Orleans, 1635–1806.

157 ———. Transportation design elements in American architecture. American Quarterly, 8:199–215, Fall 1956. illus.
Influences of boats, trains, and airplanes upon American building since the erection of the old ship meetinghouse at Hingham, Mass., in 1681.

158 LIPMAN, JEAN HERZBER. American folk art in wood, metal and stone. N. Y., Pantheon, 1948. 193p. illus.
1715——.

159 LOVE, PAUL VAN DERVEER. Patterned brickwork in the American colonies. Doctoral Dissertation, Columbia University, 1950. 179p.

160 MERCER, HENRY CHAPMAN. Ancient carpenters' tools — in eight parts. Old-Time New England, part 1, 15:164–97, Apr. 1925; part 2, 16:19–52, July 1925; part 3, 17:75–97, Oct. 1925; part 4, 16:118–37, Jan. 1926; part 5, 16:175–98, Apr. 1926; part 6, 17:63–89, Oct. 1926; part 7, 17:179–91, Apr. 1927; part 8, 18:99–108, Jan. 1928. illus.

161 PETERSON, CHARLES E. Early American prefabrication. Gazette des Beaux Arts, s.6 33:37–46, Jan. 1948. illus.

162 ———. Notes on copper roofing in America to 1802. Society of Architectural Historians. Journal, 24:313–18, Dec. 1965. illus.

163 ———. Notes on imported brick. Antiques, 62:50–51, July 1952. illus.

164 ROOS, FRANK JOHN, JR. The commemorative medal and architecture. Society of Architectural Historians. Journal, 14:3–7, May 1955. illus.
Mostly nineteenth century, on medals delineating buildings or parts of buildings. Bulfinch medal included.

165 SCULLY, VINCENT JOSEPH, JR. Romantic rationalism and the expression of structure in wood: Downing, Wheeler, Gardner, and the "stick style," 1840–1876. Art Bulletin, 35:121–42, June 1953. illus.
On their builders' guides. Based on Thesis, Yale University.

166 SLOANE, ERIC. American barns and covered bridges. N. Y., W. Funk, [1954]. 112p. illus.
Materials, tools, and construction procedures used in barns since 1620 and bridges since 1797.

167 SONN, ALBERT H. Early American wrought iron. N. Y., Charles Scribner's Sons, 1928. 3v. 320 illus.

168 STAUFFER, DAVID MCNELLY. American engravers upon copper and steel. N. Y., Grolier Club of the City of New York, 1907. 2v. illus.
Lists views.

169 STOKES, I. N. PHELPS, AND HASKELL, DANIEL C. American historical prints, early views of American cities. N. Y., New York Public Library, 1932. 327p. illus.
Covers 1497–1891.

170 STREETER, DONALD. Early wrought-iron hardware: spring latches. Antiques, 66:125–27, Aug. 1954. illus.

171 TRAIN, ARTHUR, JR. The story of everyday things. N. Y., Harper and Bros., 1941. 428p. illus.
Discussion of many items associated with living and architecture.

172 UNITED STATES. NATIONAL PARK SERVICE. Popular Study Series, no. 1, 1941.
Small pamphlets with some material on early architecture.

173 WATERMAN, THOMAS TALBOT. Architecture of the American Indians. American Anthropologist, 29:210–30, Apr.–June 1927. illus.
Classifies types.

174 ———. North American Indian dwellings. Annual Report of the Smithsonian Institution for 1924, part 1, pp. 461–85. illus.
Identifies and locates types. Bibliography.

175 WHIPPLE, HAZEL S. Further notes on the English brick myth. Antiques, 72:49, July 1957.

176 WHITE, M. E. Carpenter and blacksmith; the pioneer builders of America. The Museum. Newark, N. J., n.s. 9, 1:1–16, 1957. illus.

177 WILLIAMSON, SCOTT GRAHAM. American craftsman. N. Y., Crown Publishers, *ca.* 1940. 239p. illus.

178 Wood precedent in American architecture; views and details of Early American architecture from Maine and Georgia. American Architect, 148:59–66, June 1936. illus.

DOMESTIC

179 ALLEN, EDWARD B. Early American wall paintings, 1710–1850. New Haven, Conn., Yale University Press, 1926. 110p. illus.

180 American heritage: private homes of historic and antiquarian interest open to public inspection. Antiques, 37:281, June 1940.

181 ANDREWS, EDWARD DEMING. Shaker manner of building. Art in America, 48:38–45, Fall 1960. illus.
From 1780 on.

182 Antiques. History in houses, preserving our past across the nation. Antiques, v. 55, no. 1, Jan. 1949.
Series. Primarily views, various authors.

183 ARCHITECTS' EMERGENCY COMMITTEE. Great Georgian houses of America. N. Y., Kalkhoff Press, 1933–37. 2v. illus.
W. T. Bottomley, chairman of the committee; R. T. H. Halsey, author of Preface. V. 2 published by Charles Scribner's Sons.

184 BJERKOE, ETHEL HALL. Decorating for and with antiques. Garden City, N. Y., Doubleday and Co., 1950. 250p. illus.
On American domestic architecture, interior decoration, and furnishings.

185 BOGAN, HELEN DEAN. Old pictorial wall papers. Country Life in America, 32:48–50, July 1917. illus.

186 BROOKS, ARTHUR C. The old time house. Art World, 3:63–65, Oct. 1917. illus.

187 CANDEE, MRS. HELEN CHURCHILL (HUNGERFORD). Decorative styles and periods in the home. N. Y., Frederick A. Stokes and Co., 1906. 298p. illus.

188 CARPENTER, RALPH E. The fifty best historic American houses, Colonial and Federal, now furnished and open to the public. N. Y., E. P. Dutton and Co., 1955. 112p. illus.

189 COLEMAN, LAURENCE VAIL. Collecting old houses. Scientific Monthly, 41:461–63, Nov. 1935.

190 ———. Historic house museums. Washington, D. C., American Association of Museums, 1933. 187p. illus.
Contains sketch of the development of American building types and a directory.

191 CURTIS, E. R. Visit historic houses. Good Housekeeping, 109:110–14, July 1939. illus.

192 DESMOND, HARRY WILLIAM, AND CROLY, HERBERT. Stately homes in America from Colonial times to the present day. N. Y., D. Appleton and Co., 1903. 532p. illus.

193 DOW, JOY WHEELER. The American renaissance, a review of domestic architecture. N. Y., William T. Comstock Co., 1904. 182p. illus.

194 EBERLEIN, HAROLD DONALDSON. Early Colonial types and their lessons to present-day house-builders. Arts and Decoration, 11:224–25, Sept. 1919.

195 EDGELL, D. P. New England homes. Yankee. From v. 6, 1940——.
Title varies, series of articles on New England homes.

196 EVENTWORTH, IRVING B. Dependencies of the old-fashioned house. White Pine Series of Architectural Monographs, v. 8, no. 2, Apr. 1922. 14p. illus.
Covers 1790–1830.

197 FITZPATRICK, JOHN CLEMENT. Some historic houses: their builders and their places in history. N. Y., Macmillan Co., 1939. 160p. illus.

198 FOLSOM, MERRILL. Great American mansions and their stories. N. Y., Hastings House, 1963. 310p. illus.

199 GODDARD, PLINY EARLE. Native dwellings of North America. Natural History, 28:191–203, 1928. illus.
Mostly Southwest and West Coast.

200 GOULD, MARY EARLE. The Early American house: household life in America 1620–1850: with special chapters on the construction and evolution of old American homes; fireplaces and iron utensils; hearthside and barnyard activities. N. Y., C. E. Tuttle Co., 1965. illus.
Original edition, 1949.

201 HALSEY, RICHARD TOWNLEY HAINES. Wall papers and paint in the new American Wing. Metropolitan Museum of Art. Bulletin, 19:235–39, Oct. 1924. illus.

202 HALSEY, RICHARD TOWNLEY HAINES, AND TOWER, ELIZABETH. The homes of our ancestors as shown in the American Wing of the Metropolitan Museum of Art. N. Y., Doubleday, Page and Co., 1925. 320p. illus.
Later edition: Garden City, N. Y., Garden City Publishing Co., 1937.

203 HEWITT, EDWARD SHEPARD. Mystery of Early American doorways. Country Life in America, 39:35–39, Apr. 1921. illus.
Colonial and Early Republican.

204 Historic houses. Antiques, 40:38–42, July 1941.
A list.

205 Houses U. S. A.: a brief review of the development of domestic architecture in America, 1607–1946. Architectural Forum, 86:81–88, Jan.; 97–104, Mar.; 81–88, May 1947. illus.

206 HUNTER, GEORGE LELAND. Early American wall papers. Good Furniture Magazine, 19:175–79, July 1922. illus.

207 ISHAM, NORMAN MORRISON. Early American houses. Boston, Walpole Society, 1928. 61p. illus.

208 JONES, C., AND SCHLEISNER, W. H. Homes of the American presidents. N. Y., McGraw-Hill, 1962. 232p. illus.

209 KEEFE, CHARLES S. (ed.). The American house. N. Y., U. P. C. Book Co., 1933. 24p. illus.

210 KEITH, E. D. American wall paper discovery. Antiques, 62:216–17, Sept. 1952. illus.
Correction: 62:328, Oct. 1952.

211 KETTELL, RUSSELL HAWES (ed.). Early American rooms, 1650–1858. Portland, Me., Southworth-Anthoensen Press, 1936. 200p. illus.

212 KIMBALL, SIDNEY FISKE. Domestic architecture of the American colonies and of the early Republic. N. Y., Charles Scribner's Sons, 1922. 314p. illus.

213 LAMB, MARTHA JOANNE READE (HASH) (ed.). The homes of American authors. N. Y., D. Appleton and Co., ca. 1879. 256p. illus.

214 LATHROP, ELISE L. Historic houses of early America. N. Y., Robert M. McBride and Co., 1927. 464p. illus.
Later edition: N. Y., Tudor Publishing Co., 1937.

215 McCLELLAND, NANCY VINCENT. Furnishing the Colonial and Federal house. Philadelphia, J. B. Lippincott Co., 1936. 164p. illus.

216 ———. Historic wall-papers. New York History, 30:66–76, Jan. 1949. illus.
About the sale, manufacture, and types of American wallpapers, ca. 1700—ca. 1850.

217 MASON, GEORGE CHAMPLIN. The old house altered. N. Y., G. P. Putnam's Sons, 1878. 179p. illus.

218 MAYER, M. M. Domestic architecture of the Reign of Terror in the United States. Society of Architectural Historians. Journal, 7:25–26, July 1948.

219 MERCER, HENRY CHAPMAN. The dating of old houses. Bucks County, Pa., Bucks County Historical Society, Oct. 1923. 15p. illus.
Observations based upon notes taken upon an examination of about 120 old houses in Bucks County and Philadelphia, built in the eighteenth and early nineteenth centuries.

220 ———. The dating of old houses. Old-Time New England, 14:170–90, Apr. 1924. illus.
Concerns hardware and paneling.

221 ———. The origin of log houses in the United States. Bucks County Historical Society. Papers, 5:568–83, 1926. illus.

222 ———. The origin of log houses in the United States. Old-Time New England, 18:1–20, July; 51–63, Oct. 1927; 19:28–43, July 1928. illus.

223 NEWCOMB, REXFORD. Brief history of rural architecture in the United States. President's Conference on Home Building and Home Ownership, Washington, D. C., 1932, 7:35–56, 1932.

224 ———. The Colonial and Federal house. Philadelphia, J. B. Lippincott Co., 1933. 174p. illus.
Reprinted 1938.

225 NEWTON, ROGER HALE. Our summer resort architecture; an American phenomenon and social document. Art Quarterly, 4:297–321, 1941. illus.
Primarily after 1860.

226 NICHOLSON, ARNOLD. American houses in history. N. Y., Viking Press, 1965. 260p. illus.
Mostly exteriors.

227 Nightingale house at Providence, Rhode Island; Dower house, West Chester, Pa.; Bremo in Virginia; Rosedown, St. Francisville, La. Arts and Decoration, 39:6–13, Oct. 1933. illus.

228 PEET, STEPHEN DENISON. Ethnic styles in American architecture. American Antiquarian, 24:19–34, 59–76, Jan. 1902.

229 ———. Houses and house life among the prehistoric races. American Antiquarian, 10:333–57, 1888.

230 ——— (ed.). Village life and village architecture. American Antiquarian and Oriental Journal, 24:239–54, July and Aug. 1902. illus.
American Indian.

231 PICKERING, ERNEST. The homes of America, as they have expressed the lives of our people for three centuries. N. Y., Crowell, 1931. 284p. illus.

232 PRATT, DOROTHY, AND PRATT, RICHARD. A guide to Early American homes. N. Y., McGraw-Hill Book Co., 1956. 2v. illus.
Contents: v. 1, North. 251p; v. 2, South. 227p.

233 ———. A second treasury of Early American homes. N. Y., Hawthorne Books, 1959. 143p. illus.
First edition, 1954.

234 PRATT, RICHARD. Houses, history and people. N. Y., M. Evans, 1965. 240p. illus.

235 ———. A treasury of Early American homes. N. Y., Whittlesey House, 1949. 136p. illus.
Illustrations of exteriors and interiors of homes on Atlantic seaboard, and some on the lower Mississippi and California, 1650–1850, with explanatory text.

236 RAWSON, MRS. MARION NICHOLL. Old house picture book. N. Y., E. P. Dutton and Co., 1941. 96p. illus.

237 ROBINSON, A. G. Snapshots of cottages, old and new. Architectural Record, 36:345–50, Dec. 1914. illus.

238 ROBINSON, ETHEL FAY, AND ROBINSON, THOMAS P. Houses in America. N. Y., Viking Press, 1936. 239p. illus.

239 ROGERS, MEYRIC REYNOLD. American interior design, the traditions and development of domestic design from Colonial times to the present. N. Y., W. W. Norton, 1947. 309p. illus.

240 SCHELL, SHERRILL, AND OTHERS. Old American homes and their stories. Mentor, 11:21–36, June 1923. illus.

241 SCULLY, VINCENT JOSEPH. American villas; inventiveness in the American suburb from Downing to Wright. Architectural Review, 115:168–79, 364, Mar.–June 1954. illus.

242 SHACKLETON, ELIZABETH. Old American houses, the framed house. Saturday Evening Post, 199:30–31, 46, 48, Mar. 12, 1927. illus.

243 SHERLOCK, CHELSA C. Homes of famous Americans. Des Moines, Iowa, Meredith Publications, 1926. 2v. illus.

244 SHURTLEFF, HAROLD ROBERT (completed by S. E. Morison). The log cabin myth: a study of the early dwellings of the English colonists in North America. Cambridge, Mass., Harvard University Press, 1939. 215p. 33 illus.

Devoted to proving that log cabin construction did not originate spontaneously in the United States, with special reference to documentary sources of information.

245 WALLER, HERBERT H. Famous historical places in the United States. Boston, Meador Publishing Co., 1956. 312p. illus.

246 WHARTON, ANNE HOLLINGSWORTH. Salons Colonial and Republican. Philadelphia, J. B. Lippincott Co., 1900. 286p. illus.

247 WILLIAMS, HENRY LIONEL, AND WILLIAMS, OTTALIEK. Great houses of America. N. Y., G. P. Putnam's Sons, 1966. 295p.

248 ———. A guide to old American houses, 1700–1900. N. Y., A. S. Barnes, 1962. 168p. illus.

249 ———. Old American houses: how to restore, remodel and reproduce them. N. Y., Coward-McCann, 1957. 190p. illus.

History, origin, design, and construction of the small Colonial and Post-Colonial houses in America.

250 ———. Old American houses and how to restore them (1700–1850). Garden City, N. Y., Doubleday and Co., 1946. 239p. illus.

251 [WINCHESTER, ALICE (ed.).] Living with antiques. Antiques, v. 44, no. 1, July 1943.

Irregular series of articles on antiques in domestic settings. Primarily focuses on the objects but often gives exterior views and historical information. Good articles of 2–3 pages in length. Preceded by "Antiques in domestic settings" and "Antiques in American homes."

PUBLIC

252 ALLEN, RICHARD SANDERS. Covered bridges of the middle Atlantic states. Brattleboro, Vt., Stephen Greene Press, 1959. 120p. illus.

Basic history and reference for Delaware, Maryland, Pennsylvania, Virginia, West Virginia, and Washington, D.C.

253 ———. Covered bridges of the Northeast. Brattleboro, Vt., Stephen Greene Press, 1957. 121p. illus.

Basic history and reference for New York, New Jersey, and New England. Includes table of existing covered bridges and list of builders.

254 ARONIN, JEFFREY ELLIS. Rise of the factory style in the U. S. A. American Association of Architectural Bibliographers, University of Virginia, pub. 6, Spring 1956.

Out of print. Bibliography.

255 FORTENBAUGH, ROBERT. The nine capitals of the United States. York, Pa., Maple Press Co., 1948. 104p. illus.

On Philadelphia, Baltimore, Lancaster, York, Princeton, Annapolis, Trenton, New York, and Washington, 1774–1800.

256 General government and state capitol buildings of the United States. Richmond, Va., Allen and Ginter, 1890. 13p.

257 GREER, WILLIAM ROYAL. Gems of American architecture. St. Paul, Minn., Brown and Bigelow, 1935. 56p. illus.

Curiosa.

258 HAMMOND, JOHN MARTIN. Quaint and historic forts of North America. Philadelphia, J. B. Lippincott Co., 1915. 308p. illus.

259 HARLOW, LEWIS A. Covered bridges can talk. Coral Gables, Fla., Wake-Brook House, 1963. 84p. illus.

260 Historically famous lighthouses. Department of the Treasury, Coast Guard, 1950. 86p. illus.

261 KELLY, JOHN FREDERICK. Public buildings — part 1. Monograph Series, 16:309–36, 1930. illus.

Covers 1724–1820.

262 KLAUDER, CHARLES ZELLER, AND WISE, HERBERT C. College architecture in America and its part in the development of the campus. N. Y., Charles Scribner's Sons, 1929. 301p. illus.

263 LAHDE, CLARENCE WILLIAM. Our fourteen national capitols. [Washington, D. C., 1952.] [38p.] illus.

1754, 1765, 1774–1863.

264 LATHROP, ELISE L. Early American inns and taverns. N. Y., Tudor Publishing Co., 1935. 365p. illus.

N. Y., Robert M. McBride and Co., 1926.

265 MEEKS, CARROLL L. V. The railroad station: an architectural history. New Haven, Conn., Yale University Press, 1956. 203p. illus.

Yale Historical Publications, History of Art, 2. Originally Doctoral Dissertation, Harvard University, 1948.

266 MERRITT, ARTHUR HASTINGS. The story of American hospitals pictured on old blue china. New York Historical Society. Quarterly, 38:30–47, Jan. 1954. illus.

Thirteen hospitals, almshouses, and asylums in New York, Boston, Baltimore, Philadelphia, Delaware (Ohio), and Hartford, 1736——.

267 PANCOAST, HAZEL, AND PANCOAST, CHALMERS. Covered bridges to yesterdays. Newark, Ohio, 1959. 95p. illus.

268 PETERSEN, HEGEN. Kissing bridges. Brattleboro, Vt., Stephen Greene Press. 1965. 48p. illus.

Lists covered bridge societies.

269 SNOW, EDWARD ROWE. Famous lighthouses of America. N. Y., Dodd, Mead and Co., 1955. 314p. illus.

270 STEINMAN, DAVID B., AND WATSON, SARA RUTH. Bridges and their builders. N. Y., 1957.
Good general history.

271 STEVENSON, DAVID ALAN. The world's lighthouses before 1820. London, Oxford University Press, 1959. 310p. illus.

[U. S. public buildings.] *See* U. S. Superintendent of Documents, *Catalogue of Public Documents*, for numerous reports.

272 UNITED STATES TREASURY DEPARTMENT. History of public buildings under the control of the Treasury Department. Washington, D. C., Government Printing Office, 1901. 648p. illus.
Contains photographs and histories of post offices and other Federal buildings in all states.

273 WHITE, RICHARD GRANT. Old public buildings in America. Century Magazine, 27:677–88, Mar. 1884. illus.

274 WRISTON, B. Use of architectural handbooks in the design of schoolhouses from 1840 to 1860. Society of Architectural Historians. Journal, 22:155–60, Oct. 1963. illus.

275 ZORN, WALTER LEWIS. The capitols of the United States of America. Monroe, Mich., n.p., 1955. 176p. illus.
Primarily pictorial. 1774——.

RELIGIOUS

276 BACH, RICHARD FRANZ. Church planning in the United States — part 1. Architectural Record, 40:15–29, July 1916. illus.
Further numbers of this series give no reference to early churches.

277 BOURNE, FRANK A. Early American country churches. Architectural Record, 45:188, Feb. 1919. illus.

278 BRODERICK, ROBERT C. Historic churches of the United States. N. Y., W. Funk, [1958]. 262p. illus.

279 CAROE, ALBAN D. R. Old churches and modern craftsmanship. N. Y., Oxford University Press, 1949. 223p. illus.

280 DEXTER, HENRY MARTYN. Meeting houses considered historically and suggestively. Boston, J. E. Tilton and Co., 1859. 29p. illus.

281 DORSEY, STEPHEN PALMER. Early English churches in America, 1607–1807. N. Y., Oxford University Press, 1952. 206p. illus.
Episcopal churches from New England to Georgia.

282 DOW, JOY WHEELER. American renaissance steeples — in two parts. Architects and Builders Magazine, part 1, 6:122–31, Dec. 1904; part 2, 6:162–72, Jan. 1905. illus.
Ca. 1750—*ca.* 1820.

283 EMBURY, AYMAR, II. Early American churches. N. Y., Doubleday, Page and Co., 1914. 189p. illus.

284 ———. Early American churches — in eleven parts. Architectural Record, part 1, 30:584–96, Dec. 1911, Bruton Parish, Bennington, Guilford, and Augusta; part 2, 31:57–66, Jan. 1912, St. Peter's, Philadelphia, Pa., Farmington, Conn.; Christ Church, Hartford, Conn.; Old Swede's Church, Wilmington, Del.; part 3, 31:153–61, Feb. 1912, North and Center churches in New Haven, Conn., Christ Church and Pohick Meeting House near Alexandria, Va.; part 4, 31:256–66, Mar. 1912, Ship Meeting House, Hingham, Mass.; St. Peter's, New Kent County; St. Luke's, Smithfield; Old Meetinghouse, Lancaster, Mass.; part 5, 31:417–24, Apr. 1912, Sag Harbor, Long Island; Meetinghouse, Springfield, N. J.; King's Chapel, Boston, Mass.; St. Michael's, Charleston, S. C.; part 6, 31:547–56, May 1912, Deerfield; Winston-Salem; Old South, Boston, Mass.; Old Dutch, Tappan; part 7, 31:629–36, June 1912, Independent Presbyterian, Savannah, Ga.; First Presbyterian, Newark, N. J.; Trinity, Newport, R. I.; Park Street, Boston, Mass.; part 8, 32:81–88, July 1912, St. Paul's, Edenton, N. C.; First Baptist, Providence, R. I.; Congregational, East Avon, Conn.; Christ Church, Philadelphia, Pa.; part 9, 32:159–68, Aug. 1912, St. Paul's, St. Mark's, St. John's Chapel, City of New York; Trinity Church, Newark, N. J.; part 10, 32:257–66, Sept. 1912, First Church, Springfield, Mass.; First Church, Lenox, Mass.; Gloria Dei, Philadelphia, Pa.; Monumental Church, Richmond, Va.; part 11, 32:453–63, Nov. 1912, St. Phillip's Church, Charleston, S. C.; First Reformed Church, Hackensack, N. J.; North Reformed Church, Schvaalenburg, N. J.; First Reformed Church, New Brunswick, N. J. illus.

285 FRIEDMAN, THEODORE, AND GORDIS, ROBERT (eds.). Jewish life in America. N. Y., Horizon Press, 1955.
Includes Jewish arts and synagogue architecture in America, 1763–1953.

286 Historic churches of America: their romance and their history. . . . illustrated by etchings, photogravures and other reproductions . . . with full letter text by sixteen competent authorities, compiled from the chronicles, legends and traditions of the most famous churches, meeting houses, missions and cathedrals in the United States and adjoining countries. Philadelphia, H. L. Everett, 1890. 160p. illus.
Publication in twenty parts extended through the years 1891–94.

287 KRAHN, CORNELIUS. Developments and trends: Mennonite church architecture. Mennonite Life, 12:19–27, 34, Jan. 1957. illus.

288 PATTERSON, MARY S. Housing for the Quaker spirit. Friends Journal, 1:299–302, Nov. 5, 1955. illus.
Quaker meetinghouses, 1672———.

289 REED, HENRY HOPE. In the shadow of St. Barbara and St. Thomas: Catholic church architecture in America. Thought, 31:326–49, Autumn 1956.
Since ca. 1727.

290 RINES, EDWARD FRANCIS. Old historic churches of America, their romantic history and their traditions. N. Y., Macmillan Co., 1936. 373p. illus.

291 SELVERIAN, HARRY. A bibliography of American church architecture. American Association of Architectural Bibliographers, University of Virginia, 1958.

292 SHINN, GEORGE WOLFE. King's handbook of notable Episcopal churches in the United States. Boston, Moses King Corp., 1889. 286p. illus.

293 UPJOHN, HOBART B. Churches in eight American colonies, differing in elements of design. Monograph Series, v. 15, no. 1, 1929. 28p. illus.

Covers 1736–1835 and South Carolina, North Carolina, New York, New Jersey, Connecticut, New Hampshire, Vermont, and Massachusetts.

294 WALLINGTON, MRS. NELLIE (URNER). Historic churches of America. N. Y., Duffield and Co., 1907. 259p. illus.

295 WISCHNITZER, RACHEL BERNSTEIN. Synagogue architecture in the United States: history and interpretation. Philadelphia, Jewish Publication Society of America, 1955. 204p. illus.

Colonial

GENERAL REFERENCES

296 ALLIS, MARGUERITE. English prelude. N. Y., G. P. Putnam's Sons, 1936. 323p. illus.

297 AMERICAN SOCIETY OF LANDSCAPE ARCHITECTS. Colonial gardens; the landscape architecture of George Washington's time. Washington, D. C., United States George Washington Bicentennial Commission, 1932. 72p. illus.

298 BANNISTER, WILLIAM P. The American spirit in Colonial architecture. Dutch Boy Painter, pp. 102–7, July 1926. illus.

299 BLACKALL, CLARENCE H. Good and bad Colonial architecture. Architectural Review, n.s. 1:1–5, 13–18, Jan., Feb. 1899. illus.

300 BOYD, JOHN TAYLOR, JR. Some examples of Colonial lettering. Architectural Record, 40:588–90, Dec. 1916. illus.

301 BRIDENBAUGH, CARL. Cities in revolt; urban life in America, 1743–1776. N. Y., Alfred A. Knopf, 1955. 433p. illus.

302 ———. Cities in the wilderness; the first century of urban life in America, 1625–1742. N. Y., Alfred A. Knopf, 1955. 500p. illus.

First edition: Ronald Press, 1938. Another edition: Capricorn Books, 1964.

303 ———. The Colonial craftsman. N. Y., New York University Press, 1950. 214p. illus.

Also: Chicago, University of Chicago Press, 1961.

304 BROOKS, W. F. Colonial architecture. American Institute of Architects. Journal, 16:175–79, 224–29, May–June 1928.

305 BUCKLER, RIGGIN, AND OTHERS. Early American architectural details. Brickbuilder, continued as Architectural Forum, v. 24–27, Jan. 1915—Nov. 1917. illus. only.

Photographs and measured drawings. Mostly Colonial. New England, Maryland, and Virginia.

306 CAMPBELL, WILLIAM M. Some Colonial lettering. American Architect, 122:478–81, Nov. 1922. illus.

307 CEWIN, OLOF Z. So-called Colonial architecture of the United States. American Architect and Building News, 48:63–65, 75–77, 87–88, 97–99, 107–8, 115–18, 130–31, May 18—June 29, 1895. illus.

Probably Olof Z. Cervin.

308 CHANDLER, JOSEPH EVERETT. Colonial architecture of Maryland, Pennsylvania and Virginia. Boston, Bates, Kimball and Guild Co., 1892. 55p. illus.

309 Characteristic details of the Georgian Colonial style. American Architect, 124:557–62, Dec. 19, 1923. illus.

310 Colonial architecture and other Early American arts. Pittsburgh, Pa., Carnegie Library, 1926. 28p.

311 COONTZ, JOHN LEO. Light-houses of Colonial times. D. A. R. Magazine, 62:685–89, Nov. 1928.

312 DOW, GEORGE FRANCIS. Old English pattern books of hardware used in the building and cabinet makers' trades. Old-Time New England, 17:30–41, July 1926. illus.

313 DYER, WALTER ALDEN. Early American craftsmen: being a series of sketches of the lives of the more important personalities in early development of the industrial arts in America. N. Y., Century Co., 1915. 387p. illus.

314 EBERLEIN, HAROLD DONALDSON. The architecture of Colonial America. Boston, Little, Brown and Co., 1927. 289p. illus.
First edition, 1910.

315 ——. Decorative cast iron in Colonial America. Arts and Decoration, 6:373–77, Aug. 1914. illus.

316 ——. Doors and shutters of the Colonial period. House and Garden, 35:20–21, 60, Feb. 1919. illus.

317 ——. Varieties of Colonial architecture. Craftsman, 30:91–94, Apr. 1916.

318 EBERLEIN, HAROLD DONALDSON, AND HUBBARD, CORTLANDT VAN DYKE. American Georgian architecture. Bloomington, Indiana University Press, 1952. 55p. illus.
1750–1825.

319 EGGERS, OTTO R. Early American architecture. American Architect, 118:144, 176, 212, 250, 284, 320, 352, 380, 410, 442, 472, 500, 534, 576, 604, 642, 670, 704, 736, 788, 822, 860, Aug.–Dec. 1920; 119:14, 42, 68, 92, 120, 146, 174, 206, 244, 274, 364, 394, 426, 452, 488, 514, 554, 584, 612, 648, Jan.–June 1921; 120:12, 44, 80, 116, 152, 188, 224, 270, 346, 392, 428, 476, July–Dec. 1921; 121:12, 58, Jan. 1922. illus.
Also issued separately in portfolio by the American Architect, 1922.

320 EMBURY, AYMAR, II. The beauty of Colonial doorways. Country Life in America, 18:647–50, Oct. 1910. illus.

321 EWAN, N. R. Early brickmaking in the Colonies. Camden, N. J., Camden Historical Society, 1938.

322 Examples of old Colonial. Architectural Record, 9:109–14, July 1899. illus.

323 Georgian period; original details of measured drawings. N. Y., U. P. C. Book Co., 1922. 24p. illus.

324 GILBERT, F. MASON. Origin and characteristics of Colonial architecture. Western Architect, 14:21–22, Sept. 1909. illus.

325 GRIFFIN, MARTIN I. J. Bricks from England. American Catholic Historical Researches, n.s. 5:46–47, Jan. 1909.

326 HIGGINS, J. F. Colonial details. Architectural Forum, 42:335–36, May 1925. illus.

327 HOPKINS, ALFRED. Fences and fence posts of Colonial times. White Pine Series of Architectural Monographs, v. 8, no. 6, Dec. 1922. 16p. illus.

328 HOWELLS, JOHN MEAD. Lost examples of Colonial architecture. N. Y., Dover Publications, 1963. 244p. illus.

Buildings which have been altered or have disappeared: public buildings, churches, houses, interiors, and details. First edition: William Helburn, 1931.

329 HUME, I. N. Preservation of English and Colonial American sites. Archaeology, 14:250–56, Dec. 1961. illus.

330 ISHAM, NORMAN MORRISON. Glossary of Colonial architectural terms. N. Y., Walpole Society, 1939. 37p. illus.

331 JACKSON, JOSEPH. American Colonial architecture, its origin and development. Philadelphia, David McKay Co., 1924. 228p. illus.

First printed serially in the magazine, *Building*.

332 JONES, ALVIN LINCOLN. Under Colonial roofs. . . . Boston, Charles B. Webster, 1894. 237p.

333 KIENITZ, J. F. Basic phases of eighteenth-century architectural form. Art in America, 35:34–52, 215–31, Jan.–July 1947.

334 ———. Parallel of American styles. Art in America, 34:91–105, Apr. 1946. illus.

Relates painting, architecture, and furniture, *ca.* 1740—*ca.* 1760.

335 KIMBALL, SIDNEY FISKE. The study of Colonial architecture. Architectural Review, 6:28–29, 37–38, 76, Feb.–May 1918.

336 KOCHER, A. LAWRENCE. Color in Early American architecture. Architectural Record, 64:278–90, Oct. 1928.

337 LITCHFIELD, ELECTUS D. Colonial fences. Country Life in America, 31:61–64, Mar. 1917. illus.

338 MASON, GEORGE CHAMPLIN, JR. Colonial architecture, a preliminary report presented to the annual convention of the American Institute of Architects. American Architect and Building News, 10:71–74, 83–85, Aug. 13, Aug. 20, 1881. illus.

339 ———. Environment the basis of Colonial architecture. Philadelphia, printed by the order of the Society, 1906. 24p. illus.

Address before the Society of Colonial Wars in the Commonwealth of Pennsylvania.

340 MIDDLETON, G. A. T. English Georgian architecture, the sources of the American Colonial style. Architectural Record, 9:97–108, Oct. 1899. illus.

341 MORRISON, HUGH SINCLAIR. Early American architecture, from the first Colonial settlements to the national period. N. Y., Oxford University Press, 1952. 619p. illus.

Excellent survey of architecture, 1607–1780, from New England to Florida and California.

342 NUTTING, WALLACE. Early American hardware. Antiques, 4:78–81, Aug. 1923. illus.

343 POLLEY, G. HENRY. Architecture, interiors and furniture of the American colonies during the eighteenth century. Boston, G. H. Polley and Co., 1914. illus.

344 POPE, JOHN RUSSELL. Some Colonial doorways. Country Life in America, 48:48–49, Oct. 1925. illus. only.

345 PRIME, ALFRED COXE (comp.). The arts and crafts in Philadelphia, Maryland and South Carolina, 1721–1785. Boston, Walpole Society, 1929. 323p. illus.
Advertisements from newspapers. Some architects included.

346 ROSE, CHRISTINA LIVINGSTON. An unknown Colonial type. Country Life in America, 32:67–69, June 1917. illus.

347 ROWE, HENRY W. Reflections gleaned from a Colonial scrapbook. American Architect, 109:202–7, March 1916. illus.

348 SCHUYLER, MONTGOMERY. Education of a Colonial carpenter. Architectural Record, 19:227–29, Mar. 1906. illus.
Carpenters as designers, and builders' handbooks.

349 ———. A history of old Colonial architecture. Architectural Record, 4:312–66, Jan.–Mar. 1895. illus.
Includes Early Republican work.

350 SODERHOLTZ, ERIC ELLIS. Colonial architecture and furniture. Boston, G. H. Polley and Co., 1895. 66p. illus.

351 TELLER, MYRON S. Early Colonial hand forged iron work. Architectural Record, 57:395–416, May 1925. illus.

352 UPJOHN, RICHARD M. Colonial architecture of New York and the New England states. Proceedings of the third annual convention of the American Institute of Architects, Nov. 16–17, 1869, pp. 47–51.

353 WALLIS, FRANK EDWIN. American architecture, decoration and furniture of the eighteenth century. N. Y., Paul Wenzel, 1895. 53p. illus.

354 ———. The case for Colonial: what and why is Colonial architecture. House and Garden, 16:188–92, Dec. 1909. illus.

355 ———. Old Colonial architecture and furniture. Boston, G. H. Polley and Co., 1888. 66p. illus.

356 WARE, WILLIAM ROTCH, AND KEEFE, CHARLES S. (eds.). The Georgian period: being photographs and measured drawings of Colonial work with text. N. Y., U. P. C. Book Co., ca. 1923. 6v. 454 illus.
First appeared in 1898, New York, American Architect and Buildings News Company. Includes some Early Republican examples.

357 WATERMAN, THOMAS TILESTON. Seventeenth-century window lights. Antiques, 49:104–5, 118, Feb. 1946. illus.
Origin and development of windows.

358 WERTENBAKER, THOMAS J. American Georgian architecture. American Philosophical Society. Proceedings, 87:65–69, 1943. illus.
Abstract: *American Journal of Archaeology*, 48:99–100, Jan. 1944.

359 WERTZ, SYLVIA STARR, AND WERTZ, JOSEPH B. What and why the Palladian window. Antiques, 27:219–22, June 1935. illus.

360 WRIGHT, LOUIS BOOKER. The cultural life of the American colonies, 1607–1763. N. Y., Harper and Row, 1957. 292p. illus.
New American Nation Series.

DOMESTIC

361 ACKERMAN, PHYLLIS. Wallpapers in Early American homes; engaging facts about the first pictorial wall-coverings in this country. Arts and Decoration, 17:100–101, 138, 140, June 1922.
Primarily New England.

362 ALLEN, EDWARD B. Tudor houses of Colonial days. International Studio, 77:345–48, July 1923. illus.
Covers Bacon's castle, Province house, Boston, and houses near Charleston, S. C.

363 ———. Ye old picture wallpapers. House Beautiful, 49:369–72, 412, May 1921.

364 ARCHER, GLEASON L. How the Pilgrims built their houses. Americana, 39:147–55, 1936.

365 BRAZER, ESTHER STEVENS. Early American decorations; a comprehensive treatise. Springfield, Mass., Pond-Ekberg Co., 1940. 273p. illus.
Revealing the technique involved in the art of Early American decoration of furniture, walls, tinware, etc.; reference book for the student of early design and restoration.

366 BROWN, FRANK CHOUTEAU. Some examples of corner cupboards generally of early design and construction. Pencil Points, 21:795–810, Dec. 1940. Monograph Series, 26:177–92. illus.
Covers 1686–1770, mostly from Massachusetts.

367 CHANDLER, JOSEPH EVERETT. The Colonial house. N. Y., Robert M. McBride and Co., 1916. 341p. illus.

368 COUSINS, FRANK. Footscrapers of a bygone day. Country Life in America, 24:58, Oct. 1913. illus.

369 The doorway inside the Colonial house. Country Life in America, 31:34–35, Dec. 1916. illus.
Massachusetts and Maryland, *ca.* 1800.

370 DOW, JOY WHEELER. Colonial houses of the earliest type. American Architect, 115:701–6, May 1918. illus.

371 DRAKE, SAMUEL ADAMS. Our Colonial homes. Boston, Lothrop, Lee and Shepherd Publishing Co., 1894. 211p. illus.

372 EBERLEIN, HAROLD DONALDSON. What Early America had on its walls. International Studio, 38:52–56, Sept. 1927.
Pictorial and other decoration.

373 ELWELL, NEWTON W. Colonial furniture and interiors. Boston, G. H. Polley and Co., 1896. 69p. illus.

374 Footscrapers from Colonial houses. House and Garden, 40:49, Aug. 1921. illus.

375 FRENCH, LEIGH, JR. Colonial interiors; photographs and measured drawings of the Colonial and early Federal periods. N. Y., William Helburn, 1923. 125 illus.
This is *Colonial Interiors*, first series.

376 GLENN, THOMAS ALLEN. Some Colonial mansions and those who lived in them. Philadelphia, H. T. Coats and Co., 1899, 1900. 2v. 503p. illus.

377 HAMLIN, A. D. F. The genesis of the American country house. Architectural Record, 42:292–99, Oct. 1917.

378 HAMMOND, JOHN MARTIN. Colonial mansions of Maryland and Delaware. Philadelphia, J. B. Lippincott Co., 1914. 304p. illus.

379 HARLAND, MARION (pseud. of Mrs. M. V. Hawes Terhune). More Colonial homesteads and their stories. N. Y., G. P. Putnam's Sons, 1899. 449p. illus.

380 ———. Some Colonial homesteads and their stories. N. Y., G. P. Putnam's Sons, 1897. 511p. illus.

381 HAYWARD, ARTHUR H. Colonial lighting. Boston, B. J. Brimmer and Co., 1923. 168p. illus.
Also: Boston, Little, Brown and Co., 1927.

382 [cancelled]

383 HOLLISTER, PAUL MERRICK. Famous Colonial houses. Philadelphia, David McKay Co., 1921. 170p. illus.

384 HOLTZOPER, E. C. Doors and doorways. Country Life in America, 6:135–39, June 1904. illus.
Georgian.

385 HOUSTON, FRANK. Salvage for town betterment. House and Garden, 49:88–89, Jan. 1926. illus.
Philipse manor house, Yonkers, N. Y.; home of Chief Justice Marshall, Richmond, Va.; Stenton, Germantown, Pa.; Capen house, Topsfield, Mass.

386 LANGDON, WILLIAM CHAUNCEY. Everyday things in American life (1607–1776). N. Y., Charles Scribner's Sons, 1927. 353p. illus.
Social life and customs.

387 MCCLELLAND, ADA A. Some D. A. R. homes. D. A. R. Magazine, 50:147–57, Mar. 1917.

388 Master detail series. The Georgian Colonial house. Architectural Forum, 60:49–64, Jan. 1934. illus.

389 MILLAR, DONALD. Measured drawings of some Colonial and Georgian houses. N. Y., Architectural Book Publishing Co., 1916, 1930. 3v. illus.

390 NASH, GEORGE W. Old chimney cupboards. Architectural Record, 41:287–88, Mar. 1917. illus.

391 NEWTON, JANET FOSTER. Log cabin or frame. Antiques, 46:270–73, Nov. 1944. illus.

Arguments for and against the existence of the American-type log cabin before the eighteenth century.

392 NORTHEND, MARY HARROD. Colonial homes and their furnishings. Boston, Little, Brown and Co., 1912. 252p. illus.

393 NUTTING, WALLACE. Early American ironwork. Saugus, Mass., Wallace Nutting, 1919. 24p. illus.

Fireplace furniture and other hardware.

394 OAKLEY, IMOGENE B. Six historic homesteads. Philadelphia, University of Pennsylvania Press, 1936. 191p. illus.

Moffatt-Ladd house, Portsmouth, N. H.; Quincy mansion, Braintree, Mass.; Webb house, Wethersfield, Conn.; Jumel house, New York; Stenton, Philadelphia; Mount Clare, Baltimore.

395 PAINT MANUFACTURERS' ASSOCIATION OF THE UNITED STATES. EDUCATIONAL BUREAU. A photographic study of frame dwellings of Colonial times. Washington, D. C., Judd and Detweiler, 1915. 52 illus.

396 PAUL, M. REA. Decorative painting in Colonial times. Dutch Boy Painter, pp. 110–14, July 1926. illus.

397 PINDAR, PETER AUGUSTUS (pseud.). Small Colonial houses. Monograph Series, v. 17, no. 6, 1931. 23p.

Covers 1730–1803.

398 Preserving old houses. House and Garden, 51:106–7, 162, 164, Jan. 1927. illus.

Dyckman house, New York City; Abraham Browne house, Watertown, Mass.; Scotch Boardman house, Saugus, Mass.; Samuel Fowler house, Danvers, Mass. Comment on restoration by various societies.

399 RILEY, PHILIP, AND BOWMAN, K. J. Color in Colonial times. N. Y., Department of Research and Decoration of the National Lead Co., 111 Broadway, N. Y., n.d.

400 RILEY, PHILIP, AND COUSINS, FRANK. Landscape wall paper, famous old wall papers in famous old houses. House Beautiful, 39:148–49, Apr. 1916. illus.

401 ROBINSON, JANE TELLER. Kitchen of the Colonial house. House and Garden, 46:78–79, 90, Aug. 1924. illus.

402 ROBINSON, THOMAS P. The study of Colonial houses. House Beautiful, 48:85–88, Aug. 1920. illus.

403 SEWELL, ANNE. Wall papers of Colonial times. American Homes and Gardens, 11:204–8, June 1914. illus.

404 SMITH, ROBERT CHESTER. The eighteenth-cenutry house in America. Antiques, 66:477–80, Dec. 1954. illus.

405 SYMONDS, R. W. Georgian porticos in an American collection. International Studio, 99:15–18, July 1931.

Some English examples.

406 TUDOR, EVAN J. Georgian fireplaces and interior wall treatments. Arts and Decoration, 34:42–46, Nov. 1930. illus.

Examples from Pennsylvania museum collections.

407 WALLIS, FRANK E. The Colonial renaissance — houses of the middle and southern colonies. White Pine Series of Architectural Monographs, v. 2, no. 1, Feb. 1916. 14p. illus.

Covers 1707–1813, in Maryland and Virginia.

408 WATERMAN, THOMAS TILESTON. The dwellings of Colonial America. Chapel Hill, University of North Carolina Press, 1950. 312p. illus.

RELIGIOUS

409 ALVORD, JAMES CHURCH. Colonial churches of America. Art World, 2:286–89, June 1917.

410 GARDNER, G. R. Some remodeled Colonial churches. American Architect and Building News, 76:37–38, May 3, 1902. illus.

411 LATHROP, ELISE L. Old New England churches. Rutland, Vt., C. E. Tuttle Co., 1963. 171p. illus.

First edition, 1938.

412 ROSE, HAROLD WICKLIFFE. The Colonial houses of worship in America: built in the English Colonies before the Republic, 1607–1789, and still standing. N. Y., Hastings House, 1903. 574p. illus.

Early Republican

GENERAL REFERENCES

413 [American architecture. Contemporary discussion.] North American Review, 43:356–84, Oct. 1836.

Review (sic) of James Gallier's *The American Builder's General Price Book and Estimator.* Includes discussion of sacred, sepulchral, and domestic architecture in Philadelphia, New York, and Boston.

414- [American architecture. Contemporary discussion.] American Magazine of
421 Knowledge, 2:528, Aug. 1836. American Museum, 8:147, Oct. 1790. American Repertory of Arts and Science, 1:106–14, Mar. 1840. Brother Jonathan, 5:31–33, May 13; 61–62, May 20; 91–92, May 27; 121–22, June 3; 151–52, June 10; 181–82, June 17; 211–12, June 24; 241–44, July 1; 271–74, July 8; 301–3, July 15; 331–32, July 22; 421–22, Aug. 12, 1843. Gazette of the United States, v. 5, May 12, 1794. Literary Magazine and American Register, 1, no. 6:405–9, Mar. 1804. New York Mirror, 8:110, Oct. 9, 1830. Register of Pennsylvania, 2:271–72, Nov. 8, 1828.

422 [Architecture and democracy. Contemporary discussion.] Harbinger, 8:106, Feb. 3, 1849.

423 CAEMMERER, HANS PAUL. The influence of classical art on the architecture of the United States. Doctoral Dissertation, American University, 1938.

424 Church architecture in the United States. Literary World, 3:733, 920–21, Oct. 14, Dec. 9, 1848.

425 CLARK, T. C. Architects and architecture. Christian Examiner and Religious Miscellany, 49:251–77, Sept. 1850.

426 CLEVELAND, HENRY R. A selection from his writings. Boston, The Author, 1844. 384p.

427 [College architecture. Contemporary criticism.] Yale Literary Magazine, 18:240–44, May 1853.

428 CORNELIUS, CHARLES OVER. Some Early American doorways. Old-Time New England, 18:99–108, Jan. 1928. illus.

Doorways owned by the Metropolitan Museum, 1792—ca. 1820.

429 EBERLEIN, HAROLD DONALDSON, AND HUBBARD, CORTLANDT VAN DYKE. Colonial interiors, Federal and Greek Revival. N. Y., William Helburn, 1938. 84p. illus.

This is *Colonial Interiors*, third series. Covers Delaware, Maryland, New Hampshire, New Jersey, New York, and Pennsylvania.

430 Ecclesiastical architecture. Yale Literary Magazine, 11:65–72, Dec. 1845.
Difference in structure of houses of worship of different peoples and how these architectural works are somewhat an index of the character of the people who build them.

431 FALLON, JOHN T. Domestic architecture of the early nineteenth century. American Architecture, 110:139–44, Sept. 6, 1916.

432 GARDINER, FANNY HALE. The Octagon house. Country Life in America, 23:79–80, Mar. 1913. illus.
Orson Squire Fowler houses from several states.

433 GIEDION, SIGFRIED. Space, time and architecture, the growth of a new tradition. Cambridge, Mass., Harvard University Press, 1941. 601p. illus.
Some new material on nineteenth-century American architecture.

434 GILLET, LOUIS. L'architecture aux États-Unis et l'influence française. France-Amérique, 4ᵉ année, pp. 77–80, 154–57, 240–44, 288–91, Feb., May 1913.

435 [GILMAN, ARTHUR DELEVAN.] Architecture in the United States. North American Review, 58:436–80, Apr. 1844.
Critical discussion, primarily of public buildings in Boston, Mass.

436 GREENOUGH, HORATIO. American architecture. N. Y., G. P. Putnam and Co., 1852. 222p.
In Horatio Greenough, *Travels, Observations and Experiences of a Yankee Stonecutter*, part 1, by Horace Bender (pseud.), and in the *North American Review* in 1843. See also *Southern Literary Messenger*, 19:513–17, Aug. 1853; *Democratic Review*, 13:206–10, 1843.

437 HOLLOWAY, EDWARD STRATTON. Interior architecture of the Federal era. House and Garden, 52:104–6, Oct. 1927.

438 The introduction of iron buildings. Debow's Review, 20:641–42, May 1856.
On the proposed use of iron as a building material.

439 JACKSON, JOSEPH. The development of American architecture, 1783–1830. Philadelphia, David McKay Co., 1926. 230p. illus.

440 JARVES, JAMES JACKSON. Art hints. N. Y., Harper and Bros., 1855. 398p.
Architecture, sculpture, and painting.

441 ———. The art idea. N. Y., Hurd and Houghton, 1864. 381p.
Chapters 17 and 18 contain comments on American architecture. Other editions, 1865–77.

442 LANGDON, WILLIAM CHAUNCEY. Everyday things in American life. v. 2 (1776–1876). N. Y., Charles Scribner's Sons, 1941. 398p. illus.

443 MAJOR, HOWARD. Return of cast iron. Country Life in America, 54:69–70, Oct. 1928. illus.

444 METCALF, FRANK J. Octagon houses of Washington and elsewhere. Columbia Historical Society. Records, 26:91–105, 1924.

445 New article of commerce. New Yorker, 1:381, Sept. 3, 1836.
Houses to be floated from Pennsylvania to Mississippi.

446 Origin of classic place names in central New York. New York State Historical Association. Quarterly, 7:155–68, July 1926.

447 PRATT, RICHARD H. From Georgian to Victorian. House and Garden, 51:120–21, 142, 146, 196, Apr. 1927. illus.

Includes discussion of Asher Benjamin and Minard Lafever.

448 RANKIN, ROBERT. American architecture. Yale Literary Magazine, 10:411–14, Aug. 1845.

Townsend prize essay. Short history of the art in the Old World and how it is developing in the United States.

449 ROOS, FRANK JOHN, JR. The Egyptian style; notes on our Early American taste. Magazine of Art, 33:218–23, 255–56, Apr. 1940. illus.

450 RUSK, WILLIAM SENER. Egyptian echoes in American architecture. Americana, 28:295–98, 1934.

451 SCHMIDT, CARL F. The octagon fad. Scottsville, N. Y., 1958. 207p. illus.

452 SWAN, NORMA LIPPINCOTT. Old carved mantel-pieces. Country Life in America, 47:50–51, Apr. 1925. illus. only.

453 [THOMPSON, JOHN W.] Cast iron buildings: their construction and advantages. N. Y., J. W. Harrison, 1856. 16p. illus.

Refers to an iron building in New York City by James Bogardus.

454 TUTHILL, LOUISA CAROLINE (HUGGINS). History of architecture from the earliest times: its present condition in Europe and the United States. Philadelphia, Lindsay and Balkiston, 1848. 426p. illus.

GREEK REVIVAL

455 BIDDLE, EDWARD. Nicholas Biddle. Numismatic and Antiquarian Society of Philadelphia. Proceedings, v. 27, 1916.

456 COMSTOCK, HELEN. Some aspects of Greek Revival in America. Connoisseur, 113:114–18, June 1944, illus.

457 GOODYEAR, W. H. Greek architecture in the United States. Chautauquan, 16:3–11, 131–37, 259–67, 1892. illus.

458 Greek Revival in America. Magazine of Art, 36:288–92, Dec. 1943. illus.

Exhibition at the Metropolitan Museum of Art.

459 HAMLIN, TALBOT F. Greek Revival architecture in America. London, Oxford University Press, 1944.

Includes a list of articles in American periodicals prior to 1850 by Sarah Hamlin. Now in paperback by Dover.

460 ———. The Greek Revival in America and some of its critics. Art Bulletin, 24:244–58, Sept. 1942.

461 ———. The Greek Revival in American architecture. Columbia University Quarterly, 31:171–82, 1939.

1820's and '30's.

462 Hints to American architects. National Register, 2:209–10, Nov. 30, 1816.

On the nobleness of Grecian architecture, tracing its origin and development.

463 KIMBALL, SIDNEY FISKE. Romantic classicism in architecture. Gazette des Beaux Arts, s.6 25:95–112, Feb. 1944. illus.

464 Magnificent Greek Revival. Life, 39:58–67ff., Aug. 29, 1955. illus.

465 MAJOR, HOWARD. Domestic architecture in the early American Republic — the Greek Revival. Philadelphia, J. B. Lippincott Co., 1926. 236p. illus.
Reprint with similar title: Bronx, N. Y., Benjamin Blom, 1967. 259p. illus.

466 ———. Greek influence on American homes. Country Life in America, 47:41–43, Feb. 1925. illus.

467 ———. The Greek Revival: the American national expression. Architectural Forum, 40:45–51, Feb. 1924. illus.

468 O'DONNELL, THOMAS EDWARD. The architecture of the Greek Revival and its influence in America. Master's Thesis, University of Illinois, 1924.

469 PRATT, RICHARD H. How the Greek Revival began. House and Garden, 52:88–89, Aug. 1927. illus.

470 RALSTON, RUTH. Greek Revival architecture. Antiques, 45:76–79, Feb. 1944. illus.
1815–60.

471 SCHUYLER, MONTGOMERY. The old Greek Revival — in four parts. American Architect, part 1, 98:121–26, 128, Oct. 12, 1910; part 2, 98:201–4, 206–8, Dec. 21, 1910; part 3, 99:81–84, 86–87, Mar. 1, 1911; part 4, 99:161–66, 168, May 3, 1911. illus.
Discussion of Latrobe, Mills, Strickland, and others.

472 When civic architecture flourished; reproductions of old prints from the Greek Revival. Architectural Forum, 110:106–11, Jan. 1959. illus.

GOTHIC AND OTHER REVIVALS

473 BOAS, GEORGE (ed.). Romanticism in America. Baltimore, Johns Hopkins Press, 1940. 202p. illus.

474 BOLTON, T. Gothic Revival architecture in America: the history of a style. American Collector, 17:6–9, April; 15–18, May; 16–19, June 1948. illus.

475 CLARK, KENNETH. The Gothic Revival, an essay in the history of good taste. N. Y., Charles Scribner's Sons, 1929. 308p. illus.
Background for American Gothic.

476 EARLY, JAMES. Romantic thought and architecture in the United States. Doctoral Dissertation, Harvard University, 1953.

477 ECKELS, C. W. Egyptian Revival in America. Archaeology, 3:164–69, Sept. 1950. illus.

478 GILCHRIST, AGNES ADDISON. Romanticism and the Gothic Revival. N. Y., Richard R. Smith, 1938. 187p. illus.
A study of the rise and decline of the romantic movement in Europe and America and its effect on contemporary literature and architecture. Issued also as Doctoral Dissertation, University of Pennsylvania, 1938.

[Gothic Revival buildings, including Italian villas, etc.] See *Godey's Lady's Book*, *Peterson's Magazine*, and similar publications, *ca.* 1845—*ca.* 1870. See also entries under A. J. Downing, Samuel Sloan, Robert Mills, Richard Upjohn, etc.

479 KIENITZ, JOHN F. The generations of the 1850's, 1860's and 1870's in the fine arts of the United States in relation to parallel phases of American culture. Doctoral Dissertation, University of Wisconsin, 1938.

480 LANCASTER, CLAY. Architectural follies. American Heritage, 5:6–11, Winter 1954. illus.

1753–1884.

481 ———. Italianism in American architecture before 1860. American Quarterly, 4:127–48, Summer 1952. illus.

1800———.

482 ———. Japanese influence in America. N. Y., W. H. Rawls, 1963. 292p. illus.

On all of the arts in the United States, particularly architecture.

483 ———. Oriental forms in American architecture, 1800–1870. Art Bulletin, 29:183–93, Sept. 1947. illus.

484 MAASS, JOHN. In defense of the Victorian houses. American Heritage, 6:34–41, Oct. 1955. illus. Appended: A portfolio of Victorian architecture, by Walker Evans.

Built *ca.* 1840———.

485 ———. The gingerbread age: a view of Victorian America. N. Y., Holt, Rinehart and Winston, 1957. 212p. illus.

1837–87. Includes "American Gothic," "Italianate interlude," and "mansardic era."

486 MEEKS, CARROLL L. V. Creative eclecticism. Society of Architectural Historians. Journal, 12:15–18, Dec. 1953.

Philosophical discussion.

487 ———. Romanesque before Richardson in the United States. Art Bulletin, 35:17–33, Mar. 1953. illus.

1846–76.

488 NEWMAN, RICHARD K., JR. Yankee Gothic: medieval architectural forms in the Protestant church building of nineteenth-century New England. Doctoral Dissertation, Yale University, 1949.

489 OMOTO, SADAYOSHI. Some aspects of the so-called "Queen Anne" revival style of architecture. Doctoral Dissertation, Ohio State University, 1955. 330p.

Discussion of both England and America.

490 PEVSNER, N., AND LANG, S. Egyptian Revival. Architectural Review, 119:242–54, May 1956. illus.

Includes some American examples.

491 Steamboat Gothic. Minneapolis Institute. Bulletin, 20:161, Nov. 28, 1931.

New England

GENERAL REFERENCES

492 APPLETON, WILLIAM SUMNER. Destruction and preservation of old New England buildings. Art and Archaeology, 8:131–84, May–June 1919. illus.

493 ———. The Society for the Preservation of New England Antiquities and its work. American Society of Architectural Historians. Journal, 1:19–20, July–Oct. 1941.

494 BROWN, FRANK CHOUTEAU. Architecture 1620–1750. House and Garden, 75:35, 64, June 1939. illus.

495 ———. Architecture 1750–1850. House and Garden, 75:40–41, June 1939. illus.

496 ———. Early brickwork in New England. Pencil Points, 15:165–80, Apr. 1934. Monograph Series, 20:113–28. illus.
Covers 1668–1763 in and around Boston.

497 ———. Some interior arched openings found in northeastern Colonial work. Pencil Points, 21:651–66, Oct. 1940. Monograph Series, 26:161–76. illus.
Covers 1660–1818.

498 ———. Some New England paneled room ends from the seventeenth and early eighteenth centuries. Pencil Points, 21:379–94, June 1940. Monograph Series, 26:129–44. illus.

499 BYNE, ARTHUR G. Some century-old doorways in rural New England. Architectural Record, 30:574–83, Dec. 1911. illus. only.

500 CHAMBERLAIN, NATHAN HENRY. A paper on New England architecture. Boston, Crosby, Nichols and Co., 1858. 30p.
Read before the New England Historic Genealogical Society, September 4, 1858. Hitchcock suggests that this pamphlet is probably the first separate publication on Colonial architecture.

501 CHAMBERLAIN, SAMUEL. Ever New England. N. Y., Hastings House, 1945. 247p. illus.

502 ———. House in New England. N. Y., Hastings House, 1948. 252p. illus.
Fifth revised edition; first edition, 1937. Covers 1627–1835.

503 ———. New England doorways. N. Y., Hastings House, 1939. 101p. illus.

504 ———. The New England image. N. Y., Hastings House, 1962. 192p. illus.

505 ———. Six New England villages. N. Y., Hastings House, 1948. 104p. illus.

Descriptions and photographs of houses, 1684–1825, in Hancock, N. H., Litchfield, Conn., Little Compton, R. I., Bennington, Vt., Deerfield, Mass., and Wiscasset, Me.

506 CORSE, MURRAY PINCHOT. Colonial architecture of New England. Architecture, 47:62–63, Apr. 1923. illus. only.

507 ———. Puritan architecture. Architecture, 45:1–5, 43–46, Jan.–Feb. 1922.

508 DONNELLY, M. C. Astronomical observatories in New England. Old-Time New England, 50:72–80, Jan. 1960. illus.

509 ———. New England pyramids, 1651–1705. Society of Architectural Historians. Journal, 19:76–77, May 1960. illus.

Small spires.

510 DOW, GEORGE FRANCIS. Arts and crafts in New England, 1704–75. Topsfield, Mass., Wayside Press, 1927. 326p. illus.

Gleanings from Boston newspapers relating to printing, engraving, silversmiths, pewterers, furniture, pottery, old houses, costumes, trades and occupations, etc.

511 DRAKE, SAMUEL ADAMS. Nooks and corners of the New England coast. N. Y., Harper and Bros., ca. 1875. 459p. illus.

512 FEDERAL WRITERS' PROJECT. Here's New England! Boston, Houghton Mifflin Co., 1939. 122p. illus.

513 FORBES, ALLEN. Towns of New England and old England. N. Y., Tudor Publishing Co., 1936. illus.

514 GARDNER, GEORGE CLARENCE. Massachusetts Bay influence on Connecticut Valley Colonial. White Pine Series of Architectural Monographs, v. 11, no. 1, 1925. 17p. illus.

Covers ca. 1700–1800.

515 GRAHAM, BENJAMIN. Some New England staircases — 1670–1770. Pencil Points, 14:445–60, Oct. 1933. Monograph Series, 19:65–80. illus.

516 GRANDGENT, LOUIS. Colonial doorways. House Beautiful, 49:476–77, June 1921; 50:102–3; 200–201. illus.

Unlabeled illustrations.

517 HAMLIN, TALBOT FAULKNER. Variety and harmony. Pencil Points, 22:83–88, Feb. 1941. illus.

Examples from New England.

518 HASKELL, ARTHUR C. Early interior doorways in New England — part 1. Pencil Points, 13:680–94, Oct. 1932. Monograph Series, 18:230–44. illus.

Covers 1652–1768.

519 HAYES, MARIAN. Life and architecture in the Connecticut Valley. Doctoral Dissertation, Radcliffe College, 1945.

520 HIPKISS, EDWIN J. Early eighteenth-century American interiors. Architectural Forum, 38:35–40, Jan. 1923. illus.

521 ———. Interior woodwork in New England during the seventeenth and eighteenth centuries. White Pine Series of Architectural Monographs, v. 11, no. 2, 1925. 15p. illus.
Mostly Connecticut.

522 HOOPER, MARION, AND CRANE, CHARLES EDWARD. Life along the Connecticut River. Brattleboro, Vt., Stephen Daye Press, 1939. 120p. illus.

523 HOWE, OLIVER H. Early town planning in New England. American Architect, 118:464–69, Oct. 13, 1920. illus.

524 HOWELLS, JOHN MEAD. Architectural heritage of the Merrimack. N. Y., Architectural Book Publishing Co., 1941. 248p. illus.

525 KENNEDY, R. W. Toward an old architecture. Pencil Points, 25:78–83, Aug. 1944. illus.
Philosophical discussion of old vs. new styles.

526 KENT, LOUISE. Village greens of New England. N. Y., M. Barrows and Co., 1948. 280p. illus.
1620–1948.

527 KILHAM, WALTER H. Colonial brickwork of New England. Brickbuilder, 10:244–48; 11:3–6, 25–28, Dec. 1901—Feb. 1902. illus.

528 ———. Colonial gateways and fences in New England. House and Garden, 7:225–32, Apr. 1905. illus.

529 KINGMAN, RALPH CLARKE. New England Georgian architecture. N. Y., Architectural Book Publishing Co., 1913. illus.

530 KINGSBURY, F. D. Pattern of New England settlement as exemplified by the properties of the society; together with a comparison of ancient and modern routes of travel. Old-Time New England, 40:200–218, Apr. 1950. illus.

531 LAWRENCE, ROBERT MEANS. New England Colonial life. Cambridge, Mass., Cosmos Press, 1927. 276p. illus.

532 MERRILL, DAVID OLIVER. Isaac Damon and the architecture of the Federal period in New England with illustrations. Doctoral Dissertation, Yale University, 1965. 737p. illus.
1781–1862.

533 NASH, SUSAN HIGGINSON. New England decoration — the development of interior design — 1620–1850. House and Garden, 75:30–34, June 1939. illus.

534 [New England.] For miscellaneous titles on New England see various issues of the *New England Quarterly*.

535 [New England number.] House and Garden, v. 75, June 1939. illus.
Major articles are included elsewhere. Also includes brief references to particular houses.

536 NICHOLS, ARTHUR HOWARD. The bells of Paul and Joseph W. Revere. Boston, 1911. 40p. illus.
Reprinted from *Historical Collections of Essex Institute*, Salem, Mass.

537 PHILLIPS, J. H. Early American interiors. Architectural Review, n.s. 8:105–9, 131–37, 163–70, Apr.–June, 1919. illus.
Colonial, mostly New England.

538 POOR, ALFRED EASTON. Colonial architecture of Cape Cod, Nantucket, and Martha's Vineyard. N. Y., William Helburn, 1932. illus.

539 POWELL, LYMAN P. (ed.). Historic towns of New England. N. Y., G. P. Putnam's Sons, 1898. 599p. illus.

540 PRESSEY, PARK. Preserving the landmarks. House Beautiful, 36:97–100, Sept. 1914. illus.
Covers 1650–1808.

541 ROBERTS, GEORGE S. Historic towns of Connecticut River Valley. Schenectady, N. Y., Robson and Adee, 1906. 494p. illus.

542 ROBINSON, ALBERT GARDNER. Old New England doorways. N. Y., Charles Scribner's Sons, 1919. 21p. illus.

543 SAYLOR, HENRY H. Early American style of New England. House and Garden, 67:46–47, 78, 80–81, 92, Apr. 1935. illus.

544 Some old New England doorways, records of the craftsmanship of Colonial days. Craftsman, 22:216–19, May 1912.

545 Synopsis of New England architecture and decoration from 1620–1850. House and Garden, 75:24–25, June 1939.

546 WAILES, REX. Notes on some windmills in New England. Old-Time New England, 21:99–128, Jan. 1931. illus.

547 WARING, JANET. Early American stencils on walls and furniture. N. Y., W. R. Scott, 1937. 148p. illus.

548 WATKINS, MALCOLM. Notes on the New England blacksmith. Antiques, 51:180–82, Mar. 1947. illus.
Illustrations of architectural details: handles, latches, hinges.

549 WHIPPLE, J. RAYNER. Old New England weather vanes. Old-Time New England, 31:45–56, Oct. 1940. illus.

550 WILLARD, ASHTON R. Early architecture of New England. Western Architect, 17:64–67, July 1911. illus.
Domestic and public.

DOMESTIC

551 ACKERMAN, PHYLLIS. Wall papers, from New England houses. Antiques, 69:440–43, May 1956. illus.
1730–1860.

552 ALLEN, EDWARD B. Colonial porticoes of New England. House Beautiful, 48:102–3, Aug. 1920. illus.
Marblehead and Salem.

553 ———. Some old New England frescoes. Old-Time New England, 25:78–84, Jan. 1935. illus.
Weymouth, Mass.

554 BARTLETT, STUART. Garrison houses along the New England frontier. Pencil Points, 14:253–68, June 1933. Monograph Series, 19:33–48. illus.
Covers 1640–1750.

555 BRIGGS, MARTIN S. Homes of the pilgrim fathers in England and America (1620–1685). London, Oxford University Press, 1932. 211p. illus.

556 BROWN, FRANK CHOUTEAU. New England Colonial houses of the early portion of the eighteenth century. White Pine Series of Architectural Monographs, v. 1, no. 2, 1915. 15p. illus.

557 ———. Three-story Colonial houses of New England. White Pine Series of Architectural Monographs, v. 3, no. 1, Feb. 1917. 14p. illus.
Covers 1760–1809.

558 CHAMBERLAIN, SAMUEL. Beyond New England thresholds. N. Y., Hastings House, 1938. 95p. illus.

559 ———. A small house in the sun; the visage of rural New England. N. Y., Hastings House, 1936. 96p. illus.

560 CORNER, JAMES M., AND SODERHOLTZ, ERIC ELLIS. Examples of domestic Colonial architecture in New England. Boston, Boston Architectural Club, 1892. 50 illus.
First edition, 1891.

561 COUSINS, FRANK. Stairways of old New England. Country Life in America, 26:66–67, Oct. 1914. illus.

562 COVELL, ALWYN T. Old Chatham and neighboring dwellings south of the Berkshires. White Pine Series of Architectural Monographs, v. 5, no. 5, Oct. 1919. 14p. illus.
New York and Connecticut.

563 CRAWFORD, MARY CAROLINE. The romance of old New England rooftrees. Boston, L. C. Page and Co., 1903. 390p. illus.

564 CREESE, WALTER L. Round houses of New England. Old-Time New England, 43:85–90, Apr.–June, 1953. illus.
1829–1939.

565 DERBY, RICHARD B. Early houses of the Connecticut Valley. White Pine Series of Architectural Monographs, v. 2, no. 3, June 1916. 14p. illus.
Covers 1660–1800. Frary house and Williams house, Deerfield, Mass. Wheeler house, Orford, N. H. (1800), credited to Bulfinch.

566 DOW, GEORGE FRANCIS. Domestic life in New England in the seventeenth century. Topsfield, Mass., Perkins Press, 1925. 48p. illus.
A lecture at the opening of the American Wing of the Metropolitan Museum of Art.

567 ———. Houses of the first settlers in New England. Antiques, 18:127–30, Aug. 1930. illus.

568 ERSKINE, RALPH C. Architectural sermons in Early American homes. Arts and Decoration, 18:32–33, Feb. 1923. illus.

569 HIPKISS, EDWIN J.; KELLY, J. FREDERICK; REAGAN, OLIVER; FOSTER, WILLIAM D.; AND WELSH, LEWIS E. Early American domestic architecture. Architectural Forum, 32:53–60, Feb. 1920, Wentworth-Gardner house, Portsmouth, N. H.; 33:101–8, Sept. 1920, Wellington house near Waltham, Mass.; 33:175–82, Nov. 1920, Warner house near Chester, Conn.; 33:219–26, Dec. 1920, Jessup house, Westport, Conn.; 34:47–54, Feb. 1921, Sir William Johnson house, Fort Johnson, N. Y. illus.

570 Historic houses in New England open to the public. House and Garden, 76:65, June 1939.

[Houses, New England.] *Old-Time New England* has numerous short notes on New England houses, not listed here.

571 HOWE, LOIS L., AND FULLER, CONSTANCE. Details from old New England houses. N. Y., Architectural Book Publishing Co., 1913. 52p. illus.

572 HUNTER, WALKER C. Various types of old Colonial knockers found on houses in New England. House Beautiful, 39:12, Apr. 1916. illus.

573 LITTLE, ARTHUR. Early New England interiors . . . Salem, Marblehead, Portsmouth and Kittery. Boston, A. Williams and Co., 1878. 45p. illus.

574 LITTLE, NINA FLETCHER. On dating New England houses. Antiques, 47:155–57, 228–31, 273–76, 334–36, Mar.–June 1945. illus.
By structural elements, 1600's—1820.

575 MACDONALD, ALBERT J. Colonial brick houses of New England. Boston, Rogers and Manson Co., 1917. 55p. illus.

576 MIXER, KNOWLTON. Development of the New England homestead. House Beautiful, 62:245–46, 393–95, Sept.–Oct. 1927. illus.

577 ———. Old houses of New England. N. Y., Macmillan Co., 1927. 346p. illus.

578 NORTHEND, MARY HARROD. Historic homes of New England. Boston, Little, Brown and Co., 1914. 274p. illus.

579 ———. Old time latches and knockers. American Homes and Gardens, 5:466–68, Dec. 1908. illus.

580 ———. Old time wall papers. American Homes and Gardens, 2:403–5, June 1906. illus.

581 PEABODY, R. S. Georgian houses of New England. American Architect and Building News, 2:338–39, Oct. 20, 1877; 3:54–55, Feb. 16, 1878. illus.
First article signed, "Georgian."

582 ROBIE, VIRGINIA. A Colonial pilgrimage. House Beautiful, 15:78–83, 171–75, 315–17, Jan.–Apr. 1904; 16:13–15, Aug. 1904. illus.
Part 1. Portsmouth, N. H., and Kittery, Me.; part 2. Exeter, N. H.

583 ROBINSON, ALBERT G. Old New England houses. N. Y., Charles Scribner's Sons, 1920. 127p. illus.

584 SANBORN, KATE. Old time wall papers and decorations. House Beautiful, 12:304–8, Oct. 1902. illus.

585 SMITH, CHARLES LYMAN. Colonial doorways from a layman's standpoint. American Architect, 121:204–9, Mar. 1922. illus.
Primarily Massachusetts.

586 TEMPLE, GRACE LINCOLN. Hunting old-time wall-papers. American Magazine of Art, 11:381–90, Sept. 1920. illus.

587 WATERMAN, THOMAS TILESTON. Two eighteenth-century panelled rooms, Connecticut and Massachusetts. Architecture, 50:pl. 153, Oct. 1924. illus.
East chamber, Parker Tavern, Reading, Mass.; north parlour, house at Flanders, Conn.

588 WHITEFIELD, EDWIN. The homes of our forefathers, being a selection of the oldest and most interesting buildings, historical houses and noted places in Maine, New Hampshire and Vermont. Reading, Mass., The Author, 1886. 3p. illus.

589 ———. The homes of our forefathers, being a selection of the oldest and most interesting buildings, historical houses and noted places in Rhode Island and Connecticut. Boston, Whitefield and Crocker, 1882. 6p. illus.

590 WILLOUGHBY, CHARLES C. Houses and gardens of the New England Indians. American Anthropologist, 8:115–32. illus.
Cites early references.

591 WORTH, HENRY BARNARD. The development of the New England dwelling house. Lynn, Mass., F. S. Whitten, 1911. 24p. illus.
Reprinted from Lynn Historical Society. *Register*, 14:129–52, 1911.

PUBLIC

592 ALLEN, RICHARD SANDERS. The Connecticut River bridges. Covered Bridge Topics, 6, no. 1:6–7, 2:4–5, 3:4–7, 4:6–7, Mar.–Dec. 1948.
Covered bridges from Ascutney, Vt. to the mouth of the river, 1785——.

593 CARSON, GERALD HEWES. Country stores in early New England. Sturbridge, Mass., Old Sturbridge Village, [1955]. 15p. illus.
Old Sturbridge Village Booklet Series, 3.

594 CRAWFORD, MARY CAROLINE. Among old New England inns, being an account of little journeys to various quaint inns and hostelries of Colonial New England. Boston, L. C. Page and Co., 1907. 381p. illus.

595 DEAN, ELDON L. Early college and educational buildings in New England. Pencil Points, 15:597–612, Dec. 1934. Monograph Series, 20:177–92. illus.
Covers 1744–1829.

596 ELDEN, ALFRED. Tide-mills in New England. Old-Time New England, 25:117–27, Apr. 1935.

597 GREELEY, W. R. Flora of democracy; New England meeting houses and city halls. American Architect, 133:217–24, Feb. 1928. illus.

598 HAMILTON, EDWARD PIERCE. The New England village mill. Old-Time New England, 42:29–38, Oct. 1951. illus.
Grist and saw mills, 1632–1800.

599 MARLOWE, GEORGE FRANCIS. Coaching roads of old New England; their inns and taverns and their stories. N. Y., Macmillan Co., 1945. 200p. illus.

600 MARR, HARRIET WEBSTER. The four-square school. Antiques, 65:475–77, June 1954. illus.
New England schools, 1700–1800.

601 MEEKS, CARROLL L. V. Some early depot drawings. Society of Architectural Historians. Journal, 8:33–42, Jan. 1949. illus.
Original drawings for New England railroad stations, 1835–68.

602 NORTHEND, MARY HARROD. We visit old inns. Boston, Small, Maynard and Co., 1925. 176p. illus.

603 PRENTICE, THOMAS MORGAN. Historic taverns in New England. Connecticut Magazine, 7:459–72, 1903.

604 RIPLEY, HUBERT G. New England inns and taverns. Pencil Points, 13:804–8, Dec. 1932. Monograph Series, 18:246–60. illus.
Covers 1686–1797.

605 SCHUYLER, MONTGOMERY. Architecture of American colleges. Part 6. Dartmouth, Williams, and Amherst. Architectural Record, 28:425–42, Dec. 1910.

606 ———. Architecture of American colleges. Part 7. Brown, Bowdoin, Trinity, and Wesleyan. Architectural Record, 29:144–66, Feb. 1911.

607 SNOW, EDWARD ROWE. Famous New England lighthouses. Boston, Yankee Publishing Co., 1945. 457p. illus.

608 WAGEMANN, CLARA EOLA. Covered bridges of New England. Rutland, Vt., C. E. Tuttle Co., 1952. 151p. illus.
Census of existing covered bridges in New England and New York built since 1780. Previous edition, 1931.

609 WALES, REX. Notes on some windmills in New England. Old-Time New England, 21:99–128, Jan. 1931.

610 WALKER, C. ERNEST. Covered bridge ramblings in New England, with 100 reproductions of photographs taken by the author. Contoocook, N. H., 1959. 114p. illus.

611 ———. Covered bridges of the Connecticut River Valley in 1954. Covered Bridge Topics, 12:1, 6–8, Dec. 1954. illus.

612 WILLOUGHBY, MALCOLM F. Lighthouses of New England. Boston, T. O. Metcalf Co., 1929. 253p. illus.

RELIGIOUS

613 BACON, LEONARD. The genesis of the New England churches. N. Y., Harper and Bros., 1874. 485p. illus.

614 BACON, MRS. MARY SCHELL (HOKE). Old New England churches and their children. N. Y., Doubleday, Page and Co., 1906. 442p. illus.

615 BELLOWS, ROBERT P. Country meeting houses along the Massachusetts–New Hampshire line. White Pine Series of Architectural Monographs, v. 11, no. 5, 1925. 19p. illus.

Covers 1809–25.

616 CRAWFORD, MARY CAROLINE. The romance of old New England churches. Boston, L. C. Page and Co., 1907. 377p. illus.

617 DONNELLY, MARIAN CARD. New England meeting houses in the seventeenth century. Doctoral Dissertation, Yale University, 1955–56.

618 ———. New England meeting houses in the seventeenth century. Old-Time New England, 47:85–97, Apr.–June 1957. illus.

619 DRUMMOND, A. L. Evolution of the New England meeting house. Royal Institute of British Architects Journal, s.3 53:337–42, June 1946. illus.

620 LATHROP, ELISE. Old New England churches. Rutland, Vt., C. E. Tuttle Co., 1938. 171p. illus.

621 MARLOWE, GEORGE FRANCIS, AND CHAMBERLAIN, SAMUEL. Churches of old New England, their architecture and their architects. N. Y., Macmillan Co., 1947. 222p. illus.

622 MEADER, ROBERT F. Colonial church architecture in New England. Susquehanna University Studies, 4:63–82, Mar. 1949. illus.

1650–1850.

623 MURCHISON, KENNETH M. The spired meeting house of old New England. Arts and Decoration, 48:8–12, Mar. 1938. illus.

624 PLACE, CHARLES A. From meeting house to church in New England — in four parts. Old-Time New England, part 1, 13:69–77, Oct. 1922; part 2, 13:111–23, Jan. 1923; part 3, 13:149–64, Apr. 1923; part 4, 14:3–20, July 1923. illus.

625 PORTER, NOAH. New England meeting house. New Haven, Conn., Yale University Press, 1933. 34p.

Reprint of a paper written in 1882. Published by the Committee on Historical Publications, Tercentenary Commission of the State of Connecticut.

626 ROSS, H. C. Two interesting restorations of old New England churches. Old-Time New England, 3:2–8, Feb. 1913. illus.

Christ Church, Boston, and Center Church, New Haven.

627 SINNOTT, EDMUND WARE. Meetinghouse and church in early New England. N. Y., McGraw-Hill Book Co., 1963. 243p. illus.

628 SMITH, CHARLES LYMAN. New England churches of architectural historical interest. American Architect, 23:261–66, Mar. 1923. illus.

629 SMITH, PATRICIA ANNE. New England meeting houses and churches [1681–1829]. Society of Architectural Historians. Journal, 7:29–30, July–Dec. 1948.

Abstract of Master's Thesis, Oberlin College, 1945.

630 WATTS, HENRY F. R. Tower clocks: made before 1850. National Association of Watch and Clock Collectors. Bulletin, 4:94–102, Apr. 1950. illus.

1668–1862.

631 WEIS, FREDERICK LEWIS. Colonial clergy and Colonial churches of New England. Lancaster, Mass., 1936. 280p. illus.
Dates churches.

632 WIGHT, CHARLES ALBERT. Some old time meeting houses of the Connecticut Valley. Chicopee Falls, Mass., The Rich Print, 1911. 225p. illus.

633 WINSLOW, OLA ELIZABETH. Meetinghouse Hill, 1630–1783. N. Y., Macmillan Co., 1952. 344p. illus.
Congregational churches.

CONNECTICUT

GENERAL REFERENCES

634 ALLEN, RICHARD SANDERS. Covered bridges in Connecticut. Covered Bridge Topics, 8:1, 4–8, Dec. 1950.
Census and account of bridges built ca. 1818.

635 ALLIS, MARGUERITE. Historic Connecticut. N. Y., Grosset and Dunlap Co., 1938. 343p. illus.
Originally published as Connecticut Trilogy. Covers Hartford, Saybrook, and New Haven.

636 BESSELL, WESLEY SHERWOOD. Colonial architecture in Connecticut — in five parts. Architectural Record, part 1, 37:360–69, Apr. 1915; part 2, 37:445–52, May 1915; part 3, 37:547–56, June 1915; part 4, 38:672–80, Dec. 1915; part 5, 39:53–64, Jan. 1916. illus.

637 BICKFORD, CLARA EMERSON. The homes of our forefathers. Connecticut Magazine, 7:493–500, 1902; 8:78–84, 1903.

638 CROFUT, FLORENCE S. MARCY. Guide to the history and historic sites of Connecticut. New Haven, Conn., Yale University Press, 1937. 2v. illus.

639 DE VITO, MICHAEL C. Connecticut's old timbered crossings. Warehouse Point, Conn., De Vito Enterprises, 1964. 71p. illus.

640 EBERLEIN, HAROLD DONALDSON. Seventeenth-century Connecticut house. White Pine Series of Architectural Monographs, v. 5, no. 1, Feb. 1919. 14p. illus.

641 FEDERAL WRITERS' PROJECT. Connecticut: a guide to its roads, lore and people. Boston, Houghton Mifflin Co., 1938. 593p. illus.

642 FOSTER, WILLIAM D. River towns of Connecticut. White Pine Series of Architectural Monographs, v. 9, no. 2, Apr. 1923. 14p. illus.
Covers Hartford, Wethersfield, and Windsor.

643 GARVAN, ANTHONY N. B. Architecture and town planning in Colonial Connecticut. New Haven, Yale University Press, 1957. 166p. illus.
1633–1775. Yale Historical Publications, History of Art, 6.

644 ISHAM, NORMAN MORRISON, AND BROWN, ALBERT F. Early Connecticut houses; an historical and architectural study. Providence, R. I., Preston and Rounds Co., 1900. 303p. illus.
Now in paperback by Dover.

645 KELLY, JOHN FREDERICK. Architectural guide for Connecticut. New Haven, Conn., Yale University Press, 1935. 44p.
Published for the Tercentenary Commission of the State of Connecticut.

646 ———. Connecticut's old houses, a handbook and guide. Stonington, Conn., Pequot Press, 1963. 73p. illus.
Antiquarian and Landmarks Society of Connecticut, Connecticut Booklet No. 4.

647 ———. Early Connecticut architecture. N. Y., William Helburn, 1924. 25 illus.

648 ———. Early Connecticut architecture. 2nd ser. N. Y., William Helburn, 1931. 23p. illus.

649 ———. Early Connecticut meetinghouses; being an account of the church edifices built before 1830. N. Y., Columbia University Press, 1948. 2v. illus.
Based on parish and town records, 1636–1830.

650 ———. Early domestic architecture of Connecticut. N. Y., Dover Publications, 1963. 210p. illus.
First edition, 1924.

651 ———. Early domestic architecture of Connecticut. New Haven, Conn., Yale University Press, 1933. 30p.
Published by the Committee on Historical Publications, Tercentenary Commission of the State of Connecticut.

652 ———. Raising Connecticut meeting houses. Old-Time New England, 27:3–9, July 1936. illus.

653 ———. Three early Connecticut weather-vanes. Old-Time New England, 31:96–99, Apr. 1941. illus.

654 KELLY, JOHN FREDERICK; HAMILTON, LORENZO; AND KELLY, HENRY S. Early architecture of Connecticut. Architecture, v. 43–49, Jan. 1921—Feb. 1924.
A series of illustrations.

655 MARLOWE, GEORGE, AND CHAMBERLAIN, SAMUEL. Old Bay paths; their villages and byways and their stories. N. Y., Hastings House, 1942. 126p. illus.

656 MAY, CHARLES C. The old time mansions of northern Connecticut. Architectural Review, 12:175–78, 192, June 1921. illus.

657 National Society of Colonial Dames of America. CONNECTICUT SOCIETY. Connecticut houses. Hartford, Conn., Bulletin of the Connecticut State Library, no. 16, 1931. 39p.
List of 655 manuscript histories of historic houses. First published as *Bulletin of the Connecticut State Library*, no. 7, 1916.

658 ———. Old houses of Connecticut. New Haven, Conn., Yale University Press, 1923. 519p. illus.
Mrs. Anna Bertha Trowbridge, ed.

659 ———. Old inns of Connecticut. Hartford, Conn., Prospect Press, 1937. 253p. illus.
Marian Dickinson Terry, ed.

660 Old houses, Connecticut; views. American Institute of Architects. Journal, 8:113–15, Mar. 1920. illus. only.

661 PINDAR, PETER AUGUSTUS (pseud.). Boston Post Road. White Pine Series of Architectural Monographs, v. 6, no. 1, Feb. 1920. 14p. illus.

662 ———. Stage coach road from Hartford to Litchfield. White Pine Series of Architectural Monographs, v. 9, no. 5, Oct. 1923. 16p. illus.

Covers 1650–1833.

663 SEYMOUR, GEORGE DUDLEY. Researches of an antiquary. Five essays on early American architects. New Haven, Conn., 1928. 32p. illus.

Mentions various architects of Connecticut, including Ithiel Town.

LOCATIONS

Avon

664 MILLS, LEWIS S. The Canal Warehouse, Avon, Connecticut. The Lure of Litchfield Hills, 10:21, 26, June 1949. illus.

1827–1935.

Bethany

665 Wheeler-Beecher house, Bethany, Connecticut, built 1805. Architectural Forum, 46:193–200, Feb. 1927. illus.

Branford

666 KELLY, JOHN FREDERICK. Swain-Harrison house, Branford, Conn. Old-Time New England, 32:84–95, Jan. 1942. illus.

Ca. 1680.

Bridgeport

667 ANDREWS, W. Gothic tragedy in Bridgeport? Antiques, 72:50–53, July 1957. illus.

Gothic Revival, Alexander Jackson Davis, and the Harral-Wheeler mansion, 1846.

Brooklyn

668 KINGSLEY, LOUISE. Old Trinity Church, Brooklyn, Connecticut. Old-Time New England, 42:73–77, Jan. 1952. illus.

Episcopal, 1769–1865.

Canaan

669 PEASE, MRS. EDWIN J. Christ Church, Canaan, Connecticut. The Lure of Litchfield Hills, 10:15–16, 34–35, June 1949. illus.

Episcopal, 1814.

Canterbury

670 DANA, RICHARD H., JR. Old Canterbury on the Quinnebaug. White Pine Series of Architectural Monographs, v. 9, no. 6, Dec. 1923. 16p. illus.

Covers 1732–1815.

Chester

671 FOSTER, THEODORE. Old homes of Chester, Connecticut. West Haven, Conn., O. K. Walker, 1936. 92p. illus.

Clinton

672 CRAMER, MRS. EFFIE STEVENS. Adam Stanton house, Clinton, Conn. Old-Time New England, 22:88–95, Oct. 1931. illus.

673 WANGNER, ELLEN D. Old Adam Stanton house, Clinton, Conn. Country Life in America, 48:70–76, Aug. 1925. illus.
1789.

Darien

674 Domestic setting for antiques. Antiques, 37:75–77, Feb. 1940. illus.
Lt. William Parsons house, 1754.

675 GILLESPIE, H. S. Biography of a Colonial house. Arts and Decoration, 20:38–39, Mar. 1924. illus.

676 In the Jeffersonian tradition: Hancock house, Darien. Arts and Decoration, 41:36–38, Oct. 1934. illus.

Derby

677 SHELTON, ADA STEWART. Commodore Hull house. D. A. R. Magazine, 62:473–75, Aug. 1928.

678 STIVERS, MABEL P. Trueman Gilbert house. Old-Time New England, 19:75–79, Oct. 1928. illus.

East Haven

679 KELLY, JOHN FREDERICK. Moulthroup house, East Haven, Connecticut. Old-Time New England, 12:147–52, Apr. 1922.
Seventeenth century.

East Lyme

680 KEITH, ELMER. Thomas Lee house. Old-Time New England, 39:81–88, Apr. 1949. illus.
Before 1672.

East Windsor

681 McCLURE, DAVID. Connecticut towns: East Windsor in 1806. New Haven, Conn., Acorn Club of Connecticut, 1949. 26p.
1680–1806.

Easton

682 KELLY, JOHN FREDERICK. Seventeenth-century Connecticut log house. Old-Time New England, 31:29–40, Oct. 1940. illus.
Lt. James Bennett house, 1675–80.

Essex

683 MAGONIGLE, H. VAN BUREN. Essex, a Connecticut River town. White Pine Series of Architectural Monographs, v. 6, no. 6, Dec. 1920. 16p. illus.

Fairfield

684 CHILD, FRANK SAMUEL. An historic mansion, being an account of the Thaddeus Burr homestead, Fairfield, Connecticut. 1654–1915. 1915. 27p. illus.
1790.

Farmington

685 Ancestral home of the Whitman family of Farmington, Conn. House Beautiful, 45:89, Feb. 1919. illus.
Ca. 1660.

686 BESSELL, WESLEY SHERWOOD. Farmington, Connecticut. White Pine Series of Architectural Monographs, v. 12, no. 2, 1926. 22p. illus.
Whitman house, Cowles house, and others.

687 BRANDIGEE, ARTHUR L., AND SMITH, EDDY N. Farmington, Connecticut, village of beautiful homes. Farmington, Conn., The Authors, 1906. 213p. illus.

Franklin

688 NOTT, SAMUEL. Connecticut towns: Franklin in 1800. New Haven, Conn., Acorn Club of Connecticut, 1949. 12p.
1718–1800.

Goshen

689 NORTON, LEWIS MILLS. Connecticut towns: Goshen in 1812. New Haven, Conn., Acorn Club of Connecticut, 1949. 27p.
1731–1812.

Greenwich

690 JELCHOW, ROGER H. Northern Greenwich in Connecticut, in ye olden days before 1875. Greenwich, Conn., 1948. illus.
Mostly 1642.

691 TALCOTT, NORMAN. The tavern and the old Post Road. Connecticut Magazine, 10:647–54, Oct. 1906.
Putnam cottage (1731).

Guilford

692 ANDREWS, EVANGELINE WALKER (ed.). The Henry Whitfield house, 1639; the journal of the restoration of the old stone house, Guilford, by J. Frederick Kelly. Guilford, Conn., Henry Whitfield State Historical Museum, 1939. 60p. illus.

693 KELLY, JOHN FREDERICK. Norton house, Guilford, Conn. Old-Time New England, 14:122–30, Jan. 1924. illus.
1690.

694 ———. Restoration of the Henry Whitfield house, Guilford, Connecticut. Old-Time New England, 29:75–89, Jan. 1939. illus.
1639–40.

695 New England heritage. House Beautiful, 81:24–27, Sept. 1939. illus.
Ebenezer Scranton house, 1720.

696 Old Guilford 1639–1939. House Beautiful, 81:14–17, July–Aug. 1939. illus.

697 SNYDER, R. Rescue of a Colonial house, once the old home of L. Beecher at Guilford. American Home, 2:7–8, Apr. 1921.

698 STATE HISTORICAL MUSEUM, CONNECTICUT. Historical papers relating to the Henry Whitfield house, Guilford, Connecticut. New Haven, Conn., Tuttle, Morehouse and Taylor Press, 1911. 59p. illus.

Haddam

699 BRAINARD, NEWTON C. The East Haddam meetinghouse: who designed it? Connecticut Historical Society Bulletin, 13:4–6, Jan. 1948. illus.

700 CLARK, LEVI HUBBARD. Connecticut towns: Haddam in 1808. New Haven, Conn., Acorn Club of Connecticut, 1949. 10p.
1662–1808.

Hartford

701 KELLER, GEORGE. The old City Hall, Hartford, Connecticut. American Architect, 79:55, Feb. 14, 1903.
Also known as Old State House.

702 MERRITT, ARTHUR H. Hartford state house Staffordshire. Antiques, 33:312–13, 1938. illus.

703 MUNICIPAL ART SOCIETY, HARTFORD, CONN. Preservation and restoration of the City Hall, Hartford, Conn. Hartford, Conn., Municipal Art Society, 1906. 16p. illus.
Bulletin 6 of the society publications.

704 [State House. Contemporary description.] Atkinson's Casket, no. 8:458, Aug. 1835.

705 TALCOTT, MARY KINGSBURY. Old State House, Hartford, Connecticut. D. A. R. Nineteenth Annual Report, 289–90, 1917.
(1796). Charles Bulfinch, architect.

Lebanon

706 ARMSTRONG, ROBERT GRENVILLE. Historic Lebanon: highlights of an historic town. Lebanon, Conn., First Congregational Church, 1950. 79p. illus.
1637.

707 CHAMPE, HOWARD CRULL. Old meeting-house at Lebanon, Conn., Old-Time New England, 30:82–85, Jan. 1940. illus.

708 SIZER, THEODORE. A case-study in restoration: the Lebanon meetinghouse, Lebanon, Connecticut. Society of Architectural Historians. Journal, 14:8–11, May 1955. illus.
Designed by John Trumbull, 1804.

Litchfield

709 BULCKLEY, ALICE TALCOTT. Historic Litchfield, 1720–1907. Hartford, Conn., Hartford Press, 1907. 37p. illus.
A short account of the history of the old houses of Litchfield. Compiled from Kilborn's *History of Litchfield*, Woodruff's *History of the Town of Litchfield*, Kilborn's *History of Litchfield Tradition*.

710 Elton House at Litchfield, Connecticut. Country Life in America, 31:43, Nov. 1916. illus.

711 FRYER, AARON G. Litchfield — an American heritage. Antiques, 68:57–59, July 1955. illus.
Settled 1720.

712 GILLESPIE, HARRIET SISSON. Toll-gate Hill tavern. Country Life in America, 48:58–59, Sept. 1925. illus.

1745. Moved from Litchfield to Torrington, Conn.

713 PRICE, C. MATLACK. Historic houses of Litchfield, Connecticut. White Pine Series of Architectural Monographs, v. 5, no. 3, June 1919. 16p. illus.

Covers 1753–1832.

714 WARREN, WILLIAM LAMSON. The domestic architecture of William Sprats and other Litchfield joiners. Old-Time New England, 46:36–51, Oct.–Dec. 1955. illus.

Sprats, 1747–1810.

715 ———. William Sprats and his civil and ecclesiastical architecture in New England. Old-Time New England, 44:64–78, 103–14, Jan.–June 1954. illus.

Courthouse of Litchfield County, Conn., 1795–97, and the meetinghouse at Georgia, Vt., 1800–1802.

Middletown

716 KELLY, JOHN FREDERICK. Barnes house, Long Hill, Middletown, Connecticut. Old-Time New England, 33:46–52, Jan. 1943. illus.

Milford

717 FEDERAL WRITERS' PROJECT. History of Milford, Connecticut, 1639–1939. Bridgeport, Conn., Braunworth and Co., *ca.* 1939. 204p. illus.

Mystic

718 Our Cover. The Log of Mystic Seaport, 1:1–11, Mar. 1949. illus.

Bank, built in 1833.

Naugatuck

719 GREEN, CONSTANCE WINSOR. History of Naugatuck, Connecticut. Naugatuck, 1948. 331p. illus.

1674——.

New Canaan

720 COMSTOCK, HELEN. Windsor house at New Canaan, Connecticut. Antiques, 58:462–67, Dec. 1950. illus.

Built 1800 at Windsor, Vt., moved to New Canaan, 1936. Asher Benjamin?

721 GILLESPIE, HARRIET SISSON. The old Wardwell house, New Canaan, Connecticut. House Beautiful, 49:30–31, Jan. 1921.

New Haven

722 BALDWIN, SIMEON E. The three earliest New Haven architects. New Haven Colony Historical Society. Papers, 10:226–39, 1951.

Peter Harrison, David Hoadley, Ithiel Town, 1766–1844.

723 BROCKWAY, JEAN LAMBERT. John Trumbull as architect at Yale. Antiques, 28:114–15, 1935.

724 BROOKS, HAROLD ALLEN, JR. The home of Ithiel Town, its date of construction and original appearance. Society of Architectural Historians. Journal, 13:27–28, Oct. 1954. illus.

1836–37.

725 CHAMBERLAIN, SAMUEL, AND FRENCH, ROBERT D. The Yale Scene. New Haven, Conn., Yale University Press, 1950. 114p. illus.

726 DENISON, ROBERT C. The United Church on the Green, New Haven, Conn. New Haven, 1915. 16p.
1813–15. David Hoadley, architect.

727 KEITH, ELMER DAVENPORT, AND WARREN, WILLIAM L. Peter Banner, a builder for Yale College. Old-Time New England, 45:93–102, Apr.–June 1955; 47:49–53, Oct.–Dec. 1956; 49:104–10ff., Apr. 1959. illus.
Construction of the president's house, 1799, and his plan for Berkeley Hall, 1800.

728 O'DONNELL, THOMAS E. Home of the Greek revivalist, Ithiel Town, at New Haven, Conn. Architectural Forum, 49:71–72, June 1928. illus.

729 NEWTON, ROGER HALE. New Haven: Sachem's Wood, one of the earliest Greek Revival mansions; A. J. Davis, Arch. Old-Time New England, 33:33–36, Oct. 1942. illus.

730 SCHUYLER, MONTGOMERY. Architecture of American colleges. Part 2. Yale. Architectural Record, 26:393–416, Dec. 1909. illus.

731 SEYMOUR, GEORGE DUDLEY. Henry Caner, 1680–1731, master carpenter, builder of the first Yale College buildings, 1718, and of the rector's house, 1722. Old-Time New England, 15:99–124, Jan. 1925. illus.

732 ———. Residence and library of Ithiel Town. New Haven, Conn., 1930.
Reprinted from *New Haven*, pp. 546–60.

733 SIGOURNEY, LYDIA. Residence and library of Ithiel Town, Esq. Ladies' Companion, 10:123–26, Jan. 1839.

734 [Yale College. Contemporary description.] Philadelphia Souvenir, 1:32, 249, Feb. 5, 1828. illus.

New London

735 BODENWEIN, GORDON. New London: so-called Huguenot House, *ca.* 1759, New London, Connecticut. Old-Time New England, 34:44–48, Jan. 1944. illus.

736 [New London Exchange. Contemporary description.] Robert Merry's Museum, 6:143–45, Nov. 1843. illus.

737 ROGERS, EDNA MINER. New London, Connecticut; homes visited by Washington and Lafayette — stage coaches and taverns. Americana, 16:21–37, Jan. 1922.

New Preston

738 Cogswell tavern. New Preston, Connecticut. American Monthly Magazine, 23:360–62, Nov. 1903.
1760–62.

Noroton

739 RUSSELL, E. H. Yesterday's treasure; Milestone house, Noroton, Connecticut. Country Life in America, 59:35–42, Apr. 1931.
Built 1690 at Stratford, Conn.; moved to Noroton, 1931.

Norwalk

740 BEARD, AUGUSTUS FIELD. The building of Norwalk. New Canaan Historical Society Announcements, 4:158–70, June 1957.
1640–1861.

Norwich

741 PERKINS, MARY E. Old houses of the antient [*sic*] town of Norwich, 1660–1800. Norwich, Conn., Bulletin Co., 1895. 621p. illus.

Old Lyme

742 SPAULDING, MELVIN PRATT. Old Lyme: Roger Griswold house. Arts and Decoration, 49:2–6, Jan. 1939. illus.

Redding

743 CALLARD, SALLY. Kiln house. Antiques Journal, 7:22–23, Feb. 1952. illus.
Ca. 1723.

Salisbury

744 PETTEE, JULIA. The Rev. Jonathan Lee and his eighteenth-century Salisbury parish: the early history of the town of Salisbury, Connecticut. Salisbury, Conn., Salisbury Assoc., 1957. 242p. illus.

Saybrook

745 HOLMAN, MABEL CASSINE. The romance of a Saybrook mansion. Connecticut Magazine, 10:46–51, Jan.–Mar. 1906.

Shelton

746 MORSE, C. Z. Commodore Isaac Hull's house at Shelton, Connecticut. Old-Time New England, 26:65–68, Oct. 1935. illus.

South Coventry

747 KEITH, ELMER. The Nathan Hale houses. Antiques, 48:280–83, Nov. 1945. illus.
Richard Hale house, 1776; Strong house, Joseph Huntington house, 1763.

Southington

748 [SKILTON, JOHN DAVIS, AND SKILTON, HENRY ALSTONE.] Doctor Henry Skilton house, Southington, Hartford County, Connecticut. [Hartford?], Conn., 1930.

Stonington

749 DAVIS, SARAH M. History of an old Connecticut homestead. American Monthly Magazine, 41:45–47, Aug. 1912.
Stanton Davis homestead.

750 Hunting houses; four 19th century houses at Old Mystic and Stonington. House and Garden, 67:26–27, June 1935. illus.

751 PALMER, HENRY ROBINSON. Stonington by the sea. Stonington, Conn., Palmer Press, 1957. 95p. illus.
First edition, 1913.

752 PENTZ, M. W. Stonington, Connecticut — where the Colonial atmosphere is preserved to a marked degree. Architectural Record, 32:230–37, Sept. 1912. illus.

753 WHEELER, GRACE DENISON. The homes of our ancestors in Stonington, Connecticut. Salem, Mass., Newcomb and Gauss Co., 1903. 286p. illus.

Stratfield

754 SHELTON, PHILO. Connecticut towns: Stratfield in 1800. New Haven, Conn., Acorn Club of Connecticut, 1949. 9p.
1699–1800.

Stratford

755 CAMERON, KENNETH WALTER. The genesis of Christ Church, Stratford, Connecticut: background and earliest annals, commemoration of the two hundred fiftieth anniversary, 1707–1957. Stratford, Conn., Christ Church, 1957. 58p. illus.
Episcopal.

756 SULLIVAN, NORINE C. Time passes by this New England town. . . . Arts and Decoration, 51:18–21, Dec. 1939. illus.

757 WILCOXSON, WILLIAM H. History of Stratford, Conn., 1639–1939. Stratford, Conn., Stratford Tercentenary Commission, 1939. 783p. illus.
Numerous illustrations.

Suffield

758 TARN, DAVID E. The town of Suffield, Connecticut. White Pine Series of Architectural Monographs, v. 7, no. 6, Dec. 1921. 16p. illus.
Covers 1736–1824.

Trumbull

759 BEACH, E. MERRILL. Trumbull, church and town. . . . [Trumbull, Conn., Historical Committee], 1955. 165p. illus.
Church of Christ, 1730——.

Wallingford

760 ROYCE, LUCY ATWATER. Nehemiah Royce or Washington elm house, Wallingford, Connecticut. Old-Time New England, 25:40–49, Oct. 1934. illus.
1672.

Westbury

761 ROBERTSON, T. M. Very early American house; Guinea Hollow farm, Old Westbury. Arts and Decoration, 30:80, Mar. 1929. illus.

Wethersfield

762 PALMER, FREDERIC. The Buttolph-Williams house in Wethersfield, Connecticut. Antiques, 60:195–97, Sept. 1951. illus.
Ca. 1680.

Windham County

763 DANA, RICHARD H., JR. Old hill towns of Windham County, Connecticut. White Pine Series of Architectural Monographs, v. 10, no. 1, Feb. 1924. 16p. illus.
Covers 1808–35.

Windsor

764 DAUGHTERS OF THE AMERICAN REVOLUTION. CONNECTICUT. A memorial of the opening of the Ellsworth homestead at Windsor, Connecticut, October eighth,

nineteen hundred and three under the auspices of the Connecticut Daughters of the American Revolution. New Haven, Conn., Tuttle, Morehouse and Taylor Press, 1907. 109p. illus.

765 The Ellsworth homestead; Elmwood, the state chapter house of the Connecticut Daughters of the American Revolution. American Monthly Magazine, 23:353–58, Nov. 1903.

1740.

Woodbury

766 BESSELL, WESLEY S. Old Woodbury and adjacent domestic architecture of Connecticut. White Pine Series of Architectural Monographs, v. 2, no. 5, Oct. 1916. 14p. illus.

Jabes Bacon house (1762), Woodbury; Sanford house, Litchfield; Bostwick house, Southbury.

767 KENT, HENRY W. The Glebe-house, Woodbury, Conn. Old-Time New England, 13:169–73, Apr. 1923. illus.

1745–50.

MAINE

GENERAL REFERENCES

768 American home pilgrimages, no. 4. — Maine. American Home, 20:8–11, 54–56, Aug. 1938. illus.

Covers 1750–1890.

769 CHAMBERLAIN, SAMUEL. The coast of Maine. N. Y., Hastings House, 1941. 101p. illus.

770 DUNNACK, HENRY E. Maine forts. Augusta, Me., Charles E. Nash and Son, 1924. 252p. illus.

Covers 1607–1908.

771 FEDERAL WRITERS' PROJECT. Maine: a guide down east. Boston, Houghton Mifflin Co., 1937. 476p. illus.

772 GREEN, SAMUEL M. Thomas Lord, joiner and housewright. Magazine of Art, 40:230–35, Oct. 1947. illus.

Nineteenth century.

773 HADLOCK, WENDELL S. Recent excavations at De Monts' Colony, St. Croix Island, Maine. Old-Time New England, 44:92–99, Apr.–June 1954. illus.

French settlement on island in Passamaquoddy Bay, 1604–5.

774 HILL, W. SCOTT. Early Kennebec taverns. Sprague's Journal of Maine History, 9:21–23, Jan. 1921.

775 LUCEY, WILLIAM LEO. The Catholic Church in Maine. Francestown, N. H., M. Jones Co., [1957]. 372p. illus.

1613——.

776 MAINE WRITERS' RESEARCH CLUB (comp.). Historic churches and homes of Maine. Portland, Me., Falmouth Book House, 1937. 289p. illus.

777 MITCHELL, GEORGE R. Early architecture of Maine. Architecture, v. 37–38, Jan.–Oct. 1918. illus. only.

778 NASON, MRS. EMMA HUNTINGTON. Old Colonial house in Maine built prior to 1776. Augusta, Me., Kennebec Journal, 1908. 106p. illus.

779 NOBLE, RUTH VERRILL. Maine profile. Cambridge, Mass., Berkshire Publishing Co., [1954]. 96p. illus.

780 ORCHARD, WILLIAM C. Notes on Penobscot houses. American Anthropologist, n.s. 11:601–6, 1909. illus.

781- PORTER, FREDERICK HUTCHINSON. A survey of existing Colonial architecture
782 in Maine. Architectural Review, 7:29–32, 47–51, 94–96, Aug.–Nov. 1918; 11:13–15, 45–48, 83–88, 119–20, 155–56, 183–86, July–Dec. 1920; 12:41–46, 64, 92, 151–52, Feb.–June 1921. American Architect, 120:149–51, Aug. 1921. illus.

783 SMITH, MARION JAQUES. A history of Maine, from wilderness to statehood. Portland, Me., Falmouth Publishing House, 1949. 348p. illus.
1497–1820.

784 WALKER, C. HOWARD. Some old houses on the southern coast of Maine. White Pine Series of Architectural Monographs, v. 4, no. 2, Apr. 1918. 14p. illus.

LOCATIONS

Aroostoock County

785 ATKINSON, MINNIE. Molunkus house. Sprague's Journal of Maine History, 13:82–90, 1925.

Augusta (see also *Hallowell*)

786 BASSETT, NORMAN L. History of the Blaine mansion. Americana, 15:288–93, July 1921.

787 FEDERAL WRITERS' PROJECT. Augusta-Hallowell on the Kennebec. Augusta, Me., Augusta-Hallowell Chamber of Commerce, [ca. 1937]. 168p. illus.

788 ————. Maine's Capitol. Augusta, Me., Kennebec Print Shop, 1938. 44p.
1828–31. Charles Bulfinch, architect.

789 McLANATHAN, RICHARD B. K. Bulfinch's drawings for the Maine State House. Society of Architectural Historians. Journal, 14:12–17, May 1955. illus.

790 ————. Charles Bulfinch and the Maine State House. Doctoral Dissertation, Harvard University, 1951.

Bangor

791 CHAPMAN, HARRY J. The first Bangor city hall. Bangor Historical Society. Proceedings for 1914–15, pp. 51–56.

Bar Harbor

792 HALE, RICHARD WALDEN, JR. The story of Bar Harbor. N. Y., I. Washburn, 1949. 259p. illus.
1605————.

793 WASSON, M. Up the road to yesterday; Woodlawn, scene of the Bingham purchase. Country Life in America, 58:65–66, May 1930. illus.
1802.

Biddeford

794 HALEY, ADELAIDE. Haley house and farm, 763 Poolroad, Biddeford, Maine. Old-Time New England, 35:3–9, July 1944. illus.
1713 or 1718.

Bucksport

795 BUXTON, PHILIP W. The Jed Prouty tavern. Down East, 1:40–44, Winter 1955. illus.
1790?——.

Castine

796 STANWOOD, CORDELIA J. Castine, a village by the sea. House Beautiful, 48:92–94, 126, 128, Aug. 1920. illus.
Covers 1765—ca. 1820.

Columbia Falls

797 GOLDSMITH, MARGARET O. Ruggles house at Columbia Falls, Maine. Old-Time New England, 15:68–76, Oct. 1924. illus.

Ellsworth

798 DURNBAUGH, JERRY L. The Black house. Down East, 2:28–31, June 1956. illus.
Built for Col. John Black in 1827, now a museum.

799 STANWOOD, CORDELIA J. The story of Ellsworth, Maine. House Beautiful, 46:373–75, Dec. 1919. illus.

800 STURGES, WALTER KNIGHT. The Black house, Ellsworth — an Asher Benjamin house in Maine. Antiques, 65:398–400, May 1954. illus.
Ca. 1802 or 1824–27.

Gardiner

801 ERSKINE, ROBERT J.; SANBORN, LAUREN M.; AND COLCORD, ELMER D. The Gardiner story, 1849–1949: historical sketches of the plantation, town, city and noted people. Gardiner, Me., published by the city of Gardiner, 1949. 76p. illus.

Hallowell (see also Augusta)

802 GOLDSMITH, MARGARET O. Two early homes in Hallowell, Maine. House Beautiful, 55:361–64, Apr. 1924. illus.
Vaughan house and Merrick house, ca. 1800.

Head Tide

803 BROWN, FRANK CHOUTEAU. Congregational Church at Head Tide, Maine. Old-Time New England, 30:94–100, Jan. 1940. illus.
1838.

Kennebunk, including Kennebunkport

804 DOW, JOY WHEELER. Old-time dwellings in Kennebunkport. Kennebunk, The Star Print, 1926. 83p. illus.

805 HOWE, FLORENCE THOMPSON. Brick store museum at Kennebunk, Maine. Antiques, 38:74–75, Aug. 1940. illus.
1825.

Kittery (see also *Portsmouth*, N. H.)

806 FROST, JOHN ELDRIDGE. Colonial village. Kittery Point, Me., Gundalow Club, 1948? 82p. illus.
1647——. Originally Master's Thesis, University of New Hampshire.

807 RICHARDSON, H. T. John Bray house in Kittery, Maine. House Beautiful, 65:704–12, May 1929. illus.

808 ROBIE, VIRGINIA. Colonial pilgrimage, no. 3 — Sir William Pepperrell [*sic*] and his staircase. House Beautiful, 15:315–17, Apr. 1904. illus.
Sparhawk house, 1742.

809 VAUGHN, D. M. Afternoon at the Lady Pepperrell [*sic*] mansion. Old-Time New England, 40:157–58, Oct. 1949.

Machias

810 DONWORTH, GRACE. Burnham tavern, ancient hostelry at Machias. D. A. R. Magazine, 69:35, 1935.

Matinicus Island

811 CONDON, VESTA. An island store one hundred years ago. Old-Time New England, 32:52–56, Oct. 1941. illus.

Parkman

812 MCKUSICK, VICTOR A. Parkman, Maine, a frontier settlement. Old-Time New England, 49:41–48, Oct. 1958. illus.

Penobscot Bay Area

813 LOOMIS, CHARLES DANA. Port towns of Penobscot Bay. White Pine Series of Architectural Monographs, v. 8, no. 1, Feb. 1922. 14p. illus.

Phippsburg

814 HARRIMAN, A. J. Doorway, Thomas McCobb house, Phippsburg, Maine. Architecture, v. 51, no. 5, May 1925. illus. only.

Portland

815 ELDEN, A. Tate house, Stroudwater, Portland, Maine. Old-Time New England, 26:138–41, Apr. 1936. illus.

816 First Parish Church, Portland, Maine. Architectural Review, n.s. 6:67–69, June 1918. illus.

817 THOMPSON, FLORENCE WHITTLESEY. Early churches in Portland. Sprague's Journal of Maine History, 9:81–83, Apr. 1921.

Saco

818 FAIRFIELD, ROY P. Sands, spindles, and steeples. Portland, Me., House of Falmouth, [1956]. 461p. illus.
1603——.

South Berwick

819 BAER, ANNIE WENTWORTH. Captain Nathan Lord's house. Granite Monthly, 59:201–6, July 1927.

820 BROWN, FRANK CHOUTEAU. Interior details and furnishings of the Sarah Orne Jewett dwelling, built by John Haggins in 1774 at South Berwick, Maine. Pencil Points, 21:115–30, Feb. 1940. Monograph Series, 26:97–112. illus.

821 KINGSBURY, EDITH. Hamilton house; historic landmark, South Berwick. House Beautiful, 65:782–87, 874, June 1929. illus.
1770.

822 SHELTON, LOUISE. The garden at Hamilton house. American Homes and Gardens, 6:422–25, Nov. 1909. illus.
1770.

823 TRAFTON, BURRIN W. F., JR. Hamilton house, South Berwick, Maine. Old-Time New England, 48:57–64, Jan. 1958. illus.
1787–88.

South Windham

824 SPILLER, NELLIE D. The Parson Smith homestead, South Windham, Maine. Old-Time New England, 48:48–56, Oct.–Dec. 1957. illus.
1764.

Thomaston

825 CARLETON, SARA H. Knox mansion returns to life. National Republic, 20:24, Nov. 1932.
Replica, built 1932, of home of Major General Henry Knox, 1794.

826 GREEN, SAMUEL M. Architecture of Thomaston, Maine. Society of Architectural Historians. Journal, 10:24–32, Dec. 1951. illus.
1783——.

827 HUSSEY, MRS. LEROY FOGG. Montpelier. D. A. R. Magazine, 83:579–80, July 1949. illus.
1794–1871, and a replica erected in 1929.

Topsham

828 HARRIMAN, A. J. Doorway of the General Veasie house, Topsham, Maine. Architecture, v. 51, no. 6, June 1925; v. 52, no. 2, Aug. 1925. illus. only.

829 ——. General McLellan house, Topsham, Maine. Architecture, 52:150–52, Oct. 1925. illus. only.

Wiscasset

830 GOLDSMITH, M. O. Some old houses in Wiscasset, Maine. Architectural Forum, 45:265–72, Nov. 1926. illus.

831 HARRIMAN, A. J. Doorway of the Nickels house, Wiscasset, Maine. Architecture, 51:121–22, Apr. 1925. illus. only.

832 LOWNDES, M. Yankee mansion, known in 1790 as the Bunch of Grapes tavern, Wiscasset, Maine. House and Garden, 77:40, June 1940. illus.

833 PATTERSON, WILLIAM D. Wiscasset, Maine. White Pine Series of Architectural Monographs, v. 12, no. 6, 1926. 22p. illus.

Early Republican.

834 PINKHAM, CHARLES E. The old Lincoln County Jail. Down East, 2:28–29, 37, Aug. 1955. illus.

1809——.

835 Wiscasset open house. House Beautiful, 81:81–83, Nov. 1939. illus.

York County

836 BOURNE, EDWARD EMERSON. Garrison houses, York County. Maine Historical Society. Collections, 7:107–20, 1876.

837 PERKINS, ELIZABETH B. Old village school at York, Maine. Old-Time New England, 35:63–66, Apr. 1945. illus.

1746, restored.

York Harbor

838 VAUGHAN, DOROTHY M. Sayward-Barrell house on York River, York Harbor, Maine. Old-Time New England, 29:15–20, July 1938. illus.

Ca. 1717.

MASSACHUSETTS

GENERAL REFERENCES

839 BAGG, ERNEST NEWTON. Late eighteenth-century architecture in western Massachusetts. White Pine Series of Architectural Monographs, v. 11, no. 4, 1925. 19p. illus.

Covers 1800—*ca.* 1828.

840 BROWN, FRANK CHOUTEAU. Entrance halls and stairways, illustrated by examples from Massachusetts and central New England. Pencil Points, 20:245–60, Apr. 1939. Monograph Series, 25:17–32. illus.

Covers 1670–1820.

841 ———. Some Colonial wall cabinets and kitchen dressers, principally from early Massachusetts settlements. Pencil Points, 20:373–88, June 1939. Monograph Series, 25:33–48. illus.

Covers 1650–1786.

842 ———. Some low mantels and fireplace enframements, principally of the beginning of the nineteenth century. Pencil Points, 20:673–88, Oct. 1939. Monograph Series, 25:65–80. illus.

Covers 1687–1811 in Massachusetts.

843 BUCKLY, JULIAN. Architecture in Massachusetts during the latter part of the eighteenth century. White Pine Series of Architectural Monographs, v. 2, no. 2, Apr. 1916. 14p. illus.

844 CHAMBERLAIN, SAMUEL. Lexington and Concord. N. Y., Hastings House, 1939. 72p. illus.

845 CHANDLER, JOSEPH EVERETT. Colonial cottages of Massachusetts during the latter half of the seventeenth century. White Pine Series of Architectural Monographs, v. 1, no. 1, 1915. 13p. illus.

846 COUSINS, FRANK. Mantel details. Some of the early craftsman's work in Salem, Danversport, and Peabody, Mass., and in Portsmouth, N. H. Country Life in America, 30:46–47, May 1916. illus. only.

847 CUMMINGS, ABBOTT LOWELL. Domestic architecture of the 17th century in Massachusetts. Society of Architectural Historians. Journal, 7:30, July 1948.
Summary of Master's Thesis, Oberlin College, 1947.

848 DOW, GEORGE FRANCIS. Building agreements in seventeenth-century Massachusetts. Old-Time New England, 12:135–39, Jan. 1922; 13:28–32, July 1922; 13:131–34, Jan. 1923.

849 EMBURY, AYMAR, II. Houses in southeastern Massachusetts. White Pine Series of Architectural Monographs, v. 14, no. 1, 1928. 19p. illus.
Houses dated 1790 and earlier, in Taunton and Weymouth.

850 FEDERAL WRITERS' PROJECT. Massachusetts: a guide to its places and people. Boston, Houghton Mifflin Co., 1937. 675p. illus.

851 GARDNER, G. C. Colonial architecture in western Massachusetts. American Architect and Building News, part 1, 45:99–100, Sept. 15, 1894; part 2, 46:89–90, Dec. 1, 1894; part 3, 47:39–41, Jan. 26, 1895. illus.

852 HAMLIN, TALBOT FAULKNER. Americana: spirit of early buildings transcends periods. Pencil Points, 19:655–62, Oct. 1938. illus.
Examples from the Massachusetts coast.

853 HOUSE, ALBERT VIRGIL. The lean-to house and the life it sheltered. Danvers Historical Society. Collections, 11:113–33, 1923.

854 JACKSON, ROBERT TRACY. History of the Oliver, Vassall and Royall houses in Dorchester, Cambridge, and Medford. Genealogical Magazine, 2:3–17, Jan. 1907.

855 LORING, KATHERINE PEABODY. Earliest summer residents of the north shore and their houses. Essex Institute. Historical Collections, 68:193–208, 1932.
Ca. 1840.

856 MACKENNAL, ALEXANDER. Homes and haunts of the Pilgrim fathers. Philadelphia, J. B. Lippincott Co., 1899. 200p. illus.
Later editions to 1920.

857 MARLOWE, GEORGE FRANCIS, AND CHAMBERLAIN, SAMUEL. The Old Bay paths, their villages and byways and their stories. N. Y., Hastings House, 1942. 126p. illus.
Houses along Indian paths in the Old Bay area. Principally Massachusetts and Connecticut.

858 Minor Colonial details — part 1. Some old summer houses from eastern Massachusetts gardens. Architectural Review, n.s. 5:169–71, Aug. 1917. illus.

859 MITCHELL, GEORGE R. Early architecture of Massachusetts. Architecture, v. 43, Jan. 1921. illus. only.

860 NEWTON, BENJAMIN H. A group of early Massachusetts vestibules. Pencil Points, 15:273–88, June 1934. Monograph Series, 20:129–44. illus.

Covers 1670–1796.

861 NORTHEND, MARY HARROD. Group of Colonial doorways. American Homes and Gardens, 12:52–55, Feb. 1915. illus.

From Salem and Dedham.

862 Notes on the development of early architecture in Massachusetts. Boston, Historic American Buildings Survey and W. P. A., 1941. 35p.

863 POOR, ALFRED EASTON. Colonial architecture of Cape Cod, Nantucket, and Martha's Vineyard. N. Y., William Helburn, 1932. 147p. illus.

864 RICE, NATHAN. Dr. Paine's and other early gristmills. Worcester Historical Society. Publications, 2:247–54, 1940.

Early gristmills in Massachusetts.

865 SCHUYLER, MONTGOMERY. Architecture of American colleges. Part 10. Three women's colleges — Vassar, Wellesley, and Smith. Architectural Record, 31:513–37, May 1912. illus.

866 Three old New England houses. Magazine of History, 12:273–76, Nov. 1910.

Covers Fairbanks house, Dedham; Horseshoe (or Coffin) house, Nantucket; Whipple house, Ipswich.

867 WATKINS, WALTER KENDALL. Three contracts for seventeenth-century building construction in Massachusetts. Old-Time New England, 12:27–32, July 1921.

Contracts for houses at Malden and Boston, and King's Chapel, Boston.

868 WHITEFIELD, EDWIN. Homes of our forefathers . . . in Massachusetts. Dedham, Mass., The Author, 1892. 41p. illus.

First edition, 1879.

869 WICKHAM, JENNETTE ADAMS. Historic churches of Massachusetts. American Monthly Magazine, 39:127–32, Sept. 1911.

LOCATIONS

Amesbury

870 LONGYEAR, MARY HAWLEY. The history of a house. 2nd ed. Brookline, Mass., Longyear Foundation, 1947. 70p. illus.

Bagley house, 1819.

Amherst

871 ALLEN, MARY ADELE. Around a village green; sketches of life in Amherst. Northampton, Mass., Kraushar Press, [1939]. 94p. illus.

Includes historic sites and buildings.

872 SEE, ANNA PHILLIPS. The old Strong house, home of Mary Mattoon chapter, Amherst, Mass. D. A. R. Magazine, 55:509–14, Sept. 1921.

1744.

Andover

873 CUMMINGS, ABBOTT LOWELL. The Parson Barnard house, formerly known as the Bradstreet house in North Andover, Massachusetts. Old-Time New England, 47:28–40, Oct.–Dec. 1956. illus.
Built 1715, not as formerly stated, in 1667.

874 DOUGLAS-LITHGOW, R. A. A group of early Colonial houses at Andover, Massachusetts. Massachusetts Magazine, 5:3–9, Jan. 1912.

875 HOWES, JENNIE WRIGHT. North Andover homesteads. D. A. R. Magazine, 64:623–32, Oct. 1930.

876 LE BOUTILLIER, ADDISON B. Early wooden architecture of Andover, Mass. White Pine Series of Architectural Monographs, v. 3, no. 2, Apr. 1917. 14p. illus.
Covers 1667–1824.

877 WHITEHILL, WALTER MUIR. The North Andover hay scales. Old-Time New England, 39:35–37, Oct. 1948. illus.
Scales and small building, 1819.

Aptucxet (near *Bourne*)

878 LOMBARD, PERCIVAL HALL. Aptucxet trading post, first trading post of Plymouth Colony; its restoration on the original foundations. Old-Time New England, 23:159–74, Apr. 1933. illus.
1627.

Arlington

879 NYLANDER, ROBERT HARRINGTON. Jason Russell and his house in Menotomy. Old-Time New England, 55:29–42, Oct. 1964. illus.
Now Arlington.

Auburn

880 FEDERAL WRITERS' PROJECT. Auburn: 1837–1937. Auburn, Mass., Auburn Centennial Committee, 1937. 63p. illus.

Barnstable

881 DARLING, EDWARD, AND MILLER, WILLIAM A., JR. Three old timers: Sandwich, Barnstable, Yarmouth, 1639–1939. South Yarmouth, Cape Cod, Mass., Wayside Studio, [1939]. 47p. illus.

882 GOODELL, EDWIN B., JR. Meeting-house at West Barnstable, Mass. Old-Time New England, 21:37–42, July 1930. illus.
1719 and later.

883 SHUMWAY, HARRY IRVING. Old tavern of Cape Cod. American Cookery, 37:171–75, 1932.
Barnstable Inn.

Berkshire County and the *Berkshires*

884 BIRDSALL, RICHARD DAVENPORT. The first century of Berkshire County. Boston Public Library Quarterly, 9:20–39, Jan. 1957.
1722–1861.

885 CHAMBERLAIN, SAMUEL. The Berkshires. N. Y., Hastings House, [1956]. 103p. illus.

886 COOKE, ROBERT HILLYER. Historic homes and institutions and genealogical and personal memoirs of Berkshire County, Massachusetts. N. Y., Lewis Publishing Co., 1906. 2v. illus.

887 Federal Writers' Project. The Berkshire hills. N. Y., Funk and Wagnalls Co., 1939. 368p. illus.

888 KILHAM, WALTER H. Cabot-Lee-Kilham house, Beverly, Mass. Old-Time New England, 15:157–63, Apr. 1925. illus.

Eighteenth century.

889 PIERSON, WILLIAM H., JR. Industrial architecture in the Berkshires. Doctoral Dissertation, Yale University, 1949.

890 RAMSDELL, ROGER WEARNE. Wooden architecture in the Berkshires. White Pine Series of Architectural Monographs, v. 10, no. 5, 1924. 16p. illus.

Covers 1734–1803.

Billerica

891 EGBERT, HANS. Manning manse; an old homestead at North Billerica, Massachusetts. House Beautiful, 50:26–29, 66, July 1921. illus.

Boston — General (see also *Brookline, Cambridge, Dorchester, Roxbury*, etc.)

892 Area preservation and the Beacon Hill bill. Old-Time New England, 46:106–10, Apr. 1956.

893 BACON, EDWIN M. A guide book. Boston, Ginn and Co., 1903. 190p. illus.

894 BOSTON. MUSEUM OF FINE ARTS. Museums and some historic houses in Boston and vicinity. Boston, Museum of Fine Arts, 1934. 16p.

895 Boston, yesterday and today. [Boston, Court Square Press, 1939.] 31p. illus.

Contents include: Old North Church, by F. E. Webster; Old things in New England, by Wallace Nutting; and Historic Faneuil Hall, the cradle of Liberty, by E. H. Finnegan.

896 Boston brickwork, Colonial era. Brickbuilder, 14:27–33, Feb. 1905. illus.

897 Boston's Beacon Hill. Architectural Forum, 116:100–105, Jan. 1962. illus.

898 BROWN, FRANK CHOUTEAU. Beacon Hill, Boston, Mass. Pencil Points, 19:177–92, Mar. 1938. Monograph Series, 24:97–112. illus.

Covers 1795–1844.

899 ———. Historic Boston, Massachusetts. Pencil Points, 18:287–302, May 1937. Monograph Series, 23:1–16. illus.

Covers 1713–1826.

900 Buildings and house hardware: gleanings from eighteenth-century Boston newspapers. Old-Time New England, 17:20–29, July 1926. illus.

901 BUNTING, BAINBRIDGE. The architectural history of the Back Bay region in Boston. Doctoral Dissertation, Harvard University, 1952.

902 CHAMBERLAIN, SAMUEL. Historic Boston in four seasons. N. Y., Hastings House, 1938. 73p. illus.

903 CHAMBERLAIN, SAMUEL, AND HOWE, MARK ANTONY DE WOLFE. Boston land-marks. N. Y., Hastings House, 1946. 133p. illus.

904 CUMMINGS, ABBOTT LOWELL. Charles Bulfinch and Boston's vanishing West End. Old-Time New England, 52:31–49, Oct. 1961. illus.

905 DRAKE, SAMUEL ADAMS. Old landmarks and historic personages of Boston. Boston, James R. Osgood and Co., 1873. 484p. illus.

906 FADUM, RALPH E. Observations and analysis of building settlements in Boston. Doctoral Dissertation, Harvard University, 1950.

907 [Franklin Music Warehouse. Contemporary description.] National Register, 4:239, Oct. 11, 1817.

908 HERSEY, HORATIO BROOKS. Old West End Boston. Old-Time New England, 20:162–77, Apr. 1930. illus.

909 HITCHCOCK, HENRY-RUSSELL. Boston architecture, 1637–1954, including other communities within easy driving distance. N. Y., Reinhold Publishing Corp., [1954]. 64p. illus.

910 ———. Guide to Boston architecture; excerpts. Progressive Architecture, 35:77–78, June 1954.

911 HILHAM, WALTER H. Boston after Bulfinch, an account of its architecture 1800–1900. Cambridge, Mass., Harvard University Press, 1946. 114p. illus.

912 KIRKER, HAROLD CLARK, AND KIRKER, JAMES. Bulfinch's Boston, 1787–1817. N. Y., Oxford University Press, 1964. 305p. illus.

913 McQUADE, W. Boston accent: brisk saga of a city. Architectural Forum, 120:71–78, June 1964. illus.
Ties old traditions with new.

914 MITCHELL, GEORGE R. Boston Colonial series. Architecture, v. 47–48, Mar.–Aug. 1923. illus. only.

915 PORTER, EDWARD G. Rambles in old Boston, New England. Boston, Cupples, Hurd and Co., 1887. 439p. illus.
[Real estate properties owned by the Society for the Preservation of New England Antiquities.] Regularly mentioned in *Old-Time New England*.

916 ROSS, MARJORIE DRAKE, AND CHAMBERLAIN, SAMUEL. The book of Boston: the Victorian period, 1837 to 1901. N. Y., Hastings House, 1964. 166p. illus.

917 SCHUYLER, MONTGOMERY. Boston, Massachusetts, ancient and modern. Pall Mall Magazine, 28:325, 1902.

918 STANLEY, RAYMOND W. (ed.). Mr. Bulfinch's Boston. Boston, Old Colony Trust Co., 1963. 74p. illus.

919 TOLMAN, GEORGE R. Twelve sketches of old Boston buildings. Boston, Helio-type Printing Co., 1882. 12 illus.

920 WATKINS, WALTER KENDALL. The early use and manufacture of paper-hangings in Boston. Old-Time New England, 12:109, Jan. 1922.

921 WINSOR, JUSTIN. Memorial history of Boston. Boston, J. R. Osgood and Co., 1880–81. 4v.
V. 4, pp. 383–414 refer to architecture.

Boston — Domestic

922 AMORY, MARTHA BABCOCK. Gardiner Greene mansion on Pemberton Hill. Bostonian Society. Proceedings, Jan. 15, 1924, pp. 21–27.

923 BENTON, JOSIAH HENRY. Story of the old Boston Town House, 1658–1711. Boston, Merrymount Press, 1908. 212p. illus.

924 BERNSTEIN, ALLEN. Cornelius Coolidge, architect of Beacon Hill row houses, 1810–1840. Old-Time New England, 39:45–46, Oct. 1948.

925 BROWN, FRANK CHOUTEAU. First residential row houses in Boston; Tontine Crescent. Old-Time New England, 37:60–69, Jan. 1947. illus.
1793. Charles Bulfinch, architect.

926 BROWN, JOHN PERKINS, AND RANSOM, ELEANOR. Thomas Creese house, being a description of a typical townhouse of the early eighteenth century and containing a history of the site thereof from the time of Ann Hutchinson to the present day. Boston, J. P. Brown, 1940. illus.
1711.

927 CARRICK, ALICE VAN LEER. The Revolutionary home of Paul Revere. Country Life in America, 39:63–65, Dec. 1920. illus.
Ca. 1677.

928 CHAMBERLAIN, ALLEN. Beacon Hill, its ancient pastures and early mansions. Boston, Houghton Mifflin Co., 1925. 309p. illus.

929 CUMMINGS, ABBOTT LOWELL. Foster-Hutchinson house. Old-Time New England, 54:59–76, Jan. 1964. illus.
1689–92.

930 DOGGETT, SAMUEL BRADLEY. The model of the Bradlee-Doggett house, Hollis Street, Boston. Old-Time New England, 19:174–80, Apr. 1929. illus.

931 DOUGLAS-LITHGOW, R. A. Andrew Oliver house, Dorchester. Massachusetts Magazine, 3:57–61, Jan. 1910.

932 ———. Governor Hutchinson's house on Milton Hill. Massachusetts Magazine, 3:121–24, Apr. 1910.

933 FLICK, A. C. Old Hancock house. New York State Historical Association. Quarterly, 7:291–93, Oct. 1926.
A replica has been built at Ticonderoga, N. Y.

934 Harrison Gray Otis house. Old-Time New England, 22:151–61, Apr. 1932. illus.
Account of a loan exhibition. Built 1795, attributed to Charles Bulfinch.

935 Harrison Gray Otis house, corner Lynde and Cambridge Streets, Boston. Old-Time New England, 8:7–16, Mar. 1917. illus.
1795.

936 [Houses. Contemporary descriptions.] American Magazine of Knowledge, 2:80, Oct. 1835. The Parley, part 2:200, 1842. Southern Literary Messenger, 5:793–98, Dec. 1839.

937 INGRAHAM, F. Visit to the Harrison Gray Otis house. Old-Time New England, 29:21–31, July 1938. illus.
114 Cambridge St.

938 In the old Harrison Gray Otis house. House Beautiful, 42:246, Oct. 1919. illus.

939 John Singleton Copley's houses on Beacon Hill, Boston; correspondence between Copley and his half-brother, Henry Pelham. Old-Time New England, 25:85–95, Jan. 1935. illus.

940 [Julien house. Contemporary description.] American Magazine of Knowledge, 2:81, Oct. 1835.

941 KEYES, H. E. The Crescent that waned; Franklin Crescent, Boston. Antiques, 30:27, July 1936. illus.
1796. Charles Bulfinch, architect.

942 LAWRENCE, ROBERT MEANS. Old Park Street and its vicinity. Boston, Houghton Mifflin Co., 1922. 172p. illus.

943 LAWRENCE, SARAH B. Some old white doorways. New England Magazine, n.s. 44:635–43, July 1911.
Beacon Hill.

944 Parker-Inches-Emery house, 40 Beacon Street, Boston. Old-Time New England, 2:1–11, Aug. 1913. illus.
1818.

945 RIPLEY, HUBERT G. Boston dry points — part 4. Paul Revere house. Architectural Record, 59:388–91, Apr. 1926. illus.

946 ROBINSON, FREDERICK B. Beacon Hill house from Bulfinch designs. International Studio, 99:20–23, July 1931. illus.
Louisberg Square. After 1800.

947 STATE STREET TRUST COMPANY. Forty of Boston's historic houses; a brief illustrated description of the residences of historic characters of Boston who have lived in or near the business section. Boston, State Street Trust Co., 1912. 44p. illus.

948 WAITE, EMMA FORBES. The Tontine Crescent and its architect. Old-Time New England, 43:74–77, Jan.–Mar. 1953. illus.
1794–96. Charles Bulfinch, architect. Disappeared by 1860.

949 WATERMAN, THOMAS TILESTON. Certain brick houses in Boston from 1700–1776. Old-Time New England, 23:22–27, July 1932. illus.

950 ———. The Savage house, Dock Square, Boston. Old-Time New England, 17:107–10, Jan. 1927. illus.
1706–7.

951 WATKINS, WALTER KENDALL. The Hancock house and its builder. Old-Time New England, 17:3–19, July 1926. illus.

952 WHITEFIELD, EDWIN. Homes of our forefathers in Boston, old England and Boston, New England. Boston, The Author, 1889. 138p. illus.

Boston — Public

953 BAIL, HAMILTON VAUGHAN. Views of Harvard to 1860: an iconographic study. Harvard Library Bulletin, 2:44–82, 179–221, 309–343, Winter, Autumn 1948. illus.
1788–1839.

954 [Beacon Hill Column. Contemporary description.] American Magazine of Knowledge, 2:47, Sept. 1835.

955 BOSTONIAN SOCIETY. T Wharf, past and present. Bostonian Society. Proceedings, pp. 27–40, 1948. illus.
History, predecessors, structures built on it.

956 Boston's new Old State House. Magazine of History, 13:305–10, June 1911.

957 BROWN, ABRAM ENGLISH. Faneuil Hall and Faneuil Hall market; or Peter Faneuil and his gift. Boston, Lea and Shepherd Co., 1900. 671p. illus.
1742. Addition by Bulfinch, 1805.

958 BROWN, FRANK CHOUTEAU. John Smibert, artist, and the first Faneuil Hall. Old-Time New England, 36:61–63, Jan. 1946.
1742.

959 [Bunker Hill Monument. Details of the costs.] Niles' Weekly Register, 59:304, Jan. 9, 1841.

960 [Capitol. Contemporary description.] American Magazine of Knowledge, 2:68–69, Oct. 1835.

961 CARTER, RUTH N. The Puritan Post: a history of the postoffice in Boston. Bostonian Society. Proceedings, pp. 27–38, 1957.
1639.

962 DOUGLAS-LITHGOW, R. A. The Province house, Boston. Massachusetts Magazine, 3:199–203, July 1910.
Also known as the Peter Sergeant house, 1676.

963 DRAKE, SAMUEL ADAMS. Old Boston taverns and tavern clubs. Boston, W. A. Butterfield, 1917. 124p. illus.

964 ELIOT, WILLIAM HAVARD. Description of the Tremont house with architectural illustrations. Boston, Gray and Bowen, 1830. 36p. illus.
1828. Isaiah Rogers, architect.

965 [Exchange Coffee House. Contemporary descriptions.] National Register, 3:216–17, Apr. 5, 1817. New World, 3:96, Aug. 7, 1841.

966 FOX, THOMAS A. Brief history of the Beacon Hill State House. American Architect and Building News, 48:127–29, June 29, 1895.
1795. Charles Bulfinch, architect.

967 KIRKER, HAROLD CLARK. Boston Exchange Coffee House. Old-Time New England, 52:11–13, July 1961.
1809. Asher Benjamin, architect.

968 Massachusetts State Library, Boston. The Massachusetts State House. Boston, 1953. 155p. illus.

Erected 1795–98. Charles Bulfinch, architect.

969 NORCROSS, FREDERICK WALTER. Ye ancient inns of Boston town. New England Magazine, 25:315–25, 1901–2.

970 READ, CHARLES F. The Old State House, and its predecessor the first Town House. Bostonian Society. Proceedings. pp. 32–50, 1908.

971 Rededication of the Old State House, Boston, July 11, 1882. Boston, Printed by Order of the Council, 1885. illus.

972 RIPLEY, HUBERT G. Boston dry points — part 1. Old State House. Architectural Record, 58:542–48, Dec. 1925. illus.

973 ———. Boston dry points — part 2. Faneuil Hall. Architectual Record, 59:165–69, Jan. 1926. illus.

974 ———. Boston dry points — part 3. The Old Tremont house. Architectural Record, 59:287–91, Mar. 1926. illus.

975 ———. Boston dry points — part 5. Copley Square. Architectural Record, 59:467–71, May 1926. illus.

976 ———. Boston dry points — part 8. Old City Hall. Architectural Record, 60:363–68, Oct. 1926. illus.

1810.

977 ———. Boston dry points — part 9. Old Granary burying grounds. Architectural Record, 60:575–79, Dec. 1926. illus.

978 ———. Boston dry points — part 10. The New State House. Architectural Record, 61:315–20, Apr. 1927. illus.

Bulfinch front, 1798.

979 SPENCER, CHARLES ELDRIDGE. The First Bank of Boston, 1784–1949. N. Y., Newcomen Society in North America, 1949. 32p. illus.

The First National Bank of Boston, founded as the Massachusetts Bank.

980 THWING, LEROY L. Boston street lighting in the 18th century. Old-Time New England, 28:72–78, Oct. 1937.

981 [Triangular building. Contemporary description.] American Magazine of Knowledge, 2:80, Oct. 1835. illus.

Used as a customhouse and warehouse.

982 WILLARD, SOLOMON. Plans and sections of the obelisk on Bunker's Hill. . . . Boston, S. N. Dickinson, 1843. 31p. illus.

1824–42. Solomon Willard, architect.

Boston — Religious

983 ALLEN, ISABEL HOPKINS. Old North Church, Boston. Antiques Journal, 10:26–27, 37, July 1955. illus.

1723.

984 BABCOCK, MARY KENT DAVEY. Old Christ Church, Boston. Historical Magazine of the Protestant Episcopal Church, 8:166–69, 1939.

985 BOLTON, CHARLES KNOWLES. Christ Church, Salem Street, Boston, 1723. Boston, The Church, 1912. 49p. illus.
Second edition, 1930.

986 BROWN, FRANK CHOUTEAU. Early Boston churches. Pencil Points, 18:799–814, Dec. 1937. Monograph Series, 23:81–96. illus.

987 BROWN, GILBERT PATTEN. The real Old North Church; a landmark of the Republic. Granite Monthly, 45:159–62, May 1913.
Christ Church (1723).

988 COLE, WILLIAM I. Early churches at the North End, Boston. New England Magazine, 26:241–56, 1902. illus.

989 FAGAN, JAMES O. The Old South; or the romance of early New England history. Boston, George H. Ellis Co., 1923. 141p. illus.
Old South Church (1729).

990 FOOTE, HENRY WILDER. Annals of King's Chapel, from the Puritan age of New England to the present day. Boston, Little, Brown and Co., 1882–96. 2v. illus.
1749. Peter Harrison, architect.

991 FRENCH, WILLARD. Paul Revere's Old North Church. Architectural Record, 19:215–22, Mar. 1906. illus.

992 GREENE, JOHN GARDNER. Charles Street Meeting-house, Boston. Old-Time New England, 30:86–93, Jan. 1940.
1807. Asher Benjamin, architect.

993 LEAHY, WILLIAM AUGUSTINE. Catholic churches of Boston and vicinity and St. John's Seminary, Brighton. Boston, McClellan, Hearn and Co., 1892. 43p. illus.

994 METCALF, PRISCILLA. Boston before Bulfinch: Harrison's King's Chapel. Society of Architectural Historians. Journal, 13:11–14, Mar. 1954. illus.
English models for this church, 1749.

995 Old South meeting house. Stone and Webster. Journal, 46:506–14, Apr. 1930.

996 OLD SOUTH SOCIETY. Our heritage, Old South Church, 1669–1919. Norwood, Mass., Plimpton Press, 1919.

997 ———. The two hundred and fiftieth anniversary of the founding of the Old South Church in Boston. Norwood, Mass., Plimpton Press, 1919. 138p. illus.

998 PLACE, CHARLES A. New South Church, Boston, Mass. Old-Time New England, 11:51–53, Oct. 1920. illus.

999 Preservation of Park Street Church, Boston. Boston, 1903. Pamphlet.
1809. Peter Banner, architect.

1000 PRESSEY, PARK. Early Boston churches. Old-Time New England, 41:56–60, Jan. 1951. illus.
Thirteen church societies and their buildings, 1632–1727.

1001 STRICKLAND, CHARLES RUTAN. Rebuilding the Old North Church steeple. Antiques, 68:54–56, July 1955. illus.

1002 [Trinity Church. Contemporary description.] Boston Musical Gazette, 1:100, Oct. 17, 1838.

Bradford

1003 CARY, GEORGE E. The First Church of Christ, Bradford, Massachusetts. Essex Institute. Historical Collections, 86:1–14, Jan. 1950. illus.

    1849——.

Braintree

1004 Quincy homestead, Braintree, Mass. Antiquarian, 2:15–17, June 1924. illus.

1005 SHUSTER, RUTH W. Gathered in 1707 . . . a history of the First Congregational Church, Braintree, Massachusetts, 1707–1957. [Braintree? Mass., 1957.] 138p. illus.

Brookfield

1006 GILLESPIE, HARRIET S. Brookfield tavern restored. House Beautiful, 51:44–46, Jan. 1922. illus.

    1771.

Brookline

1007 AMORY, MARGOT. Captain Cook cottage, Brookline, Massachusetts. House Beautiful, 62:646–49, Dec. 1927. illus.

1008 CANDAGE, RUFUS G. F. Gridley house, Brookline and Jeremy Gridley. Brookline Historical Society. Publications, no. 1:3–32, 1903.

1009 1827 Gothic; home of R. S. Humphrey, a famous one-acre estate in Brookline. House and Garden, 73:38–40, May 1938. illus.

1010 GODDARD, JULIA. The Goddard house, Warren Street, Brookline, built about 1730; its owners and occupants. Brookline Historical Society. Proceedings, pp. 16–34, 1903.

1011 LITTLE, NINA FLETCHER. Some old Brookline houses built in this Massachusetts town before 1825 and still standing in 1948. Brookline, Brookline Historical Society, 1949. 160p. illus.

    1736–1825.

1012 STEARNS, CHARLES H. The Sewall house. Brookline Historical Society. Proceedings, pp. 35–45, 1903.

Cambridge

1013 BAIL, HAMILTON VAUGHAN. Views of Harvard: a pictorial record to 1860. Cambridge, Mass., Harvard University Press, 1949. 264p. illus.

    1693–1858. Reprinted from *Harvard Library Bulletin*, 1947–49.

1014 BROWN, FRANK CHOUTEAU. Old Judge Lee house, Cambridge, Mass. Architectural Review, 4:77–78, May 1916. illus.

1015 BULFINCH, ELLEN SUSAN. The Tudor house at Fresh Pond. Cambridge Historical Society. Publications, 3:100–109, 1908.

1016 CAMBRIDGE HISTORICAL COMMISSION. Survey of architectural history in Cambridge; report one: East Cambridge. Cambridge, Mass., 1965. 101p. illus.

    1642——.

1017 CAMBRIDGE HISTORIC DISTRICTS STUDY COMMITTEE. Final report of the Historic Districts Study Committee. Cambridge, Mass., 1962. illus.

1018 CAPEN, OLIVER BRONSON. Country homes of famous Americans. Part 6. Ralph Waldo Emerson. Country Life in America, 6:40–43, May 1904. illus. 1828.

1019 ———. Country homes of famous Americans. Part 9. Henry Wadsworth Longfellow. Country Life in America, 6:346–49, 363, Aug. 1904. illus.
Vassall-Craigie-Longfellow house, 1759.

1020 CHAMBERLAIN, SAMUEL. Historic Cambridge in four seasons. N. Y., Hastings House, 1942. 73p. illus.

1021 CHAMBERLAIN, SAMUEL, AND MOFFAT, DONALD. Fair Harvard. N. Y., Hastings House, 1948. 104p. illus.

1022 CHANDLER, JOSEPH EVERETT. Judge Joseph Lee house, Cambridge, Mass. House Beautiful, 51:108–10, Feb. 1922. illus.

1023 COGSWELL, CHARLES N. Cambridge, Massachusetts. Part 1. Pencil Points, 18:589–604, Sept. 1937. Monograph Series, 23:49–64. illus.

1024 ———. Cambridge, Massachusetts. Part 2. Pencil Points, 18:665–80, Oct. 1937. Monograph Series, 23:65–80. illus.
Covers 1686–1808.

1025 CONANT, KENNETH. Group of old Cambridge houses. House Beautiful, 53:33–36, Jan. 1923. illus.

1026 DANA, HENRY WADSWORTH LONGFELLOW. Chronicles of the Craigie house; the coming of Longfellow. Cambridge Historical Society. Proceedings, 25:19–60, 1938–39. illus.
Contains an 1815 sketch of the house (1759).

1027 ———. Longfellow house, Cambridge, Mass. Old-Time New England, 38:81–96, Apr. 1948. illus.
Sometimes called Vassall-Craigie-Longfellow house, 1759.

1028 DAUGHTERS OF THE AMERICAN REVOLUTION. MASSACHUSETTS. An historic guide to Cambridge, compiled by members of the Hannah Winthrop Chapter, National Society, Daughters of the American Revolution. Cambridge, Mass., 1907. 207p. illus.

1029 First college building in the U. S. A. The Month at Goodspeed's Book Shop, 22:15–19, Oct. 1950. illus.
The "Old College" of Harvard, 1638–79.

1030 FRASER, ESTHER STEVENS. Cinderella house; John Hicks house, Cambridge, Mass. Country Life in America, 47:70–76, Dec. 1924. illus.

1031 ———. John Hicks house. Cambridge Historical Society. Proceedings, 20:110–24, 1934.

1032 ———. John Hicks house, Cambridge, Mass. Old-Time New England, 22:99–113, Jan. 1932. illus.
1760.

1033 ———. Painted decoration in Colonial homes. Cambridge Historical Society. Proceedings, 21:50–57, 1936.

1034 GOZZALDI, MARY ISABELLA. A few old Cambridge houses. Cambridge Historical Society. Proceedings, 6:17–26, 1912.

1035 GOZZALDI, MARY ISABELLA; DANA, ELIZABETH ELLERY; AND POTTINGER, DAVID T. The Vassall house. Cambridge Historical Society. Proceedings, 21:78–118, 1936.

1036 HARVARD UNIVERSITY. Education, bricks, and mortar: Harvard buildings and their contribution to the advancement of learning. Cambridge, 1949. 99p. illus.
1642———.

1037 LEBARON, FRANCIS. The Washington-Craigie-Longfellow house. Washington's headquarters and Longfellow's home in Cambridge, Mass. Century, 73:487–98, Feb. 1907.

1038 LILLIE, RUPERT BALLOU. Cambridge in 1775. Wenham? Mass., 1949. 42p. illus.
Description of topography, streets, and buildings in 1775.

1039 ———. Gardens and homes of the Loyalists. Cambridge Historical Society. Proceedings, 26:49–62, 1940.

1040 MOORE, MRS. JAMES L. The Fayerweather house. Cambridge Historical Society. Publications, 25:86–94, 1939.

1041 MORISON, SAMUEL ELIOT. Conjectural restoration of the Old College at Harvard. Old-Time New England, 23:131–58, Apr. 1933. illus.
1638.

1042 Painters in the house; Elmwood, home of J. R. Lowell. Mentor, 14:14–16, Aug. 1926. illus.

1043 RUGGLES, HENRY STODDARD. Ruggles mansion. Cambridge, Massachusetts. N. Y. Genealogical and Biographical Records, 56:101, Apr. 1925.

1044 Ruggles mansions built in 1641 and 1764. House Beautiful, 48:89, Aug. 1920. illus.
1641 house has been destroyed.

1045 SCHUYLER, MONTGOMERY. Architecture of American colleges. Part 1. Harvard. Architectural Record, 26:243–69, Oct. 1909. illus.

1046 WATKINS, LURA WOODSIDE. Cambridge glass, 1818 to 1888: the story of the New England Glass Company. Boston, Little, Brown, [1953, c. 1930]. 199p. illus.
Appendix: other Cambridge factories.

1047 WHEELWRIGHT, JOHN BROOKS. Valentine-Fuller house, Cambridgeport, Massachusetts. Old-Time New England, 28:68–71, Oct. 1937.
Ca. 1847.

Cape Ann (see also *Gloucester*)

1048 BARTLETT, STUART. Later dwelling architecture of Cape Ann. Part 1. Pencil Points, 15:379–94, Aug. 1934. Monograph Series, 20:145–60. illus.
Covers 1740–1820, Gloucester and Rockport.

1049 ———. Later dwelling architecture of Cape Ann. Part 2. Pencil Points, 15:501–16, Oct. 1934. Monograph Series, 20:161–76. illus.

1050 BREWSTER, DANIEL O. The cottages of Cape Ann — part 1. Pencil Points, 14:535–50, Dec. 1933. Monograph Series, 19:81–96. illus.
Covers 1665–1825.

1051 BROWN, FRANK CHOUTEAU. Cape Ann: some earlier Colonial dwellings in and about Annisquam, Massachusetts. Pencil Points, 14:69–84, Feb. 1933. Monograph Series, 19:1–16. illus.
Covers 1650–1715.

1052 CHAMBERLAIN, SAMUEL. Gloucester and Cape Ann. N. Y., Hastings House, 1938. 73p. illus.

1053 FRANKLIN, M. S. Cottage interiors of Cape Ann. Pencil Points, 15:65–80, Jan. 1934. Monograph Series, 20:97–112. illus.

Cape Cod (see also *Barnstable* and *Yarmouth*)

1054 BANGS, M. R. Cape Cod where houses were built to suit the land. House Beautiful, 60:252–58, Sept. 1926. illus.

1055 BOICOURT, JANE. Antiques on Cape Cod. Antiques, 61:530–33, June 1952. illus.
Survey of architecture, 1630's–1850.

1056 CARRICK, ALICE VAN LEER. Oldest house on Cape Cod. Country Life in America, 44:42–45, Sept. 1923. illus.
Dillingham house, Brewster (1660).

1057 CHAMBERLAIN, SAMUEL. Cape Cod in the sun. N. Y., Hastings House, 1937. 95p. illus.

1058 CONNALLY, ERNEST ALLEN. Cape Cod house: an introductory study. Society of Architectural Historians. Journal, 19:47–56, May 1960. illus.

1059 EARLY, ELEANOR. And this is Cape Cod! Boston, Houghton Mifflin Co., 1936. 223p. illus.

1060 EDWARDS, AGNES. Cape Cod — new and old. Boston, Houghton Mifflin Co., 1918. 239p. illus.

1061 First functionable homes; proportion and patterns; durable house of Cape Cod. Life, 38:124–25, 128–31, Apr. 18, 1955. illus.

1062 READ, EDWARD SEARS. Cape Cod farm and village houses. Architectural Forum, 39:7–10, July 1923. illus.

Carlisle

1063 WILKINS, MRS. B. P. Century-old houses of Carlisle. Old-Time New England, 23:44–55, Oct. 1932. illus.

Clinton

1064 STONE, CHRISTOPHER C. Old houses in Clinton. Clinton Historical Society. Papers, 1:39–43, 1912.

Colrain

1065 JOHNSON, KARLTON C. The venerable house, 1750–1950; the story of the Congregational Church, Colrain, Massachusetts. Colrain, Mass., published by F. S. Apte, S. W. Coombs, and K. S. Johnson for the Colrain Congregational Church, 1950. 44p. illus.

Concord

1066 BARTLETT, GEORGE B. Concord: historic, literary and picturesque. 15th ed. Boston, Lothrop, Lee and Shepard Publishing Co., 1895. 200p. illus.

1067 BROWN, FRANK CHOUTEAU. Some records of old Concord, first inland township of Massachusetts. Pencil Points, 13:332–46, May 1932. Monograph Series, 18:181–96. illus.

Includes Bedford, Groton, Shirley Center.

1068 CAPEN, OLIVER BRONSON. Country homes of famous Americans. Part 4. Henry David Thoreau. Country Life in America, 5:285–88, Feb. 1904. illus.

Birthplace, Concord, before 1800. Description of Walden Pond hut, *ca.* 1845.

1068A ———. Country homes of famous Americans. Part 8. Nathaniel Hawthorne. Country Life in America, 6:242–45, 282, 283, July 1904. illus.

Old Manse, 1765. Wayside, original house, *ca.* 1750, many additions.

1069 FRENCH, ALLEN. Old Concord. Boston, Little, Brown and Co., 1915. 186p. illus.

1070 KEYES, JOHN S. Story of an old house. Concord Antiquarian Society. Publications, no. 5, 1903. 17p. illus.

Smedley-Jones house.

1071 LATHROP, M. L. Literary shrine open to visitors; home of three authors, the Wayside, Concord, Massachusetts. Library Journal, 58:362, Apr. 15, 1933.

1072 LOTHROP, MARGARET M. The Wayside: home of authors. N. Y. American Book Co., [1940]. 202p. illus.

Danvers

1073 ALLEN, NELLIE BURNHAM. The old farmhouse on the Newburyport Turnpike. Danvers Historical Society. Collections, 37:1–17, 1949. illus.

Allen farm house, built 1803–4.

1074 ALLEN, RUTH HOWARD. Some Putnam houses on Locust Street. Danvers Historical Society. Collections, 27:29–39, 28:46–52, 1939–40.

1075 ———. Some Putnam houses on Locust Street. Danvers Historical Society. Collections, 37:53–62, 1949. illus.

House built by Samuel Putnam, 1813.

1076 BROWN, FRANK CHOUTEAU. Danvers (old Salem Village), Massachusetts — part 1. Pencil Points, 19:719–34, Nov. 1938. Monograph Series, 24:161–76. illus.

Covers 1648–1812.

1077 ———. Danvers (old Salem Village), Massachusetts — part 2. Pencil Points, 19:783–98, Dec. 1938. Monograph Series, 24:177–92. illus.

Covers 1670–1809.

1078 Contract and expense account for building the Samuel Fowler house, Danversport, 1810. Essex Institute. Historical Collections, 67:46–48, 1931.

Also appeared in *Old-Time New England*, 21:185–87, 1931.

1079 An early East Danvers house. Danvers Historical Society. Collections, 3:59–63, 1915.

Built 1641 or 1642 by Richard Ingersoll.

1080 FALES, WINNIFRED. Lindens, a house with a history. Country Life in America, 33:46–49, Mar. 1918. illus.

Before 1754. Moved to Washington, D. C.: *New York Times*, Dec. 5, 1937, section 9.

1081 HOUSE, ALBERT VIRGIL. Historic cellar holes. Danvers Historical Society. Collections, 15:87–107, 1927.

Notes on houses.

1082 Lindens, built in Danvers, Massachusetts, in 1754, re-erected and furnished in Washington, D. C. in 1938. Antiques, 33:67, 76–79, Feb. 1938. illus.

1083 PERLEY, SIDNEY. Nurse house. Essex Institute. Historical Collections, 62:1–3, Jan. 1926.

Rebecca Nurse house.

1084 PHILBRICK, JULIA A. Old Putnam houses in Danvers. Danvers Historical Society. Collections, 5:70–73, 1917.

1085 PRIEST, GEORGE F. Old houses of Salem Village. Danvers Historical Society. Collections, 3:1–12, 1915.

1086 PUTNAM, ALFRED P. Danvers people and their homes. Danvers Historical Society. Collections, 9:57–64, 1921; 11:50–54, 1923; 17:55–73, 1929.

1087 Samuel Fowler house, Danversport, Mass. Old-Time New England, 3:1–6, Mar. 1912. illus.

1809.

1088 TAPLEY, HARRIET S. Old tavern days in Danvers. Danvers Historical Society. Collections, 8:1–32, 1920.

1089 WINSLOW, ANNIE M. First Baptist Church. Danvers Historical Society. Collections, 37:47–52, 1949. illus.

First Baptist Church, 1781–1948.

Dedham

1090 APPLETON, WILLIAM SUMNER. Scenic wallpaper from East Dedham, Massachusetts. Old-Time New England, 22:51–58, Oct. 1931. illus.

1091 Oldest frame dwelling in the United States, the Fairbanks house, Dedham, Massachusetts. Mentor, 16:30–31, Apr. 1928. illus.

Deerfield

1092 ANTIQUES. Deerfield issue. Antiques, 70:173–296, Sept. 1956. illus.

Primarily antiques, some interior views.

1093 CHAMBERLAIN, SAMUEL, AND FLYNT, HENRY N. Historic Deerfield: houses and interiors. N. Y., Hastings House, 1965. 182p. illus.

Revised and enlarged edition of *Frontier of Freedom*, 1952 and 1957.

1094 COLEMAN, EMMA L. Frary house, Deerfield, Massachusetts. Old-Time New England, 23:88–98, Jan. 1933. illus.
1683 and later.

1095 FLYNT, HENRY N. Old Deerfield, a living community. Art in America, 43:40–47ff., May 1955. illus.

1096 HADDON, RAWSON W. Old Deerfield, Massachusetts. White Pine Series of Architectural Monographs, v. 6, no. 5, Oct. 1920. 14p. illus.

1097 Old Deerfield, containing an appreciation of early New England as evidenced by the now standing seventeenth century houses of Deerfield. Boston, Pinkham Press, 1928. 24p. illus.

1098 SCALES, JOHN LONGFELLOW. The Longfellow garrison. American Monthly Magazine, 38:246–51, May 1911.

1099 SHELDON, GEORGE, AND SHELDON, J. M. ARMS. The Rev. John Williams house. Deerfield, Mass., 1918. 32p. illus.
1707.

1100 SHELDON, J. M. ARMS. Old Indian house at Deerfield, Mass., and the effort made in 1847 to save it from destruction. Old-Time New England, 12:99–108, Jan. 1922. illus.

1101 ———. Revolutionary history of a New England homestead; Colonel Joseph Stebbins homestead in Deerfield, Massachusetts. Deerfield, Mass., 1925. 50p. illus.
Ca. 1772.

1102 Story of Deerfield, based on information supplied by H. N. Flynt. Antiques, 60:108–12, Aug. 1951. illus.
1669——.

1103 Three old Deerfield fireplaces, belonging to the latter half of the eighteenth century. Architectural Review, 5:113, June 1917. illus.

1104 WHITING, MARGARET C. Old-time mural and floor decorations in Deerfield and vicinity. Pocumtuck Valley Memorial Association. Proceedings, 6:272–81, 1921.

Dennis (see *Yarmouth*)

Dorchester

1105 STARK, JAMES HENRY. History of the old Blake house, and a brief sketch of the Dorchester Historical Society. [Dorchester?], Mass., 1907. 13p. illus.

1106 STONE, ELMA A. The old Trescott house. Hyde Park Historical Register, 3:73–76, Apr. 1903.

Duxbury

1107 ALDEN, EDWARD SMITH. Alden homestead, Duxbury, Mass. . . . Holyoke, Mass., Alden Press, 1932. 64p.

1108 BAXTER, SYLVESTER. Alden house at Duxbury, Massachusetts. Architectural Record, 49:399–408, May 1921. illus.
1655.

1109 HALL, GERTRUDE. Charm of old Duxbury: an historic Massachusetts Bay town and its delightful old and new houses. Indoors and Out, 2:161–69, July 1903. illus.

Essex

1110 Dow, GEORGE FRANCIS. The Choate house at Essex, Massachusetts, and its recent restoration. Old-Time New England, 12:6–13, July 1921. illus.
1725.

1111 LITTLE, NINA FLETCHER. John Cogswell's grant and some of the houses thereon, 1636–1839; with special reference to the Jonathan Cogswell house, which stands at the end of Spring Street, Essex, Massachusetts. Essex Institute. Historical Collections, 76:152–73, 1940.

1112 [cancelled].

Framingham

1113 First Baptist Church, Framingham Centre, Massachusetts. Architectural Review, n.s. 6:41–45, May 1918. illus.

1114 FISHER, CHARLES P. Structural history of the Pike-Haven-Foster house, Framingham, Massachusetts. Old-Time New England, 45:28–36, Oct.–Dec. 1954. illus.
1696–1860.

Gloucester (see also *Cape Ann*)

1115 BROOKS, ALFRED MANSFIELD. The Gloucester model. Essex Institute. Historical Collections, 76:43–45, 1940.
Scale model of present Main Street, Gloucester, Mass., done 1830.

1116 BROWN, FRANK CHOUTEAU. Interior details and furnishings of the William Haskell dwelling, built before 1650 at West Gloucester, Massachusetts. Pencil Points, 20:113–28, Feb. 1930. Monograph Series, 25:1–17. illus.

1117 CHAMBERLAIN, SAMUEL, AND HOLLISTER, PAUL. Beauport at Gloucester, the most fascinating house in America. N. Y., Hastings House, 1951. 84p. illus.

1118 LITTLE, MRS. BERTRAM K. Old White-Ellery house, Gloucester, Massachusetts. Old-Time New England, 37:53–59, Jan. 1947. illus.
1704.

Granville

1119 WILSON, ALBION BENJAMIN. History of Granville, Massachusetts. n.p., 1954. 381p. illus.

Groveland

1120 NORTHEND, MARY HARROD. House with a history. American Homes and Gardens, 9:128–31, Apr. 1912. illus.
Savony house. Before 1777.

1121 POORE, ALFRED. The houses and buildings of Groveland, Massachusetts. Essex Institute. Historical Collections, 46:193–208, 289–304, July–Oct. 1910; 47:25–40, 133–48, 261–76, Jan.–July 1911.
Compiled in 1854.

Hadley

1122 HUNTINGTON, JAMES LINCOLN, AND CHAMBERLAIN, SAMUEL. Forty acres; the story of the Bishop Huntington house. N. Y., Hastings House, 1949. 68p. illus.
1752.

Hancock

1123 ANDREWS, EDWARD DEMING. Hancock Shaker Village. Art in America, 51:44–47, Dec. 1963. illus.
1780's on.

Hatfield

1124 MILLER, MARGARET. Reminiscences of an old meeting house. Pocumtuck Valley Memorial Association. Proceedings, 6:95–105, 1921.

Haverhill

1125 BACON, EDGAR MAYHEW. Country homes of famous Americans. Part 3. John Greenleaf Whittier. Country Life in America, 5:209–13, 256, Jan. 1904. illus.
Birthplace near Haverhill (1668) house at Amesbury.

1126 Contract-specifications covering construction of the old Saltonstall house at Haverhill, Mass., executed in 1788. Architectural Record, n.s. 6:75, May 1918. illus.

1127 SALTONSTALL, NATHANIEL; MARSH, MOSES; AND CARLTON, AMOS. An eighteenth-century builder's contract. Old-Time New England, 46:81–83, Jan.–Mar. 1956. illus.
1788. Includes specifications for a house.

Hingham

1128 CORSE, MURRAY P. Old Ship meeting-house in Hingham, Mass. Old-Time New England, 21:19–30, July 1930. illus.

1129 DAUGHTERS OF THE AMERICAN REVOLUTION. MASSACHUSETTS. Hingham; a story of its early settlement and life, its ancient landmarks, its historic sites and buildings. Hingham, Mass., Old Colony Chapter, D. A. R., 1911. 123p. illus.

1130 RUSSELL, ELIZABETH H. Old Ordinary at Hingham, Massachusetts, an ancient tavern. House Beautiful, 58:109–12, 156–57, Aug. 1925. illus.
Before 1700.

1131 SHUMWAY, HARRY IRVING. Grandfather among the taverns. American Cookery, 39:139–46, 1934.
Old Ordinary.

1132 STARK, GLADYS TEELE DETWYLER. The Old Ship meeting house of Hingham, Massachusetts. Boston, Beacon Press, 1951. 32p. illus.
1635.

Holyoke

1133 BAGG, EDWARD PARSONS, AND BAGG, AARON MOORE, JR. The first hundred years of the Second Congregational Church of Holyoke, 1849–1949. Holyoke, Mass., 1949. 68p. illus.

Ipswich

1134 Cap't. Matthew Perkins house, Ipswich, Mass. Old-Time New England, 15:125–27, Jan. 1925. illus.
Ca. 1638.

1135 [Houses of Ipswich.] *See* Chronicle report of the 250th anniversary exercises of Ipswich, Mass. Ipswich, 1884. 74p. illus.

1136 The Thimbles, Ipswich, Massachusetts. House Beautiful, 42:150–51, Aug. 1917. illus.

1137 WATERMAN, THOMAS TILESTON. Staircase, Corbett house, Ipswich, Mass. Architecture, v. 50, no. 4, pl. 154, Oct. 1924. illus. only.

1138 WATERS, THOMAS FRANKLIN. Early homes of the Puritans, and some old Ipswich houses. Salem, Mass., Salem Press Co., 1898. 106p. illus.

1139 ———. Glimpses of everyday life in old Ipswich. Salem, Mass., Ipswich Historical Society, 1925. 39p. illus.

1140 ———. Ipswich in Massachusetts Bay colony. Ipswich, Mass., Ipswich Historical Society, 1905. 2v. illus.
Another edition, 1917.

1141 Whipple house, Ipswich, Mass. Antiquarian, 1:23, 25, Dec. 1923. illus.
Ca. 1640 and later.

Lancaster

1142 BROWN, JOHN P. Notes on the Bulfinch church at Lancaster, Massachusetts. Old-Time New England, 27:148–51, Apr. 1937. illus.

1143 PLACE, CHARLES A. Bulfinch church, Lancaster, Mass. Architectural Forum, 34:191–98, June 1921. illus.
1816. Charles Bulfinch, architect.

1144 SAFFORD, MARION FULLER. Historical sketch of the First Church of Lancaster. Lancaster, Mass., The Church, 1916. 16p.

Lenox

1145 LYNCH, FREDERICK. The church on the Lenox Hilltop and round about it. New England Magazine, 23:192–211, Oct. 1900. illus.
Brief discussion of the architecture.

Lexington

1146 PIPER, FRED SMITH. Architectural yesterdays in Lexington; a fragmentary account of some of the older buildings and their builders. Lexington Historical Society. Proceedings, 4:114–26, 1912.

Lowell

1147 COOLIDGE, JOHN. Mill and mansion. N. Y., Columbia University Press, 1942.
A study of architecture and society, 1820–65.

1148 GRIFFIN, SARA SWAN. Old homes and historic byways of Lowell. Lowell Historical Society. Contributions, 1:451–66, 1913.

1149 THOMPSON, ELLEN STRAW. Rediscovering an old house. New England Magazine, 37:185–92, Oct. 1907.

Spalding house, 1670.

Lynn

1150 HAWKES, NATHAN MORTIMER. Hearths and homes of old Lynne, with studies in local history. Lynn, Mass., Nichols, 1907. 350p. illus.

1151 MACKENZIE, NEIL D. The first parish meetinghouse, Lynnfield Center, Massachusetts. Old-Time New England, 45:103–6, Apr.–June 1955. illus.

Built 1714.

Malden

1152 COREY, DELORAINE PENDRE. The Old Brick. Malden Historical Society. Register, 6:6–12, 1920.

Brick meetinghouse, 1803.

1153 WATKINS, WALTER KENDALL. Malden's old meeting houses. Malden Historical Society. Register, 2:33–53, 1912.

Mansfield

1154 COPELAND, JENNIE F. Fisher-Richardson house. Old-Time New England, 21:168–78, Apr. 1931. illus.

1700.

Marblehead

1155 ALDRICH, WILLIAM TRUMAN. Marblehead, its contribution to eighteenth and early nineteenth century American architecture. White Pine Series of Architectural Monographs, v. 4, no. 1, Feb. 1918. 14p. illus.

1156 BROWN, FRANK CHOUTEAU. Old Marblehead — part 1. Pencil Points, 19:313–28, May 1938. Monograph Series, 24:113–28. illus.

Covers 1683–1750.

1157 ———. Old Marblehead, Massachusetts — part 2. Pencil Points, 19:455–70, July 1938. Monograph Series, 24:129–44. illus.

Covers 1648–1824.

1158 ———. Old Marblehead, Massachusetts — part 3. Pencil Points, 19:591–606, Sept. 1938. Monograph Series, 24:145–60. illus.

Covers 1729–68.

1159 CHADWELL, PAULINE SOROKA. Colonel Jeremiah Lee mansion. Antiques, 48:353–55, Dec. 1945. illus.

1768.

1160 CHAMBERLAIN, SAMUEL. Old Marblehead. N. Y., Hastings House, 1940. 72p. illus.

1161 FOWLER, SAMUEL PAGE. The King Hooper house and its early occupants. Danvers Historical Society. Collections, 1:87–89, 1913.

1745. Extracts from a letter from Samuel Page Fowler, May 5, 1875.

1162 SPALDING, DEXTER EDWIN. King Hooper mansion, a famous Colonial residence in Marblehead, Massachusetts. House Beautiful, 52:106–8, Aug. 1922. illus.

1163 WORTHINGTON, FREDERICK WILLIAM. The King Hooper house. American Homes and Gardens, 11:273–75, 285, Aug. 1914. illus.

Marlborough

1164 Contract to build a minister's house at Marlborough, Mass., in 1661. Old-Time New England, 24:142, Apr. 1934.

Marshfield

1165 BRADFORD, GERSHOM. The unknown Webster. Old-Time New England, 44:55–63, Oct.–Dec. 1953. illus.
Daniel Webster, 1824–52. Includes his country estate.

1166 EATON, WALTER PRICHARD. Winslow house at Marshfield, Mass. House Beautiful, 50:184–87, 224–26, Sept. 1921. illus.
1699.

1167 Marshfield, 70°-40′W : 42°-5′N; the autobiography of a Pilgrim town . . . 1640–1940. Marshfield, Mass., Marshfield Tercentenary Committee, 1940. 334p. illus.

1168 ROBINSON, THOMAS P. Historic Winslow house at Marshfield, Mass. Old-Time New England, 11:107–12, Jan. 1921. illus.

1169 SWAN, MABEL M. Two early Massachusetts houses. Antiques, 52:106–9, Aug. 1947. illus.
Winslow house, Marshfield, 1699; Sever house, Kingston, 1760.

Martha's Vineyard

1170 CHAMBERLAIN, SAMUEL. Martha's Vineyard. N. Y., Hastings House, 1941. 73p. illus.

Medford

1171 BROOKS, MRS. ALFRED, AND MANN, MOSES W. Colonial houses — old and new. Medford Historical Society. Register, 15:67–72, July 1912.

1172 COOLIDGE, RUTH DAME. The Craddock house, past and future. Medford Historical Society. Register, 29:37–56, Sept. 1926.
Also known as the Peter Tufts house (1677–80).

1173 FULLER, GEORGE S. T. History of the Royall house and its occupants. Medford Historical Society. Register, 29:1–11, Mar. 1926.
Before 1697, 1750 and later.

1174 GILL, ELIZA M. At Medford's old civic center. Medford Historical Society. Register, 25:11–15, 27, Mar.–June 1922.

1175 Isaac Royall house on the Plantation, Medford, Massachusetts. American Architect and Building News, 24:171–72, Oct. 13, 1888. illus.

1176 MANN, MOSES W. Dr. Osgood's house. Medford Historical Society. Register, 23:38–40, June 1920.
1785.

1177 ———. Renovation of the Peter Tufts house. Medford Historical Society. Register, 29:70–75, Dec. 1926.

1178 ———. The Touro house and its owner. Medford Historical Society. Register, 23:78–83, Dec. 1920.
Before 1822.

1179 ———. The Tufts family residences. Medford Historical Society. Register, 18:60–67, July 1915.

1180 Medford disaster of 1850. Medford Historical Society. Register, 42:59–64, 1939.
Destruction by fire of twenty-five buildings, 1850.

1181 WILD, HELEN TILDEN (comp.). The building of the Town House. Medford Historical Society. Register, 9:40–43, Jan. 1906.
Compiled from the town records.

1182 ———. The old Royall house. Salem, Mass., Salem Press Co., 1908. 8p. illus.
Reprinted from *Massachusetts Magazine*, v. 1, no. 3.

Middlesex County

1183 DRAKE, SAMUEL ADAMS. Historical fields and mansions of Middlesex. Boston, James R. Osgood and Co., 1874. 442p. illus.

1184 FORBES, HARRIETTE M. Some seventeenth century houses of Middlesex County, Massachusetts. Old-Time New England, 29:90–105, Jan. 1939. illus.
At Sherborn, Wayland, Lincoln, Stow.

Milton

1185 HAMILTON, EDWARD PIERCE. A history of Milton. Milton, Mass., Milton Historical Society, 1957. 275p. illus.

Nantucket

1186 CHAMBERLAIN, SAMUEL. Nantucket. N. Y., Hastings House, 1939. 73p. illus.

1187 CROSBY, EVERETT U. 95% perfect, the older residences of Nantucket. Nantucket, Mass., Inquirer and Mirror Press, 1937.

1188 DOUGLAS-LITHGOW, R. A. Jethro Coffin's home, "the oldest house" in Nantucket, 1686–1910. Massachusetts Magazine, 4:23–28, Jan. 1911.

1189 DUPREY, KENNETH. Old houses on Nantucket. N. Y., Architectural Book Publishing Co., 1959. 242p. illus.

1190 ELDRIDGE, GERALD E. Nantucket lighthouses. Historic Nantucket, 4:25–29, July 1956.
1746–1955.

1191 FOWLKES, GEORGE ALLEN. A mirror of Nantucket; an architectural history of the island, 1686–1850. Plainfield, N. J., 1959. 136p. illus.

1192 GARDNER, ARTHUR H. The Big Shop. Nantucket Historical Association. Proceedings, 22:35–43, 1916.
Ca. 1800.

1193 HAMLIN, TALBOT F. Nantucket. Architectural Review, 102:53–57, July 1947. illus.

1194 HINCHMAN, LYDIA S. Maria Mitchell house and memorial. Nantucket, Mass. Old-Time New England, 16:105–17, Jan. 1926. illus.
(1818).

1195 HUSBAND, J. Notable restoration; residence of F. H. B. Byrne, Nantucket. House Beautiful, 63:421–24, Apr. 1928. illus.

1196 ———. 1724: house of E. Tuttle, Nantucket. House Beautiful, 61:637–39, May 1927. illus.

1197 LEACH, ROBERT J. The first two Quaker meetinghouses on Nantucket. Nantucket Historical Association. Proceedings, 1950, pp. 24–33. illus.
1710–62.

1198 LINTON, MARY J. More of Nantucket; an early Quaker house. House Beautiful, 54:360, 404, 405, Oct. 1923. illus.
Ca. 1700.

1199 MACKAY, HELEN G. Houses of Nantucket, and a bit of its history. House Beautiful, 52:220–21, 250–51, Sept. 1922. illus.
Covers 1686 — ca. 1820.

1200 MACY, WILLIAM F. Nantucket's oldest house (1686) the Jethro Coffin house, the Horseshoe house. Nantucket, Mass., Inquirer and Mirror Press, 1929. 35p. illus.

1201 Nantucket renaissance: the Jared Coffin house; E. E. Coffin, arch.; interiors by J. Hendrix. Interior Design, 35:100–105, Jan. 1964. illus.
1845. Restored 1942.

1202 PAGE, FRANCES. The great hall. Historic Nantucket, 4:13–20, Apr. 1957. illus.
Athenaeum, rebuilt in 1847, condemned for public use in 1917, recently restored.

1203 PAGE, MARIAN. Historic restorations: the Jared Coffin house. Interiors, 123:58–63ff., Jan. 1964. illus.
1845.

1204 RIPLEY, HUBERT G. The Jethro Coffin house at Sunset Hill, sometimes called the Horseshoe house. American Institute of Architects. Journal, 16:218–23, June 1928. illus.

1205 SCHWEINFURTH, J. A. Early dwellings of Nantucket. White Pine Series of Architectural Monographs, v. 3, no. 6, Dec. 1917. 14p. illus.

1206 ———. Nantucket revisited. American Architect, 110:301–8, 311–13, Nov. 15, 1916. illus.

1207 STEVENS, WILLIAM OLIVER. Nantucket, the far-away island. N. Y., Dodd, Mead and Co., 1936. 313p. illus.

New Bedford

1208 CRAPO, HENRY HOWLAND. Old buildings in New Bedford. Old Dartmouth Historical Sketches, 23:17–29, 1909.

1209 DOW, JOY WHEELER. A house of the transitional style. Architectural Review, n.s. 2:75–77, June 1901. illus.
Bennett house, ca. 1840.

1210 Rosé, Grace Norton. Past century charm of New Bedford. Architectural Record, 33:424–33, May 1913. illus.

1211 Worth, Henry B. The homesteads at Apponagansett before 1710. Old Dartmouth Historical Sketches, 25:6–9, 1909.
Near New Bedford.

Newbury

1212 Brown, Frank Chouteau. Dwellings of Newbury Old Town. Pencil Points, 14:169–84, Apr. 1933. Monograph Series, 19:17–32. illus.
Covers 1645–97.

1213 Huse, Mabel Hale. The old home. Boston, Meador Publishing Co., [1957]. 69p. illus.
Caleb Moody house.

1214 Ilsley house, Newbury, Mass. Old-Time New England, 2:10–13, Aug. 1911. illus.
Ca. 1670.

1215 Kingsbury, Felicia Doughty. A roof-tree that grew — the Tristam Coffin house, Newbury. Old-Time New England, 40:180–86, Jan. 1950. illus.
Ca. 1653.

1216 One of the oldest houses in New England, the Spences house, 1651, Newbury, Mass. Country Life in America, 30:38–39, June 1916. illus.

1217 Spring, James W. The Coffin house in Newbury, Massachusetts. Old-Time New England, 20:3–29, July 1929. illus.

Newburyport

1218 Barriskill, James M. Newburyport theatre in the early nineteenth century. Essex Institute. Historical Collections, 93:279–314, Oct. 1957.
1811–25.

1219 ———. Newburyport theatre in the Federal period. Essex Institute. Historical Collections, 93:1–35, Jan. 1957.
1799–1811.

1220 Brigham, Clarence Saunders. Timothy Dexter mansion prints. Essex Institute. Historical Collections, 91:193–94, July 1955. illus.
Engravings. 1810?–1859?

1221 Driver, J. P. Newburyport and its business district. Old-Time New England, 54:87–95, Apr. 1964. illus.

1222 Fisher, Richard Arnold. Old houses in and around Newburyport, Massachusetts. White Pine Series of Architectural Monographs, v. 3, no. 3, June 1917. 15p. illus.
Covers 1646–1810.

1223 Hale, Albert. Old Newburyport houses. Boston, W. B. Clarke and Co., 1912. 68p. illus.

1224 Huse, Caleb. The Coffin house, Newburyport, Massachusetts. Old-Time New England, 27:69–72, Oct. 1936.
Nineteenth-century description.

1225 MEAD, EDWIN DOAK. The Old South pilgrimage to Newburyport. Boston, 1900. 14p.

Reprinted from *New England Magazine*, July 1900.

1226 SWAN, MABEL M. Ship carvers of Newburyport. Antiques, 48:78–81, Aug. 1945. illus.

Architectural details by ship carvers, 1746–1858.

Norton

1227 COPELAND, JENNIE FREEMAN. The Rev. Pitt Clarke house. Old-Time New England, 41:7–10, July 1950. illus.

1796.

Peabody

1228 UNDERWOOD, MRS. GEORGE L. The Derby-Osborn farm, Peabody, with its McIntire summer house and barn. Old-Time New England, 16:55–64, Oct. 1925. illus.

1793–94. Now at Glen Magna Farms, Danvers.

Pelham

1229 SEE, ANNA PHILLIPS. Ancient Pelham and the oldest town hall in New England. D. A. R. Magazine, 56:286–92, May 1922.

Town hall, 1743.

Petersham

1230 COOLIDGE, MABEL COOK. The history of Petersham, Massachusetts. Petersham Historical Society, 1948. 408p. illus.

1730———.

Pigeon Cove

1231 WILLIAMS, THOMAS. Some old houses of Pigeon Cove, Massachusetts. Pencil Points, 14:349–64, July 1933. Monograph Series, 19:49–64. illus.

Covers 1676–1778.

Plymouth

1232 [Allyn house. Contemporary description.]American Magazine of Useful and Entertaining Knowledge, 3:37, Oct. 1836.

1233 BAUM, DWIGHT JAMES. Pilgrimage to Plymouth. Architecture, 44:265–88, 328–33, Sept.–Nov. 1921. illus.

1234 PRATT, WALTER MERRIAM. The Mayflower Society house: being the story of the Edward Winslow house, the Mayflower Society, and the Pilgrims. Cambridge, Mass., Private Printing, University Press, 1950. 32p. illus.

1754. Now headquarters of the Society of Mayflower descendants. Massachusetts.

1235 Restoring Colonial houses, Plymouth, Massachusetts. Architectural Record, 75:530–32, June 1934. illus.

1236 STODDARD, FRANCIS R., JR. The old Thomas house at Plymouth. Massachusetts Magazine, 3:269–71, Oct. 1910.

1237 ———. The old Warren house at Plymouth. Massachusetts Magazine, 4:105–9, Apr. 1911.

1238 ———. The Winslow house. Massachusetts Magazine, 5:102–4, Apr. 1912.

1239 STRICKLAND, CHARLES R. Architecture of Plimoth plantation. American Institute of Architects. Journal, 31:13–18, Jan. 1959. illus.

1240 ———. First permanent dwellings at Plimoth plantation. Old-Time New England, 40:162–69, Jan. 1950. illus.
   Ca. 1620.

1241 WOOD, JOHN SUMNER. Cupid's path in ancient Plymouth: the last Pilgrim houses. [Germantown? Md., 1957.] 112p. illus.
   1620———.

Quincy

1242 ADAMS, HENRY, II. The Adams mansion. Old-Time New England, 19:3–17, July 1928. illus.
   1731.

1243 ———. The birthplace of Presidents John and John Quincy Adams, Quincy, Massachusetts. Old-Time New England, 26:78–99, Jan. 1936. illus.

1244 ANNABLE, I. K. Historical notes of the Crombie Street Congregational Church. Essex Institute. Historical Collections, 77:204–17, July 1941.

1245 COYLE, EDITH WOODBURY. The Quincy homestead. Old-Time New England, 19:147–58, Apr. 1929. illus.
   1706 and earlier.

1246 CUSHING, ARTHUR BOARDMAN. The Dorothy Quincy homestead, Quincy, Mass. Massachusetts Magazine, 4:96–98, Apr. 1911.

1247 EDWARDS, WILLIAM CHURCHILL. Historic Quincy, Massachusetts. City of Quincy, 1957. 415p. illus.
   First edition, 1945.

1248 NORTHEND, MARY HARROD. Dorothy Quincy house. House and Garden, 25:97–101, Feb. 1914. illus.
   1623.

1249 WHITNEY, FREDERICK AUGUSTUS. Historical sketch of the Old Church, Quincy, Massachusetts. Albany, N. Y., J. Munsell Co., 1864. 17p.

Reading

1250 HOWARD, LOEA PARKER. The Parker tavern; being an account of a most interesting house built by Abraham Bryant in 1694, together with some facts about early owners. Reading, Mass., Reading Antiquarian Society, 1930. 31p. illus.

Roxbury

1251 CORDINGLEY, W. W. Shirley Place, Roxbury, Massachusetts. Old-Time New England, 12:51–63, Oct. 1921. illus.
   1748.

1252 LANG, WILLIAM BAILEY. Views, with ground plans of the Highland cottages at Roxbury, designed and erected by W. B. Lang. Boston, The Author, 1845. 2p. illus.

1253 RUSSELL, FRANCIS. Lost elegance. American Heritage, 8:36–39, 107, June 1957. illus.

Shirley Place, sometime between 1731–56.

Salem

1254 BELKNAP, HENRY WYKOFF. The 17th century house. Salem, Mass., Newcomb and Gauss Co., 1930. 8p. illus.

John Ward house, 1684.

1255 BRAGDON, CLAUDE FAYETTE. Six houses in Salem. American Architect and Building News, 39:41–43, Jan. 21, 1893. illus.

1256 BRAY, OSCAR S. Restoring historic wharf at Salem, Mass. Civil Engineering, 10:105–7, 1940.

1257 BROWN, FRANK CHOUTEAU. Gardner-White-Pingree house, built in Salem, Massachusetts, in 1804 by Samuel McIntire, architect. Pencil Points, 21:515–30, Aug. 1940. Monograph Series, 26:145–60. illus.

1258 ———. Salem, Massachusetts. Pencil Points, 18:305–20, May 1937. Monograph Series, 23:17–32. illus.

Covers 1668–1810. Includes a location map of old buildings.

1259 [cancelled]

1260 CARRICK, ALICE VAN LEER. House of seven gables. Country Life in America, 39:45–47, Apr. 1921. illus.

Ca. 1668.

1261 CHAMBERLAIN, SAMUEL. Historic Salem in four seasons. N. Y., Hastings House, 1938. 73p. illus.

1262 ———. Salem interiors; two centuries of New England taste and decoration. N. Y., Hastings House, 1950. 176p. illus.

1263 Contract for building the prison in Salem for the County of Essex, 1764. Essex Institute. Historical Collections, 68:299–302, 1932.

1264 CORNING, C. H. Chestnut Street associates, Salem, Mass. Old-Time New England, 42:102–5, Apr. 1952. illus.

1265 COUSINS, FRANK. Colonial architecture, series 1. Fifty Salem doorways. N. Y., Doubleday, Page and Co., 1912. 50p. illus.

1266 COUSINS, FRANK, AND RILEY, PHILIP M. The Colonial architecture of Salem. Boston, Little, Brown and Co., 1919. 282p. illus.

1267 ———. Six old Salem doorways. Architectural Record, 42:393–99, Oct. 1917. illus.

1268 ———. The wood-carver of Salem; Samuel McIntyre, his life and work. Boston, Little, Brown and Co., 1916. 168p. illus.

1269 CUMMINGS, ABBOTT LOWELL. Samuel McIntire and his sources. Essex Institute. Historical Collections, 93:149–66, Apr. 1957.

His relation to builders and carvers.

1270 DOW, GEORGE FRANCIS. The Colonial village built at Salem, Massachusetts, in the spring of 1930. Old-Time New England, 22:3–14, July 1931. illus.

1271 Dow, Joy Wheeler. Salem enchantment. House Beautiful, 12:334–44, Nov. 1922. illus.

1272 Downs, J. Derby and McIntire. Metropolitan Museum. Bulletin, n.s. 6:73–81, Oct. 1947. illus.

1273 Emmerton, Caroline O. Chronicles of three old houses. Boston, Thomas Todd Co., 1935. 57p. illus.
House of Seven Gables (*ca.* 1688), Hathaway house (1682), and Retire Beckett house (1655).

1274 Essex Institute. Visitor's guide to Salem. Salem, Mass., Essex Institute, 1927. 249p. illus.

1275 Four doors by Samuel McIntire. House Beautiful, 39:75, Feb. 1916. illus.

1276 Franklin, M. S. Public buildings — part 2. Recording the architecture of late Colonial times in Salem, Massachusetts. Pencil Points, 13:408–22, June 1932. Monograph Series, 18:198–212. illus.
Covers 1782–1828.

1277 Hayden, Barbara E. Central Street, Salem, and the Ingalls house. Essex Institute. Historical Collections, 85:58–91, Jan. 1949.
1630–1910.

1278 Hunt, W. H. Old Salem houses. American Architect, 119:507–13, 522, Apr. 1921. illus.

1279 ———. Samuel McIntyre housewright-architect, Salem, Mass. American Architect, 119:415–22, 428, Apr. 1921. illus.

1280 Kimball, Sidney Fiske. The Derby room and its furnishings. Pennsylvania Museum. Bulletin, 25:11–17, Apr. 1930. illus.
A room from the Elias Hasket Derby house.

1281 ———. Elias Hasket Derby mansion in Salem. Essex Institute. Historical Collections, 60:273–92, Oct. 1924.

1282 ———. Mr. Samuel McIntire, carver, the architect of Salem. Portland, Me., Southworth-Anthoensen Press, 1940. 157p. illus.

1283 ———. Samuel McIntire. Essex Institute. Historical Collections, 93:122–48, Apr. 1957. illus.
His life in Salem as a designer.

1284 Larkin, Oliver W. Samuel McIntire and the arts of post-Colonial America. Essex Institute. Historical Collections, 93:211–21, Apr. 1957.

1285 List of houses built in Salem from 1750–1773. Essex Institute. Historical Collections, 58:292–96, Oct. 1922.

1286 MacDonald, Albert J. Selected interiors of old houses in Salem and vicinity. . . . Boston, Rogers and Manson Co., 1916. 55p. illus.

1287 McDonald, Edith W. The woodcarver of Salem. Stone and Webster. Journal, 46:53–63, 1930.
Samuel McIntire.

1288 MacSwiggan, Amelia E. Samuel McIntire — Salem's illustrious carver. Antiques Journal, 9:13–17, 23, Jan. 1954. illus.

1289 Merrill, Walter McIntosh. New evidence that Samuel McIntire designed Hamilton Hall. Essex Institute. Historical Collections, 91:79, Jan. 1955. illus.
Unsigned architect's drawing, *ca.* 1806.

1290 Messer, Nellie Stearns. The Ropes Memorial at Salem, Massachusetts. Old-Time New England, 14:146–63, Apr. 1924. illus.
1719.

1291 Northend, Mary Harrod. Historic doorways of old Salem. Boston, Houghton Mifflin Co., 1926. 96p. illus.

1292 ———. Memories of old Salem. N. Y., Moffat, Yard and Co., 1917. 341p. illus.

1293 ———. The old Cook-Oliver house in Salem. American Homes and Gardens, 11:308–11, Sept. 1914. illus.
1804. Samuel McIntire, architect.

1294 ———. Old fences in Salem and Newburyport. American Homes and Gardens, 11:48–52, Feb. 1914. illus.

1295 ———. Pierce-Nichols house at Salem. American Homes and Gardens, 12:183–87, June 1915. illus.
1782. Samuel McIntire, architect.

1296 Notes on the Derby houses from the Derby ledgers. Essex Institute. Historical Collections, 69:90–95, 1933.
Eighteenth-century building costs.

1297 Old John Ward house, built 1684, now at Essex Institute Museum Yard, Salem, Mass. American Architect, 134:10, July 1928. illus.

1298 Perley, Sidney. The court houses in Salem. Essex Institute. Historical Collections, 47:101–23, Apr. 1911.

1299 Phillips, James Duncan. Salem in the eighteenth century. Boston, Houghton Mifflin Co., 1937. 533p. illus.

1300 ———. Salem in the seventeenth century. Boston, Houghton Mifflin Co., 1933. 426p. illus.

1301 Porter, Frederick Hutchinson. The Pineapple house, Salem, Mass. Architectural Review, n.s. 6:70, April 1918. illus.
In Brown Street Court. *Ca.* 1740.

1302 Riley, Philip M. Inside a McIntire house. Country Life in America, 24:52–54, Oct. 1913. illus.

1303 ———. In the spirit of old Salem. House Beautiful, 39:72–74, Feb. 1916. illus.
Covers 1690–1800.

1304 Riley, Philip M., and Cousins, Frank. Windows of old Salem. Country Life in America, 28:48–49, Oct. 1915. illus.

1305 Robb, Gordon. Gate and posts, Baldwin-Lyman house, Salem, Mass., built in 1808. Brickbuilder, 24:265–66, Nov. 1915. illus.

1306 ROBOTTI, FRANCES DIANA. Chronicles of old Salem: a history in miniature . . . illustrated from the collections of the Essex Institute. Salem, Mass., 1948. 129p. illus.

1626–1933.

1307 RYAN, MARGARET. The Assembly house at Salem; built in 1782 and now restored to its former glory. House Beautiful, 50:89–92, Aug. 1921. illus.

1308 SALEM, MASS., BOARD OF PARK COMMISSIONERS. Colonial village built at Salem, Mass., to commemorate the three hundredth anniversary of the arrival of the Winthrop fleet, June 12, 1630. Salem, 1930. 8p.

1309 ———. Guide to Salem, 1630. Salem, 1930. 32p. illus.

Manual for participants and spectators at the pageant of the arrival of Governor Winthrop in the ship Arabella, June 1930.

1310 Selected interiors of old houses in Salem and vincinity. Boston, Rogers and Manson Co., 1919. 55p. illus.

1311 SMALL, EDWIN W. Derby house, part of Salem maritime national historic site. Old-Time New England, 47:100–107, Apr. 1957. illus.

1761. For Elias H. Derby on Derby Street.

1312 STOW, CHARLES MESSER. Samuel McIntire of Salem. Antiquarian, 12:36–38, 66, 68, Feb. 1929. illus.

1313 SWAN, MABEL MUNSON. A factual estimate of Samuel McIntire. Essex Institute. Historical Collections, 93:200–210, Apr. 1957. illus.

1314 WATERMAN, THOMAS TILESTON. Staircase, Witch house, Salem, Mass. Architecture, 50:pl. 155, Oct. 1924. illus. only.

1315 WHIPPLE, SHERMAN L., AND WATERS, THOMAS FRANKLIN. Puritan homes. Ipswich Historical Society. Publications, no. 27, 1929. 99p. illus.

1316 WINCHESTER, ALICE. The Pingree house in Salem. Antiques, 49:174–77, Mar. 1946. illus.

1804–5.

1317 WISWALL, RICHARD HALL. Notes on the building of Chestnut Street. Essex Institute. Historical Collections, 75:203–33, 1939.

Saugus

1318 CUMMINGS, ABBOTT LOWELL. The "Scotch"-Boardman house, a fresh appraisal. Old-Time New England, 43:56–73, 91–102, Jan.–June 1963. illus.

Ca. 1651.

1319 FIRST IRON WORKS ASSOCIATION. First Iron Works Gazette, 1951–53. 3v., 12 8p. issues. illus.

Restoration of the Hammersmith Iron Works.

Shelburne

1320 BARDWELL, LEILA STONE. Vanished homes of rural Shelburne, Mass. D. A. R. Magazine, 91:117–24, Feb. 1957.

Settled in 1759.

Shrewsbury

1321 General Artemas Ward homestead, Shrewsbury, Mass. Old-Time New England, 17:147–55, Apr. 1927. illus.

1730.

Somerville

1322 BROWN, FRANK CHOUTEAU. Joseph Barrell estate, Somerville, Mass.: Charles Bulfinch's first country house. Old-Time New England, 38:53–62, Jan. 1948. illus.

1792, enlarged in 1816, demolished about 1896.

South Walpole

1323 SHUMWAY, HARRY IRVING. Tavern as it used to be. American Cookery, 38:139–46, 1933.

Fuller's tavern, 1807.

1324 SHURROCKS, ALFRED F. Fuller's tavern, South Walpole, Mass. Old-Time New England, 18:146–57, Apr. 1928. illus.

1325 WHITING, HARRY A. Old Fuller's tavern reopens. Old-Time New England, 18:158–59, Apr. 1929.

Southwick

1326 MERRILL, D. Isaac Damon and the Southwick Column Papers. Old-Time New England, 54:48–58, Oct. 1963. illus.

Documents associated with the construction of the Congregational Church, Southwick, Mass., 1824, and discussion of his architecture.

Springfield (see also *West Springfield*)

1327 Alexander house — Linden Hall, State Street, Springfield, Mass. Old-Time New England, 30:35–40, Oct. 1939. illus.

Designed by Asher Benjamin in 1811.

1328 PHILLIPS, JULIA BOWLES. Romance of Linden Hall. Old-Time New England, 40:227–38, Apr. 1950. illus.

The Alexander house, description from 1886.

1329 TOBEY, FRANK G. Old State Street, its residences and the people who lived in them. Connecticut Valley Historical Society. Papers, 4:184–202, 1912.

1330 TOMLINSON, JULIETTE. The Alexander house. William's Scrapbook, [pp. 3–7], Mar. 1952. illus.

1811–12. Designed by Asher Benjamin.

1331 ———. The John Mills house on Crescent Hill — Henry A. Sykes, architect. William's Scrapbook, [pp. 1–4], Jan. 1952. illus.

1849.

1332 ———. Reuben Bliss house of Springfield. Antiques, 61:346–47, Apr. 1952. illus.

Built *ca.* 1753–60; demolished 1926–27, rooms preserved in the Smithsonian Institution and the Brooklyn Museum.

1333 ———. Ten famous houses of Springfield. Springfield, Mass., Connecticut Valley Historical Museum, 1952. 32p. illus.

1752———.

Stockbridge

1334 Colonial restoration; so-called Mission House, Stockbridge, Mass. Antiques, 18:216–19, Sept. 1930. illus.

1739.

1335 STEELE, F. Mission House; oldest house in Stockbridge. House Beautiful, 68:26–33, 54–57, July 1930. illus.

Stotham

1336 RIPLEY, HUBERT G. New England village. White Pine Series of Architectural Monographs, v. 6, no. 2, Apr. 1920. illus.

Covers Cadwallader Simpkins house, Jenks-Greenleaf house, Salmon-White house, Podbury-Ives house, and Obadiah Witherspoon house.

Sturbridge

1337 ANTIQUES. Old Sturbridge Village. Antiques, 68:222–67, Sept. 1955. illus.

Reproduction of an eighteenth-century town, near Springfield.

1338 CHAMBERLAIN, SAMUEL. Old Sturbridge Village, a photographic impression. N. Y., Hastings House, 1951. 68p. illus.

1339 ———. A tour of Old Sturbridge Village. N. Y., Hastings House, 1955. 72p. illus.

1340 COMSTOCK, HELEN. Old Sturbridge Village. Connoisseur, 125:41–42, Mar. 1950. illus.

1341 CUMMINGS, ABBOTT LOWELL. Architecture in early New England. Sturbridge, Mass., Old Sturbridge Village, 1958. Unpaged. illus.

Old Sturbridge Village Booklet Series, 7.

1342 CURTIS, JOHN OBED. Early well house, Sturbridge, Massachusetts. Old-Time New England, 53:79–82, Jan. 1963. illus.

Late eighteenth century.

1343 ———. Moving historic buildings. American Institute of Architects. Journal, 43:41–46, Mar. 1965. illus.

Buildings moved to Old Sturbridge Village.

1344 FENNELLY, CATHERINE MARY. The New England village scene: 1800. Sturbridge, Mass., Old Sturbridge Village, [1955]. 15p. illus.

Old Sturbridge Village Booklet Series, 1.

1345 WATKINS, M. Old Sturbridge Village. American Collector, 16:6–7ff., Mar.; 8–9ff., Apr. 1947. illus.

1346 WELLS, R. D. History lives and is taught anew at Old Sturbridge Village. Old-Time New England, 40:101–7, July 1949. illus.

Sudbury

1347 CARRICK, ALICE VAN LEER. Wayside Inn. House Beautiful, 65:536–42, Apr. 1929. illus.

1348 CHAMBERLAIN, SAMUEL. Longfellow's Wayside Inn; a camera impression. N. Y., Hastings House, 1938. 72p. illus.

1686 and later.

1349 EATON, FLORENCE TAFT. Longfellow's Wayside Inn. Landmark, 10:301–4, May 1928.

1350 Inn where the tales were told. Mentor, 4:33, Aug. 1926. illus.

1351 LAWRENCE, C. A. Longfellow's Wayside Inn. Arts and Decoration, 6:548–51, Oct. 1916. illus.

1352 LORING, CHARLES G. Red Horse tavern. Garden and Home Builder, 43:435–43, July 1926. illus.

1353 MEAD, LUCIA AMES. How the old Wayside Inn came back. Old-Time New England, 22:41–45, July 1931. illus.

1354 POWELL, SUMNER C. Seventeenth-century Sudbury. Society of Architectural Historians. Journal, 11:3–15, Mar. 1952. illus.

1638–86.

1355 SEABURY, JOSEPH S. The Wayside Inn. House Beautiful, 36:32–39, July 1914. illus.

1356 WINCHESTER, ALICE. Longfellow's Wayside Inn at South Sudbury, Massachusetts. Antiques, 74:138–39, Aug. 1958.

Taunton

1357 APPLETON, WILLIAM SUMNER. East Taunton: Deane-Barstow house, built in 1807. Old-Time New England, 35:55–56, Jan. 1945. illus.

Topsfield

1358 BESTON, HENRY B. An Old World house on a new world lane. House Beautiful, 46:80–81, Aug. 1919. illus.

Capen house, 1683.

1359 The building of the Congregational meeting house in 1842. Topsfield Historical Society. Collections, 20:86–88, 1915.

1360 MILLAR, DONALD. Seventeenth century New England house. Architectural Record, 38:348–61, Sept. 1915. illus.

Capen house.

1361 ———. Seventeenth century New England house. Old-Time New England, 11:3–8, July 1920. illus.

Capen house.

1362 PEABODY, CHARLES JOEL. The story of a Peabody house and its neighborhood. Topsfield Historical Society. Collections, 26:113–20, 1921.

1782.

1363 PERLEY, SIDNEY. Topsfield houses and lands. Topsfield Historical Society. Collections, 29:49–98, 1928.

Uxbridge

1364 Well-preserved Colonial home of Revolutionary times. House Beautiful, 52:560–61, Dec. 1922. illus.

Waltham

1365 ALLEN, GORDON. The Vale. Old-Time New England, 42:81–87, Apr. 1952. illus.

Lyman house, 1793. Samuel McIntire, architect.

1366 LITTLE, BERTRAM K. A McIntire country house. . . . The Vale in Waltham, Massachusetts. Antiques, 63:506–8, June 1953. illus.

1793——.

1367 MAILLOUX, KENNETH FRANK. The Boston Manufacturing Company of Waltham, Massachusetts, 1813–1848: the first modern factory in America. Doctoral Dissertation, Boston University, 1957. 239p.

1368 MAYALL, ROBERT NEWTON. Country seat of a gentleman: "The Vale." Old-Time New England, 43:36–41, Oct.–Dec. 1952. illus.

Lyman house, 1793——.

1369 ORCUTT, P. D. Gore Place, Waltham, Massachusetts, the beginnings of a restoration. American Architect, 150:67–74, June 1937.

Rebuilt between 1799 and 1804. Sometimes credited to Bulfinch.

Watertown

1370 BROWN, FRANK CHOUTEAU. Watertown, Massachusetts. Pencil Points, 18:323–38, May 1937. Monograph Series, 23:33–48. illus.

Covers 1663–1806.

Wayland

1371 First Parish Church, 1814, Wayland, Massachusetts. Architectural Forum, n.s. 6:95, May 1918. illus.

Wenham

1372 APPLETON, WILLIAM SUMNER. Description of Robert McClaflin's house. Old-Time New England, 16:157–67, Apr. 1926. illus.

Seventeenth century.

Westborough

1373 WESTBOROUGH, MASSACHUSETTS, HISTORICAL SOCIETY. More old houses in Westborough. n.p., 1908. illus.

1374 ——. Other old houses in Westborough. n.p., 1911. illus.

1375 ——. Some old houses in Westborough, Mass., and their occupants. n.p., 1906. 70p. illus.

Some tipped-in photographs.

Westfield

1376 ISHAM, NORMAN MORRISON. Colonial doorway from the Connecticut Valley. Metropolitan Museum of Art. Bulletin, 12:32–34, Feb. 1917. illus.

West Springfield

1377 [STORROW, HELEN O.?] Storrowton, a New England village. Boston, Mass., Thomas Todd Co., 1930. 25p. illus.

Storrowton comprises a group of houses, 1767–1834, moved to the grounds of the Eastern States Exposition.

1378 [cancelled].

Williamstown

1379 ADRIANCE, VANDERPOEL. New foundations. Williamstown, Mass., 1940. 24p. Mimeographed.

Describes buildings in Williamstown which have been moved to new sites.

1380 GRANT, CHARLES C. Rebuilding of the First Congregational Church of Williamstown, Massachusetts. Architectural Record, 32:249–57, Oct. 1915. illus.

1381 MILHAM, WILLIS I. Early American observatories. Which was the first astronomical observatory in America? Williamstown, Mass., Williams College, 1938. 58p. illus.

Describes eleven observatories erected and equipped before 1840.

1382 PERRY, ARTHUR LATHAM. Williamstown and Williams College. Williamstown, Mass., 1899. 847p. illus.

1383 WATERMAN, THOMAS TILESTON. The President's house, Williams College, Mass. American Architect, 130:269–80, Oct. 1926. illus.

Wollaston

1384 Colonial Josiah Quincy homestead, Wollaston. Old-Time New England, 28:85–89, Jan. 1938.

Worcester

1385 Contracts to build the Stephen Salisbury mansion in Worcester, Massachusetts in 1772, and a store house in 1790. Old-Time New England, 20:178–85, Apr. 1930.

1386 [Court house and prison, 1732. Description.] Worcester Magazine and Historical Journal, 2:204, July 1826.

1387 CRANE, ELLERY BICKNELL (ed.). Historic homes and institutions and genealogical and personal memoirs of Worcester County, Massachusetts, with a history of the Worcester Society of Antiquity. N. Y., Lewis Publishing Co., 1907. 4v. illus.

1388 CUTLER, W. WALDO. Isaiah Thomas house, Worcester, Massachusetts. Old-Time New England, 18:133–40, Jan. 1928. illus.

1782.

1389 FORBES, MRS. HARRIETTE M. Elias Carter, architect, of Worcester, Massachusetts. Old-Time New England, 11:58–71, Oct. 1920. illus.

1390 ———. The Salisbury mansion, Worcester, Massachusetts. Old-Time New England, 20:99–111, Jan. 1930. illus.

1772.

1391 ISHAM, NORMAN MORRISON. The Stephen Salisbury house in Worcester and its restoration. Old-Time New England, 20:111–20, Jan. 1930. illus.

1392 The passing of the Baldwin house. Worcester Magazine, 6:80–86, Sept. 1903.

1393 SAWYER, C. H., AND DRESSER, L. Salisbury houses. Worcester Museum. Annual, 5:64–92, 1946. illus.

Three buildings in Worcester, 1772———.

1394 TYMESON, MILDRED McCLARY. Worcester centennial, 1848–1949. . . . Worcester, Mass., 1948. 83p. illus.

1395 WAITE, EMMA F. Old-time taverns of Worcester. Worcester Society of Antiquities. Proceedings, 19:70–82, 1903.

1396 WHEELER, HENRY M. A New England house one hundred years ago. Worcester Society of Antiquities. Proceedings, 19:358–94, 1903.

1397 WORCESTER BANK AND TRUST COMPANY. Some historic houses of Worcester; a brief account of the houses and taverns that fill a prominent part in the history of Worcester. . . . Worcester, Mass., 1919. 71p. illus.

Yarmouth

1398 HOWES, THOMAS PRINCE. Ancient houses. Yarmouthport, Mass., C. W. Swift, 1911. 6p.
Covers Yarmouth and Dennis.

NEW HAMPSHIRE

GENERAL REFERENCES

1399 BAER, ANNIE WENTWORTH. Ricker Inn. New Hampshire, 61:160–68, Apr. 1929.
Late eighteenth and early nineteenth century.

1400 BLOSSOM, DEBORAH. Home of the month. New Hampshire Profiles, v. 5——, 1956.
Illustrated monthly installments on the architecture and furnishings of New Hampshire houses built between 1737 and 1938.

1401 COLBY, FREDERICK MYRON. Granite state rooftrees. Granite State Magazine, 1:13–17, Jan. 1906.

1402 ——. Old rooftrees of New Hampshire. Magazine of History, 4:160–65, Sept. 1906; 6:276–80, Nov. 1907.

1403 FEDERAL WRITERS' PROJECT. Hands that built New Hampshire. Brattleboro, Vt., Stephen Daye Press, 1940. 288p. illus.
Some material on architects and builders.

1404 ——. New Hampshire: a guide to the Granite State. Boston, Houghton Mifflin Co., 1938. 559p. illus.

1405 FERGUSON, A. E. Early dwellings in New Hampshire. White Pine Series of Architectural Monographs, v. 12, no. 5, 1926. 19p. illus.
Colonial.

1406 FORD, DAN. Our disappearing covered bridges. New Hampshire Profiles, 3:8–13, Nov. 1954. illus.
1790——.

1407 GEORGES, JUSTINE FLYNT. House of the month. New Hampshire Profiles, 2:35–46, Jan.; 29–40, Apr.; 27–36, Nov. 1953. illus.
Boardman-Marvin house, Portsmouth, *ca.* 1800; Sanborn house, Hampton Falls, 1685; farmhouse by David Bennett, Northwood Ridge, 1840.

1408 HENNESSY, WILLIAM G. New Hampshire homes — then and now. New Hampshire Profiles, 3:14–19, Mar. 1954. illus.

Types of houses: saltbox, Pre-Revolutionary, Georgian, and Greek Revival.

1409 KENYON, THEDIA COX. New Hampshire covered bridge sketchbook. Sanbornville, N. H., Wake-Brook House, 1955. 71p. illus.

Includes list of existing covered bridges in New Hampshire.

1410 MEADER, ROBERT F. W. New Hampshire meeting houses. New Hampshire Profiles, 2:17–23, May 1953. illus.

1650——.

1411 SPEARE, EVA A. Colonial meeting-houses of New Hampshire compared with their contemporaries in New England. Littleton, N. H., Courier Printing Co., 1938. 238p. illus.

Published under auspices of Daughters of Colonial Wars, State of New Hampshire.

1412 STANIELS, EVA F. T. Historic inns. Granite Monthly, 44:17–20, Jan. 1912.

1413 WOOD, HELEN M. Historic churches of New Hampshire. American Monthly Magazine, 38:300–301, June 1911.

1414 WOOD, JAMES A. New Hampshire homes. Concord, N. H., The Author, 1895.

LOCATIONS

Allentown

1415 DOWST, JOHN. The old Allentown meeting house. Granite Monthly, 44:5–11, Jan. 1912.

1815.

Amherst

1416 HOWE, LOIS LILLEY. Colonel Robert Means house at Amherst, New Hampshire. White Pine Series of Architectural Monographs, v. 13, no. 5, 1927. 19p. illus.

Ca. 1775.

Boscawen

1417 VAUGHAN, DOROTHY M. Old Bonney Tavern, Boscawen, New Hampshire. Old-Time New England, 31:57–61, Jan. 1941. illus.

1787.

Bradford

1418 MORSON, WILLIAM TAYLOR. Another old New England farmhouse restored. Antiques, 54:32–35, July 1948. illus.

Reply: J. Lipman. 54:275, Oct. 1948. Built by Joshua Eaton, about 1814.

Conway

1419 WALKER, C. ERNEST. Covered bridges of Conway, N. H. Covered Bridge Topics, 12:3, 7, Summer 1954. illus.

1846–1952.

Dover

1420 FLANDERS, LOUIS W. Garrisons of ancient Dover, New Hampshire. Old-Time New England, 17:51–62, Oct. 1926. illus.

1421 STEVENS, LYDIA A. The Varney-Ham house. Granite State Magazine, 3:233–39, June 1907.

On Garrison Hill (1694).

Dublin

1422 Beginnings of a New Hampshire town church as instanced at Dublin; excerpts. Old-Time New England, 37:7–11, July 1946. illus.

Dunbarton

1423 CORSE, MURRAY PINCHOT. Stark mansion, Dunbarton, New Hampshire. Architecture, 47:123, Apr. 1923. illus.

Durham

1424 Bunker Garrison house, Durham, New Hampshire. Old-Time New England, 1:1–7, Feb. 1911. illus.

Ca. 1694.

Exeter

1425 JENKINS, FREDERICK WARREN. The old Garrison house of Exeter. Granite Monthly, 34:386–90, May 1903.

(Between 1650 and 1658.)

1426 NORTHEND, MARY HARROD. Ladd-Gilman house, Exeter, New Hampshire. American Homes and Gardens, 11:409–13, Dec. 1914. illus.

1721.

1427 ROBIE, VIRGINIA. Colonial pilgrimage — part 4. House in governor's land. House Beautiful, 16:13–15, Aug. 1904. illus.

Gilman house, before 1747.

1428 ROGERS, GEORGE B. The Gilman house. Exeter, N. H., News-Letter Press, 1906. 32p. illus.

Fitzwilliam

1429 SHUMWAY, HARRY IRVING. Two taverns and a village green. American Cookery, 40:203–9, 1935.

Gilmanton

1430 WILKENS, LAUROSE. The old Smith shop. New Hampshire Profiles, 2:90–91, June 1953. illus.

Gilmanton Iron Works, 1780, destroyed in 1952.

Hanover

1431 LENNING, HENRY F. A history of Dartmouth Hall. Master's Thesis, Dartmouth College, 1937.

Harrisburg

1432 HUXTABLE, A. L. New England Mill Village, Harrisburg, N. H. Progressive Architecture, 38:139–40, July 1957. illus.

1810——.

Haverhill

1433 GREER, LOIS GOODWIN. General Montgomery house at Haverhill, New Hampshire. House Beautiful, 57:48–49, 74, 76–78, Jan. 1925. illus.

Hopkinton

1434 BRADLEY, DUANE. From dream to reality. New Hampshire Profiles, 3:20–24, Mar. 1954. illus.

Restoration of Cape Cod cottage, *ca.* 1770.

Jaffrey

1435 BRADFORD, L. M. The historic Baker house. Americana, 7:833–34, Sept. 1912. Colonial.

Keene

1436 SHUMWAY, HARRY IRVING. Old tavern of New Hampshire. American Cookery, 37:251–55, 302–4, 1932.

Sawyer Tavern.

Lisbon

1437 LONG, ELLA, AND PICKWICK, HAZEL. Early floor decoration in a New Hampshire farmhouse. Decorator, 3:14–15, Winter 1948–49. illus.

Before 1815.

Manchester

1438 BLOOD, GRACE HOLBROOK. Manchester on the Merrimack: the story of a city. Manchester, N. H., L. A. Cummings Co., 1948. 353p. illus.

1751——.

Middleton

1439 ALLEN, EDWARD B. Frescoed walls of the Meeting House at Middleton, New Hampshire. Old-Time New England, 20:129–33, Jan. 1930. illus.

New Castle

1440 WINGATE, KATHERINE H. G. The historic church of New Castle, New Hampshire. D. A. R. Magazine, 50:309–17, May 1917.

Congregational Church.

New Lisbon

1441 CHANDLER, JOSEPHINE CRAVEN. Cobleigh Tavern, Gunthwaite, now New Lisbon, New Hampshire. Old-Time New England, 24:38–45, Oct. 1933. illus.

Orford

1442 HODGSON, ALICE DOAN. Back to beginnings. New Hampshire Profiles, 3:23–26, Jan. 1954. illus.

Restoration of Samuel Morey house, 1792.

Peterboro

1443 NORTHEND, MARY HARROD. Remodeling of an old tavern in Peterboro, New Hampshire. House Beautiful, 48:110–13, Aug. 1920. illus.

Wilson Tavern, Colonial.

Plaistow

1444 CARD, MARIAN. A small New England church. Old-Time New England, 43:4–6, July–Sept. 1952. illus.

1837. Includes account of earlier structure, 1728–1837.

Portsmouth

1445 BREWSTER, CHARLES WARREN. Rambles about Portsmouth — first series. 2nd ed. Portsmouth, N. H., L. H. Brewster, 1873. 381p.

Sketches of persons, localities, and incidents of two centuries; principally from tradition and unpublished documents. First edition: Portsmouth, N. H., C. W. Brewster and Son, 1859–69. 2v.

1446 CHAMBERLAIN, SAMUEL. Portsmouth, New Hampshire. N. Y., Hastings House, 1940. 73p. illus.

1447 CORNELIUS, CHARLES OVER. Wentworth-Gardner house. Metropolitan Museum of Art. Bulletin, 14:24–31, Feb. 1919. illus.

1448 DeNORMANDIE, JAMES. Three old churches. Boston, George H. Ellis, 1912. 7p. illus.

Reprinted from *The Portsmouth Book*.

1449 FISHER, ROBERT. Houses in old Portsmouth. International Studio, 80:478–81, Mar. 1925.

1450 GEORGES, JUSTINE FLYNT. The Portsmouth of long ago. New Hampshire Profiles, 2:39–42, July 1953. illus.

Eighteenth-century houses and cemeteries.

1451 The grace of a doorway. New Hampshire Profiles, 3:26–27, Aug. 1954. illus.

Primarily photographs of front entrances of old houses in Portsmouth.

1452 HOWELLS, JOHN MEAD. Architectural heritage of the Piscataqua; houses and gardens of the Portsmouth district of Maine and New Hampshire. N. Y., Architectural Book Publishing Co., 1938. 217p. illus.

Bibliographical note on pp. xvii–xx, books on architecture and the allied crafts used in America prior to 1830.

1453 LITCHFIELD, ELECTUS D. Portsmouth, New Hampshire, an early American metropolis. White Pine Series of Architectural Monographs, v. 7, no. 1, Feb. 1921. 14p. illus.

Covers 1720–89.

1454 MOSES, J. M. John Mason's three great houses. Granite Monthly, 50:116–19.

On the Piscataqua River.

1455 NORTHEND, MARY HARROD. Historic Wentworth house. American Homes and Gardens, 5:106–9, Mar. 1908. illus.

1750.

1456 ———. Jacob Wendell house. American Homes and Gardens, 11:200–203, June 1924.

1789.

1457 ORCUTT, PHILIP DANA. Moffatt-Ladd house, its garden and its period, 1763. Portsmouth, New Hampshire Society of Colonial Dames of America, 1935. 48p. illus.

1458 Portsmouth, Colonial metropolis. House and Garden, 7:33, June 1940. illus.

1459 ROBIE, VIRGINIA. Colonial pilgrimage — part 1. Bit of old Portsmouth. House Beautiful, 15:77–83, Jan. 1904. illus.

Warner house, 1718; Langdon house, 1780.

1460 ———. Colonial pilgrimage — part 2. An old mansion by the sea. House Beautiful, 15:171–75, Feb. 1904. illus.

Benning Wentworth house, 1750.

1461 SHERWIN, HARRY E. Fort Constitution. New Hampshire Profiles, 1:32–34, 63, Dec. 1951. illus.

1623.

1462 STURGIS, RICHARD CLIPSTON. Architecture of Portsmouth. Boston, George H. Ellis, 1912. 20p. illus.

Reprinted from *The Portsmouth Book.*

1463 VAUGHAN, DOROTHY M. Gov. John Langdon Memorial Mansion at Portsmouth, N. H. Old-Time New England, 39:1–6, July 1948. illus.

1783.

1464 ———. Haven and Parry houses, Pleasant Street, Portsmouth, New Hampshire. Old-Time New England, 34:6–9, July 1943. illus.

1752 and post-Revolutionary War.

1465 Wentworth-Gardner house, Mechanic Street, Portsmouth, New Hampshire. Old-Time New England, 30:34, July 1939. illus.

1760.

Salmon Falls

1466 BAER, ANNIE WENTWORTH. Colonel John Wentworth and his Salmon Falls house. Granite Monthly, 59:103–11, Apr. 1927.

1467 BROWN, FRANK CHOUTEAU. Interior details and furnishings of the Colonel Paul Wentworth mansion, built in 1701 at Salmon Falls, New Hampshire, and moved to Dover, Massachusetts, in 1937. Pencil Points, 20:509–24, Aug. 1939. Monograph Series, 25:49–64. illus.

1468 ———. Oldest remaining Wentworth mansion. Old-Time New England, 19:51–66, Oct. 1928. illus.

1701.

1469 CHANDLER, J. C. Paul Wentworth house, the house that made history. Good Housekeeping, 97:76–77, Dec. 1933. illus.

Sandown

1470 HENNESSY, WILLIAM G. The old church at Sandown. New Hampshire Profiles, 3:28–32, Aug. 1954. illus.

1772.

1471 PRESSEY, P. When grandma went to meeting as a little girl; the old meeting-house at Sandown, N. H. Old-Time New England, 35:60–62, Apr. 1945. illus.

1472 WINCHESTER, ALICE. Meeting house at Sandown. Antiques, 48:336–37, Dec. 1945. illus.

1773–74.

Warner

1473 COLBY, FREDERICK MYRON. Granite State rooftrees. Historic houses of Warner. Granite State Magazine, 1:177–81, Apr. 1906; 2:75–80, Aug. 1906.

Weare

1474 TAYLER, WILLIAM WALLACE. Captain Samuel Philbrick house, Weare, New Hampshire. Dearborn, Mich., 1933. 31 numbered leaves.

RHODE ISLAND

GENERAL REFERENCES

1475 DOWNING, ANTOINETTE FORRESTER. Early homes of Rhode Island. Richmond, Va., Garrett and Massie, 1937. 408p. illus.

1476 FEDERAL WRITERS' PROJECT. Rhode Island; a guide to the smallest state. Boston, Houghton Mifflin Co., 1937. 500p. illus.

1477 FOWLER, A. N. Rhode Island mill towns. Pencil Points, 17:271–86, May 1946. Monograph Series, 22:17–32. illus.
Covers 1809–35.

1478 HITCHCOCK, HENRY-RUSSELL, JR. Rhode Island architecture. Providence, Rhode Island Museum Press, 1939. 69p. illus.

1479 ISHAM, NORMAN MORRISON, AND BROWN, ALBERT F. Early Rhode Island houses, an historical and architectural study. Providence, Preston and Rounds, 1895. 100p. illus.
Covers 1701–1830.

1480 JENKS, GROVER L. Dwellings in northeastern Rhode Island and the Smithfields. Pencil Points, 16:317–32, June 1935. Monograph Series, 21:33–48.
Covers 1701–1825.

1481 LASWELL, GEORGE D. Corners and characters of Rhode Island. Providence, The Oxford Press, 1924. illus.

1482 MILLER, WILLIAM D. Early houses of the King's Province in the Narragansett country. Wakefield, R. I., privately printed, 1941. 33p. illus.

1483 NATIONAL SOCIETY OF COLONIAL DAMES. Old houses in the south colony of Rhode Island — part 1. Providence, 1932. 63p. illus.

1484 RHODE ISLAND HISTORICAL SOCIETY. Report of the Committee on Marking Historical Sites in Rhode Island, made to the General Assembly at its January session, 1913. Providence, E. L. Freeman Co., 1914. 183p. illus.
Governor Bull house, Newport; house and home-lot of Roger Williams, Providence; Fort Independence; Reynolds house, Bristol; General Nathanael Greene house, Coventry.

1485 Two centuries of architecture in Rhode Island. Architectural Forum, 71:supp. 16–17, Aug. 1939. illus.

LOCATIONS

Blackstone Valley

1486 BROWN, FRANK CHOUTEAU. Rhode Island houses along the Blackstone River Valley. Pencil Points, 16:197–212, Apr. 1935. Monograph Series, 21:17–32. illus.

Covers 1684–1790.

Bristol

1487 BURLEIGH, WILLIAM J. Houses of Bristol, Rhode Island — part 1. Pencil Points, 17:335–49, June 1936. Monograph Series, 22:33–48. illus.

Covers late seventeenth and early eighteenth centuries.

1488 ———. Houses of Bristol, Rhode Island — part 2. Pencil Points, 17:447–62, Aug. 1936. Monograph Series, 22:49–64. illus.

Covers eighteenth and early nineteenth centuries.

1489 DOW, JOY WHEELER. Bristol renaissance. White Pine Series of Architectural Monographs, v. 3, no. 5, Oct. 1917. 14p. illus.

Classic Revival houses; DeWitt-Colt, DeWolfe-Myddleton, Parker-Borden, and Cabot-Church houses.

1490 ———. Doorways of the Bristol renaissance. Architectural Review, n.s. 3:28–30, Mar. 1901. illus.

1491 MINER, LILIAN BURLEIGH. Old homes of Bristol, Rhode Island. House Beautiful, 46:218–20, Oct. 1919. illus.

1492 ———. Old treasures of Bristol, Rhode Island. House Beautiful, 47:42–44, Jan. 1920. illus.

Centerdale

1493 CADY, JOHN HUTCHINS. The Thomas Clemence house. Rhode Island Historical Society. Collections, 34:65–77, July 1941. illus.

Ca. 1680.

Coventry

1494 GENERAL NATHANAEL GREENE HOMESTEAD ASSOCIATION. Home of General Nathanael Greene at Coventry, Rhode Island. Coventry, R. I., General Nathanael Greene Homestead Association, 1925. 61p. illus.

East Greenwich

1495 PRESTON, HOWARD W. General Varnum house. Rhode Island Historical Society. Collections, 20:115–20, Oct. 1927.

(1773).

Johnston

1496 CADY, JOHN HUTCHINS. The Thomas Clemence house, 38 George Waterman Road, Johnston, R. I. Old-Time New England, 39:17–24, July 1948. illus.

About 1680.

Lincoln

1497 GARDNER, HENRY W. Some early single room houses of Lincoln, Rhode Island. Pencil Points, 16:93–108, Feb. 1935. Monograph Series, v. 21, no. 1. illus.

Covers 1687–1700.

1498 KETTELL, RUSSELL HAWES. Repair and preservation of Eleazer Arnold's splendid mansion. Old-Time New England, 43:28–35, Oct.–Dec. 1952. illus.
1687.

Little Compton

1499 HALDEN, JOHN C. Little Compton and Tiverton Four Corners. Pencil Points, 17:707–22, Dec. 1936. Monograph Series, 22:81–96. illus.
Covers 1684–1745.

Middletown

1500 LATTU, ARLENE MURRAY RINGER. Taylor-Chase-Smythe house: John Taylor, a founder of Middletown, Rhode Island, 1702–1740. [Newport, R. I., Naval Supply Depot, 1954.] 31 leaves. illus.
Ca. 1702–27.

Narragansett

1501 BELCHER, HORACE G. Old Rocky Point. Rhode Island History, 7:33–50, April 1948. illus.
Resort on Narragansett Bay, 1847–1947.

1502 HANSCOM, R. M. Colonial homes nearly two centuries old; Captain Gardiner place, Narragansett, Rhode Island. Arts and Decoration, 34:76, Nov. 1930. illus.

1503 UPDIKE, WILKINS. History of the Episcopal Church in Narragansett, Rhode Island, including a history of other Episcopal churches in the state, by Wilkins Updike. With a transcript of the Narragansett Parish Register, from 1718–1774; an appendix containing a reprint of a work entitled: America Dissected, by Reverend James MacSparran, D.D., and copies of other old papers; (portraits and views of historic places). Boston, D. B. Updike, 1907. 3v. illus.

Newport

1504 ALLEN, F. J. The ruined mill, or Round Church of the Norsemen, at Newport, Rhode Island, U. S. A., compared with the Round Church at Cambridge and others in Europe. Cambridge, England, 1921. 16p. illus.
Reprinted from the Cambridge Antiquarian Society. *Communications*, 22:91–107, 1921.

1505 Ayrault house, Newport, R. I. American Institute of Architects. Journal, 25:162–63, Apr. 1956. illus.
Contains details from the Stuyvesant house, New York City, 1810.

1506 BRIGHAM, HERBERT OLIN. The old stone mill. Newport, R. I., Franklin Printing House, 1948. 32p.
1677——.

1507 CLARK, KENNETH. Newport, an early American seaport. White Pine Series of Architectural Monographs, v. 8, no. 3, June 1922. 16p. illus.
Colonial houses.

1508 CONANT, KENNETH J. Newport tower or mill. Rhode Island History, 7:2–7, Jan. 1948.
Comments on Hjalmar R. Holand's *America, 1355–1364*, N. Y., 1946, and Philip Ainsworth Means, *Newport Tower*, N. Y., 1942.

1509 COVELL, ELIZABETH BENTLEY (GREENE). Historic houses of old Newport. Country Life in America, 43:64–66, Feb. 1923. illus.

1510 ———. Historic types of Newport houses. Newport Historical Society. Bulletin 48, 1924. 13p.

1511 ———. The old Robinson house, one of the landmarks of Newport, Rhode Island. House Beautiful, 58:382, Oct. 1925. illus.

1512 COVELL, WILLIAM KING. Newport, Rhode Island, houses before and after. Old-Time New England, 25:128–35, Apr. 1935; 28:1–3, July 1937. illus.
Photographs of sites after demolition of early houses.

1513 DOWNING, ANTOINETTE FORRESTER, AND SCULLY, VINCENT JOSEPH, JR. The architectural heritage of Newport, Rhode Island, 1640–1915. Cambridge, Mass., Harvard University Press, 1952. 241p. illus.

1514 EDWARD, JAMES GIBSON. The Newport story. [Newport, R. I., 1952.] 71p. illus. 1639——.

1515 GALE, MRS. MARIE J. Some old Newport houses. Newport, R. I., Newport Historical Society. 25p.
Newport Historical Society, Bulletin 36.

1516 GODFREY, WILLIAM S., JR. The archaeology of the old stone mill in Newport, Rhode Island. American Antiquity, 17:120–29, Oct. 1951. illus.
Evidence, 1677–1885, concerning the date of the tower.

1517 ———. Digging a tower and laying a ghost: the archaeology and controversial history of the Newport Tower. Doctoral Dissertation, Harvard University, 1952.

1518 Historic Newport. Interior Design, 32:143–49ff., Nov. 1961. illus.

1519 HOLAND, HJALMAR RUED. The Newport Tower: Norse or English? American Scandinavian Review, 37:230–36, Sept. 1949. illus.

1520 ———. The Newport Tower mystery. Rhode Island History, 12:56–62, 83–89, Apr.–July 1953. illus.

1521 ———. The origin of the Newport Tower. Rhode Island History, 7:65–73, July 1948. illus.
Reply to Kenneth J. Conant's attack on his America, 1355–1364.

1522 ISHAM, NORMAN MORRISON. Colony house at Newport, Rhode Island. Old-Time New England, 8:3–20, Dec. 1917. illus.
1738–39.

1523 ———. The old Brick Market or old City Hall, Newport, Rhode Island. Old-Time New England, 6:2–11, Jan. 1916. illus.
1761. Peter Harrison, architect.

1524 ———. Trinity Church in Newport, Rhode Island, a history of the fabric. Boston, D. B. Updike, 1936. 111p. illus.
1725.

1525 KING, DAVID. Historical sketch of the Redwood Library and Athenaeum in Newport, Rhode Island. Providence, Providence Press Co., 1876. 12p.

(1750). Peter Harrison, architect. Earlier edition?: Boston, John Wilson and Sons, 1860. 53p.

1526 MACDONALD, WILLIAM. The Old State House at Newport. Newport Historical Society. Bulletin 11, 1914. 11p.

Also known as the Old Colony House, 1739.

1527 MASON, GEORGE CHAMPLIN. Annals of the Redwood Library and Athenaeum. Newport, R. I., published by the Redwood Library, 1891. 528p. illus.

1528 ———. Annals of Trinity Church, Newport, Rhode Island. Newport, R. I., George H. Carr, 1890. illus.

1725.

1529 ———. Reminiscences of Newport. Newport, R. I., C. E. Hammett, Jr., 1884. 407p. illus.

1530 Maudsley-Gardner-Watson-Pitman house. Old-Time New England, 28:79–84, Jan. 1938. illus.

Eighteenth century.

1531 MEANS, PHILIP AINSWORTH. Newport Tower. N. Y., Henry Holt and Co., 1942. 365p. illus.

1532 NEWPORT HISTORICAL SOCIETY. The story of the Old City Hall. Newport Chamber of Commerce, n.d. Pamphlet.

1533 O'LOUGHLIN, KATHLEEN MERRICK. Newport Tower. St. Catharines, Ontario, 1948. 20p.

1534 PAGE, MARION. Historic restorations: Hunter house. Interiors, 120:104–11ff., Apr. 1961. illus.

1535 PELL, HERBERT. The old stone mill, Newport. Rhode Island History, 7:105–19, Oct. 1948.

1536 POHL, FREDERICK J. A key to the problem of the Newport Tower. Rhode Island History, 7:75–83, July 1948.

1537 POWEL, MARY EDITH. A few words about some old buildings in Newport. Newport, R. I., Newport Historical Society. 1925. 36p. illus.

Newport Historical Society, Bulletin 55.

1538 SHELTON, F. H. More light on the old mill at Newport. Newport, R. I. Newport Historical Society. 1917. 24p. illus.

Newport Historical Society, Bulletin 21.

1539 STEVENS, MAUD LYMAN. Antiquities of Newport, Rhode Island. Old-Time New England, 21:51–59, Oct. 1931. illus.

Better-known buildings.

1540 ———. A history of the Vernon house in Newport, Rhode Island. Newport, R. I., Charity Organization Society, 1915. 58p. illus.

1758.

1541 ———. The old Hazard house. Newport, R. I., Newport Historical Society. 1920.

Newport Historical Society, Bulletin 33.

1542 ———. Wanton-Lyman-Hazard house, Newport, Rhode Island. Old-Time New England, 18:21–34, July 1927. illus.

(After 1675.)

1543 TERRY, RODERICK (ed.). History of the Old Colony House at Newport as recorded by early and modern writers. Newport Historical Society. Bulletin, 63:1–36, Oct. 1927.

1544 Touro Synagogue, Newport, Rhode Island. Newport Society of Friends of Touro Synagogue National Historic Shrine, 1948. 55p. illus.

1658———. Peter Harrison, architect.

North Kingston

1545 CADY, JOHN HUTCHINS. Cocumscussoc. Old-Time New England, 39:61–70, Jan. 1949. illus.

About 1680. Richard Smith, Jr., architect.

North Smithfield

1546 FRANKLIN, M. S. Houses and villages of North Smithfield, Rhode Island. Pencil Points, 16:431–46, Aug. 1935. Monograph Series, 21:49–64. illus.

Covers 1714–1836.

Providence

1547 BROWN, FRANK CHOUTEAU. Providence, Rhode Island, Georgian mansion, the house founded by John Brown, Esq., 1786. Pencil Points, 17:97–112, Feb. 1936. Monograph Series, 22:1–16. illus.

1786. Joseph Brown, architect.

1548 CADY, JOHN HUTCHINS. The civic and architectural development of Providence, 1636–1950. Providence, Book Shop, 1957. 320p. illus.

1549 ———. The Providence Market House and its neighborhood. Rhode Island History, 11:97–116, Oct. 1952. illus.

1744———. Erected 1773–75.

1550 ———. Weybosset bridge. Rhode Island History, 8:13–20, Jan. 1949.

Nine bridges, 1660–1904.

1551 CHAPIN, HOWARD M. The lands and houses of the first settlers of Providence. Rhode Island Historical Society. Collections, 12:1–8, Jan. 1919.

1552 DOWNING, ANTOINETTE FORRESTER. New light on the Sullivan Dorr house. Rhode Island History, 16:33–40, Apr. 1957. illus.

Includes information from receipted bills, construction 1809–10.

1553 ISHAM, NORMAN MORRISON. The design of the John Brown house: headquarters of the Rhode Island Historical Society . . . edited by John Hutchins Cady. Rhode Island History, 7:126–28, Oct. 1948.

1786.

1554 ———. The house of Roger Williams. Rhode Island Historical Society. Collections, 18:33–39, Apr. 1925.

1555 ———. Providence and its Colonial houses. White Pine Series of Architectural Monographs, v. 4, no. 3, June 1918. 15p. illus.
Covers 1700–1820.

1556 ———. Meeting-house of the First Baptist Church in Providence, a history of the fabric. Providence, Akerman-Standard Co., 1925. 33p. illus.
Dedicated May 28, 1775. Joseph Brown, architect.

1557 KING, HENRY M. First Baptist Church; oldest church of any denomination in Rhode Island and the oldest Baptist church in America. Old-Time New England, 34:38–43, Jan. 1944. illus.

1558 MERCHANTS NATIONAL BANK OF PROVIDENCE. Old Providence; a collection of facts and traditions relating to various buildings and sites of historic interest in Providence. Providence, 1918. 65p. illus.

1559 MINER, GEORGE LELAND. Angell's Lane: the history of a little street in Providence. Providence, Akerman-Standard Press, 1948. 198p. illus.
Thomas Street, 1636———.

1560 MINER, LILIAN BURLEIGH. Through the streets of old Providence. House Beautiful, 44:152–54, 170, Aug. 1918. illus.

1561 Nightingale house at Providence. Arts and Decoration, 39:6–7, Oct. 1933. illus.
1792. Attributed to Caleb Ormsbee.

1562 OVERBY, OSMUND R. The architecture of College Hill, 1770–1900. Doctoral Dissertation, Yale University, 1963. 459p. illus.

1563 PRESTON, HOWARD WILLIS. Notes on old Providence. The old County House in Providence. Providence, Preston and Rounds, 1918. 8p.
Reprinted from Rhode Island Historical Society. *Collections*, v. 11, April 1918.

1564 Providence is rich in Federal mansions. House and Garden, 77:28–29, June 1940. illus.

1565 Stephen Hopkins house, Providence, Rhode Island. Antiques, 46:210–11, Oct. 1944. illus.
1708, enlarged 1743.

Roslyn

1566 BROWER, MARION WILLETTS, AND MCGEE, DOROTHY HORTON. The story of Roslyn Grist Mill. Roslyn, R. I., Board of Trustees, Roslyn Grist Mill, 1953. 16p. illus.
1698.

Tiverton (see also *Little Compton*)

1567 MACKAY, H. G. Winnisemet farm; Nathaniel Briggs house, near Tiverton, Rhode Island. House Beautiful, 53:632–33, June 1923.

1568 PARKER, RODERICK H. Tiverton, Rhode Island, and some of its early dwellings. Pencil Points, 17:575–89, Oct. 1936. Monograph Series, 22:65–80. illus.
Covers *ca.* 1700–1818.

Warren

1569 RUSSELL, J. FENIMORE. Some old houses of Warren, Rhode Island — in two parts. Pencil Points, 16:539–54, 635–50, Oct., Dec. 1935. Monograph Series, 21:65–80, 81–96. illus.

Part 1 covers 1820–25; part 2 covers 1789–1820.

Warwick

1570 WELLMAN, RITA. Governor Greene house in Rhode Island. International Studio, 99:25–26, July 1931. illus.

1680 and later.

Wickford

1570A CUMMINGS, J. H. An old church and glebe. International Studio, 81:293–96, July 1925. illus.

St. Paul's.

1571 UPDIKE, DANIEL BERKELEY. Restoration of a Colonial altarpiece. Old-Time New England, 22:188–92, Apr. 1932. illus.

In St. Paul's Church, 1707.

1572 WHITE, HUNTER C. Old St. Paul's in Narragansett. [Wakefield? R. I.], 1957. 56p. illus.

St. Paul's Church (Episcopal), also called the Old Narragansett Church, 1707——.

1573 ———. Wickford and its old houses. Providence, Reynolds Press, 1936. 35p.

VERMONT

GENERAL REFERENCES

1574 ALLEN, RICHARD SANDERS. How they built the covered bridges. Vermont Life, 11:50–57, Autumn 1956. illus.

1575 ———. Undercover work in Vermont . . . the story of Vermont's covered bridges. Vermont Life, 8:36–41, Spring 1954. illus.

On eight types of wooden construction. 1804 and later.

1576 BURTON, ARTHUR GIBBES. Vermont portraits: a series of historical buildings, sites, and scenes. Vermont History, 21:199–202, July–Oct. 1954; 23:39–42, 129–32, 221–24, 319–22, Jan.–Oct. 1955; 24:47–50, 145–48, 243–46, Jan.– July 1956. illus.

Drawings, no text.

1577 CHAPPELL, GEORGE S. Colonial architecture in Vermont. White Pine Series of Architectural Monographs, v. 4, no. 6, Dec. 1918. 14p. illus.

1578 CONGDON, HERBERT WHEATON. The covered bridge. Brattleboro, Vt., Stephen Daye Press, 1941. 150p. illus.

Later edition, 1959.

1579 ———. Old Vermont houses. Brattleboro, Vt., Stephen Daye Press, 1940. 190p. illus.

Popular sketch from earliest buildings up to 1850. Includes courthouses, taverns, and churches.

1580 COURIER, THEODORE. Covered bridges in Vermont. Vermont Quarterly, 18:22–28, Jan. 1950.
1785——.

1581 CRANE, CHARLES EDWARD. Let me show you Vermont. N. Y., Alfred A. Knopf, 1937. 347p. illus.

1582 FEDERAL WRITERS' PROJECT. Vermont: a guide to the Green Mountain State. Boston, Houghton Mifflin Co., 1937. 392p. illus.

1583 FORBES, P. P. American home pilgrimages — part 10, Vermont. American Home, 26:38, 40–43, June 1941. illus.

1584 GREENE, STEPHEN, AND OTHERS (eds.). A treasury of *Vermont Life*. Woodstock, Vt., Countryman Press, 1956. 191p. illus.
Undated excerpts from the magazine, *Vermont Life*.

1585 LOVELL, FRANCES S. Some covered bridges in Bennington, Windham, and Windsor counties. Vermont Life, 5:22–25, Summer 1951. illus.
1840–79.

1586 SWARTWOUT, EGERTON. Some old-time churches of Vermont. White Pine Series of Architectural Monographs, v. 13, no. 6, 1927. 20p. illus.
Covers 1787–1821.

LOCATIONS

Bennington

1587 BAYHAN, RICHARD S. (ed.). Historical sketch of buildings now or once located in the village on the hill at Bennington, Vermont, formerly known as Bennington Center, and now called Old Bennington. Cleveland, Ohio, Central Publishing Co., 1930. 50p. illus.

1588 BONHAM, EUPHA. Historic Bennington. Vermont Life, 3:12–17, Autumn 1948. illus.
1763–1948. Description, some historical references.

1589 BOOTH, VINCENT RAVI. Restoration of the old First Church of Bennington, Vermont. Old-Time New England, 30:72–81, Jan. 1940. illus.
1805. Attributed to Asher Benjamin.

1590 CLARK, CAMERON. Houses of Bennington, Vermont and vicinity — used as a study of Colonial textures. White Pine Series of Architectural Monographs, v. 8, no. 5, Oct. 1922. 16p. illus.

1591 Colonial craftsman's home; Georgian mansion near Bennington built in 1795 by Judge Lyman Norton, still occupied by his descendants. House and Garden, 75:68–69, June 1939. illus.

1592 Historic Bennington. House Beautiful, 82:22–24, July–Aug. 1940. illus.

1593 SERBE, MILTON J. Old Bennington's historic church. D. A. R. Magazine, 67:77–80, 1933.

1594 SPARGO, JOHN. Covered wooden bridges of Bennington and vicinity. Bennington, Vt., Bennington Historical Museum and Art Gallery, 1953. 20p. illus.

Brandon

1595 SHUMWAY, HARRY IRVING. Direct from the quarry. House Beautiful, 46:78–79, Aug. 1919. illus.

Early nineteenth-century houses.

Brookline

1596 MARCH, HAL L., JR. Blunderbuss Academy; or, the strange case of Brookline's round schoolhouse. Vermont Life, 4:46–48, Summer 1950. illus.

Planned by John Wilson, 1821.

Caledonia County

1597 GLOVER, WALDO F. Old Scotland in Vermont. Vermont History, 23:92–103, Apr. 1955. illus.

Five stone houses, 1798–1812.

Castleton

1598 WAITE, FREDERICK CLAYTON. The first medical college in Vermont: Castleton, 1818–1862. Montpelier, Vt., Vermont Historical Society, 1949. 280p. illus.

Castleton Medical College.

Cavendish

1599 GAY, LEON S. Dwellings from the hills. Vermonter, 39:225–31, 1934.

1600 ———. The Salmon Dutton house. Vermont Quarterly, 18:175–78, Oct. 1950. 1782.

Concord

1601 WALTER, MABEL HALL. Judge Hibbard house, Concord, Vermont. Old-Time New England, 24:93–96, Jan. 1934. illus.

Ca. 1814.

Fairlee

1602 ROBINSON, PHILIP G. (ed.). The town under the cliff: a history of Fairlee, Vermont. Fairlee, Vt., [1957]. 187p. illus.

Lyndon

1603 WALTER, MABEL HALL. Cahoon house, Lyndon, Vermont. Old-Time New England, 26:106–19, Jan. 1939. illus.

Newbury

1604 MUNSELL, L. Town house neighborhood, Newbury, Vermont. Old-Time New England, 32:57–62, Oct. 1941. illus.

Newfane

1605 CUDWORTH, ADDISON E. Genealogy of the Windham County Court House. Vermont Historical Society. Proceedings, 1923, 1924, and 1925, pp. 220–28.

Norwich

1606 WHITE, PHILIP AYLWIN, AND JOHNSON, DANA DOANE. Early houses of Norwich, Vermont. Hanover, N. H., Dartmouth College, 1938. 51p. illus.

Richmond

1607 DIMICK, KATHRYN M. Vermont's most interesting church. Vermont Quarterly, 18:110–14, July 1950.

About the old Round Church, Richmond, Vt., "a regular polygon of sixteen sides," 1813——.

Rockingham (near *Bellows Falls*)

1608 DESMOND, H. W. A forgotten Colonial church. Architectural Record, 14:94–106, Aug. 1903. illus.

1609 HAYES, LYMAN SIMPSON, AND HAYES, WILLIAM DANFORTH. The old Rockingham meeting house, erected 1787 and the first church in Rockingham, Vermont, 1773–1840. Bellows Falls, Vt., P. H. Gobie Press, 1915. 102p. illus.

1610 LOVELL, FRANCES STOCKWELL. Rockingham meeting house. Vermont Life, 3:44–47, Autumn 1948. illus.

1787——.

Rutland

1611 SWAN, MRS. ALTON. History of the First Parish Congregational Church of Rutland, Vt. D. A. R. Magazine, 91:730–34, June 1957.

1780——.

Shaftsbury

1612 GALE, DAVID C. The old Joshua Monroe mansion. Old-Time New England, 31:74–80, Jan. 1941. illus.

1798–1812. Now known as the Iron Kettle Farm.

Shelburne

1613 NATIONAL SOCIETY FOR THE PRESERVATION OF COVERED BRIDGES. The covered bridge of Shelburne Museum, Vt. Covered Bridge Topics, 12:3, 6–7, Spring 1954. illus.

Built *ca.* 1845 across the Lamoille River at Cambridge.

1614 WINCHESTER, ALICE. Shelburne Museum. Antiques, 66:110–21, Aug. 1954. illus.

Particularly the Cavendish house (1782) and the Vermont house (1790).

Waterford

1615 WALTER, MABEL HALL. Pike-Streeter tavern, Waterford, Vermont. Old-Time New England, 22:15–22, July 1931. illus.

1800.

Weathersfield Bow

1616 MORSE, ETHEL C. The old Stone Church of Weathersfield Bow. Vermont Life, 5:46–48, Autumn 1950. illus.

East Congregational Church, 1838——.

West Newbury

1617 WELLS, FREDERIC P. Union meeting house at West Newberry. . . . Vermonter, 39:36–43, 1934.

1833.

Weston

1618 BOOTHBY, R. E. Farrar-Mansur house. Vermonter, 39:175–76, 1934.

Windham County

1619 MORSE, VICTOR L. Windham County's famous covered bridges. Brattleboro, Vt., Book Cellar, 1960. 43p. illus.

Earlier edition.

1620 WALKER, C. ERNEST. Covered bridges of Windham County, Vermont. Covered Bridge Topics, 13:3, 7, Fall 1955. illus.

Since 1835.

Windsor

1621 Constitution House. Vermont Life, 3:14–15, Winter 1949. illus.

Tavern, before 1777.

Windsor County

1622 ALLEN, RICHARD SANDERS. Rare old covered bridges of Windsor County, Vermont. Brattleboro, Vt., Book Cellar, 1962. 42p. illus.

1623 GAY, LEON S. Dwellings from the hills. Vermont Life, 5:29–33, Autumn 1950. illus.

Stone buildings in southern Windsor County. Flourishing 1832.

1624 WALKER, C. ERNEST. The covered bridges of Windsor County, Vermont. Covered Bridge Topics, 13:3–6, Dec. 1955. illus.

Since 1830.

Middle Atlantic States

GENERAL REFERENCES

1625 ALLBEE, BURTON HIRAM. Ancient Dutch houses in America; historic structures left by the Hollanders. Journal of American History, 3:286–92, 1908.

1626 BAILEY, ROSALIE FELLOWS. Pre-Revolutionary Dutch houses and families in northern New Jersey and southern New York. N. Y., William Morrow and Co., 1936. 612p. illus.

1627 EMBURY, AYMAR, II. The Dutch Colonial house, its origins, design, modern plan and construction. N. Y., McBride, Nast and Co., 1913. 108p. illus.

1628 ———. Dutch Colonial type of house. House and Garden, 17:46–49, Feb. 1910. illus.
Suggesting adaptations of the style.

1629 HAYES, JOHN RUSSELL. Old meeting-houses. Philadelphia, The Biddle Press, 1909. 44p. illus.
Second edition: titled *Old Quaker Meeting-Houses*, 1911. 74p. illus.

1630 HIGGINS, HENRY. Some interesting old Dutch houses. House Beautiful, 45:35–37, 52, Jan. 1919. illus.
In New Jersey, New York, and Pennsylvania.

1631 MEIXNER, ESTHER CHILSTROM. Swedish landmarks in the Delaware Valley. Swedish Pioneer Historical Quarterly, 7:21–34, Jan. 1956.
On surviving buildings in Pennsylvania, Delaware, and New Jersey erected by Swedes between 1654 and 1760.

1632 NASH, GEORGE W. Some Early American hardware, Dutch Colonial examples. Architectural Record, 34:329–33, Oct. 1913. illus.

1633 PENNYPACKER, ISAAC R. The Dutch on the Delaware. American Mercury, 2:345–50, 1924.

1634 RATHMELL, JAMES K., JR. Delaware River covered bridges. Covered Bridge Topics, 15:1, 5, Oct. 1957. illus.
Pennsylvania and New Jersey, 1806———.

1635 ROGERS, MRS. HENRY WADE. Dutch Colonial farmhouses. House Beautiful, 16:15–17, Oct. 1904. illus.
Covers examples in New Jersey and New York.

1636 SCHUYLER, MONTGOMERY. Dutch origins of American architecture. Architectural Record, 4:313–66, April–June 1895. illus.

1637 SCOTT, W. W. Dutch buildings, customs, habits. . . . Americana, 16:368–79, Oct. 1922.

1638 SLOCUM, S. E. Early Dutch Colonial architecture. American Architect, 105:1–10, 12, Jan. 7, 1914. illus.

1639 WALLACE, PHILIP B., AND DUNN, WILLIAM ALLEN. Colonial churches and meeting-houses, Pennsylvania, New Jersey and Delaware. N. Y., Architectural Book Publishing Co., 1931. 313p. illus.
This is *Colonial Architecture in Old Philadelphia* (sic), v. 3.

1640 WARD, CHRISTOPHER LONGSTRETH. The Dutch and Swedes on the Delaware, 1609–1664. Philadelphia, University of Pennsylvania Press, 1930. 393p. illus.

1641 ———. New Sweden on the Delaware. Philadelphia, University of Pennsylvania Press, 1938. 160p. illus.

1642 WERTENBAKER, THOMAS JEFFERSON. The founding of the American civilization: the middle colonies. N. Y., Charles Scribner's Sons, 1938. illus.
Documented sketch describing the origin and use of the horizontal log cabin among the eighteenth-century German colonists of Pennsylvania, pp. 298–307.

1643 WISE, HERBERT CLIFTON, AND BEIDLEMAN, FERDINAND H. Colonial architecture for those about to build: being the best examples, domestic, municipal and institutional, in Pennsylvania, New Jersey and Delaware with observations of the local building art of the eighteenth century. Philadelphia, J. B. Lippincott Co., 1913. 270p. illus.

DELAWARE

1644 ANTIQUES. Winterthur Museum issue. Antiques, 60:347–476, Nov. 1951. illus.
Principally articles on period rooms.

1645 BENNETT, GEORGE FLETCHER. Early architecture of Delaware. Wilmington, Del., Historical Press, 1932. 213p. illus.

1646 CORKRAN, L. C. Peter Marsh, two centuries, and our heritage; The Homestead, Rehoboth Neck, Sussex County. American Home, 12:132–35, Aug. 1934. illus.

1647 A Delaware shrine. Hobbies, 54:34–35, Sept. 1949.
New Castle, 1682–1854.

1648 EBERLEIN, HAROLD DONALDSON, AND HUBBARD, CORTLANDT V. D. Historic houses and buildings of Delaware. Dover, Del., Public Archives Commission, 1962. 227p. illus.

1649 FEDERAL WRITERS' PROJECT. Delaware; a guide to the First State. N. Y., Viking Press, 1938. 550p. illus.

1650 ———. New Castle on the Delaware. Wilmington, Del., W. N. Cann, 1937. 142p. illus.

1651 FERGUSON, WILLIAM E. Early iron works in southern Delaware. Delaware Folklore Bulletin, 4:13–14, 16, Apr. 1954.
1750–1836.

1652 FOSTER, WILLIAM D. New Castle, Delaware, an eighteenth century town. White Pine Series of Architectural Monographs, v. 12, no. 1, 1926. 19p. illus.

1653 FRYER, AARON. The story of New Castle. Antiques, 60:113–17, Aug. 1951. illus.
1651——.

1654 Historic American buildings; Old Swedes, Holy Trinity Church, Wilmington, Delaware. Architectural Forum, 61:445–52, Dec. 1934. illus.

1655 KRUSE, ALBERT. An impression of the old manner of building in New Castle, Delaware. Delaware History, 4:171–206, June 1951. illus.
Architect's examination of structures built 1707–1858.

1656 MACDONALD, BETTY. Historic landmarks of Delaware and the eastern shore. Wilmington, Del., Delaware State Society, Daughters of the American Colonists, 1963. 109p. illus.

1657 Master detail series. Historic American buildings: Amstel, Van Dyke and Chancellor Kensey Johns houses, New Castle. Architectural Forum, 65:125–32, Aug. 1936.

1658 MOORE, MRS. FRANCIS HARDY. The removal and restoration of the old First Presbyterian Church of Wilmington, Delaware. Presbyterian Historical Society. Journal, 10:208–16, June 1920.

1659 Old buildings in New Castle, Delaware. American Architect, 141:49–56, Feb. 1936. illus.

1660 WATERSTON, ELIZABETH. Churches in Delaware during the Revolution, with a brief account of their settlement and growth. Wilmington, Del., Historical Society of Delaware, 1925. 117p. illus.

1661 WESLAGER, CLINTON ALFRED. Brandywine Springs: the rise and fall of a Delaware resort. Wilmington, Del., Hambleton Co., 1949. 124p. illus.
1826——.

1662 ——. Historic New Castle. Delaware Cavalcade, 1:8–9, 22–24, Summer 1950. illus.
1651——.

1663 ——. Log structures in New Sweden during the seventeenth century. Delaware History, 5:77–95, Sept. 1952. illus.
1638–1700.

1664 WISE, HERBERT CLIFTON. George Read II house, at New Castle, Delaware. White Pine Series of Architectural Monographs, v. 11, no. 6, 1925. 21p. illus.
1791–1801.

1665 WOLCOTT, DANIEL F. The restoration of the courthouse in New Castle. Delaware History, 7:193–206, Mar. 1957. illus.
Ca. 1732, with later additions.

NEW JERSEY

GENERAL REFERENCES

1666 Antiques. New Jersey issue. Antiques, 62:161–248, Sept. 1952. illus.

1667 Black, William Nelson. Colonial buildings in New Jersey. Architectural Record, 3:245–62, Jan.–Mar. 1894. illus.

1668 Blauvelt, Hiram. Some Jersey Dutch Colonial hardware. New Jersey Historical Society. Proceedings, 13:30–38, July 1928.

1669 Boyd, John T., Jr. Some early Dutch houses in New Jersey — in three parts. Architectural Record, part 1, 36:31–48, July 1914; part 2, 36:148–58, Aug. 1914; part 3, 36:220–30, Sept. 1914. illus.

1670 Card, Marian. Early church architecture in New Jersey; summary. Society of Architectural Historians. Journal, 7:30, July 1948.
Ca. 1620–1819. Abstract of Master's Thesis, Oberlin College.

1671 Cawley, James S. Historic New Jersey in pictures. Princeton, N. J., Princeton University Press, 1939. 95p. illus.

1672 Coleman, Oliver. Dutch byways in New Jersey. House and Garden, 8:1–8, July 1905. illus.

1673 De Lagerberg, Lars. New Jersey architecture, Colonial and Federal. Springfield, Mass., private printing by W. Whittum, 1956. 316p. illus.
1610–1836. Photographs and 551 plates of drawings made between 1906 and 1915. Introductory text only.

1674 Dennis, Helen Dean. The Elisha Boudinot house, Newark, N. J. New Jersey Historical Society. Proceedings, 67:253–60, Oct. 1949. illus.

1675 Ellis, Rowland C. Colonial Dutch houses in New Jersey. Newark, N. J., Carteret Book Club, 1933. 60p. illus.
Twenty wood engravings.

1676 Embury, Aymar, II. Three old Dutch roads and the houses along them. Country Life in America, 16:591–94, 656, 658, 660, 662, Oct. 1909. illus.
Ca. 1750—ca. 1850. Between Jersey City and the Ramapo Mountains.

1677 Federal Writers' Project. New Jersey: a guide to its present and past. N. Y., Viking Press, 1939. 750p. illus.

1678 ———. New Jersey: a profile in pictures. N. Y., M. Barrows and Co., 1939. 59p. illus.

1679 ———. Stories of New Jersey, its significant places, people and activities. N. Y., M. Barrows and Co., 1938. illus.

1680 ———. Swedes and Finns in New Jersey. Bayonne, N. J., Jersey Printing Co., 1938. 165p. illus.

1681 Gowans, Alan. Architecture in New Jersey, a record of American civilization. Princeton, N. J., Van Nostrand, 1944. 161p. illus.
New Jersey Historical Series, v. 6.

1682 GROSVENOR, JEWETT A. Wooden architecture of the lower Delaware Valley. White Pine Series of Architectural Monographs, v. 6, no. 3, June 1920. 14p. illus.

Covers 1740–1813.

1683 LOVE, PAUL VAN DERVEER. Patterned brickwork in southern New Jersey. New Jersey Historical Society. Proceedings, 73:182–208, July 1955. illus.

1691–1831.

1684 MICKLEWRIGHT, ALBERT E. Early architecture of New Jersey. Series of measured drawings. Architecture, v. 35–37, Jan. 1917–May 1918. illus. only.

1685 MILLS, WEYMER JAY. Historic houses of New Jersey. Philadelphia, J. B. Lippincott Co., 1903. 348p. illus.

1686 PERRY, MATILDA HARDENDORF. Historic churches of New Jersey. American Monthly Magazine, 41:129–31, Sept. 1912.

1687 SOCIETY OF COLONIAL WARS. NEW JERSEY. Historic roadsides. Princeton, N. J., 1928. 115p. illus.

Location map and bibliography.

1688 TURNER, GORDON B. Colonial New Jersey, 1703–1763. New Jersey Historical Society. Proceedings, 70:229–45, Oct. 1952.

1689 TURNER, WILLIAM S. New Jersey architecture. New Jersey Historical Society. Proceedings, 55:289–95, 1937.

1690 WEISS, HARRY BISCHOFF, AND SIM, ROBERT J. The early grist and flouring mills of New Jersey. Trenton, N. J., New Jersey Agricultural Society, 1956. 135p. illus.

1691 WENDEHACK, CLIFFORD C. Early Dutch houses of northern New Jersey. White Pine Series of Architectural Monographs, v. 11, no. 3, 1925. 19p. illus.

Covers 1670–1837.

1692 W. P. A. Architectural Survey: New Jersey's architectural growth to 1860. Architect and Engineer, 135:70–71, Oct. 1938. illus.

LOCATIONS

Allentown

1693 BOYD, JOHN TAYLOR, JR. House of John Imlay, Esq., an eighteenth century dwelling, Allentown, New Jersey. Monograph Series, v. 15, no. 3, 1929. 21p. illus.

Ca. 1790.

Bergen County

1694 BLAUVELT, H. Migration of an ancestral home; New Jersey Dutch Colonial house. House and Garden, 52:112–13, 162, 164, 166, 202, Nov. 1927. illus.

Demarest house, *ca.* 1750.

1695 Old Dutch houses in Bergen County. New Jersey Historical Society. Proceedings, 9:273–75, July 1924.

Bound Brook

1696 GOLDSMITH, MARGARET O. Pre-Revolutionary farmhouse. House Beautiful, 54:610–12, Dec. 1923.

Built before 1722. Staats farm.

Bridgeton

1697 MULFORD, WILLIAM CORNWALL. The old Broad Street Presbyterian Church in Bridgeton, N. J. Vineland Historical Magazine, 35:112–17, July–Oct. 1950.

1792——.

Burlington County

1698 MILLS, ROBERT. A model jail of the olden time. Designs for a debtors' gaol, and work-house for felons for Burlington County, State of New Jersey. N. Y., Russell Sage Foundation, 1928. 2p. illus.

Camden

1699 BOYER, CHARLES S. The old houses in Camden, New Jersey. Camden, N. J., The Author, 1920. 15p. illus.

Annals of Camden, no. 1.

Cape May County

1700 BROWN, KENNETH O. The Cape May Point Lighthouse. Cape May County Magazine of History and Genealogy, 3:70–74, June 1949.

1701 CAMPBELL, CLARE. Cape May Court House Post Office is one hundred years old. Cape May County Magazine of History and Genealogy, 3:265–69, June 1953. illus.

1853.

1702 FITZPATRICK, HELENA WAY. Some old houses of Cape May County. Part 3: Villas to Cape May. Cape May County Magazine of History and Genealogy, 3:214–24, June 1952. illus.

1702–1846.

1703 ——. Some old houses of Cape May County, New Jersey. Wildwood, N. J., The Leader, 1951. 20p. illus.

1702–1851.

1704 STAUFFER, M. CATHARINE. The First Baptist Church of Cape May County. Cape May County Magazine of History and Genealogy, 3:187–92, June 1952. illus.

First Baptist Church, Cape May Court House, 1712——.

Dover

1705 ENGLE, CAROLINE KIRKHAM. 100 years: Saint John's Parish in Dover, New Jersey, 1849–1949. Dover, 1949. 97 leaves. illus.

Episcopal.

Dunellen

1706 FEDERAL WRITERS' PROJECT. The story of Dunellen. Dunellen, N. J., Art Color Printing Co., 1937. 111p. illus.

Elizabeth

1707 DIX, WARREN R. Old houses of Elizabethtown; the Belcher mansion, 1046 East Jersey Street, Elizabeth. Union County Historical Society. Proceedings, 8:68–82, 1923.

Before 1742.

1708 ———. Old houses of Elizabethtown; the Governor Belcher mansion. New Jersey Historical Society. Proceedings, 8:169–85, 1923.

1709 ———. Old houses of Elizabethtown; part 2, the Hetfield house. New Jersey Historical Society. Proceedings, 12:298–302, 1928.

Heathfield or Hetfield house was acquired by Matthias Heathfield (Hetfield, Hattfield), December 5, 1673.

1710 FIELD, MRS. EDWARD M. Historical Elizabeth — two famous mansions. New Jersey Historical Society. Proceedings, 13:393–99, Oct. 1928.

General Winfield Scott mansion (destroyed) and Elias Boudinot mansion (*ca.* 1752).

1711 HUTCHINSON, ELMER T. The old Wheat Sheaf Inn. New Jersey Historical Society. Proceedings, n.s. 5:246–48, Oct. 1920.

1730.

1712 LAMB, MRS. MARTHA L. House of Elias Boudinot and Governor Livingston. Magazine of American History, 21:361–80, May 1889. illus.

Governor Livingston home is Liberty Hall. Both Pre-Revolutionary.

Flemington

1713 DEATS, HIRAM EDMUND. Dedication of the restored Fleming house. Flemington, N. J., H. E. Deats, 1928. 8p. illus.

(1756). Reprinted from *Hunterdon County Democrat*, June 21, 1928.

Greenwich

1714 ANDREWS, BESSIE AYERS. Colonial and old houses at Greenwich, N. J. Vineland, N. J., G. E. Smith, 1907. 87p. illus.

Hackensack

1715 PEARMAN, JOSEPH BERNARD. An old homestead of Colonial New Jersey. American Homes and Gardens, 10:267–70, 300, Aug. 1913. illus.

Brinckerhoff house.

Hudson County

1716 LOWE, DAVID G. Requiem for a Court House. American Heritage, 17:26–29, 72–74, Oct. 1966. illus.

Hudson County Court House, original building was Greek Revival.

Jersey City

1717 GRUNDY, J. OWEN. Prior's Mill; a Revolutionary landmark. New Jersey Historical Society. Proceedings, 16:174–79, 1931.

1760.

Matawan

1718 FEDERAL WRITERS' PROJECT. Matawan, 1686–1936. Matawan, N. J., Matawan Journal, *ca.* 1936. 95p. illus.

Middlesex County

1719 FEDERAL WRITERS' PROJECT. Monroe Township, Middlesex County, New Jersey, 1838–1938. New Brunswick, N. J., 1938. 140p. illus.

Middleton

1720 Ancient dwellings restored; Marlpit Hall, Middleton. Antiques, 30:30, July 1936. illus.

Ca. 1680.

Monmouth County

1721 ELDRIDGE, SARAH E. "Old Tennent" historic church, Monmouth County, New Jersey. American Monthly Magazine, 39:240–42, Nov. 1911.

The First Presbyterian Church of the County of Monmouth.

1722 FREIDAY, DEAN. Tinton Manor: the Iron Works. New Jersey Historical Society. Proceedings, 70:250–61, Oct. 1952.

1674–83.

Morristown and *Morris County*

1723 Early continental structures being rebuilt at Morristown National Historical Park. Pencil Points, 15:supp. 15–16, Apr. 1934. illus.

1724 EDWARDS, CARL IRVING. Pequannock Township 1740–1956: a town's growth in words and pictures. [Pequannock Township? N. J., 1956.] 68p. illus.

Morris County.

1725 HOFFMAN, PHILIP H. (comp.). History of the Arnold tavern, Morristown, N. J. Morristown, N. J., Chronicle Press, 1903. 28p. illus.

Views of historic buildings.

1726 HUDSON, J. PAUL. The Ford mansion at Morristown, New Jersey. Antiques, 55:127–29, Feb. 1949. illus.

1774——.

1727 Morristown National Historical Park. Washington, D. C., Government Printing Office, 1940. 16p. illus.

1728 VOGT, GRACE J. Schuyler-Hamilton house, Morristown, N. J. D. A. R. Magazine, 59:569–73, Sept. 1925.

1729 Washington's headquarters at Morristown, New Jersey. Antiques, 36:245, Nov. 1939. illus.

Ca. 1772.

Mount Holly

1730 WOOLMAN, FENIMORE C. The Burlington County Courthouse at Mount Holly, New Jersey. White Pine Series of Architectural Monographs, v. 12, no. 3, 1926. 19p. illus.

1796.

New Albion

1731 LINDSAY, G. C. Plantagenet's Wigwam. Society of Architectural Historians. Journal, 17:31–35, Winter 1958. illus.

Seventeenth century. One of a series.

New Brunswick

1732 ATKINSON, JOSEPHINE. Buccleuch, historic homestead of New Brunswick. D. A. R. Magazine, 61:179–86, Mar. 1927.
1729.

1733 ATKINSON, MARY J. The old taverns of New Brunswick. Somerset County Historical Quarterly, 3:9–18, Jan. 1914.

1734 BENEDICT, WILLIAM H. Early taverns in New Brunswick. New Jersey Historical Society. Proceedings, n.s. 3:129–46, July 1918.

Newark

1735 FARRAND, WILSON. A brief history of the Newark Academy, 1774–1792–1916. Contribution to the celebration of the 250th anniversary of the founding of Newark, May 1916. Newark, N. J., Baker Printing Co., 1916. 20p. illus.

1736 WHITE, M. E. Schoolhouse in the garden; the old stone schoolhouse built in 1784. Newark, N. J., The Museum, n.s. 9, no. 2:14–16, 1957. illus.

Perth Amboy

1737 McGINNIS, WILLIAM CARROLL. The Westminster. New Jersey Historical Society. Proceedings, 74:203–7, July 1956. illus.
1764——.

1738 MILLER, GEORGE J. Westminster — story of a Colonial house. New Jersey Historical Society. Proceedings, 15:465–84, Oct. 1930.
1764.

Princeton

1739 CLEMENT, JOHN. Coxe Hall. New Jersey Historical Society. Proceedings, 3rd ser. 9:27–37, Jan. 1914.

1740 Dean's House, Princeton. American Institute of Architects. Journal, 9:124–27, Mar. 1948. illus.
1756.

1741 FEDERAL WRITERS' PROJECT. Old Princeton's neighbors. Princeton, N. J., Graphic Arts Press, *ca.* 1939. 96p. illus.

Covers Cedar Grove, Jugtown, Princeton Basin, Penn's Neck, Dutch Neck, Grover's Mills, Aqueduct, Kingston.

1742 GAUSS, KATHERINE. Historic house in Princeton, New Jersey. House Beautiful, 66:632, 634, 636, 638, Nov. 1929. illus.

1756. Home of the Dean of the Faculty of Princeton University, formerly the President's home.

1743 ——. Two hundred years of Morven I Record. House Beautiful, 62:50–51, 87–90, July 1927. illus.
Richard Stockton house, 1701.

1744 SCHUYLER, MONTGOMERY. The architecture of American colleges. Part 3. Princeton. Architectural Record, 27:129–60, Feb. 1910.

1745 WILSON, H. L. MCGILL. Miller Chapel. Princeton Seminary. Bulletin, 43:24–27, Winter 1950.

Presbyterian, 1817.

Salem County

1746 EBERLEIN, HAROLD DONALDSON. Early brick houses of Salem County, New Jersey. American Architecture and Architectural Review, 120:139–48, Aug. 1921. illus.

1747 SICKLER, JOSEPH SHEPPARD. Old houses of Salem County. Salem, N. J., Sunbeam Publishing Co., 1949. 110p. illus.

1687–1815. First edition, 1934.

1748 TELLER, RAYMOND J. The Geiger house, Salem County, New Jersey. American Catholic Historical Society. Record, 68:121–28, Sept.–Dec. 1957.

1743. Matthias Geiger, architect.

Somerset County

1749 HANSEN, ANDREW. The Van Harlingen homestead — seat of Queen's College in 1780. Somerset County Historical Quarterly, 6:173–76, July 1917.

Trenton

1750 COTTRELL, ALDEN TUCKER. The old barracks at Trenton. Trenton, N. J., Old Barracks Assoc., 1951. 14p. illus.

1758.

1751 GODFREY, CHARLES E. Dutch Trading Post, Trenton, New Jersey. Trenton Historic Society, 1919. 8p. illus.

1752 Mappa house, Trenton, N. J. American Architect, 104:61–68, Aug. 13, 1913. illus.

1753 RANDOLPH, MRS. EDWARD F. William Trent — his country home. D. A. R. Magazine, 83:813–15, Oct. 1949. illus.

1719. Established as a museum in 1929.

1754 [State House. Description of the building.] Gazette of the United States, 4:139, Sept. 29, 1792.

1755 WOODRUFF, JOHN W. The evolution of a house, 1802–1808. New Jersey Historical Society. Proceedings, 68:83–92, Apr. 1950. illus.

Oaklands, by George W. Woodruff.

Troy Hills

1756 HOWELL, CATHERINE S. The Howell homestead of Troy Hills. New Jersey Historical Society. Proceedings, n.s. 6:152–56, July 1921.

Union

1757 DIEDRICH, MARIO CHARLES. Our town: a brief little history of the early days, growth, and development of the Township of Union. Union, N. J., Union Center National Bank, 1948. 34p. illus.

1664——.

NEW YORK

GENERAL REFERENCES

1758 American home pilgrimages — part 7. Eastern New York, Manhattan and Long Island. American Home, 22:68, 70, 72, 75, 77, 78, 104–9, 112, 113, June 1939. illus.

1759 ANDERSON, STOTT. Guide to the covered bridges of New York State. n.p., 1962. 38p. illus.

1760 ANDREWS, EDWARD DEMING. Communal architecture of the Shakers. Magazine of Art, 30:710–15, Dec. 1937.
Mostly New Lebanon and Watervliet.

1761 BETTS, BENJAMIN F. Early architecture of western New York. Architecture, v. 33–34, Jan.–Nov. 1916. illus., with two pages of text.

1762 COMSTOCK, HELEN. New York's country houses; impressions of nineteenth century artists at New York Historical Society. Connoisseur, 139:134–35, Apr. 1957. illus.

1763 CONOVER, JEWEL HELEN. Nineteenth century houses in western New York. Albany, State University of New York, 1966. 161p. illus.

1764 FEDERAL WRITERS' PROJECT. New York: a guide to the Empire State. N. Y., Oxford University Press, 1940. 800p. illus.

1765 GUTHE, C. E. Historic house museums in New York State. Museum News, 25:6–8, Nov. 15, 1947.

1766 HUXTABLE, ADA LOUISE. The architecture of New York; a history and guide. Garden City, N. Y., Doubleday and Co., Anchor Books, 1964. 6v. illus.
Contents: v. 1, Classic New York: Georgian gentility to Greek elegance; v. 2, Victorian New York: growth, grandeur and the romantic mood; v. 3, Building for business: the Iron Age and palaces of trade.

1767 KING, DOROTHY. Old mantels. House Beautiful, 47:406–7, May 1920. illus.

1768 Master detail series. Historic American buildings: Jan Breese house, East Greenbush; house at Russia; Beverwyck, W. P. Van Rensselaer house, Rensselaer. Architectural Forum, 63:39–50, July 1935. illus.

1769 MERRILL, ARCH. Covered bridges in New York State. New York History, 33:84–93, Jan. 1952. illus.
1805——.

1770 Octagonal buildings in New York State. Information and photographs supplied by Stephen R. Leonard, Sr., compiled by Ruby M. Rounds. Cooperstown, N. Y., New York State Historical Association, 1954. 22p. illus.
Houses, barns, schools, etc. 1840–1925.

1771 PETERICH, GERDA. Cobblestone architecture of upstate New York. Society of Architectural Historians. Journal, 15:12–18, May 1956. illus.
1828–54. Materials and masonry of the cobblestone walls.

1772 ROUNDS, RUBY M. (ed.). Octagon buildings in New York State (as of February 1952). New York History, 33:212–20, 322–32, Apr.–July 1952. illus. List, alphabetical by counties, of 120 houses, 1848——.

1773 SCHMIDT, CARL F. Cobblestone architecture. Rochester, N. Y., Great Lakes Press, 1944. 104p. illus.

Mostly western N. Y., *ca.* 1825–65, where several hundred were built. There are other cobblestone buildings in areas where New York state residents migrated.

1774 SCHUYLER, MONTGOMERY. The architecture of American colleges. Part 9. Union, Hamilton, Hobart, Cornell, and Syracuse. Architectural Record, 30:549–73, Dec. 1911. illus.

1775 ——. The small city house in New York. Architectural Record, 8:357–88, Apr.–June 1899.

1776 STOTZ, CHARLES M. Early architecture of central New York. Architecture, v. 48, 50, Nov. 1923–Aug. 1924. illus. only.

1777 ——. Early architecture of western New York. Architecture, v. 47, May 1923. illus. only.

1778 TALLMAN, CARL C. Colonial architecture of central New York. Architectural Review, 6:73–74, May 1918. illus. only.

1779 ——. Early wood-built houses of central New York. White Pine Series of Architectural Monographs, v. 4, no. 5, Oct. 1918. 14p. illus.

Covers 1800–38 in Finger Lakes region.

LOCATIONS

Albany

1780 ALLEN, RICHARD SANDERS. Covered bridges of Albany County, N. Y. Covered Bridge Topics, 12:1, 6–7, Summer 1954. illus.

1820–1933.

1781 [Brick theatre. Contemporary description.] Minerva, 1:279, Dec. 7, 1822.

1782 CUTLER, C. B. Albany Academy — in two parts. Architectural Record, part 1, 39:132–43, Feb. 1916; part 2, 39:247–64, Mar. 1916. illus.

1783 DYKEMAN, JOHN L. Doorways, Albany, New York. Architecture, v. 38, no. 6, Dec. 1918. illus. only.

1784 ——. Lancaster School, Albany, New York. Architecture, 36:245–46, Dec. 1917.

1816, now Albany Medical College.

1785 ——. New York State National Bank, Philip Hooker, architect, 1803. Architecture, 34:271–72, pl. 191–92, Dec. 1916. illus.

1786 ——. Stonework, door and window heads, Albany, New York. Architecture, v. 38, no. 6, Dec. 1918. illus. only.

1787 ——. Three Albany doorways. Architecture, 35:71–72, Apr. 1917. illus. only.

1788 ———. Three Hooker churches. Architecture, 39:123–25, May 1919. illus.
Some scattered plates adjacent to this article and in v. 40.

1789 FEDERAL WRITERS' PROJECT. Albany — past and present. Albany, 1938. 28p.
illus.

1790 LAMB, MRS. MARTHA L. The Van Rensselaer manor. Magazine of American
History, 11:1–32, Jan. 1884. illus.

1791 Opening of the Schuyler mansion at Albany, New York, Oct. 17, 1917. American Scenic and Historic Preservation Society. Annual Report, 23:607–24, 1918.

1792 RALSTON, R. Van Rensselaer manor house, Albany. Metropolitan Museum of
Art. Bulletin, 26:supp. 4–9, Dec. 1931.
Moved to Williamstown, Mass.

1793 REYNOLDS, MARIUS T. Colonial buildings of Rensselaerwyck. Architectural
Record, 4:415–38, Apr., June 1895. illus.

1794 SCHUYLER, GEORGINA. The Schuyler mansion at Albany, New York, residence
of Major-General Philip Schuyler, 1762–1804. American Scenic and Historic
Preservation Society. Reports, 17:603–40, 1912.

1795 The Spirit of '76. The Schuyler mansion at Albany, residence of Major-
General Philip Schuyler, 1762–1804. N. Y., The DeVinne Press, 1911. 43p.
illus.

Auburn

1796 BONTA, EDWIN. Along the Seneca Turnpike: introducing a distinct type of
Post-Colonial house. Architectural Record, 40:505–15, Dec. 1916. illus.

1797 First Presbyterian Church, Auburn, N. Y. Architectural Review, n.s. 6:74–
75, May 1918. illus.
1817.

Aurora

1798 BETTS, BENJAMIN F. Colonial lodge building at Aurora, New York. Architectural Review, 5:172, pl. 49–54, Aug. 1917. illus.

Barneveld

1799 ALGER, ELIZABETH D. Mappa Hall. North Country Life, 4:18–22, Summer
1950. illus.
House, 1809.

Beacon

1800 WEST, MRS. HAL R. Madam Brett homestead. D. A. R. Magazine, 89:687, 700,
June 1955. illus.
1708–1895.

Belvidere

1801 THORNTON, WINIFRED KNIGHT. A history of the Church mansion, Belvidere.
New York History, 31:294–307, July 1950. illus.
For Philip Church, 1807———, on the Genesee.

Brewster

1802 SMITH, AMY ADELLE. Forgotten things. North Country Life, 3:51–52, 53–55, 57–59, Winter–Fall 1949. illus.

Elisha Brewster house, 1825, cobblestone schoolhouse and cemetery of Brewster settlement. Includes covered bridge at Dexter.

Bronxville

1803 BURNETT, BERTRAND G. Masterston homestead — Bronxville. Westchester County Historical Society. Bulletin, 7:65–69, 1931.

Brooklyn

1804 DILLARD, MAUD ESTHER. Old Dutch houses of Brooklyn. N. Y., Richard R. Smith, 1945.

Reviews: *Antiques*, 48:370, Dec. 1945. New York Historical Society. *Quarterly Bulletin*, 29:249–51, Oct. 1945.

1805 LANCASTER, CLAY. Old Brooklyn Heights: New York's first suburb; including detailed analyses of 619 century-old houses. Rutland, Vt., C. E. Tuttle Co., 1961. 183p. illus.

Brownville

1806 FAIRBANKS, J. House of a distinguished pioneer, built by J. Brown in Brownville, New York. House Beautiful, 64:534, Nov. 1928. illus.

1811.

Buffalo

1807 Buffalo's architecture in review. Art News, 38:8–9, 17, Jan. 20, 1940.

Review of an exhibition.

1808 City's architecture from 1816 to 1940; photographs. Architectural Review, 87:147, Apr. 1940.

1809 [Eagle Street Theatre. Contemporary description.] New York Mirror, 13:121, Oct. 17, 1835.

Cazenovia

1810 Lorenzo, and the Meadows. House and Garden, 78:14–15, Aug. 1940. illus. (1807).

Chautauqua County

1811 STARR, SYLVIA, AND WERTZ, JOSEPH B. Architecture that came from Athens. House and Garden, 64:49–51, July 1933. illus.

Examples from Ashville, Panama, Chautauqua, and Westfield.

Clinton

1812 PILKINGTON, WALTER. The Kirkland cottage. Clinton, N. Y., Hamilton College, 1953. 13p. illus.

1792.

Cohoes

1813 ALLEN, RICHARD SANDERS. Spanning the Mohawk at Cohoes, New York. Covered Bridge Topics, 12:1, 4, Spring 1954. illus.

Covered bridges, 1795–1871.

Constable

1814 HOUGH, MARJORIE G. Constable Hall: pioneer manor house. North Country Life, 2:14–18, Winter 1948. illus.

1810–17.

Cooperstown

1815 JONES, LOUIS CLARK. Cooperstown. Cooperstown, N. Y., Otsego County Historical Society, 1949. 86p. illus.

1769——.

1816 MACFARLANE, JANET R. The schoolhouse at the corners. New York History, 30:122–27, Jan. 1949. illus.

School house, Otsego County, before 1828. Now in Farmers' Museum, Cooperstown.

1817 WHITING, FRANK P. Cooperstown in the days of our forefathers. White Pine Series of Architectural Monographs, v. 9, no. 3, June 1923. 16p. illus.

Covers 1790–1831.

Croton-on-Hudson

1818 ALBEE, ALLISON. The Van Cortlandt manor house: fact and fancy. Westchester County Historical Society. Quarterly Bulletin, 30:3–17, Jan. 1954. illus.

Ca. 1640–1709.

1819 Mr. Rockefeller's latest gift: Van Cortlandt manor restored. Connoisseur, 144:280–81, Jan. 1960. illus.

Enlarged in eighteenth century.

1820 PAGE, MARIAN. Historic restorations: Van Cortlandt manor. Interiors, 121:96–101ff., Aug. 1961. illus.

Cutchogue

1821 BROWN, FRANK CHOUTEAU. The old house at Cutchogue, Long Island. Old-Time New England, 31:10–21, July 1940. illus.

Horton-Wickham-Landon house, 1649.

1822 Old house, built 1649, Cutchogue, Long Island. Antiques, 32:294–95, June 1941. illus.

Dobbs Ferry

1823 CHAMBERS, WALTER B. Messmore Kendall residence at Dobbs Ferry. Westchester County Historical Society. Bulletin, 7:49–58, 1931.

1824 GILLESPIE, HARRIET SISSON. Restoration of Washington's headquarters at Dobbs Ferry, the Philip VanBrugh Livingston manor. House Beautiful, 53:254–56, 284–85, Mar. 1923. illus.

(*Ca.* 1700).

Dutchess County (see also *Rhinebeck*)

1825 FEDERAL WRITERS' PROJECT. Dutchess County. Philadelphia, William Penn Association of Philadelphia, 1937. 166p. illus.

1826 HASTINGS, HELEN M. Some landmarks of Dutchess County. Architectural Record, 45:276–80, May 1919. illus.

1827 NEWLIN, LILIAN WASHBURN. An old homestead on the Hudson. House Beautiful, 36:73–76, Aug. 1914. illus.

Mount Gulian, 1740 and later. Near Fishkill Landing.

1828 REYNOLDS, HELEN WILKINSON. Dutchess County doorways. . . . New York, W. F. Payson Co., 1931. 280p. illus.

Covers 1730–1830.

1829 SPURLING, GENEVIEVE BROWN. Old Brown homestead in The Orchard. Dutchess County Historical Society. Year Book 54–57.

1753, near Rhinebeck.

East Avon

1830 FULTON, G. JR. Taintor homestead, East Avon, N.Y., built in 1812. Architectural Forum, 45:249–56, Oct. 1926. illus.

East Chester

1831 HALBERT, WILLIAM CARTER. Saint Paul's Church in the town of East Chester. Westchester Historian, 32:63–68, 98–102, Summer, Fall 1956. illus.

Episcopal, 1761——.

Easthampton

1832 GILLESPIE, HARRIET SISSON. John Howard Payne homestead. Country Life in America, 26:69–72, Oct. 1914. illus.

1833 KAUFFMAN, ELIZABETH, AND KAUFFMAN, CYRUS. John Howard Payne homestead, the shrine of homes — Home, Sweet Home. House Beautiful, 54:16–19, 68–70, July 1923. illus.

Ca. 1666.

1834 SINGLETON, ESTHER. Home, Sweet Home. . . . Antiquarian, 3:5–8, 26, Nov. 1924. illus.

Esopus (see *Ulster County*)

Fayetteville

1835 GILLESPIE, HARRIET SISSON. Restoration in an old coach town, Fayetteville, New York. Arts and Decoration, 35:70, Sept. 1931. illus.

Fishkill

1836 VER NOOY, AMY PEARCE. "Fowler's Folly" and its builder. Dutchess County Historical Society. Year Book, 33:50–82. illus.

An octagon house built by Orson Squire Fowler, *ca.* 1847–56.

Flushing

1837 HORTON, H. P. The Bowne house, Freedom's Shrine. Long Island Forum, 12:107, June 1949. illus.

By John Bowne, Quaker, 1661. Now a museum.

Genesee Valley

1838 BRAGDON, CLAUDE FAYETTE. Colonial architecture in the Genesee Valley. American Architect, 43:141–42; 45:26–27; 46:11–12, 1894. illus.

These volumes also contain scattered measured drawings on this subject.

1839 ———. Colonial architecture in the Genesee Valley. Rochester Historical Society Publishing Fund Series, 2:251–60, 1923.

Geneva

1840 ROSE, CHRISTINA LIVINGSTON. Main Street, Geneva, New York. House Beautiful, 39:98–99, Feb. 1916. illus.
Ca. 1820.

1841 SMITH, WARREN HUNTING. An elegant but salubrious village, a portrait of Geneva, New York. Geneva, N. Y., W. F. Humphrey, 1931. 146p. illus.

Haverstraw

1842 BLAUVELT, H. Treason house; the Smith house at West Haverstraw, New York. Mentor, 16:35–37, July 1928. illus.

Hempstead

1843 BINSSE, HARRY LORIN. Rock Hall, an American manorial estate. Antiquarian, 16:34–38, 70, 1931.
Covers 1732–1806.

Hudson Valley (see also town and county names)

1844 ANTIQUES. Hudson River Valley issue. Antiques, 60:1–72, July 1951. illus.
Contents include Schuyler mansion (1762) by Helen Comstock and some Albany views by Ledyard Cogswell, Jr.

1845 CARMER, CARL LAMSON. The Hudson. N. Y., Farrar and Rinehart, 1939. 434p. illus.
Rivers of America series. Material on A. J. Downing.

1846 EBERLEIN, HAROLD DONALDSON. Manors and historic homes of the Hudson Valley. Philadelphia, J. B. Lippincott Co., 1924. 328p. illus.

1847 ———. Old houses of the Hudson Valley. Country Life in America, 47:45–47, 68–70, Oct., Nov. 1924. illus.

1848 EBERLEIN, HAROLD DONALDSON, AND HUBBARD, CORTLANDT VAN DYKE. Historic houses of the Hudson Valley. N. Y., Architectural Book Publishing Co., 1942. 207p. illus.

1849 GOODWIN, MRS. MAUD WILDER. Dutch and English on the Hudson, a chronicle of Colonial New York. New Haven, Conn., Yale University Press, 1919. 243p. illus.
Other editions, 1920, 1921. *Chronicles of America* series, v. 7.

1850 REYNOLDS, HELEN WILKINSON. Dutch houses in the Hudson Valley before 1776. N. Y., Payson and Clarke, 1929. 467p. illus.
New edition: N. Y., Dover, 1965.

1851 [TURNER, A. A.] Villas on the Hudson. . . . N. Y., D. Appleton and Co., 1860. 3p. 52 illus.

1852 WHITTEMORE, HENRY. Homes on the Hudson; historical, descriptive. N. Y., Artotype Publishing Co. 1p. 43 illus.
Hitchcock suggests that this book probably appeared in London in 1858–59.

1853 WILSTACH, PAUL. Hudson River landings. Indianapolis, Ind., Bobbs-Merrill Co., 1933. 311p. illus.

Hurley (see *Ulster County*)

Irvington

1854 MAXWELL, PERRITON. Sunnyside, a home and a shrine. American Homes and Gardens, 5:396–99, Oct. 1908. illus.

1650 and *ca.* 1830–40. Home of Washington Irving.

1855 ROWELL, H. G. Interior architecture of Sunnyside. American Collector, 16:16–18ff., Oct. 1947. illus.

1856 VAUGHN, M. Donor of Sunnyside and its restoration. American Collector, 16:9ff., Oct. 1947. illus.

Ithaca

1857 [The Clinton house. Contemporary description.] Atkinson's Casket, 2:85–86, Feb. 1832.

Jefferson County

1858 DeKAY, CHARLES. Old houses of Jefferson County. Architectural Record, 20:103–15, Aug. 1906. illus.

Johnstown

1859 VROOMAN, JOHN J. The restoration of an historic house. New York History, 30:97–101, Jan. 1949.

Johnson Hall, 1762.

Katonah

1860 Second transformation of an eighteenth century residence. House and Garden, 59:99–101, Apr. 1931. illus.

Kingston (see *Ulster County*)

Lewis County

1861 ALLEN, KATHERINE. Old stone house of Lewis County, New York. D. A. R. Magazine, 57:663–74, Nov. 1923.

Built in late eighteenth century for Hezekiah M. Tallcott.

Livingston County

1862 ANDERSON, HOMER G. The four wooden covered bridges which at one time spanned the Genesee River in Livingston County, New York. Covered Bridge Topics, 14:5, Fall 1956; 4, 7, Jan. 1957. illus.

From 1803.

Long Island, including *Staten Island* (see also city names)

1863 ABBOTT, MABEL. The old Tollhouse at Rossville. Staten Island Institute of Arts and Sciences. Proceedings, 11:70–73, Apr. 1949. illus.

Erected on Staten Island by Richmond Plank Road Co., 1853. Still standing.

1864 BORSIG, TET. Long Island studies. Pencil Points, 22:267–74, Apr. 1941. illus.

1865 BROWN, EDNA A. East Marion Baptist Church. Long Island Forum, 19:82, 88, May 1956.

Southold town, 1810–1908.

1866 Conservation of a relic of Colonial days: house of E. N. Wicht, Douglaston, Long Island, N. Y. American Architect, 126:285–92, Sept. 1924. illus.

1867 CUSHING, CHARLES P. Ben Franklin answers Lord Howe. Mentor, 17:1–6, July 1929.

Conference house, Staten Island. Before 1700. Also known as Billopp house.

1868 DOUBLEDAY, RUSSELL. Long Island. N. Y., Doubleday, Doran and Co., 1939. 80p. illus.

1869 EBERLEIN, HAROLD DONALDSON. Manor houses and historic homes of Long Island and Staten Island. Philadelphia, J. B. Lippincott Co., 1928. 318p. illus.

1870 Eight old Long Island houses. American Institute of Architects. Journal, 12:110–17, Mar. 1924. illus. only.

1871 FANNING, RALPH. Some Post-Colonial remains on Long Island. American Architect, 110:367–71, Dec. 1916. illus.

1872 GIBBS, IRIS, AND BIGGS, ALONZO. Powell's purchase revisited. Long Island Forum, 16:63–66, 73, Apr. 1953. illus.

Includes Thomas Powell's house, 1700.

1873 GILLESPIE, HARRIET SISSON. Historic Dutch houses upon Staten Island. Country Life in America, 31:74–75, Apr. 1917. illus.

1874 GOTTESMAN, RITA S. Rock Hall. Antiques, 50:386–87, Dec. 1946. illus.

Ca. 1767, Nassau County.

1875 Historic Billopp house on Staten Island, now to be included in a new park. Americana, 10:961–67, Nov. 1915.

Before 1688. Reprints from the *News Letter*, March 14, 1903, and the *New York Times*, September 7, 1913. This *News Letter* is probably the one published at St. George, Staten Island.

1876 HORTON, H. P. The Commack Methodist Church. Long Island Forum, 20:47–48, Mar. 1957. illus.

1877 HUNTINGTON HISTORICAL SOCIETY. Long Island's domestic architecture: old churches, mills; special exhibition. . . . Huntington, N. Y., Huntington Historical Society, 1920. 8p. illus.

1878 ISHAM, NORMAN MORRISON. An example of Colonial panelling, Woodbury, Long Island. Metropolitan Museum of Art. Bulletin, 6:112–16, May 1911. illus.

1879 JACOBSEN, MRS. J. N. Voorlezer's house in Richmondtown, Staten Island, New York. Antiques, 54:175–77, Sept. 1948. illus.

Restoration of school and church building built ca. 1695.

1880 LOWEREE, HARRY W. Lighthouses of Nassau County. Long Island Forum, 14:3–4, 9, Jan. 1951. illus.

1806——.

1881 ——. The old Dodge homestead. Long Island Forum, 12:89, 93, May 1949. illus.

Constructed by Thomas Dodge in 1721.

1882 McMILLEN, LORING. Our vanishing landmarks. Staten Island Historian, 9:28–29, Oct.–Dec. 1948.

List of buildings constructed on Staten Island before 1809 that are still standing and another list of those destroyed.

1883 MACOSKEY, ARTHUR R. (ed.). Long Island gazetteer, a guide to historic places. Brooklyn, N. Y., Eagle Library, 1939. 144p. illus.

1884 MEIER, EVELYN ROWLEY. Grist mill at Wading River. Long Island Forum, 16:113–14, June 1953. illus.

1704–1900.

1885 MORAN, WILLIAM EDGAR. Settlements on the eastern end of Long Island. White Pine Series of Architectural Monographs, v. 5, no. 2, Apr. 1919. 14p. illus.

Covers 1660–1800.

1886 Past is not for burning; eighteenth century cottage near Montauk. House Beautiful, 99:143–47ff., May 1957. illus.

1887 PATTERSON, EDWARD D. Indian alliances and forts: lost to history? Nassau County Historical Journal, 18:17–27, Spring 1957.

Seventeenth century.

1888 SOLECKI, RALPH S. A seventeenth-century fireplace at Maspeth, Long Island. Washington Academy of Science. Journal, 38:324–29, Oct. 1948. illus.

1889 VAN ANDA, G. H. Old Long Island houses. American Institute of Architects. Journal, 9:161–68, May 1921; 11:355–63, Sept. 1923; 12:110–17, Feb. 1924. illus. only.

1890 WAILES, REX. Windmills of eastern Long Island. Newcomen Society. Transactions, 15:117–51, 1936.

Seventeenth to nineteenth centuries.

1891 WINSCHE, RICHARD A. Miller Mott, Patchogue pioneer. Long Island Forum, 20:45–46, Mar. 1957. illus.

A gristmill built by Charles Mott, *ca.* 1815, burned, 1931.

1892 WOOD, CLARENCE ASHTON. Suffolk's tiniest town. Long Island Forum, 11:147–48, 153, Aug. 1948. illus.

About Shelter Island, 1641–1743.

Ludlowville

1893 TALLMAN, CARL C. Doorway, Miller house at Ludlowville, New York. Architecture, v. 40, no. 2, pl. 128, 129, Aug. 1919. illus. only.

Mohawk Valley

1894 CROUSE, NELLIS M. Forts and block houses in the Mohawk Valley. New York State Historical Association. Proceedings, 14:75–90, 1915.

Colonial.

1895 FREY, S. L. An old Mohawk Valley house. Magazine of American History, 8:337–45, May 1882.

1896 [Mohawk Valley architecture issue.] House and Garden, v. 78, Aug. 1940. illus.

Includes Cazenovia and Syracuse.

Mount Vernon

1897 WINTJEN, JULIA TREACY. Along the road to Bedford and Vermont: a colonial highway through Mount Vernon. Mount Vernon, N. Y., Mount Vernon Public Library, 1949. 28p. illus.

1664———.

New Lebanon

1898 HOPPING, D. M. C., AND WATLAND, GERALD R. The architecture of the Shakers. Antiques, 72:335–39, Oct. 1957. illus.

1811–46 at New Lebanon, N. Y., and South Union and Pleasant Hill, Ky.

New Paltz (see *Ulster County*)

New York City — General References

1899 ANDREWS, WILLIAM LORING. New Amsterdam, New Orange, New York; a chronologically arranged account of engraved views of the city from the first picture published in 1651 until the year 1800. N. Y., Dodd, Mead and Co., 1897. 142p. illus.

1900 Architectural criticism of 1854. American Institute of Architects. Journal, 1:273–78, June 1944.

Excerpts from an unsigned article: "New York Daguerreotyped." *Putnam's Monthly Magazine*, Mar. 1854.

1901 [Architecture in New York.] Putnam's Monthly Magazine, 1:121–36, 353–68, 763–86; 2:1–16, 233–48; 3:10–15, 141–52, 233–48, 1853, 1854. illus.

Many types of buildings: Colonial, Classic Revival, and contemporary.

1902 BANK OF MANHATTAN COMPANY, NEW YORK. Historic buildings now standing in New York, which were erected prior to eighteen hundred. N. Y., Bank of Manhattan Co., 1914. 45p.

1903 BLUNT, EDMUND MARCH. Blunt's stranger's guide to the city of New York. N. Y., 1817. illus.

Description of public buildings, dwelling houses, etc. Variant editions by Andrew T. Goodrich in 1818 and 1825.

1904 BOLTON, REGINALD PELHAM. Bolton priory at Pelham Manor. Westchester County Historical Society. Bulletin, 6:54–58, July 1930.

1838.

1905 ———. Washington Heights, Manhattan; its eventful past. N. Y., Dyckman Institute, 1924. 366p. illus.

1906 Bourne's views in . . . New York. N. Y., 1831. 35 illus.

Public buildings, most of which have been destroyed.

1907 BROWN, HENRY COLLINS. Glimpses of old New York. N. Y., H. C. Brown, 1917. illus.

1908 BURNHAM, ALAN. The New York architecture of Richard Morris Hunt. Society of Architectural Historians. Journal, 11:9–14, May 1952. illus.

1856–95.

1909 ———. New York landmarks; a study and index of architecturally notable structures in Greater New York. Middletown, Conn., Wesleyan University Press, 1963. 430p. illus.

Published under the auspices of the Municipal Art Society of New York.

1910 Check list of engraved views of the city of New York in the New York Public Library. New York Public Library. Bulletin, 5:222–26, 1901.

1911 CITY HISTORY CLUB OF NEW YORK. Landmarks of New York; an historical guide to the metropolis. N. Y., City History Club of New York, 1923. 261p. illus.

Published in 1909 and 1913 under title, *Historical Guide to the City of New York.*

1912 DiMARIANO, JOHN. Some doorways of older New York. Architectural Record, 45:169–75, Feb. 1919. illus. only.

1913 ———. Some drawings of older New York. Architectural Record, 48:159–65, Aug. 1920. illus. only.

1914 DUNSHEE, KENNETH HOLCOMB. As you pass by. N. Y., Hastings House, 1952. 270p. illus.

Manhattan Island's streets and buidings, 1609———.

1915 FAY, THEODORE SEDGWICK. Views in New York and its environs. . . . N. Y., Peabody and Co., 1831. 58p. illus.

Drawings by A. J. Davis, J. H. Dakin, and others.

1916 FEDERAL WRITERS' PROJECT. New York City guide: a comprehensive guide to the five boroughs of the metropolis — Manhattan, Brooklyn, the Bronx, Queens and Richmond. N. Y., Random House, 1939. 708p. illus.

Historic houses indexed and illustrated.

1917 ———. New York panorama: a comprehensive view of the metropolis. N. Y., Random House, 1938. 526p. illus.

Some mention, but no illustrations of historic houses.

1918 FRANCIS, C. S. Francis; new guide to the cities of New York and Brooklyn, and the vicinity. N. Y., 1853. illus.

1919 GAMBARO, E. JAMES. Little old New York. American Institute of Architects. Journal, 17:100–108, Mar. 1952.

1920 GERARD, JAMES W. Old Dutch streets of New York, under the Dutch. N. Y., D. Taylor, 1874. 65p.

A paper read before the New York Historical Society, June 2, 1874.

1921 GLENROIE, ROBERT WILLIAM. Unknown views of old New York. New York Historical Society. Quarterly, 34:12–17, 124–33, Jan.–Apr. 1950. illus.

The William Burgis view of Fort George, *ca.* 1730–31; Joel H. Barlow's New York, in 1840's, 1850's, and 1860's.

1922 GOTTESMAN, RITA. Discarded heritage; New York architecture. Antiques, 33:248–49, May 1938. illus.

Ca. 1650.

1923 HADDON, RAWSON WOODMAN. Varick Street, which is in Greenwich Village, Manhattan, a narrative and some pen drawings. Architectural Record, 35:49–57, Jan. 1914. illus.

1924 HAMLIN, TALBOT FAULKNER. The rise of eclecticism in New York. Society of Architectural Historians. Journal, 11:3–8, Feb. 1952. illus.
1826–69.

1925 HUXTABLE, A. L. Preservation in New York. Architectural Review, 132:83–85, Aug. 1962. illus.

1926 JACKSON, HUSON. New York architecture, 1650–1952. N. Y., Reinhold Publishing Corp., 1952. 72p. illus.

1927 Jones and Newman's pictorial directory of New York, exhibiting a continued series of colored elevations, of all dwellings, stores and public buildings fronting on the principal streets. In 4 parts. N. Y., 1848. illus.

1928 KOUWENHOVEN, JOHN ATLEE. The Columbia historical portrait of New York: an essay in graphic history. Garden City, N. Y., Doubleday and Co., 1953. 550p. illus.
Pictorial and cartographic representations of New York City, 1614–1953.

1929 LAMB, MRS. MARTHA L. The golden age of Colonial New York. Magazine of American History, 24:1–30, July 1890. illus.

1930 ———. Historic houses and landmarks. Magazine of American History, 21:1–23, Jan.; 22:177–207, Mar. 1889. illus.

1931 LEVY, FLORENCE N. Art in New York: a guide to things worth seeing. N. Y., Municipal Art Society, 1935. 134p. illus.

1932 McMILLEN, LORING. Architectural traditions of New York. Antiques, 56:100–102, Aug. 1949. illus.
Ca. 1662–1830.

1933 MELICK, HARRY C. W. The first real estate development in the Bronx. New York Historical Society. Quarterly Bulletin, 32:33–39, Jan. 1948. illus.
On Fordham manor, 1668–71.

1934 MOTT, HOPPER STRIKER. The New York of yesterday. N. Y., G. P. Putnam's Sons, 1908. 597p. illus.

1935 MUNICIPAL ART SOCIETY OF NEW YORK. Index of architecturally historic structures in New York City. N. Y., 1957. 31 leaves.
1660–1930. Listed by boroughs, with architect, date, and style.

1936 MYER, JOHN. Gothic Revival in New York. Museum of the City of New York. Bulletin, 3:50–56, Apr. 1940. illus.

1937 New York Gothic. Pencil Points, v. 22, July 1940.
Exhibition at the Museum of the City of New York.

1938 Old buildings of New York City, with some notes regarding their origin and occupants. N. Y., Brentano and Co., 1907. 179p. illus.

1939 Old New York — 1940. House Beautiful, 82:26–29, June 1940. illus.

1940 [PASKO, W. W.] Index to engravings in Valentine's *Manual*. Old New York, 1:25, 105, 165, Aug. 1889.

1941 PETERSON, ARTHUR EVERETT. Thirty historic places in Greater New York. Published by the City History Club of New York in cooperation with the New York World's Fair, 1939. 68p. illus.

1942 RODGERS, CLEVELAND, AND RANKIN, REBECCA BROWNING. New York: the world's capital city, its development and contributions to progress. N. Y., Harper, 1948. 398p. illus.
1609–1948.

1943 Shifting New York scene. Antiques, 39:304–5, June 1941. illus.
Review of an exhibition at New York Historical Society, "New York as the artist knew it from 1626 to 1940."

1944 SIMITIERE, P. E. DU. Architectural lions of New York, 1767. Society of Architectural Historians. Journal, 11:21, May 1952. illus.
Architectural sculpture.

1945 Some suburbs of New York. Lippincott's Magazine, 8:9–23, 113–25, July–Aug. 1884. illus.
New Jersey, Westchester, and Long Island.

1946 STEVENS, JOHN AUSTIN, JR. Colonial New York. N. Y., J. F. Trow and Co., 1867. 172p.
Covers 1768–84.

1947 STOKES, ISAAC NEWTON PHELPS. Iconography of Manhattan Island. N. Y., R. H. Dodd, 1915–28. 6v. illus.
Covers 1489–1909. Compiled from original sources and illustrated by photo-intaglio reproductions of important maps, plans, views, and documents in various collections.

1948 ———. New York past and present, its history and landmarks 1524–1939; one hundred views reproduced and described from old prints, etc., and modern photographs. . . . N. Y., Plantin Press, 1939. 96p. illus.

1949 The tercentenary of the city of New York and our neighborhood. N. Y., St. Mark's Church in-the-Bouwerie, 1953. 24p. illus.
Landmarks and historic buildings of the Lower East Side, 1653———.

1950 VAIL, R. W. G. Unknown views of old New York; purchase of Manhattan Island, 1626. New York Historical Society. Quarterly, 39:380–84, Oct. 1956. illus.

1951 WALLACE, W. H. Views and prints of old New York . . . 1633–1878. Journal of American History, 17:149–68, 1923.

1952 WALLIS, F. A. New Amsterdam and its hinterland. Architectural Forum, 50:473–81, Apr. 1929. illus.

New York City — Domestic

1953 ADAMS, H. M. Old New York in the new. Good Housekeeping, 74:26–27, Mar. 1922.
Covers Dyckman house, Poole house, and others.

1954 BERTON, G. Hamilton Grange today. Mentor, 17:36–37, July 1939. illus.
1802. John McComb, architect.

1955 BOLTON, REGINALD PELHAM. Washington's headquarters. New York. A sketch of the history of the Morris mansion (or Jumel mansion) in the city of New York, used by Washington as his headquarters in 1776. New York, American Scenic and Historic Preservation Society, 1903. 40p. illus.

1956 [Crystal Palace, New York World's Fair, 1853. Drawings of this and other buildings for the same fair, proposed but not executed.] American Architect, 147:33, Oct. 1935. illus.

1957 DEAN, BASHFORD, AND WELCH, ALEXANDER MCMILLAN. The Dyckman house. American Scenic and Historic Preservation Society. Reports, 22:459–84, 1917.

1958 ———. Dyckman house, built about 1783, restored and presented to the city of New York in 1916. N. Y., The Gillis Press, 1916. 47p. illus.

1959 DECKER, H. K. Saving the Audubon home. Bird Lore, 34:100–102, Jan. 1932.
Minnie's Land, occupied by Audubon in 1852.

1960 DITMAS, CHARLES ANDREWS. Historic homesteads of Kings County. Brooklyn, N. Y., The Author, 1909. 120p. illus.

1961 [Dutch houses. Contemporary descriptions.] New York Mirror, 10:241–43, Feb. 2, 1833; 12:153, Nov. 15, 1834.

1962 ELDREDGE, ALICE. The old Jumel mansion. Americana, 4:986–90, Dec. 1909.

1963 EMBURY, AYMAR, II. Farmhouses of New Netherlands. White Pine Series of Architectural Monographs, v. 1, no. 3, Dec. 1915. 14p. illus.
Covers 1656–1825.

1964 [E. W. King house. Contemporary description.] Atkinson's Casket, 10:457, Oct. 1831.
At Rodman's Neck, Pelham.

1965 FOWLER, LEMUEL HOADLEY. Some forgotten farmhouses on Manhattan Island. White Pine Series of Architectural Monographs, v. 9, no. 1, Feb. 1923. 14p. illus.
Covers Jumel and Dyckman houses.

1966 FRASER, GEORGIA. The stone house at Gowanus, scene of the battle of Long Island; Stirling's headquarters, Cornwallis' redoubt, occupied by Washington; Colonial residence of Dutch architecture; built by Nicholas Vechte, 1699. N. Y., Witter and Kintner, 1909. 161p. illus.
In Prospect Park, Brooklyn.

1967 HADDON, RAWSON WOODMAN. Roger Morris house, or Jumel mansion. New York City — in two parts. Architectural Record, part 1, 42:47–62, July 1917; part 2, 42:127–39, Aug. 1917. illus.
(Ca. 1765).

1968 HOLLISTER, P. My pilgrimage to the Jumel mansion. Country Life in America, 42:58–60, Oct. 1922. illus.

1969 Jumel mansion. Literary Digest, 115:27–28, Apr. 29, 1933. illus.

1970 LANDY, J. Domestic architecture of the robber barons in New York City. Marsyas, 5:63–85, 1947–49. illus.

1971 McCLELLAND, NANCY V. The historic Morris-Jumel mansion. American Society Legion of Honor Magazine, 19:61–72, Spring 1948.

"Mount Morris" built by Roger Morris on Washington Heights beside the Hudson, 1765. Later acquired by Stephen Jumel in 1810.

1972 MILLER, AGNES. The Macomb house: presidential mansion. Michigan History, 37:373–84, Dec. 1953.

Built by Alexander Macomb, 1787, used as Washington's residence in 1790 and torn down 1848–51.

1973 MOSES, LIONEL. Some houses of old New York. Art World, 3:437–39, Feb. 1918. illus.

1974 PELLETREAU, WILLIAM S. Early New York houses. N. Y., Francis P. Harper, 1900. 243p. illus.

1975 ———. Historic homes and institutions and genealogical and family history of New York. N. Y., Lewis Publishing Co., 1907. 4v. illus.

1976 PINTARD, MRS. The Walton mansion house, Pearl St. . . . New York Mirror, 9:289, Mar. 17, 1832. illus.

1977 PUMPELLY, JOSIAH COLLINS. The old Morris house, afterwards the Jumel mansion; its history and traditions. New York Genealogical and Biographical Society. Publications, 34:80–89, Apr. 1903.

1978 ———. Washington headquarters. Americana, 6:351–60, Apr. 1911.

Morris-Jumel house.

1979 ROSS, WILLIAM. Street houses of the city of New York. Architectural Record, 9:53–56, 1899.

Written in 1834.

1980 SHELTON, WILLIAM HENRY. The Jumel mansion. Art World, 2:245–50, June 1917. illus.

1981 ———. The Jumel mansion, being a full history of the house on Harlem Heights, built by Roger Morris before the Revolution. Boston, Houghton Mifflin Co., 1916. 257p. illus.

1982 ———. Wall paper in the Jumel mansion. Architectural Record, 43:189–90, Feb. 1918. illus.

1983 STAPLEY, MILDRED. The last Dutch farmhouses in New York City. Architectural Record, 32:22–36, July 1912. illus.

1984 STOCKTON, HELEN HAMILTON. Motoring to three manors. Americana, 16:335–46, Oct. 1922.

Covers Claverack house, Oak Hill, and the Van Cortland house.

1985 STODOLA, GILBERT I. Electric lighting of an old Colonial house: Jane Teller mansion. House Beautiful, 51:309–11, 356, Apr. 1922.

1986 [Stuyvesant mansion. Contemporary description.] New York Mirror, 9:201, Dec. 31, 1831. illus.

1987 [Washington's residence, Cherry Street. Contemporary description.] New Pictorial Family Magazine, 2:69–72, 1845.

1988 WHITE, RICHARD GRANT. Old New York and its houses. Century Magazine, 26:845–54, Oct. 1883.

New York City — Public

1989 ALLEN, ISABEL HOPKINS. New York's City Hall. Antiques Journal, 9:8–9, 37, Sept. 1954. illus.

1812.

1990 ANDREWS, WILLIAM LORING. The iconography of the Battery and Castle Garden. N. Y., Charles Scribner's Sons, 1901. 43p. illus.

1991 [Astor house. Contemporary description.] American Magazine of Knowledge, 2:260, Feb. 1836.

1834–39. Isaiah Rogers, architect. Also known as Park Hotel.

1992 BAYLES, WILLIAM HARRISON. Old taverns of New York. Journal of American History, 18:19–30, 115–30, 211–29, 317–22, 1924; 23:113–34, 153–97, 217–45, 1929; 24:150–67, 220–47, 1930; 25:117–35, 205–27, 1931; 27:83–99, 187–201, 1933.

1993 ———. Old taverns of New York. N. Y., Frank Allaben Genealogical Co., 1915. 489p. illus.

Dutch taverns, the Coffee House, the Black Horse, Merchant's Coffee House, tavern signs, the King's Arms, Hampden Hall, the Province Arms, Fraunces' Tavern, the Tontine Coffee House, the City Hotel, the Shakespeare Tavern, road houses.

1994 Bill for the Croton Reservoir. New York Public Library. Bulletin, 31:155–58, Mar. 1927.

The Egyptian reservoir that stood on the site of the present library building, erected 1838–42. James Renwick, architect. Description of the Croton aqueduct: *New Yorker*, 10:9, Sept. 19, 1840.

1995 [Bowery Theatre. Contemporary description.] Atkinson's Casket, 6:265, June 1829.

1996 [Custom House. Contemporary descriptions.] Atkinson's Casket, 1:12, Jan. 1831. Monthly Chronicle, 3:320–26, July 1842. New World, 1:270, Sept. 26, 1840. Niles' Weekly Register, 46:385, Aug. 2, 1834.

Also known as the Sub-treasury. 1834–41. Ithiel Town and Alexander J. Davis, architects.

1997 DEPEYSTER, FREDERIC. History of the Tontine building, founded 1792, demolished in May, 1855. N. Y., 1855. illus.

Reprinted from Valentine's *Manual* for 1852, with additions.

1998 DROWNE, HENRY RUSSELL. A sketch of Fraunces' Tavern and those connected with its history. N. Y., Sons of the Revolution in the State of New York, 1949. 35p. illus.

1719. First edition, 1919, 23p.

1999 [Federal Hall. Contemporary description.] Columbia Magazine, 3:473, Aug. 1789.

2000 [Holt's Hotel. Contemporary description.] Atkinson's Casket, 8:361, Aug. 1833. illus.

2001 KENNION, JOHN W. Architects' and builders' guide. N. Y., Fitzpatrick and Hunter, 1868. 108p. illus.

Subtitle: "An elaborate description of all the public, commercial, philanthropic, literary and ecclesiastical buildings already constructed, and about to be erected next spring in New York and its environs, with their cost respectively, and the names of the architects and builders."

2002 LEWIS, STANLEY T. The New York theater: its background and architectural development: 1750–1853. Doctoral Dissertation, Ohio State University, 1954. 2v. 599p.

Discusses background to theater's architectural trends, relationships to other contemporary buildings. Many of theaters discussed no longer extant.

2003 McQUADE, WALTER. Measured drawings of New York City Hall. Architecture, v. 35–36, Jan.–July 1917. illus. only.

2004 [Masonic Hall. Contemporary descriptions.] American Magazine of Knowledge, 1:109–10, Nov. 1834. Ladies Companion, 6:255, Apr. 1837.

Gothic, 1825.

2005 MAY, CHARLES C. The New York City Hall — in three parts. Architectural Record, part 1, 39:299–319, Apr. 1916; part 2, 39:474–90, May 1916; part 3, 39:513–35, June 1916. illus.

Completed 1811. Joseph F. Mangin and John McComb, Jr., architects.

2006 [Merchants' Exchange. Contemporary descriptions.] American Penny Magazine, 1:536, Sept. 27, 1845. Atkinson's Casket, 1:12, Jan. 1831. Broadway Journal, 1:76, Feb. 1, 1845. Ladies' Companion, 6:255, Apr. 1837. New Yorker, 4:734, Feb. 1838.

First Merchants' Exchange completed May, 1827, burned 1835. Some of these references are critical as well as descriptive and include discussions of other buildings.

2007 MOTT, HOPPER STRIKER. Cato's Tavern. Americana, 11:123–31, Apr. 1916.

Located on Boston Post Road about four miles north of the City Hall.

2008 ———. Dyde's taverns. . . . Americana, 11:416–26, Oct. 1916.

2009 ———. The windmills of Manhattan; the story of the original industry on this island. Americana, 9:551–67, July 1914.

2010 NEW YORK HISTORICAL SOCIETY. Report on the preservation of the aquarium (Castle Garden) by a committee of the Society's trustees. New York Historical Society. Quarterly Bulletin, 25:48–50, Apr. 1941. illus.

Before 1812. Destroyed 1941.

2011 Original plans of the City Hall, New York. American Architect, 23:43–46, Feb. 5, 1908. illus.

Drawn in 1802. John McComb, Jr., architect.

2012 PIERCE, MRS. MELUSINA FAY. Landmark of Fraunces' Tavern. N. Y., American Scenic and Historic Preservation Society, 1901. 44p. illus.

2013 PLACZEK, ADOLF. Design for Columbia College, 1813. Society of Architectural Historians. Journal, 11:22–23, May 1952. illus.

By James Renwick, Sr.

2014 [Public buildings. Contemporary description.] New York Mirror, 7:89–90, Sept. 26, 1829. illus.

2015 Ross, WILLIAM. Descriptive account of the improvements lately made at the Custom House, New York. Architectural Record, 9:57–64, 1899. illus.

The Sub-treasury, Wall Street. Written in 1835.

2016 RUDY, SOLOMON WILLIS. The College of the City of New York: a history, 1847–1947. N. Y., City College Press, 1949. 492p. illus.

Master's Thesis, Columbia University.

2017 SCHUYLER, MONTGOMERY. The architecture of American colleges. Part 4. New York City colleges. Architectural Record, 27:443–69, June 1910. illus.

2018 ———. The New York City Hall. Architectural Record, 23:387–90, May 1908. illus.

2019 ———. The restoration of Fraunces' Tavern. Architectural Record, 24:444–48, Dec. 1908. illus.

2020 STURGES, W. K. Cast iron in New York. Architectural Review, 114:232–37, Oct. 1953. illus.

2021 [United States Branch Bank. Contemporary description.] Atkinson's Casket, 1:12, Jan. 1831. illus.

1822–24. Also known as the Assay Office. Façade moved from 15 Wall Street to the American Wing of the Metropolitan Museum of Art. Martin Thompson, architect.

2022 VAN DERPOOL, JAMES GROTE. A restoration problem at Hamilton Grange. Columbia Library Columns, 4:11–23, Feb. 1955. illus.

Built 1801–2 by John McComb.

2023 WHITING, M. A. Federal Hall. Stone and Webster. Journal, 48:454–60, 1931.

Covers 1699–1813.

2024 WILDE, EDWARD SEYMOUR. New York City Hall. Century, 27:865–72, Apr. 1884. illus.

Issued as a reprint, 1893.

New York City — Religious

2025 ALLEN, ISABEL HOPKINS. St. Paul's Chapel. Antiques Journal, 10:14–15, 38, Jan. 1955. illus.

Episcopal, 1766.

2026 [B. W.] New York and Brooklyn churches. . . . [N. Y.?], Nelson and Phillips, 1874. 128p. illus.

2027 BRUMBAUGH, C. E. B. Some New York churches during the Revolution. American Monthly Magazine, 40:1–6, Jan. 1912.

2028 CHORLEY, EDWARD CLOWES (ed.). Quarter of a millennium: Trinity Church in the city of New York, 1697–1947. Philadelphia, Church Historical Society, 1948. 162p. illus.

2029 CLARKE, NELL RAY. Old Trinity, New York. Landmark, 6:37–40, Jan. 1924.
Completed 1846. Richard Upjohn, architect.

2030 DISOSWAY, GABRIEL POILLON. Earliest churches of New York and its vicinity.
N. Y., J. G. Gregory, 1865. 416p. illus.

2031 EDELBLUTE, LUCIUS AARON. The history of the Church of the Holy Apostles,
1844–1944. N. Y., 1949. 280p. illus.
Protestant Episcopal church in Manhattan (former village of Chelsea).

2032 HADDON, RAWSON WOODMAN. St. John's Chapel, Varick Street, New York
City. Architectural Record, 35:389–403, May 1914. illus.
1807. John McComb, architect.

2033 HALL, EDWARD HAGAMAN. The First Presbyterian Church of New York.
American Scenic and Historic Preservation Society. Reports, 22:567–667,
1917.

2034 HERTEL, FREDRIKA W. A guide to historic St. Mark's Church in-the-Bouwerie.
N. Y., 1949. 19p. illus.
1660——.

2035 NEW YORK. TRINITY CHURCH. A guide book to Trinity Church and the parish
of Trinity Church in the city of New York, founded 1697. N. Y., 1950. 59p.
illus.
First edition, 1944.

2036 [St. George's Church, Stuyvesant Square.] Literary World, 3:853–54, Nov. 25,
1848.
1847.

2037 [St. John's Chapel. Contemporary description.] Christian Journal and Literary
Register, 11:145–47, May 1827.

2038 St. John's Chapel, New York. Architectural Record, 27:125–26, Jan. 1910.
illus.

2039 [St. Thomas' Church. Contemporary descriptions.] American Penny Maga-
zine, 2:600, Oct. 24, 1846. Monthly Repository and Library of Entertaining
Knowledge, 4:357–58, Mar. 1834.
Early structure destroyed 1905.

2040 SCHUYLER, MONTGOMERY. Trinity's architecture. Architectural Record,
25:411–25, June 1909. illus.
Includes other New York churches.

2041 STEWART, WILLIAM RHINELANDER. Grace Church and old New York. N. Y.,
E. P. Dutton and Co., 1924. 542p. illus.
1846. James Renwick, architect.

2042 TEALL, GARDNER. An antiquarian shrine: St. Mark's-in-the-Bouwerie. Antiques
Journal, 4:11–12, Oct. 1949. illus.
Consecrated 1799.

2043 WINGATE, CHARLES F. Saint Paul's Chapel in New York City. American Scenic and Historic Preservation Society. Reports, 22:435–58, 1917.
Begun 1764. James McBean, architect.

Newburgh

2044 BARCK, D. C. First historic house museum: Washington's Newburgh head-quarters, 1750, 1850. Society of Architectural Historians. Journal, 14:30–32, May 1955. illus.

2045 BARCLAY, DAVID. Old houses and historic places in the vicinity of Newburgh, N. Y. Newburgh, N. Y., Journal Print, 1909. 211p. illus.
Newburgh Bay and the Highlands Historical Society, Publication 15.

2046 CORNING, AMOS ELWOOD. The story of the Hasbrouck house, Washington's headquarters, Newburgh, New York. [Board of Trustees, State of New York, of Washington's Headquarters], 1950. 68p. illus.
1750. Jonathan Hasbrouck, architect.

2047 WEED, RAPHAEL A. Some Newburgh doorways and their owners. Newburgh Historical Society. Publication 26. 11p.

Onondaga County

2048 SYRACUSE UNIVERSITY. SCHOOL OF ARCHITECTURE. Architecture worth saving in Onondaga County. Syracuse, N. Y., Syracuse University Press, 1964.

Orange County

2049 MOFFATT, ALMET S. Old churches of Orange County, New York. Washington-ville, N. Y., 1927. 32p.

2050 SEESE, MILDRED N. Master builders of Middletown, 1856–1956. [Goshen, N. Y., The Bookmill, 1957.] 269p. illus.

2051 ———. Old Orange houses. Middletown, N. Y., The Whitlock Press, 1941. 2v. illus.

Orleans County

2052 COLE, MARC W. A master builder of the early nineteenth century. Country Life in America, 29:22–23, Feb. 1916.
On Cyrus Wetherill. Active in Orleans County, N. Y., 1814–35.

Oswego

2053 WATERBURY, EDWIN M. Old Fort Ontario now New York State historic site. Sons of the American Revolution. Magazine, 46:16–20, July 1951. illus.
Oswego, 1755–56.

Oyster Bay

2054 CARRICK, ALICE VAN LEER. Historic Raynham Hall. Country Life in America, 48:68–70, June 1925. illus.
1740.

2055 HORTON, H. P. Raynham Hall in Oyster Bay. Long Island Forum, 14:63, 75, Apr. 1951. illus.
1740.

2056 IRVIN, FRANCES. Historic Oyster Bay. Oyster Bay, L. I., 1953. 24p. illus.
First edition, 1926. Deals particularly with Raynham Hall, 1740.

Owego

2057 TROWBRIDGE, ALEXANDER B. Greek Revival in Owego and nearby New York towns, some suggested antidotes. White Pine Series of Architectural Monographs, v. 7, no. 3, June 1921. 16p. illus.

Pawling

2058 STEARNS, AMANDA AKIN. Ancient homes and early days of Quaker Hill. Quaker Hill, N. Y., Akin Hall Association, 1913. 44p. illus.

Peekskill

2059 Boscobel, restoration. Interior Design, 34:126–31, May 1963. illus.

2060 COMSTOCK, HELEN. Boscobel, a Hudson River country house built in 1805. Connoisseur, 152:2–9, Jan. 1963. illus.

2061 LANCASTER, CLAY. Save Boscobel! Antiques, 49:244–45, Apr. 1946. illus.
1790's.

2062 MATHIEU, JOSEPH. Boscobel restoration. American Institute of Architects. Journal, 36:29–34, July 1961.
1804.

Poughkeepsie

2063 VER NOOY, AMY; VAN WYCK, EDMUND; AND MYLOD, FRANK V. The Glebe house and the people who lived there. Dutchess County Historical Society. Year Book, 38:58–73, 1955.
1767.

Rensselaer County

2064 FOERSTER, BERND. Architecture worth saving in Rensselaer County, New York. Troy, N. Y., Rensselaer Polytechnic Institute, 1965. 207p. illus.

2065 KELLER, WILLIAM A. Rensselaerville, an old village of the Helderbergs. White Pine Series of Architectural Monographs, v. 10, no. 4, 1924. 16p. illus.
Early nineteenth century.

Rhinebeck

2066 PAULMIER, HILAH. The oldest hotel in America. D. A. R. Magazine, 52:91–92, Feb. 1918.

2067 STRONG, MRS. JACOB H. The old stone church. Dutchess County Historical Society. Year Book, 40:29–31, 1957.
Church of St. Peter the Apostle, Lutheran, Rhinebeck, N. Y., founded 1729.

Rochester

2068 FAIRCHILD, HERMAN LEROY, AND WARNER, J. FOSTER. Building stones of Rochester; nature's contribution to local edifices. Rochester Historical Society. Publication, 12:131–56, 1933.

2069 FEDERAL WRITERS' PROJECT. Rochester and Monroe County. Rochester, N. Y., Scrantom's Publishers, 1937. 440p. illus.

2070 FOREMAN, EDWARD H. First families of Rochester and their dwellings. Rochester Historical Society. Publication Fund Series, 4:353–56, 1925.

2071 HERSEY, CARL K. The architecture of Woodside. Scrapbook, 1:3–5, 4–7, 1950. illus.

By Albert Badger for Silas O. Smith, 1838–40. Now headquarters of the Rochester Historical Society.

2072 LEE, FLORENCE. The old stone lighthouse at Charlotte. Museum Service, 30:42–43, Mar. 1957. illus.

Erected at mouth of the Genesee River, 1822.

2073 McKELVEY, BLAKE. Old and new landmarks and historic houses. Rochester, N. Y., Rochester Public Library, 1950. 24p. illus. Also: Rochester History, v. 12, nos. 2, 3, Apr. 1950.

2074 RECORD, DON C. The old Rochester Savings Bank Building: seed bed of culture. Genesee Country Scrapbook, 6:8–10, 12, 1955.

Built 1857, demolished 1955.

2075 SCHMIDT, CARL FREDERICK. Greek Revival architecture in the Rochester area. Scottsville, N. Y., 1946. illus.

2076 ———. Jonathan Child and his house. Rochester, N. Y., 1962. 43 leaves. illus.

1837.

2077 SCHMIDT, CARL FREDERICK, AND SCHMIDT, ANN. Architecture and architects of Rochester, N. Y. Rochester, Rochester Society of Architects, 1959. 188p. illus.

2078 SCHOLD, JOAN LYNN. Campbell-Whittlesey house in Rochester, New York. Antiques, 49:366–68, June 1946. illus.

1835–36.

Rockland County

2079 BLAUVELT, GEORGE A. Suffern's tavern. New York State Historical Association. Journal, 6:136–40, Apr. 1925.

2080 GILLESPIE, HARRIET SISSON. A typical old Dutch farmhouse. American Homes and Gardens, 12:76–80, Mar. 1915. illus.

1758.

Rome

2081 GRAVES, HAROLD F. Black River Canal. North Country Life, 2:16–19, Summer 1948. illus.

Canal from Lyons Falls to Rome, N. Y., 1838–1922.

Rosendale (see *Ulster County*)

Roslyn

2082 GERRY, PEGGY NEWBAUER, AND GERRY, ROGER. Old Roslyn. [Roslyn, N. Y.], Bryant Library, 1954. 40p. illus.

1685—*ca.* 1873.

Rutgers

2083 BOGARDUS, DONALD FRED. This house with glory: a history of Rutgers Presbyterian Church. N. Y., Rutgers Presbyterian Church, 1948. 62p. illus.

1798.

Rye

2084 HALBERT, WILLIAM CARTER. The Jay estate. Westchester Historian, 31:98–103, Oct. 1955. illus.

Built by Peter Jay (1704–82) in 1745, torn down 1836–38; new house built by John Jay.

2085 McKAY, ELLEN COTTON. A history of the Rye Presbyterian Church. Rye, N. Y., Presbyterian Church, [1957]. 260p. illus.

1660——.

2086 SEACORD, MORGAN H. The square house. Westchester Historian, 31:44–48, 81–84, 110–13, Apr. 1955; 32:14–15, 50–52, Spring 1956. illus.

Before 1754.

Sackett's Harbor

2087 BRAGDON, CLAUDE FAYETTE. Colonial work in Sackett's Harbor. American Architect and Building News, 34:9–10, Oct. 1891. illus.

2088 DeKAY, CHARLES. Old houses in Jefferson County. Architectural Record, 20:103–15, Aug. 1916. illus.

Early Republican.

Sag Harbor

2089 WILLEY, NANCY BOYD. Built by whalers: a tour of historic Sag Harbor and its Colonial architecture. Sag Harbor, N. Y., Old Sag-Harbor Committee, 1948. 31p. illus.

First edition, 1945.

Saratoga

2090 SNELL, CHARLES W. Saratoga, National Historical Park, New York. Washington, D. C., 1950. 36p. illus.

National Park Service. Historical Handbook Series, no. 4.

Saugerties

2091 RONY, LILA RUSSELL JAMES. Echoes of two centuries, Saugerties: a quaint village of yesterday. House Beautiful, 52:332–33, 380, 382, Oct. 1922. illus.

Scarsdale

2092 CARPENTER, RALPH E., JR. Mowbra Hall — an "eighteenth-century" dwelling house; rooms assembled from demolished eighteenth-century residences. Antiques, 61:438–41, May 1952. illus.

Reconstructed 1950–51.

2093 GILLESPIE, HARRIET SISSON. Wayside, an old homestead in Scarsdale, New York — *ca.* 1725. House Beautiful, 54:144–45, 186, Aug. 1923. illus.

2094 The Powdermill House, Scarsdale. Westchester County Historical Bulletin, 24:74–76, July 1948.

House with adjacent powdermill, about 1784.

2095 SMITH, FRANK MACGREGOR. Wayside — the new and the old. Westchester County Historical Society. Quarterly Bulletin, 30:49–55, Apr. 1954. illus.
Scarsdale, *ca.* 1729.

Schenectady

2096 ALLEN, RICHARD SANDERS. The Schenectady Scotia Bridge. Covered Bridge Topics, 6:4–5, Dec. 1948.
Toll bridge built by Theodore Burr, 1808–73.

2097 Historic house regains its youth; Governor Yates house, Schenectady, New York. House and Garden, 65:55–57, May 1934. illus.

2098 HUNGERFORD, EDWARD. Gentleman of the North; Constable Hall in the Black River Valley country. House Beautiful, 63:757, 800–802, June 1928.
1819.

2099 LARRABEE, H. A. Joseph Jacques Ramée and America's first unified college plan. N. Y., [American Society of the French Legion of Honor], 1934. 7p. illus.
Franco-American Pamphlet Series, no. 1. Union College.

2100 MOHR, WILLIAM D. The story of the Mohawk Bridge. Covered Bridge Topics, 14:1, 6, Fall 1956; 14:5–6, Jan. 1957. illus.
Spanned the Mohawk, 1808–74.

2101 TUNNARD, CHRISTOPHER. Minerva's Union. Architectural Review, 101:57–62, Jan. 1947. illus.
Union College, 1818, by Joseph Jacques Ramée.

2102 VAN DER BOGERT, G. Y. Stockade story. American Institute of Architects. Journal, 40:42–48, Oct. 1963. illus.
Restoration project.

Schoharie County

2103 MATTICE, PAUL B. Old grist mills along the Schoharie. Schoharie County, N. Y., Historical Review, 12:3–9, May 1949. illus.
1713–1930.

2104 SHAFER, DON CAMERON. The Schoharie forts. County Historical Review, 14:3–13, May 1950. illus.
Upper Fort, Middle Fort, and Lower Fort, 1777–1950.

Schuylerville

2105 COREY, ALBERT B. The story behind the Schuyler mansion. American Heritage, n.s. 1:46–51, Winter 1950. illus.
By Philip Schuyler, 1767.

Scotia

2106 BUTTON, H. V. Glen-Sanders house at Scotia, New York. House Beautiful, 48:24–25, July 1920. illus.

2107 SHAFER, DON CAMERON. A treasure house of Colonial days. American Homes and Gardens, 11:123–25, Apr. 1914. illus.
Glen-Sanders near Schenectady (1713–66).

Sennett

2108 TALLMAN, CARL C. Doorway, Soule house, Sennett, New York. Architecture, v. 39, no. 4, pl. 62, Apr. 1919. illus. only.

Skaneateles

2109 TALLMAN, CARL C. Doorway, Barber house, Skaneateles, New York. Architecture, v. 40, no. 2, pl. 130, Aug. 1919. illus. only.

2110 ———. Measured drawings of the Austin house, Skaneateles, New York. Architecture, v. 39, no. 4, Apr. 1919. illus. only.

Staten Island (see *Long Island*)

Syracuse

2111 McKEE, HARLEY JAMES. Greek Revival weighlock, Syracuse, 1849–1850. Society of Architectural Historians. Journal, 19:172–73, Dec. 1960. illus.

Tappan

2112 BLAUVELT, H. The old stone house where Major Andre was imprisoned. Mentor, 16:33–35, Feb. 1928. illus.
1755.

Tarrytown

2113 BACON, EDGAR MAYHEW. Country homes of famous Americans. Part 1. Washington Irving. Country Life in America, 4:406–10. illus.

2114 CONKLIN, MARGARET SWANCOTT. Historical Tarrytown and North Tarrytown (a guide). [Tarrytown, N. Y., Tarrytown Historical Society, 1939.] 58p. illus.

2115 Historical piece hunted; Philipse Castle to be restored. Library Journal, 65:497, June 1, 1940.
1638.

2116 LANCASTER, CLAY. Architecture of Sunnyside. American Collector, 16:13–15, Oct. 1947. illus.

2117 ORMSBEE, T. H. Glory of an old Dutch home in America: Philipse Castle. American Collector, 13:7–9ff., May 1944. illus.

2118 ———. Historic Philipse house at Tarrytown restored. American Collector, 12:5ff., June 1943.

2119 PAGE, MARIAN. Historic restorations: three eras of Lyndhurst. Interiors, 125:104–11ff., Sept. 1965. illus.
Built 1840 by Alexander Jackson Davis.

2120 RABSON, BARRIE. Irving's Sunnyside. New York Folklore Quarterly, 7:205–16, Autumn 1951.
Ca. 1656.

Ticonderoga

2121 BOSSOM, ALFRED C. The restoration of Fort Ticonderoga. American Scenic and Historic Preservation Society. Reports, 18:610–18, 1923.

2122 DOWLING, R. L. Fort Ticonderoga. Antiques, 50:26–28, July 1946. illus.
Originally Fort Carillon, 1755.

2123 TOWER, ELIZABETH A. John Hancock house. Ticonderoga, N. Y., New York State Historical Association, 1926. illus.

Replica of the original Hancock house on Beacon Hill, Boston, Mass.

Troy

2124 ALLEN, RICHARD SANDERS. The Troy–Green Island bridge. Covered Bridge Topics, 6:4–5, Mar. 1948.

Railroad bridges, 1835–84.

2125 [St. Paul's Church. Contemporary description.] Monthly Repository and Library of Entertaining Knowledge, 2:49–50, July 1831.

2126 SHAFER, CARL SHURZ. A landmark on the Hudson. American Homes and Gardens, 12:15, Jan. 1915. illus.

Lansing house, 1771.

Tuckahoe

2127 KILLEFFER, DAVID HERBERT. The first 150 years of St. John's Church, 1798–1948. Tuckahoe, N. Y., St. John's Church, 1948. 63p. illus.

Lutheran.

2128 St. John's Church — Tuckahoe. From notes furnished by Leroy Lockwood. Westchester County Historical Bulletin, 24:124–28, Oct. 1948. illus.

In Yonkers suburb. 1798.

Ulster County

2129 ALLEN, RICHARD SANDERS. Covered bridges of Ulster County, New York. Covered Bridge Topics, 13:1, 4–6, Summer 1955. illus.

1836.

2130 ———. Covered bridges of Ulster County, New York. Ulster County Historical Society. Proceedings for 1947–53, pp. 17–23.

Account of thirty-five bridges, 1836———, of which five survive.

2131 EBERLEIN, HAROLD DONALDSON. Hurley Town, a New Netherland suburb. American Suburbs, pp. 264–67, May 1911. illus.

2132 GILLESPIE, HARRIET SISSON. Early Dutch architecture in the Hudson Valley; Brykill manor near Kingston. Arts and Decoration, 35:28–29, June 1931. illus.

1736 and later.

2133 HAASBROUCK, G. B. D. Old stone houses of Esopus. Ulster County Historical Society. Proceedings for 1934–35, pp. 15–28, 1935.

2134 The Hardenbergh house at Rosendale. Olde Ulster, 5:51–54, Feb. 1909.

2135 HASTINGS, HELEN M. Old stone houses of Esopus. Architectural Record, 49:91–95, Jan. 1921. illus.

2136 HEIDGERD, WILLIAM. The Ezekiel Elting brick house, New Paltz, New York. Ulster County Historical Society. Proceedings for 1947–53, pp. 67–69.

1800———.

2137 KEEFE, CHARLES S. Development of the American doorway. American Architect, 113:818–23, June 19, 1918. illus.

Examples from Kingston.

2138 KING, DOROTHY. Dutch Colonial houses in Kingston, New York. House Beautiful, 47:36–37, Jan. 1920. illus.

2139 LeGALLIENNE, RICHARD. Old Kingston. Harper's Magazine, 23:917–26, Nov. 1911. illus.

2140 MacKENSIE, ALAN. Old stone houses of Rosendale. Ulster County Historical Society. Proceedings for 1930–31, pp. 30–37, 1931.
Particularly Jacob Rutsen house.

2141 MILLAR, DONALD. Quaint Dutch survival, Jean Hasbrouck house, New Paltz, New York. Architectural Record, 59:229–32, Mar. 1926. illus.
Near Poughkeepsie, 1712.

2142 NASH, GEORGE W. The old stone church at Hurley. Olde Ulster, 8:171–79, June 1912.

2143 ———. The old stone school house at Hurley. Olde Ulster, 8:198–204, July 1912.

2144 NASH, WILLIS G. Some historic houses in Marbletown. Ulster County Historical Society. Proceedings for 1935–36, pp. 34–39, 1936.

2145 The old stone church at Warwarsing. Olde Ulster, 3:114–19, Apr. 1907.

2146 PENNINGTON, DOROTHY KING. Dutch Colonial houses in Kingston, New York. House Beautiful, 47:36–37, Jan. 1920. illus.

2147 TELLER, MYRON S., AND BEVIER, LOUIS. A history of the Bevier house. Ulster County Historical Society. Proceedings for 1947–53, pp. 24–29. illus.
Near Kingston, 1715———.

Utica

2148 Historic restorations: Fountain Elms. Interiors, 120:100–105ff., Feb. 1961. illus.
1850's.

West Point

2149 [West Point. Contemporary description.] Ladies' Companion, July 1844. illus.

Westchester County (see also town names)

2150 BARR, LOCKWOOD. Hunter's Island. Westchester County Historical Bulletin, 29:31–35, Apr. 1953. illus.
Includes mansion by John Hunter, *ca.* 1813.

2151 HAACKER, FREDERICK C. The Cortlandt furnace. Westchester County Historical Society. Quarterly Bulletin, 30:123–29, Oct. 1954. illus.
Iron Works on Croton River, *ca.* 1750–57.

2152 HALBERT, WILLIAM CARTER. Westchester historic buildings. Westchester Historian, 31:4–7, 48–50, Jan.–Apr. 1955.
Annotated list.

2153 HANSEN, HARRY, AND CHAMBERLAIN, SAMUEL. North of Manhattan: persons and places of old Westchester. . . . N. Y., Hastings House, 1950. 181p. illus.
Includes Philipse manor, Philipse Castle, and Sunnyside.

2154 LANDER, RICHARD N. The Tripp Sawmill on Byram River. Westchester County Historical Bulletin, 29:49–52, Apr. 1953. illus.
Ca. 1826–98.

2155 STONE, SUSANNE. Some historic houses of Westchester County. New York State Historical Association. Proceedings, 9:292–98, 1910.

2156 WALRADT, ARTHUR E. Old Westchester taverns. Westchester County Historical Society. Bulletin, 15:1–8, 37–44, 56–64, 1939.

2157 WEEKS, LYMAN HORACE. The Rochambeau house. Americana, 5:961–63, Sept.–Oct. 1910.

2158 WESTCHESTER COUNTY HISTORICAL SOCIETY. An old Bedford home. Westchester County Historical Bulletin, 28:34–40, Apr. 1952. illus.
Maple Grove, 1757——.

2159 WHITE, STEPHEN F. Some old churches of Westchester County. Westchester County Magazine, 3:3–5, May 1909.

White Plains

2160 BOLTON, REGINALD PELHAM. The Hammond house. 1927. 21p.

2161 SMITH, WILSON CAREY. The Miller house; Washington's headquarters at White Plains, N. Y. Magazine of American History, 8:108–18, Aug. 1881. illus.

Wyoming

2162 BARNES, KATHERINE. A Castile landmark: the Van Arsdale house. Historical Wyoming, 8:66–74, Apr. 1955. illus.
Built by Ziba Hurd, 1817.

2163 Covered bridge days. Historical Wyoming, 9:97–101, July 1956; 10:11, Oct. 1956. illus.
Since 1835.

2164 FRENCH, ROBERT H. A. P. Sherril and his country emporium. New York Folklore Quarterly, 12:271–78, Winter 1956. illus. Also: Historical Wyoming, 9:46–52, Jan. 1956. illus.
Built at Pike in 1842.

Yonkers

2165 BOLTON, REGINALD PELHAM, AND MORGAN, H. SEACORD. Philipse manor hall, Yonkers. Westchester County Historical Society. Bulletin, 9:4–7, 1933.
1682 and later.

2166 GLOAG, JOHN. In old New York; Philipse manor hall, Yonkers. Country Life, London, 88:460–61, Nov. 23, 1940. illus.

2167 HALL, EDWARD HAGAMAN. Philipse manor hall, Yonkers, New York, the site, the building and its occupants. N. Y., American Scenic and Historic Preservation Society, 1912. 255p. illus.

2168 HUNTLEY, R. Decorative accessories of the period. American Collector, 13:16–17, May 1944. illus.
Philipse manor house.

2169 ORMSBEE, T. H. Beekman wing. American Collector, 13:10–11, May 1944. illus.

2170 The story of Philipse manor. Catholic World, 130:568–75, Feb. 1930.

2171 TORREY, RAYMOND H. Philipse manor hall, Yonkers. Scenic and Historic America, 4:3–28, 1935.

Youngstown

2172 McCLELLAN, S. GROVE. Old Fort Niagara. American Heritage, 4:32–41, Summer 1953. illus.

    1678———. Restored 1934.

PENNSYLVANIA

GENERAL REFERENCES

2173 ADAMS, RUTH. Pennsylvania Dutch art. Cleveland, World Publishing Co., [1950]. 64p. illus.

American Arts Library. Covers 1682–1850.

2174 ALLEN, GEORGE H. Some European origins of early Pennsylvania architecture. American Journal of Archaeology, 40:126, Jan. 1936.

Abstract of a paper submitted to the thirty-seventh general meeting of the Archaeological Institute of America, 1935.

2175 American home pilgrimages — part 9. Western Pennsylvania. American Home, 24:38, 40–41, Oct. 1940. illus.

2176 ARCHAMBAULT, A. MARGARETTA (ed.). A guide book of art, architecture, and historic interests in Pennsylvania. Philadelphia, John C. Winston Co., 1924. 509p. illus.

2177 Architectural overtones: Pennsylvania barns; photographs. American Architect, 151:43–50, Sept. 1937. illus.

2178 BINING, ARTHUR CECIL. Pennsylvania iron manufacture in the eighteenth century. Harrisburg, 1938. 227p. illus.

2179 BRUMBAUGH, G. EDWIN. Colonial architecture of the Pennsylvania Germans. Lancaster, Pa., Pennsylvania German Society. Proceedings for 1930, v. 41, 1933. 60p. illus.

Exteriors, interiors, details, building methods.

2180 COMINGS, MARION. Pioneer architecture of western Pennsylvania. Carnegie Magazine, 11:305–8, Mar. 1938. illus.

2181 DICKSON, HAROLD EDWARD. A hundred Pennsylvania buildings. State College, Pa., Bald Eagle Press, [1954]. [125p.] illus.

Photographs with historical text, 1643———.

2182 EMBURY, AYMAR, II. Pennsylvania farmhouses, examples of rural dwellings of a hundred years ago. Architectural Record, 30:475–85, Nov. 1911. illus.

2183 FEDERAL WRITERS' PROJECT. Harmony Society in Pennsylvania. Philadelphia, William Penn Association, 1937. 38p. illus.

2184 ———. Pennsylvania: a guide to the Keystone State. N. Y., Oxford University Press, 1940. 660p. illus.

2185 ———. Pennsylvania cavalcade. Philadelphia, University of Pennsylvania Press, 1942. 462p. illus.

2186 FEGLEY, H. WINSLOW. Among some of the older mills in eastern Pennsylvania. Norristown, Pa., Pennsylvania German Society, 1930. 76p. illus.

2187 HARK, ANN. Who are the Pennsylvania Dutch? House and Garden, 79:21–64, June 1941. illus.

2188 HARPSTER, JOHN W. Eighteenth century inns and taverns of western Pennsylvania. Western Pennsylvania Historical Magazine, 19:5–16, 1936.

2189 HORST, MELVIN, AND SMITH, ELMER L. Covered bridges of Pennsylvania Dutchland. Akron, Pa., Applied Arts, 1960. 42p. illus.

2190 ISRAEL, CORA M. Historic churches of Pennsylvania. American Monthly Magazine, 41:10–16, July 1912.

2191 KAUFFMAN, HENRY J. The summer house. Dutchman, 8:2–7, Summer 1956. illus.

On small stone or brick houses close to Pennsylvania farmhouses, used for washing, baking, etc., eighteenth and nineteenth centuries.

2192 KLEES, FREDERIC. The Pennsylvania Dutch. N. Y., Macmillan Co., 1950. 451p. illus.

1683———.

2193 KOCHER, A. LAWRENCE. Early architecture of Pennsylvania — in fourteen parts. Architectural Record, part 1, 48:513–40; part 2, 49:31–47; part 3, 49:135–55; part 4, 49:233–48; part 5, 49:310–30; part 6, 49:409–22; part 7, 49:519–35; part 8, 50:27–43; part 9, 50:147–57; part 10, 50:214–26; part 11, 50:398–406; part 12, 51:507–20; part 13, 52:121–32; part 14, 52:434–44, Dec. 1920—Nov. 1922. illus.

2194 LANDIS, H. K. Early kitchens of the Pennsylvania Germans. Pennsylvania German Society. Proceedings, v. 47, part 3, 1939. illus.

2195 LEARNED, MARION DEXTER. The German barn in America. Philadelphia, University of Pennsylvania. Bulletin, 15th ser., no. 3, part 5, pp. 338–49.

2196 LICHTEN, FRANCES. Folk art of rural Pennsylvania. N. Y., Charles Scribner's Sons, 1946. 276p. illus.

2197 LIPPINCOTT, HORACE MATHER. Quaker meeting house. Germantowne Crier, 7:7–9, Dec. 1955.

General essay on such structures since 1686.

2198 Master detail series. Early architecture of western Pennsylvania; Meason house and Johnston house. Architectural Forum, 66:229–36, Mar. 1937. illus.

2199 Master detail series. The Pennsylvania farm house. Architectural Forum, 60:369–84, May 1923. illus.

2200 MERCER, HENRY C. A list of furnaces in Colonial Pennsylvania, 1720–62. Pennsylvanian, 5:35, Apr. 1948.

2201 NUTTING, WALLACE. Pennsylvania beautiful. Framingham, Mass., Old America Co., 1924. 302p. illus.

Pennsylvania Dutch area.

2202 Penn-land. House Beautiful, 82:76–77, May 1940. illus.

Covers *ca.* 1790–1800, Pennsylvania, New Jersey, and Maryland.

2203 PENNSYLVANIA. DEPT. OF FORESTS AND WATERS. The old wooden covered bridge. Pennsylvania Forests and Waters, 4:34–35, 47, Mar.–Apr. 1952. illus. 1804——.

2204 PENNSYLVANIA. GENERAL ASSEMBLY. JOINT STATE GOVERNMENT COMMISSION. Catalog of historical buildings, sites, and remains in Pennsylvania. Harrisburg? Pa., 1949. 58p.

Designed to show historical places that should be preserved. Arranged alphabetically by counties.

2205 Pennsylvania German barns. Emmaus, Pa., Pennsylvania German Folklore Society, 1958. 336p. illus.

2206 PETERSON, CHARLES E. Eight-sided schoolhouses, 1800–1840. Society of Architectural Historians. Journal, 12:21–22, Mar. 1953. illus.

Southeastern Pennsylvania.

2207 PRICE, B. LLEWELLYN. Early stonework of eastern Pennsylvania. House Beautiful, 67:58–59, 95–97, Jan. 1930. illus.

Covers Bull house, Warwick, and Chew mansion, Germantown.

2208 RAYMOND, ELEANOR. Early domestic architecture of Pennsylvania. N. Y., William Helburn, 1931. 158p. illus.

2209 RICCARDI, SARO JOHN. Pennsylvania Dutch folk art and architecture. New York Public Library. Bulletin, 46:471–83, June 1942.

Selected, annotated bibliography.

2210 RICE, WILLIAM S. Early Pennsylvania arts. School Arts Magazine, 32:395–400, 408–9, Mar. 1933.

Includes architectural line drawings.

2211 ROBACKER, EARL FRANCIS. The Dutch touch in iron. Dutchman, 8:2–6, Spring 1957. illus.

Ironwork of decorated hinges, door pulls, hasps, trivets, etc.

2212 ROSENBERGER, JESSE LEONARD. In Pennsylvania-German land, 1928–1929. Chicago, University of Chicago Press, 1929. 90p. illus.

2213 SACHSE, JULIUS FRIEDRICH. The wayside inns on the Lancaster roadside between Philadelphia and Lancaster. Lancaster, Pa., New Era Printing Co., 1912. 77p. illus.

Reprint from Pennsylvania German Society. *Proceedings*, v. 21.

2214 SCHUYLER, MONTGOMERY. Architecture of American colleges. Part 5. University of Pennsylvania, Girard, Haverford, Lehigh and Bryn Mawr colleges. Architectural Record, 28:183–212, Sept. 1910. illus.

2215 SHOEMAKER, ALFRED LEWIS (ed.). The Pennsylvania barn. Lancaster, Pa., Pennsylvania Dutch Folklore Center, [1955]. 96p. illus.

Types, materials and decorations of barns; inventory of barns from tax records of 1798; essay on hex signs.

2216 STARRETT, C. V. American home pilgrimage — part 9. Western Pennsylvania. American Home, 24:38, 40–41, Oct. 1940. illus.

2217 STOTZ, CHARLES MORSE. Early architecture of western Pennsylvania. N. Y., published by William Helburn for the Buhl Foundation, Pittsburgh, 1936. 290p. illus.

A record of building before 1860, based upon the western Pennsylvania architectural survey, a project of the Pittsburgh Chapter of the American Institute of Architects.

2218 ———. Early architecture of western Pennsylvania, an exhibition of drawings and photographs. Carnegie Magazine, 9:239–43, Jan. 1936. illus.

2219 ———. Old architecture of Pennsylvania. Architecture, 49:79, Mar. 1924. illus. only.

2220 TRUMP, ROBERT T. American door hardware, 1640–1840. Montgomery County Historical Society. Bulletin, 9:171–74, Oct. 1954. illus.

Pennsylvania Dutch locks, thumb latches, and hinges.

2221 VAN STONE, JAMES W. Fortified houses in western Pennsylvania. Pennsylvania Archaeology, 20:19–24, Jan.–June 1950.

Characteristics of forts, blockhouses, stations, and fortified dwellings, 1758–94.

2222 WESLAGER, CLINTON ALFRED. Log houses in Pennsylvania during the seventeenth century. Pennsylvania History, 22:256–66, July 1955.
Ca. 1643——.

2223 WHARTON, ANNE HOLLINGSWORTH. In old Pennsylvania towns. Philadelphia, J. B. Lippincott Co., 1920. 352p. illus.

2224 A working bibliography of art in Pennsylvania. Pennsylvania Historical and Museum Commission, Harrisburg, 1948. 148p. Mimeographed.

2225 YODER, DON. Plain Dutch and gay Dutch: two worlds in the Dutch country. Dutchman, 8:34–55, Summer 1956. illus.

Pennsylvania Mennonites, particularly the Amish, since the eighteenth century.

LOCATIONS

Altoona

2226 DICKSON, H. E. Baker mansion, Altoona, Pa. Society of Architectural Historians. Journal, 17:25–29, Mar. 1958. illus.

Berks County

2227 ESHELMAN, JOHN E. Society of Friends and their meeting houses in Berks County. Berks County Historical Review, 1:34–40, 1936.
1718–1800.

2228 ———. The Society of Friends, and their meeting houses, in Berks County. Historical Review of Berks County, 19:104–9, 117–23, July–Sept. 1954. illus. 1718–1940.

2229 HEYDINGER, EARL J. Covered bridges in Berks County, 1954. Historical Review of Berks County, 19:115, July–Sept. 1954.
A census.

2230 HOCH, DANIEL K. Journey to Weiser Park. Historical Review of Berks County, 15:238–41, July–Sept. 1950. illus.
By Conrad Weiser, 1730, and its recent restoration.

2231 HURWITZ, ELIZABETH ADAMS. Decorative elements in the domestic architecture of eastern Pennsylvania. Dutchman, 7:6–29, Fall 1955. illus.

2232 KENNEDY, DEAN. Century old farmhouses, Oley Valley, Berks County, Pennsylvania. Pencil Points, 13:540–54, Aug. 1932. Mongraph Series, 18:214–28. illus.
Covers 1733–1800.

2233 MAGEE, JAMES F., JR. Berks County paper mills, paper makers, and watermarks 1747–1832. Berks County Historical Review, 13:76–78, Apr. 1948. illus.

2234 MONTGOMERY, RICHARD S. Houses of the Oley Valley. Dutchman, 6:16–26, Winter 1954. illus.
1732———.

Bethlehem

2235 KAUFFMAN, HENRY J. Moravian architecture in Bethlehem. Dutchman, 6:12–19, Spring 1955. illus.
1741———.

2236 MAURER, J. A., AND SCHUCHARD, H. K. Moravian buildings in Bethlehem. Archaeology, 3:226–32, Dec. 1950. illus.

2237 MURTAGH, WILLIAM JOHN. Moravian architecture and city planning: a study of eighteenth century Moravian settlements in the American colonies with particular emphasis on Bethlehem, Pennsylvania. Doctoral Dissertation, University of Pennsylvania, 1963. 461p.

2238 [Reichel, William Cornelius.] Old Sun Inn at Bethlehem, Pa., 1758. . . . Doylestown, Pa., W. W. H. Davis, 1877. 48p. illus.

2239 SNYDER, KARL H. Moravian architecture of Bethlehem, Pennsylvania. White Pine Series of Architectural Monographs, v. 13, no. 4, 1927. 19p. illus.
Covers 1745–1803.

Bristol

2240 GREEN, DORON. A history of the old homes on Radcliffe Street, Bristol, Pennsylvania. . . . Bristol, Pa., [Press of Bristol Printing Co.], 1938, 319p. illus.

2241 HUTTON, ANN HAWKES. House of Decision, December, 1776. Philadelphia, Dorrance, [1956]. 151p. illus.
Thompson-Neely house, 1702.

2242 MAULE, JOHN C. Friends' old meeting house in Bristol, Pennsylvania. Bucks County Historical Society. Papers, 4:92–96, 1917.

Bucks County (see also town names)

2243 BUCKS COUNTY HISTORICAL SOCIETY. Collection of papers read before the Bucks County Historical Society. Doylestown, Pa., The Society, 1926. 769p. illus.

Covers: homes of George Taylor, Norse mills of Colonial times in Pennsylvania, octagonal schoolhouses, early courthouses of Bucks County, old Heath mill and its early owners, origin of log houses in the United States (Henry Mercer), Neshaminy Presbyterian Church.

2244 JENKINS, ARTHUR H. The mills along the Pennypack. Old York Road Historical Society. Bulletin, 18:33–39, 1954.

Montgomery and Bucks counties, since 1697.

2245 Old stone houses in Bucks County: exterior views. American Architect, 149:43–50, Oct. 1936. illus.

2246 PAXSON, HENRY D. Log houses of Bucks County. Bucks County Historical Society. Papers, 4:204–9, 1917.

2247 SMITH, JAMES KELLUM. Bucks County Colonial. House and Garden, 69:21–23, 74, Jan. 1936. illus.

2248 WATSON, HENRY WINFIELD. The Growden mansion. Bucks County Historical Society. Collections, 2:251–56, 1909.

Carlisle

2249 Dickinson College. Portfolio, v. 5, 1811.

Old West, 1804. Benjamin Latrobe, architect.

2250 FLOWER, MILTON EMBICK. Carpenters' companies and Carlisle architecture. Carlisle, Pa., Hamilton Library and Historical Association of Cumberland County, 1955. 28p. illus.

2251 HOPWOOD, JOSEPHINE L. R. Forgotten shrines: Penn's landing place is in weeds and Pennsylvania's oldest house crumbles from lack of care. Commonwealth, 2:22–23, Mar. 1948. illus.

About Penn's landing place at Upland and Caleb Pusey house in old Chester, 1682——.

2252 NORTON, PAUL FOOTE. Latrobe and Old West at Dickinson College. Art Bulletin, 33:125–32, June 1951. illus.

1804.

2253 SPONSLER, GEORGE C., JR. Mantel in Blaine house, Carlisle, Pa., built about 1780. American Architect, 128:491–92, Dec. 1925. illus. only.

Chester County

2254 BRAZER, CLARENCE WILSON. Colonial Court House, Chester, Pennsylvania. Architectural Record, 60:527–32, Dec. 1926. illus.

1724.

2255 DELAWARE COUNTY HISTORICAL SOCIETY. Bicentennial celebration of the erection in 1724 of the old Colonial Court House, Chester, Pennsylvania. Chester, Pa., Chester Times, 1924. 24p. illus.

2256 Dower house, West Chester, Pennsylvania. Arts and Decoration, 38:8–9, Oct. 1933. illus.

2257 HARVEY, EVANGELINE LUKENA. Old Washington Inn. Friends' Historical Association. Bulletin, 21:84–86, 1932.

1747.

2258 PETERSON, CHARLES C. Architecture of Chester County, Pa. Society of Architectural Historians. Journal, 19:82–83, May 1960. illus.

2259 PRESCOTT, CHARLOTTE. Great American patriot; Mordecai Hayes house on the Brandywine River. Better Homes and Gardens, 19:28–29, 90–91, June 1941. illus.

1770 and later.

2260 SOCIETY OF ARCHITECTURAL HISTORIANS AND THE FINE ARTS DEPARTMENT OF SWARTHMORE COLLEGE. Early architecture of Chester County, Pennsylvania; an exhibition of photographs . . . of the American Buildings Survey. Swarthmore, Pa., 1960. 25 leaves.

Cumberland County

2261 ALLEN, RICHARD SANDERS. Covered bridges over Conodoguinet Creek. Covered Bridge Topics, 11:1, 4, 6, Winter 1953.

1824——.

Daylesford

2262 COPELAND, J. L. Blue Ball Inn, Daylesford, Pennsylvania. House Beautiful, 65:712–20, May 1929. illus.

Delaware County

2263 KENT, DONALD H. The birthplace of John Morton. Chronicle, 3:3–5, Spring-Summer 1956. illus.

Log and stone structure in Prospect Park, 1684, 1698, 1806.

Eagle's Mere

2264 WOOD, THOMAS KENNETH. The house in the clearing. Now and Then, 9:75–77, 94–96, Jan.–Apr. 1949.

Stone house built before 1849 for Emile C. Geyelin.

Ephrata

2265 BRUMBAUGH, G. EDWIN. Medieval construction at Ephrata. Antiques, 46:18–20, July 1944. illus.

Restoration of Ephrata Saal, 1740.

2266 BRUMBAUGH, MARTIN GROVE. Outline for historical romance — history of the Ephrata Society in the eighteenth century, Pennsylvania. Norristown, Pa., Pennsylvania German Society, 1930. 12p. illus.

2267 JAYNE, HORACE H. F. The Cloisters at Ephrata. American Magazine of Art, 29:594–98, 620–22, Sept. 1936. illus.

Ca. 1740.

2268 PUGH, ANNA ELOISE. The old cloister at Ephrata, Pennsylvania. D. A. R. Magazine, 51:146–49, Sept. 1917.

Erie

2269 FEDERAL WRITERS' PROJECT. Erie; a guide to the city and county. Philadelphia, William Penn Association of Philadelphia, 1938. 134p. illus.

Fort Washington

2270 ZIEGLER, C. A. The Highlands, Skippack Pike, above Fort Washington, Pa. Architectural Review, n.s. 23:1–2, Jan. 1918. illus.
1796.

Germantown (see *Philadelphia*)

Gettysburg

2271 STAUFFER, ELMER C. Conewago Chapel. Dutchman, 7:28–33, Spring 1956. illus.
Catholic building erected near Gettysburg, 1787–1850.

Greene County

2272 PARRY, MARY SAMMONS. Greene County forts and block-houses. D. A. R. Magazine, 59:234–36, Apr. 1925.

Harrisburg

2273 CUMMINGS, HUBERTIS MAURICE. Pennsylvania's state houses and capitols. Pennsylvania History, 20:409–16, Oct. 1953. illus.
1729——.

2274 ——. Stephen Hills and the building of Pennsylvania's first capitol. Pennsylvania History, 20:417–37, Oct. 1953. illus.
1819–97.

2275 Description of the state capitol of Pennsylvania, now building at Harrisburg. Analectic Magazine, n.s. v. 2, July 1820.

Kennett Square

2276 MERRICK, H. S. Homestead of the 18th century: Longwood, Kennett Square. Arts and Decoration, 38:8–12, Jan. 1933. illus.

Kinzer

2277 WINTERMUTE, H. OGDEN. Bleak house. Antiques Journal, 3:8–9, Oct. 1948. illus.
Near Kinzer. Built *ca.* 1835.

Lancaster

2278 BYRNE, JACOB HILL. Typical old Lancaster buildings and architecture. Lancaster County Historical Society. Papers, 26:138–43, June 1922.

2279 Four Early American mantels. Architectural Record, 34:225–31, Sept. 1913. illus.
Diller house.

2280 HENSEL, WILLIAM UHLER. The passing of an old landmark. Lancaster County Historical Society. Papers, 18:251–74, Dec. 4, 1914.
Shippen house.

2281 ———. The Shippen house. Lancaster County Historical Society. Papers, 14:125–43, 1910.

Destroyed.

2282 KAUFFMAN, HENRY J. Church architecture in Lancaster County. Dutchman, 6:16–27, Summer 1955. illus.

1740–1820.

2283 KOCHER, ALFRED LAWRENCE. The early architecture of Lancaster County, Pennsylvania. Lancaster County Historical Society. Papers, 24:91–106, 1920.

Colonial.

2284 LANDIS, D. B. Lancaster houses of 150 years ago. Lancaster County Historical Society. Papers, 26:136–37, June 1922.

Lebanon County

2285 DOWNS, JOSEPH. The house of the miller at Mill Bach. Philadelphia, Pennsylvania Museum of Art, 1929. 32p. illus.

Illig's Mill.

2286 MILLAR, DONALD. An eighteenth century German house in Pennsylvania. Architectural Record, 63:161–68, 1928. illus.

Lehigh County

2287 LEHIGH COUNTY HISTORICAL SOCIETY. Proceedings, v. 18, Aug. 1950.

Land titles, settlements, and buildings, 1734———. Includes accounts of the Troxell house, 1744, cellars and barns.

2288 ROBERTS, CHARLES R. Historic buildings of the Lehigh Valley. Pennsylvania-German, 8:72–73, 169–70, 598, 599, Feb., Apr., Dec. 1907.

2289 WILLIAMS, DAVID G. Grouse Hall: the shooting box of Lynford Lardner. Lehigh County Historical Society. Proceedings, 19:37–59, 1951. illus.

Hunting lodge, ca. 1745.

2290 ———. The lower Jordan Valley: Pennsylvania German settlement. Allentown, Pa., 1950. 181p. illus.

2291 ———. Peter Blank log house in the lower Jordan Valley. Lehigh County Historical Society. Proceedings, 19:61–72, 1951. illus.

Ca. 1840.

Ligonier

2292 SIPE, CHESTER HALE. Fort Ligonier and its times: a history of the first English fort west of the Allegheny Mountains and an account of many thrilling, tragic, romantic, important but little known Colonial and Revolutionary events in the region where the winning of the west began. Harrisburg, Pa., The Telegraph Press, 1932. 699p. illus.

Based primarily on Pennsylvania archives and Colonial records laid out in 1816.

Merion

2293 BARKER, CHARLES R. Colonial taverns of Lower Merion. Pennsylvania Magazine of History, 52:205–28, July 1928.

2294 ———. Old mills of Mill Creek, Lower Merion. Pennsylvania Magazine of History, 50:1–22, Jan. 1926.

Montgomery County

2295 HOCKER, EDWARD W. Mill Grove. Picket Post, 36:17–21, Apr. 1952. illus. 1749——.

Morrisville

2296 EASTWOOD-SIEBOLD, LLOYD. An appreciation of Pennsbury, manorial home in America of William Penn, proprietor. Picket Post, no. 26:18–19, Oct. 1949.

2297 EBERLEIN, HAROLD DONALDSON, AND HUBBARD, CORTLANDT VAN DYKE. Pennsbury manor: William Penn's dream fulfilled. American Collector, 17:6–8ff., Sept. 1948. illus.
Covers 1683–1775. House re-created 1937——.

2298 MELVIN, FRANK W. The romance of the Pennsbury manor restoration. Pennsylvania History, 7:142–52, 1940.

Muncy

2299 COOPER, THOMAS. The building of a backwoods house. Now and Then, 10:305–7, Jan. 1954.
Tavern, 1794. Reprinted from *Now and Then*, v. 5, 1934.

Northampton County

2300 FEDERAL WRITERS' PROJECT. Northampton County guide. Bethlehem, Pa., Times Publishing Co., *ca.* 1939. 246p. illus.

Northumberland County

2301 CARTER, JOHN H. Spread Eagle Manor: ancient gateway to Northumberland County. Northumberland County Historical Society. Proceedings, 16:21–27, 1948. illus.
1676–1808.

Philadelphia — General References (including *Germantown*)

2302 BARTON, GEORGE. Little journeys around old Philadelphia. Philadelphia, Peter Reilly Co., 1925. 325p. illus.
Historic churches and houses.

2303 BENDINER, ALFRED. Bendiner's Philadelphia. N. Y., A. S. Barnes, 1964. 175p. illus.

2304 CARPENTERS' COMPANY OF THE CITY AND COUNTY OF PHILADELPHIA. Recording the celebration of the two-hundredth anniversary of the Carpenters' Company of the city and county of Philadelphia, Pa., and the one-hundred-fiftieth anniversary of the first meeting of the First Continental Congress, September 25, 1924. Philadelphia, Carpenters' Company of the City and County of Philadelphia, 1925. 114p. illus.

2305 CARRICK, ALICE VAN LEER. Farm that came back: Todmorden farm. Country Life in America, 47:38–41, Nov. 1924.
1790, near Philadelphia.

2306 [Chestnut Street and Arch Street. Descriptions of the buildings.] Ariel, 2:94, Oct. 4, 1828; 5:384, Mar. 17, 1832. Atkinson's Casket, 12:553–54, Dec. 1828. Hazard's Register of Pennsylvania, 10:94, Aug. 11, 1832.

2307 COUSINS, FRANK, AND RILEY, PHILIP M. Colonial architecture of Philadelphia. Boston, Little, Brown and Co., 1920. 248p. illus.

2308 DAVIS, LEICESTER K. Early architecture of Germantown. House Beautiful, 68:253–55, 274, Sept. 1930.

2309 EBERLEIN, HAROLD DONALDSON. Three types of Georgian architecture — the evolution of the style in Philadelphia — in two parts. Architectural Record, part 1, 34:56–77, July 1913; part 2, 37:159–76, Feb. 1915. illus.

2310 EBERLEIN, HAROLD DONALDSON, AND HUBBARD, CORTLANDT VAN DYKE. Portrait of a Colonial city; Philadelphia, 1670–1838. Philadelphia, J. B. Lippincott Co., 1939. 580p. illus.

2311 ELLIOTT, HUGER. Architecture in Philadelphia and a coming chance. Architectural Record, 23:295–309, Apr. 1908. illus.

2312 FARIS, JOHN T. Old roads out of Philadelphia. Philadelphia, J. B. Lippincott Co., 1917. 327p. illus.

2313 ———. Romance of old Philadelphia. Philadelphia, J. B. Lippincott Co., 1918. 336p. illus.

2314 FEDERAL WRITERS' PROJECT. Philadelphia: a guide to the nation's birthplace. Philadelphia, William Penn Association of Philadelphia, 1937. 704p. illus.

2315 FITZ-GIBBON, COSTEN. Architectural Philadelphia — yesterday and today. Architectural Record, 34:20–45, July 1913. illus.

2316 GERMANTOWN HISTORICAL SOCIETY. Historic Germantown, from the founding to the early part of the nineteenth century: a survey of the German township. Philadelphia, American Philosophical Society. Memoirs, no. 39, 1955. 154p. illus.

Contents include: Grant Miles Simon, the architecture, pp. 27–141.

2317 GILLINGHAM, HAROLD E. Some early brickmakers of Philadelphia. Philadelphia Magazine of History, 53:1–27, Jan. 1929.

2318 GOFORTH, WILLIAM DAVENPORT, AND MCAULEY, WILLIAM J. Old Colonial architectural details in and around Philadelphia. N. Y., William Helburn, 1890. 2p. 50pl.

2319 GRAY, WILLIAM F. Philadelphia's architecture. Philadelphia, City History Society of Philadelphia, no. 12, 1915. 376p. illus.

2320 HAMLIN, TALBOT FAULKNER. Some Greek Revival architects of Philadelphia. Pennsylvania Magazine of History and Biography, 65:121–44, Apr. 1941. illus.

2321 Historic Philadelphia from the founding until the early nineteenth century. American Philosophical Society. Transactions, v. 43, pt. 1, 1953. 331p. illus.

2322 JACKSON, JOHN W. A tour of old Germantown. Germantowne Crier, 1:9–10, 28–30, May 1949. illus.

Describes eleven homes and shrines, 1728———.

2323 JACKSON, JOSEPH. Early Philadelphia architects and engineers. Philadelphia, privately printed, 1923. 285p. illus.

This work originally appeared serially in the magazine, *Building*, during the years 1922–23.

2324 ———. Encyclopaedia of Philadelphia. Harrisburg, Pa., National Historical Association, 1931–33. 4v. illus.

2325 LAFORE, LAURENCE DAVIS, AND LIPPINCOTT, SARAH LEE. Philadelphia; the unexpected city. Garden City, N. Y., Doubleday and Co., 1965. 178p. illus.

2326 LIPPINCOTT, HORACE MATHER. Early Philadelphia: its people, life and progress. Philadelphia, J. B. Lippincott Co., 1917. 339p. illus.

2327 [Metal house. Description.] Godey's Lady's Book. 52:299, Apr. 1856.

Illustration and description of this section of L. Johnson's foundry in Philadelphia.

2328 [New buildings. Contemporary descriptions.] Ariel, 4:190, Mar. 19, 1831. Niles' Weekly Register, 37:39, Sept. 12, 1829; 47:280–81, Dec. 27, 1834.

2329 Old doorways, Philadelphia, Pa. Architecture, v. 39, no. 3, Mar. 1919. illus. only.

2330 PENN MUTUAL LIFE INSURANCE COMPANY. Independence Square neighborhood. Philadelphia, Penn Mutual Life Insurance Co., 1926. 155p. illus.

Historical notes on Independence and Washington squares, lower Chestnut Street, and the insurance district along Walnut Street.

2331 PHILADELPHIA MUSEUM OF ART. Two centuries of Philadelphia architectural drawings. Philadelphia, Society of Architectural Historians and Philadelphia Museum of Art, 1964.

2332 PULLINGER, HERBERT. Old Germantown. Philadelphia, David McKay Co., 1926. 57p. illus.

2333 ———. Philadelphia, past and present. Boston, L. Phillips, 1915. 2p. 25 illus.

2334 REPS, JOHN WILLIAM. William Penn and the planning of Philadelphia. Town Planning Review, 27:27–39, Apr. 1956.

1681–90.

2335 SACHSE, JULIUS FRIEDRICH. Quaint old Germantown in Pennsylvania. Pennsylvania German Society. Proceedings, v. 23, 1912.

Sixty sketches by John Richards.

2336 SALOMONSKY, VERNA COOK. Old hardware from Philadelphia and Annapolis. Architectural Record, 48:169–73, Aug. 1920. illus.

2337 SIMON, GRANT MILES. Some accounts of the singular beginnings of Philadelphia. [Philadelphia, Carpenters' Co. and the Philadelphia Chapter of the American Institute of Architects, 1957.] 56p. illus.

1682, sites of historic interest.

2338 SIMS, JOSEPH PATTERSON, AND WILLING, CHARLES. Old Philadelphia Colonial details. N. Y., Architectural Book Publishing Co., 1914. 55 illus.

2339 SMITH, R. C. Two centuries of Philadelphia architecture, 1700–1900. American Philosophical Society. Transactions, 43, no. 1:289–303, 1953. illus.

2340 TATUM, GEORGE B. Penn's great town; 250 years of Philadelphia architecture illustrated in prints and drawings. Philadelphia, University of Pennsylvania Press, 1961. 352p. illus.

2341 WAINWRIGHT, NICHOLAS BIDDLE. Scull and Heap's map of Philadelphia. Pennsylvania Magazine of History and Biography, 81:69–75, Jan. 1957. illus.
Map of Philadelphia, 1752. Includes a perspective view of the State House.

2342 WALLACE, PHILIP B., AND DUNN, A. G. Colonial ironwork in old Philadelphia; the craftsmanship of the early days of the Republic. N. Y., Architectural Book Publishing Co., 1930. 157p. illus.

2343 WATSON, JOHN FANNING. Annals of Philadelphia and Pennsylvania in the olden time. Philadelphia, E. S. Stuart, 1898. 3v. illus.
First edition, 1830.

2344 ———. Historic tales of olden time concerning Philadelphia and Pennsylvania. Philadelphia, E. Littell and Thomas Holden, 1833. 316p. illus.

2345 WEINY, DANIEL W. Early architecture of Germantown, Pa., ca. 1768. Architecture, v. 46, no. 6, Dec. 1922. illus. only.

2346 WESTCOTT, THOMPSON. Historic mansions and buildings of Philadelphia, with some notice of their owners and occupants. Philadelphia, Porter and Coats, 1877. 528p. illus.

2347 WHITE, THEOPHILUS BALLOU. Philadelphia architecture in the 19th century. Philadelphia, University of Pennsylvania Press, 1953. 128p. illus.
Exhibition catalogue, Philadelphia Art Alliance.

2348 ZIEGLER, CARL A. Carpenters' Company, organized in Philadelphia in 1724. American Architect, 126:313–18, Oct. 8, 1924. illus.

2349 ———. Early American cornices of Philadelphia. American Architect, 126:1–10, July 2, 1924. illus.

2350 ———. Fort Mifflin. American Architect, 121:47–50, Jan. 18, 1922. illus.
Ca. 1812.

Philadelphia — Domestic

2351 BACON, EDGAR MAYHEW. Country homes of famous Americans, part 2. The home of John Bartram. Country Life in America, 5:27–30, 72, 73, illus.
Ca. 1731.

2352 BEARD, DONALD S. Upsala: a monument to gracious living. Germantowne Crier, 1:11–12, May 1949. illus.
By John Johnson, III, 1798–1800.

2353 BROWNBACK, G. E. Heivert Papen and the Papen house of Germantown, Pennsylvania. Penn Germania, n.s. 1:78–80, Feb. 1912.

2354 CHILD, JOHN S. Another Germantown landmark in danger. Germantowne Crier, 5:15, 17, Sept. 1953. illus.
Believed to have been built by Squire Peter Baynton, ca. 1803.

2355 CLAY, E. B. Reliving the days of Washington; Colonial mansions in Fairmount Park. Ladies' Home Journal, 49:14–15, June 1932. illus.

2356 [Colonnade Row. Contemporary description.] Atkinson's Casket, 11:505, Nov. 1832. illus.

2357 COMSTOCK, HELEN. Mount Pleasant "the most elegant seat in Pennsylvania." Connoisseur, 156:226–31, Aug. 1964. illus.

2358 DOWNS, JOSEPH. Cedar Grove, built 1721–1725, retains its original furnishings. Good Housekeeping, 94:60–61, 255, May 1932. illus.
Was at Frankford, now in Fairmount Park.

2359 ———. An eighteenth century Philadelphia mansion. Antiquarian, 16:26–30, 66, May 1931.
Woodford (before 1730).

2360 ———. Mount Pleasant, an old Philadelphia house of 1761. Good Housekeeping, 94:58–59, Feb. 1932. illus.

2361 ———. Strawberry mansion, 1728 — an historic house of Philadelphia. Good Housekeeping, 94:54–58, Jan. 1932.

2362 ———. Woodford — a Colonial house of 1734–56. Good Housekeeping, 95:54–55, Oct. 1932. illus.

2363 EASTWICK, MRS. ANDREW M. Bartram Hall. Philadelphia City Historical Society. Publications, 2:209–13, 1930.
1851. Not the John Bartram house, 1731.

2364 EBERLEIN, HAROLD DONALDSON. Colonial seats in Fairmount Park, Philadelphia. American Homes and Gardens, 12:255–60, Aug. 1915. illus.

2365 ———. Restored Quaker farmhouse. House and Garden, 42:56–57, Oct. 1922.
Netherfield, in Huntington Valley, 1700 and 1800. Near Philadelphia.

2366 EBERLEIN, HAROLD DONALDSON, AND LIPPINCOTT, HORACE MATHER. Colonial homes of Philadelphia and its neighborhood. Philadelphia, J. B. Lippincott Co., 1912. 365p. illus.

2367 ELKINTON, KATHERINE. "Button Hill" near Chew's Woods. Germantowne Crier, 5:11, 21, Mar. 1953. illus.
1727–1800.

2368 EVANS, ABEL J. Chalkley Hall in retrospect. Germantowne Crier, 7:14–15, 25, Mar. 1955. illus.
1723, destroyed 1954.

2369 Fairmount Park. Interior Design, 34:127–31, Mar. 1963. illus.

2370 FRYER, AARON G. Elfreth's Alley, Philadelphia. Antiques, 63:49–51, Jan. 1953. illus.
Originally known as Gilbert's Alley, since 1740 known as Elfreth's Alley.

2371 GERMANTOWN HISTORICAL SOCIETY. Annual historic tour of old Germantown. Germantowne Crier, 6:14–15, May 1954. illus.
Brief histories of eleven houses, 1738–1900.

2372 ———. Park houses. Germantowne Crier, 6:20–21, Mar. 1954. illus.
Fairmount Park, Philadelphia, 1743——.

2373 GILLINGHAM, MRS. H. E. House beautiful of long ago; Mount Pleasant in Fairmount Park, Philadelphia. House Beautiful, 60:46–47, July 1926. illus.

2374 HAINES, ROBERT BOWNE, III. "Wyck." Germantowne Crier, 2:7–9, Sept. 1950. illus.
Ca. 1690.

2375 HAVERSTICK, HORACE. The Billmeyer house: read before the Site and Relic Society, February 7th, 1902. Germantowne Crier, 6:12, 22, Mar. 1954.
Ca. 1730.

2376 HINDERMYER, GILBERT. Wyck, an old house and garden at Germantown, Philadelphia. House and Garden, 2:545–59, Nov. 1902. illus.

2377 HOCKER, EDWARD W. Harkness house: the "brick building" on Market Street. Germantowne Crier, 1:11–12, 27–31, Jan. 1949. illus.
1794——.

2378 HOLLOWAY, EDWARD STRATTON. Pennsylvania Colonial homestead, Walnut Grove farm. House Beautiful, 48:379–81, 416, Nov. 1920. illus.
Eighteenth century, near Philadelphia.

2379 HORNOR, W. M., JR. Mount Pleasant, 1761. American Institute of Architects. Journal, 15:272–78, Aug. 1927. illus.

2380 House of William Penn's secretary. Touchstone, 5:64–69, Apr. 1919. illus.
Stenton, 1727.

2381 HUTCHINS, FRANK W. The Washington house in Philadelphia. D. A. R. Magazine, 61:34–40, 123–29, 198–203, Jan., Feb., Mar. 1927.
House occupied by Washington as President.

2382 JACKSON, JOHN W. Morris house: the presidential mansion in November 1793. Germantowne Crier, 1:9–10, 23, Jan. 1949. illus.
Variously called the Deschler-Franks-Perot-Morris house, 1772.

2383 KIMBALL, MARIE G. Revival of the Colonial; Philadelphia restores its old houses on the Schuylkill. Architectural Record, 62:1–17, July 1927. illus.

2384 ——. Roughing it in Philadelphia: Mount Pleasant. Virginia Quarterly Review, 14:416–24, July 1938.

2385 KIMBALL, SIDNEY FISKE. Belmont, Fairmount Park. Pennsylvania Museum. Bulletin, 22:333–45, Mar. 1927. illus.

2386 ——. Philadelphia's Colonial chain. Art and Archaeology, 21:150–54, Apr.–May 1926. illus.
Houses in Fairmount Park.

2387 KURJACK, DENNIS C. The "President's house" in Philadelphia. Pennsylvania History, 20:380–94, Oct. 1953. illus.
Morris house, 1792–97, demolished 1829.

2388 ——. Who designed the "President's house?" Society of Architectural Historians. Journal, 12:27–28, May 1953. illus.
1791–92.

2389 LAW, MARGARET LATHROP. Philadelphia's Colonial chain. Architecture, 56:1–7, 85–92, July, Aug. 1927. illus.

2390 LIPPINCOTT, HORACE MATHER. Some old Quaker houses in the Philadelphia neighborhood. Friends' Historical Association. Bulletin, 24:57–76, 1935.

2391 [Loxley house. Contemporary description.] Atkinson's Casket, 9:409, Sept. 1830. illus.

2392 LUDLUM, MABEL STEWART. The story of Strawberry mansion. Pennsylvania Museum. Bulletin, v. 26, pt. 2, 1931. 14p. illus.

1797. Benjamin Latrobe, architect. Probably the first Gothic Revival structure in the United States.

2393 McCALL, ELIZABETH B. Old Philadelphia houses on Society Hill, 1750–1840. N. Y., Architectural Books, 1966. 192p. illus.

2394 Mount Pleasant, Fairmount Park, Philadelphia. Philadelphia, Pennsylvania Museum and School of Industrial Art, 1927. 31p. illus.

2395 MURTAGH, WILLIAM JOHN. The Philadelphia row house. Society of Architectural Historians. Journal, 16:8–13, Dec. 1957. illus.

2396 The Papen-Johnson house in existence 1698–1883; the first specimen of German architectural skill in stone in Germantown, Pennsylvania. Americana, 7:1123–26, Dec. 1912.

2397 PENNSYLVANIA MUSEUM OF ART. ASSOCIATE COMMITTEE OF WOMEN. Chain of Colonial houses. Philadelphia, 1932. 25p. illus.

A guide book to the nine houses in Fairmount Park under the management of the Pennsylvania Museum.

2398 PETERS, RICHARD, JR. Belmont mansion. Numismatic and Antiquarian Society of Philadelphia. Proceedings, v. 30, 1925.

1742 and later.

2399 Restoration of Kenwood, a Regency house; Leigh French, Jr., and Eberlein, Harold Donaldson, architects. Architectural Forum, 51:519–28, Oct. 1929.

At Bethayres, near Philadelphia.

2400 [Robert Morris' house. Contemporary description.] Atkinson's Casket, 2:73, Feb. 1832.

2401 TILLOTSON, HENRY S. Historic old Chew house. Mentor, 17:32–33, July 1929. illus.

Begun 1761.

2402 Two Tucker beakers with views of the Woodlands and the Solitude, two historic houses. Philadelphia Museum. Bulletin, 54:67–70, Spring 1959. illus.

2403 WAINWRIGHT, NICHOLAS B. Colonial grandeur in Philadelphia: the house and furniture of General John Cadwalader. Philadelphia, Historical Society of Pennsylvania, 1964. 169p. illus.

Pre-Revolutionary house reconstructed from bills and family papers.

2404 WALLACE, PHILIP B. Colonial houses, Philadelphia, Pre-Revolutionary period. N. Y., Architectural Book Publishing Co., 1931. 248p. illus.

This is *Colonial Architecture in Old Philadelphia*, v. 2.

2405 WIREMAN, KATHERINE RICHARDSON. "Roxborough Plantation" 1705 to 1840; "Carlton" 1840 to 1948. Germantowne Crier, 1:9–10, 25, Dec. 1949. illus.

Philadelphia — Public

2406 [Academy of Natural Sciences. Contemporary description.] Atkinson's Casket, 10:469, Oct. 1831.

2407 ALLEN, RICHARD SANDERS. Covered bridge sesqui-centennial. Covered Bridge Topics, 12:1–2, Dec. 1954.

"First recorded" American covered bridge spanning the Schuylkill, 1805–50.

2408 [Bank of the United States. Contemporary descriptions.] Atkinson's Casket, 11:505, Nov. 1829. National Register, 13:321, Nov. 20, 1819.

1818–24. Credited to William Strickland by Agnes Addison.

2409 BIDDLE, EDWARD. Girard College. Numismatic and Antiquarian Society of Philadelphia. Proceedings, 28:199–215, 1919.

2410 BRABAZON, THOMAS. Our earliest civic center, the Independence Hall group in Philadelphia. Architectural Record, 34:1–19, July 1913. illus.

2411 BRUMBAUGH, G. E. Independence Hall area: rebirth of the old city. American Institute of Architects. Journal, 28:294–98, Sept. 1957.

2412 CLARKE, J. SELLER. The old Independence Hall group at Philadelphia. Western Architect, 35:86–87, July 1926. illus.

2413 COHEN, CHARLES J. The origin of Carpenters' Hall, Philadelphia, with incidents of the neighborhood. Numismatic and Antiquarian Society of Philadelphia. Proceedings, 28:123–66, 1919.

1770–92. Robert Smith, architect.

2414 Congress Hall restored. Architectural Record, 35:97–100, Jan. 1914. illus.

2415 COTTER, J. L. Digging an historical shrine: Philadelphia's Independence Park. Expedition, 2:28–32, Spring 1960. illus.

2416 [Dorsey's Gothic Museum. Contemporary description.] Atkinson's Casket, 10:457, Oct. 1830. illus.

2417 EBERLEIN, HAROLD DONALDSON. Fairmount Waterworks, Philadelphia. Architectural Record, 62:57–67, July 1927. illus.

1815. Benjamin Latrobe, architect.

2418 EBERLEIN, HAROLD DONALDSON, AND HUBBARD, CORTLANDT VAN DYKE. Diary of Independence Hall. Philadelphia, J. B. Lippincott Co., 1948. 378p. illus.

2419 EDMONDS, FRANKLIN DAVENPORT. Public school buildings of the city of Philadelphia from 1745 to 1845. Philadelphia, 1913. 180p. illus.

2420 ETTING, FRANK. Historical account of the old Pennsylvania State House, now known as the Hall of Independence. Boston, James R. Osgood and Co., 1876. 204p. illus.

2421 [Exchange Building. Contemporary descriptions.] Atkinson's Casket, 2:74, Feb. 1833. Knickerbocker, 3:396, May 1834.

1832–34. William Strickland, architect.

2422 FITZ-GIBBON, COSTEN. Latrobe and the Center Square Pump House. Architectural Record, 62:18–22, July 1927. illus.
1801.

2423 GARDNER, ALBERT TEN EYCK. A Philadelphia masterpiece: Haviland's prison. Metropolitan Museum of Art. Bulletin, 14:103–8, Dec. 1955. illus.
1828.

2424 GILCHRIST, AGNES ADDISON. Girard College: an example of the layman's influence on architecture. Society of Architectural Historians. Journal, 16:22–25, May 1957.
Influence of Nicholas Biddle on the design by Thomas U. Walter, 1833–46.

2425 [Girard College.] Franklin Institute of Philadelphia. Journal, v. 25–32, 1838–41.

2426 GRAHAM, R. E. Taverns of Colonial Philadelphia. American Philosophical Society. Transactions, 43, no. 1:318–25, 1953. illus.

2427 HALLER, MABEL. Early Moravian schools of Germantown. Germantowne Crier, 6:20–22, May 1954.
1742–63.

2428 HAVILAND, JOHN. Description of Haviland's design for the new penitentiary, now erecting near Philadelphia, accompanied by a bird's eye view. Philadelphia, Robert Desilver, 1824. 12p. illus.

2429 JACKSON, J. How Independence Hall was built. American Institute of Architects. Journal, 26:160–66, Oct. 1945. illus.

2430 JAMES, REESE DAVIS. Cradle of culture, 1800–1810: the Philadelphia stage. Philadelphia, University of Pennsylvania Press, 1957. 156p. illus.
On the Chestnut Street Theatre.

2431 JOHNSON, GEORGE CLARENCE. The old Concord schoolhouse. Germantowne Crier, 2:16–17, 30–31, June–Sept. 1950. illus.
1775——.

2432 KIMBALL, SIDNEY FISKE. The Bank of Pennsylvania, 1799, an unknown masterpiece of American classicism. Architectural Record, 44:132–39, Aug. 1918. illus.
Benjamin Latrobe, architect.

2433 ———. The Bank of the United States, 1818–24. Architectural Record, 58:581–94, Dec. 1925. illus.

2434 LINGELBACH, WILLIAM E. The story of "Philosophical Hall." American Philosophical Society. Proceedings, 94:185–213, June 1950. illus.
1769.

2435 [Literary and Scientific Institutions of Philadelphia. Contemporary discussion.] Hazard's Register of Pennsylvania, 12:294–95, Nov. 9, 1833.

2436 [Masonic Hall. Contemporary description.] Atkinson's Casket, 5:217–18, May 1829.

2437 MASSEY, JAMES C. Carpenters' School, 1833–42. Society of Architectural Historians. Journal, 14:28–29, May 1955. illus.

School of Architecture, Philadelphia.

2438 [Merchant's Hotel. Contemporary description.] Atkinson's Casket, 6:280–81, 1837. illus.

2439 Moved again: First Bank of the United States at 120 South Third Street, Philadelphia. Society of Architectural Historians. Journal, 15:2, Oct. 1956. illus.

2440 Mr. Nicholas Biddle and the architecture of Girard College. Pennsylvania Magazine of History and Biography, v. 18, 1894.

2441 [Naval Asylum. Contemporary description.] Atkinson's Casket, 12:553–54, Dec. 1832. illus.

2442 [Pennsylvania Hotel. Contemporary descriptions.] Hazard's Register of Pennsylvania, 16:287, Oct. 31, 1835. Weekly Magazine, 1:328–30, Apr. 14, 1798.

William Strickland, architect.

2443 PETERSON, CHARLES E. Benjamin Loxley and Carpenters' Hall. Society of Architectural Historians. Journal, 15:23–26, Dec. 1956. illus.

1770.

2444 ———. Early architects of Independence Hall. Society of Architectural Historians. Journal, 11:23–26, Oct. 1952. illus.

Edmund Woolley, Robert Mills, and John Haviland, 1735–1828. Includes several documents.

2445 ———. Early prisons. Society of Architectural Historians. Journal, 12:26–28, Dec. 1953. illus.

Walnut Street Prison, Philadelphia, 1774–75, and the Virginia Penitentiary, Richmond, 1797–1823.

2446 [Philadelphia Arcade. Contemporary description.] Atkinson's Casket, 12:560, Dec. 1832. illus.

2447 [Philadelphia Museum. Contemporary description.] Niles' Weekly Register, 54:356–57, Aug. 4, 1838.

2448 Reminiscences of Carpenters' Hall, in the city of Philadelphia, and extracts from the ancient minutes of the proceedings of the Carpenters' Company of the City and County of Philadelphia. Philadelphia, Crissey and Markley, 1858. pp. 1–41, 1–21, 1–57.

Pages 1–57 contain catalogue of books in the library of the Carpenters' Company in 1857. Also included are lists of officers and members from 1763.

2449 RILEY, EDWARD M. Independence, National Historical Park, Philadelphia, Pa. Washington, D. C., 1954. 68p. illus.

National Park Service. Historical Handbook Series, no. 17.

2450 SCATTERGOOD, DAVID. Handbook of Girard College. Philadelphia, D. Scattergood, 1888. 64p. illus.

2451 ———. Handbook of the Statehouse at Philadelphia. Philadelphia, D. Scattergood, 1890. 64p. illus.

2452 SMITH, ROBERT CHESTER. John Notman and the Athenaeum Building. [Philadelphia, 1951.] 50p. illus.

Library, 1847. Includes catalogue of drawings associated with the building, 1834–45.

2453 [State House. Contemporary descriptions.] Atkinson's Casket, 4:169–70, Apr. 1829; 12:553, Dec. 1831. Philadelphia Monthly Magazine, pp. 333–34, June 1798.

2454 TOLLES, FREDERICK BARNES. Meeting house and counting house: the Quaker merchants of Colonial Philadelphia, 1682–1763. Chapel Hill, University of North Carolina Press, 1948. 292p. illus.

2455 TURNER, WILLIAM L. The early buildings of the University of Pennsylvania. General Magazine and Historical Chronicle, 53:1–16, Autumn 1950. illus.

1740–1829.

2456 WALTER, THOMAS USTICK. Report of the architect of the Girard College for Orphans to the Building Committee. [Philadelphia, 1834–50.] 14 pamphlets.

2457 WILLIAMS, GEORGE W. The King of Prussia Inn. Germantowne Crier, 5:9, 22, Sept. 1953.

Reprinted from the *Independent-Gazette*, 1896. On a Germantown house, built 1740, demolished 1910.

2458 YARDLEY, ERNEST HOWARD. The Wissahickon's inns and interests. Germantowne Crier, 7:13–18, 24, Dec. 1955. illus.

Since 1681.

Philadelphia — Religious

2459 BARRATT, NORRIS STANLEY. Outline of the history of Old St. Paul's Church, Philadelphia, with an appeal for its preservation, together with articles of agreement, abstract of title, list of rectors, vestrymen, and inscriptions of tombstones and vaults. Philadelphia, Colonial Society of Pennsylvania, 1917. 327p. illus.

2460 BRONNER, EDWIN BLAINE. The Center Square Meetinghouse and the other meetinghouses of early Philadelphia. Friends Historical Association. Bulletin, 44:67–73, Autumn 1955. illus.

1683–1828.

2461 ———. Early years of Arch Street Meeting House. Friends Journal, 1:199–201, Sept. 24, 1955. illus.

1693–1811.

2462 FARIS, JOHN T. Old churches and meeting houses in and around Philadelphia. Philadelphia, J. B. Lippincott Co., 1926. 261p. illus.

2463 MILLER, RICHMOND P. Race Street Meeting House. Friends Historical Association. Bulletin, 46:3–9, Spring 1957.

1856.

2464 St. James of Kingsess Church. The Old Swede's Church of St. James of Kingsess, 1762. Philadelphia, M. C. Callahan, 1911. 13p. illus.

Lutheran.

2465 SIZER, THEODORE. Philadelphia's First Presbyterian Church by "Mr. Trumbul." Society of Architectural Historians. Journal, 9:20–22, Oct. 1950. illus.

1794. Tentatively attributed to John Trumbull.

2466 WATSON, JOHN FANNING. The Swede's Church and house of Sven Sener. Philadelphia, G. E. Callahan and D. S. Callahan, 1907. 13p. illus.

1677. Reprinted from *Annals of Philadelphia* by John F. Watson. First edition, 1830.

2467 WISCHNITZER, RACHEL BERNSTEIN. The Egyptian Revival in synagogue architecture. American Jewish Historical Society. Publications, 41:61–75, Sept. 1951. illus.

Mikve Israel Synagogue designed by William Strickland, 1820–25, and Beth Israel Synagogue, 1847–49.

2468 ———. Thomas U. Walter's Crown Street Synagogue, 1848–49. Society of Architectural Historians. Journal, 13:29–31, Dec. 1954. illus.

Egyptian Revival.

Pittsburgh

2469 BELL, RAYMOND MARTIN. Early Methodist church buildings in the Pittsburgh Conference. Washington, Pa., 1950. 7p.

1785–99.

2470 DAVIS, MRS. ELVERT M. Fort Fayette. Western Pennsylvania Historical Magazine, 16:65–84, Apr. 1927.

Before 1812.

2471 FEDERAL WRITERS' PROJECT. Tales of pioneer Pittsburgh. Philadelphia, William Penn Association, *ca.* 1937. 28p. illus.

2472 LORANT, STEFEN. Pittsburgh; the story of an American city. With contributions by Henry Steele Commager and others. Garden City, N. Y., Doubleday and Co., 1964. 520p. illus.

2473 MACPHERSON, L. C. Monongahela house. Western Pennsylvania Historical Magazine, 3:194–97, Oct. 1920.

2474 MARTIN, PARK H. City of Bridges. Carnegie Magazine, 23:154–58, Dec. 1949. illus.

Bridges in Pittsburgh, 1818–1949.

2475 MILLER, ANNIE CLARK. Old houses and estates in Pittsburgh. Western Pennsylvania Historical Magazine, 9:129–68, July 1926.

2476 Pittsburgh rediscovers an architect pioneer, Frederick Scheibler; summary of a paper by J. K. Shear. Architectural Record, 106:98–100, July 1949. illus.

2477 [St. Paul's. Contemporary description.] Niles' Weekly Register, 36:333, July 18, 1829.

2478 SCHMERTZ, ROBERT W. Architecture in Pittsburgh dating up to 1900. Carnegie Magazine, 23:78–82, Oct. 1949. illus.

Ca. 1800–1900.

2479 UNIVERSITY OF PITTSBURGH. HENRY CLAY FRICK FINE ARTS DEPT. HONORS SEMINAR. Reflections of changing taste in Pittsburgh architecture. Carnegie Magazine, 31:27–32, Jan. 1957. illus.

Since 1794.

2480 VAN TRUMP, JAMES D. St. Peter's, Pittsburgh, by John Notman. Society of Architectural Historians. Journal, 15:19–23, May 1956. illus.

Episcopal church designed in 1851.

Pottstown

2481 Unknown historic mansion of Pennsylvania; Bessybell, near Pottstown, Pa. Country Life in America, 33:50–51, Jan. 1918. illus. only.

Sunbury

2482 BECK, LOUISE B. The old Scott house. Northumberland County Historical Society. Proceedings, 6:226–32, 1934.

1796.

2483 GEARHART, HEBER G. Maclay-Wolverton house. Northumberland County Historical Society. Proceedings, 5:149–59, 1933.

1773.

Tinicum Island

2484 SUTTON, ISAAC CRAWFORD. Printzhof. Pennsylvania History, 20:395–98, Oct. 1953. illus.

Swedish log dwelling near Pennsylvania shore of the Delaware, 1643——.

Valley Forge

2485 PINKOWSKI, EDWARD. Washington's officers slept here: historic homes of Valley Forge and its neighborhood. Philadelphia, Sunshine Press, 1953. 278p. illus.

Thirty-four buildings existing in 1777.

2486 VALLEY FORGE HISTORICAL SOCIETY. The quarters of General Washington's staff. Picket Post, 43:6–23, Jan. 1954. illus.

History and description of twenty-three buildings in the vicinity of Valley Forge in 1777.

2487 Washington's headquarters at Valley Forge. Antiques, 38:10, 18–19, July 1940. illus.

1758.

West Bradford

2488 BRAZER, CLARENCE W. Primitive Hall and its furniture. Antiques, 53:55–57, Jan. 1948. illus.

1738. Joseph Pennock, architect.

Whitemarsh

2489 DEGN, WILLIAM L. The history of Hope Lodge. Montgomery County Historical Society. Bulletin, 1:324–26, 1939.

Manor house, 1721.

York County

2490 STAIR, J. WILLIAM. Brick-end barns. Dutchman, 1:14–33, Fall 1954. illus.

1800–50. On construction and design.

Southern States

GENERAL REFERENCES

2491 ALTSCHULER, J. A. Colonial architecture of the Carolinas. Architecture, v. 43–49, June 1921–July 1924. illus. only.

2492 BIBB, A. B. Old Colonial works of Virginia and Maryland — in seven parts. American Architecture and Building News, part 1, 25:279–81, June 1889; part 2, 25:303–5, June 1889; part 3, 26:71–73, Aug. 1889; part 4, 26:123–24, Sept. 1889; part 5, 26:161–63, Oct. 1889; part 6, 31:133–35, May 1891; part 7, 34:130–32, Nov. 1891. illus.

2493 BODINE, A. AUBREY. Chesapeake Bay and Tidewater. [N. Y.], Hastings House, 1954. 144p. illus.

Author's photographs of historical buildings and sites in Maryland, Virginia, and Delaware with brief text.

2494 BOYNTON, HENRY DELANO. Capitols of the South. Philadelphia, The Edgell Co., 1917. 31p. illus.

2495 BROWN, GLENN. Old Colonial works in Virginia and Maryland. American Architect and Building News, 22:198–99, 242–43, 254, Oct.–Nov. 1887. illus.

2496 CLARK, CHARLES B. (ed.). The eastern shore of Maryland and Virginia. N. Y., Lewis Historical Publishing Co., 1950. 3v. v. 1 and 2, 1182p. v. 3, 350p. illus. 1607——.

2497 COFFIN, LEWIS A., JR., AND HOLDEN, ARTHUR C. Brick architecture of the Colonial period in Maryland and Virginia. N. Y., Architectural Book Publishing Co., 1919. 147p. illus.

2498 CORNER, JAMES M., AND SODERHOLTZ, ERIC ELLIS. Examples of domestic Colonial architecture in Maryland and Virginia. Boston, Boston Architectural Club, 1892. 53p. illus.

2499 CRANE, EDWARD ANDREW, AND SODERHOLTZ, ERIC ELLIS. Examples of Colonial architecture in Charleston, South Carolina and Savannah, Georgia. Boston, Boston Architectural Club, 1895. 52 illus.

2500 DAVIS, BRINTON B. Architecture of the Old South. Methodist Quarterly Review, 69:238–43, Apr. 1920.

2501 Deep South; pilgrimage through the plantation country. House and Garden, 76:28–49, Nov. 1939. illus.

Mississippi and Louisiana.

2502 DENMARK, E. R. Architecture of the Old South, 1640–1850. Atlanta, Ga., Southern Architect and Building News, 1926. 75p. illus.

2503 ELWELL, NEWTON D. Architecture, furniture and interiors of Maryland and Virginia during the 18th century. Boston, G. H. Polley and Co., 1897. 63p. illus.

2504 FANNING, RALPH STANLEE. The classical revival in the South. Georgia Review, 8:52–60, Spring 1954.

1790–1865.

2505 FORMAN, HENRY CHANDLEE. The architecture of the Old South: the Medieval style, 1585–1850. Cambridge, Mass., Harvard University Press, 1948. 203p. illus.

Medieval English architectural influence in the states from Virginia to Georgia.

2506 ———. Beginning of American architecture. College Art Journal, 6:125–32, 1946. illus.

A chapter from his *Architecture of the Old South*.

2507 Frances Benjamin Johnston: her photographs of our old buildings. Magazine of Art, 30:548–55, Sept. 1937. illus.

2508 Historic and scenic reaches of the nation's capital. National Geographic Magazine, July 1938.

A spot map locating most of the important architectural examples in Delaware, Maryland, and Virginia.

2509 HORTON, CORINNE. Georgian houses of the far South. House and Garden, 6:260–67, Dec. 1904. illus.

2510 HORTON, MRS. THADDEUS. Amateur architects of the South. Architecture, 37:127–32, May 1918. illus.

2511 ———. Classic houses of the South, old and new. House Beautiful, 12:84–90, July 1902. illus.

Covers President Polk house, Dunleith, Fort Hill, Hermitage, Arlington.

2512 ———. Colonial houses of the South. Country Life in America, 12:639–44, Oct. 1907. illus.

2513 ———. Old South in American architecture. Uncle Remus' Home Magazine, v. 26–27, Oct. 1909—Apr. 1910. illus.

2514 Houses of the Old South. American Architect, 147:57–64, Sept. 1935. illus.

2515 JONES, RUTH IRENE. Ante-bellum watering places of the Mississippi Gulf Coast. Journal of Mississippi History, 18:268–301, Oct. 1956.

On Bay St. Louis, Pass Christian, Mississippi City, Biloxi, Ocean Springs, and Pascagoula as summer resorts, 1813–60, with detailed account of their hotels.

2516 KEMPTON, CHRISTINE HUDSON. Old mansions in environs of Washington. House Beautiful, 54:364–65, Oct. 1923. illus.

Poplar Hill, Mount Airy, Lothian.

2517 KENNEDY, J. ROBIE, JR. Examples of Georgian and Greek Revival work in the far South. Architectural Record, 21:215–21, Mar. 1907. illus.

2518 LANCASTER, CLAY. Some octagonal forms in Southern achitecture. Art Bulletin, 28:103–11, June 1946. illus.

2519 LAUGHLIN, C. J. River houses of the great plantations. American Heritage, 7:54–63, June 1956. illus.

2520 [Lighthouse designed by B. H. Latrobe.] American Register, 1:28–29, 1806–7.
Designed for the government for an island in the Mississippi.

2521 LINCOLN, FAY S. Ante-bellum architecture of the South; catalog of photographs of F. S. Lincoln. [N. Y., 1939.] 15p. illus.

2522 McDERMOTT, JOHN FRANCIS (ed.). The French in the Mississippi Valley. Urbana, University of Illinois Press, 1965.
Significant chapter on architecture.

2523 MAJOR, HOWARD. Southern plantation homes. House and Garden, 50:112–13, 126, 130, Nov. 1926. illus.
Classic Revival, Mississippi and Louisiana.

2524 MISH, MARY VERNON. Frontier homes of the Potomac. D. A. R. Magazine, 85:903–7, 993, Nov. 1951. illus.
On characteristic architecture of dated stone houses on the Upper Potomac, 1750–1804.

2525 MUMFORD, LEWIS. The South in architecture. N. Y., Harcourt, Brace and Co., 1941. 147p. illus.
An estimate of the South's contribution to architecture. The Dancy lectures, Alabama College.

2526 NEWCOMB, REXFORD. Spanish-Colonial architecture in the United States. N. Y., J. J. Augustin, 1937. 169p. illus.
Some material on the Southern states.

2527 NICHOLS, J. B. A historical study of Southern Baptist church architecture. Doctoral Dissertation, Southwestern Baptist Theological Seminary, 1954.

2528 PARKS, HAMILTON. The Colonial domestic architecture of the Old South in relation to its environmental background. Master's Thesis, University of Illinois, 1933. 145 leaves.

2529 PETERSON, CHARLES E. Ante-bellum houses of the Mississippi Valley, a catalogue of an exhibition of new photographs and measured drawings. St. Louis, Department of the Interior, National Park Service, Historic American Buildings Survey, Cental Unit, Oct. 1940. 16p. Mimeographed.
Includes Ohio Valley.

2530 ———. French landmarks along the Mississippi. Antiques, 53:286–88, Apr. 1948. illus.
1682———. Mississippi, Louisiana, and Illinois.

2531 REPS, JOHN W. Tidewater colonies: Francis Nicholson's Tidewater capitals. Town Planning Review, 34:32–38, Apr. 1963. illus.

2532 ———. Tidewater colonies, town planning in the 17th century. Town Planning Review, 34:27–38, Apr. 1963. illus.

2533 SALE, MRS. EDITH DABNEY (TUNIS). Colonial interiors. N. Y., William Helburn, 1930. 95p. illus.

This is *Colonial Interiors*, second series. Covers Virginia, Maryland, and North Carolina.

2534 SANFORD, TRENT ELWOOD. The architecture of the Southwest: Indian, Spanish, American. N. Y., W. W. Norton and Co., 1950. 312p. illus.

100 B.C.—1945, includes Texas.

2535 SCHUYLER, MONTGOMERY. Architecture of American colleges. Part 8. The Southern colleges. Architectural Record, 30:57–84, July 1911.

2536 SMITH, J. FRAZER. White pillars. N. Y., William Helburn, 1941. 252p. illus.

Early life and architecture of the lower Mississippi Valley.

2537 SMITH, MARY LORRAINE (ed.). Historic churches of the South: a collection of articles published in Holland's, the Magazine of the South. Atlanta, Ga., Tupper and Love, [1952]. 125p. illus.

1661——.

2538 SPRUILL, JULIA CHERRY. Virginia and Carolina homes before the Revolution. North Carolina Historical Review, 12:320–40, 1935.

2539 UNITED STATES. NATIONAL PARK SERVICE. Region one, Richmond, Va., Regional Review, v. 1, no. 1, July 1938.

Some scattered material on early architecture.

2540 WATERMAN, THOMAS TILESTON. Notes on decorative cast iron. Magazine of Art, 32:584–87, 601, Oct. 1939. illus.

Alabama, Louisiana, North Carolina, and South Carolina.

2541 WAYLAND, JOHN WALTER. Historic homes of northern Virginia and the eastern panhandle of West Virginia. Staunton, Va., McClure Printing Co., 1937. 625p. illus.

2542 WHITEHEAD, RUSSELL F. Old and New South; a consideration of architecture in the southern states. Architectural Record, 30:1–40, July 1911. illus.

2543 WORTHINGTON, ADDISON F. Old Maryland and Virginia farms. Architectural Review, n.s. 6:71–72, Apr. 1918. illus.

Colonial.

ALABAMA

2544 [Alabama architecture.] A series of seventy-two articles in the magazine section of the *Birmingham News*, between May 1934 and July 1937, the first twelve by E. Walter Burkhardt, the following sixty by Marian Feare.

2545 Alabama number. Southern Magazine, v. 1, no. 5, 1934. 60p. illus.

Description of historic homes.

2546 BRANNON, PETER A. Some early taverns in Alabama. Arrow Points, 5:52–58, Sept. 1922.

2547 CURTIS, N. C. Ante-bellum houses of central Alabama. American Institute of Architects. Journal, 8:388–98, Nov. 1920. illus.

2548 FEDERAL WRITERS' PROJECT. Alabama: a guide to the deep South. N. Y., Richard R. Smith Co., 1941. 442p. illus.

2549 HAMMOND, RALPH CHARLES. Ante-bellum mansions of Alabama. N. Y., Architectural Book Publishing Co., 1951. 196p. illus.

2550 KEENE, ELIZABETH KATHERINE. Domestic architecture in Montgomery, Alabama, before 1860. Boulder, Colo., 1945.

2551 KENNEDY, J. ROBIE, JR. Examples of the Greek Revival period in Alabama — in two parts. Brickbuilder, part 1, 13:121–24, June 1904; part 2, 13:144–47, July 1904. illus.

Part 1, Tuscaloosa; part 2, the Black Belt. *Ca.* 1820—*ca.* 1840.

2552 ———. Greek Revival of the far South — Tuscaloosa, Alabama. Architectural Record, 17:388–99, May 1905. illus.

2553 LEE, MARY WELCH. Old homes of Talladega County. Alabama Historical Quarterly, 10:81–93, 1948. illus.

After 1832, Kingston, Mt. Ida, Selwood, Thornhill, Alpine.

2554 NATIONAL LEAGUE OF AMERICAN PEN WOMEN. BIRMINGHAM BRANCH. Historic homes of Alabama and their traditions. Birmingham, Ala., Birmingham Publishing Co., 1935. 314p. illus.

2555 SIMPSON, JAMES B. Alabama State Capital: an historical sketch. Alabama Historical Quarterly, 18:80–125, Spring 1956.

First published 1898. On the capitals and capitol buildings of Alabama, 1817–98.

2556 Story of Gaineswood; details of the building of a famous plantation house. House and Garden, 76:41–43, Nov. 1939. illus.

1849 at Demopolis.

2557 WARREN, WILLIAM T. Address before the American Institute of Architects. The Octagon, May 1931.

Principally on Alabama architecture.

ARKANSAS

2558 Arkansas number. Southern Magazine, v. 2, no. 4, 1935. 48p. illus.

2559 BROUGH, CHARLES HILLMAN. Points and places of historical interest in Arkansas. Arkansas Historical Association. Publications, 1:286–301, 1906.

2560 [cancelled].

2561 FEDERAL WRITERS' PROJECT. Arkansas: a guide to the state. N. Y., Hastings House, 1941. 447p. illus.

2562 FIELD, BENJAMIN, JR. The Weaver homestead in Little Rock. Arkansas Historical Quarterly, 10:328–38, Winter 1951.

1836.

2563 Historic Old Wolf House is interesting county landmark. Rayburn's Ozark Guide, 7:29–30, Summer 1949. illus.

Reprinted from *Baxter Bulletin*, Norfork, 1809.

2564 HOOD, BOBBIE SUE. The Albert Pike home. Arkansas Historical Quarterly, 13:123–26, Spring 1954.

Little Rock, 1840.

2565 KENNAN, CLARA B. Arkansas's Old State House. Arkansas Historical Quarterly, 9:33–42, Spring 1950. illus.

1833.

2566 LEMKE, WALTER J. Fayetteville, Arkansas: some old Fayetteville homes photographed and described. [Fayetteville, Ark.], 1951. 16p. illus.

1836–71.

2567 VAUGHAN, MYRA McALMONT. A history of the Old State House. Arkansas Historical Association. Publications, 3:249–55, 1911.

2568 WOODWARD, MARY DAVID. "Frog Level," oldest house in Columbia County. Arkansas Historical Quarterly, 8:327–30, Winter 1949.

Frazier Plantation house, 1852.

DISTRICT OF COLUMBIA

Washington — City (including *Georgetown*)

2569 AMERICAN INSTITUTE OF ARCHITECTS. WASHINGTON CHAPTER. A guide to the architecture of Washington, D. C. Washington, D. C., Washington-Metropolitan Chapter AIA, 1965. 211p. illus.

2570 ———. WASHINGTON-METROPOLITAN CHAPTER. Washington architecture, 1791–1957. New York, Reinhold Publishing Corp., [1957]. 96p. illus.

2571 BAKER, GEOFFREY. The Smithsonian. Magazine of Art, 34:128–33, Mar. 1941. illus.

1852. James Renwick, architect.

2572 BEALE, MARIE OGE. Decatur House and its inhabitants. [Washington, D. C.? 1954.] 156p. illus.

1818. B. H. Latrobe, architect.

2573 BLAIR, GIST. Lafayette Square. Columbia Historical Society. Records, 28:133–73, 1926.

2574 BROWN, B. T. One of the finest examples of the early Federal home: Dumbarton house in Georgetown. Arts and Decoration, 45:28–31, Nov. 1936. illus.

Between 1780 and 1795.

2575 BROWN, GLENN. Brief description and history of the Octagon house, Dr. William Thornton, architect. Washington, D. C., 1903. 4p. illus.

2576 ———. The making of a plan for Washington city. Columbia Historical Society. Records, 6:1–10, 1903.

L'Enfant's plan.

2577 ————. The Octagon, Dr. William Thornton, architect. Washington, D. C., American Institute of Architects, 1915. 25p. illus.
(1799–1800).

2578 ————. The plan of L'Enfant for the city of Washington and its effect upon the future development of the city. Columbia Historical Society. Records, 12:1–20, 1909.

2579 BRYAN, WILHELMUS BOGART. Dreamers as capital city builders. Columbia Historical Society. Records, 40–41:53–61, 1940.
Brief sketches of Law, Blodget, and Thornton.

2580 ————. Hotels of Washington prior to 1814. Columbia Historical Society. Records, 7:71–106, 1904. illus.

2581 ————. Something about L'Enfant and his personal affairs. Columbia Historical Society. Records, 2:111–17, 1899.

2582 CAEMMERER, HANS PAUL. The Federal city. D. A. R. Magazine, 67:477–81, 1933.

2583 ————. Historic Washington, capital of the nation. Washington, Columbia Historical Society, 1948. 98p. illus.
Covers 1789–1948.

2584 ————. Manual on the origin and development of Washington. Washington, D. C., Government Printing Office, 1939. 365p. illus.
Seventy-fifth Congress, third session, Senate Document 178.

2585 ————. Washington, the national capital. Washington, D. C., Government Printing Office, 1932. 736p. illus.
Seventy-first Congress, third session, Senate Document 332. Contains a list of books on Washington, pp. 721–22.

2586 [Capital. Contemporary description.] Cabinet of Religion, New York, 2:383–86, Oct. 6, 1829.

2587 Capital's most-haunted house to become a public monument: Octagon house. Newsweek, 16:35, July 29, 1940.

2588 CLARK, ALLEN C. The Abraham Young mansion. Columbia Historical Society. Records, 12:53–70, 1909.

2589 ————. Old mills. Columbia Historical Society. Records, 31–32:81–115, 1930.
District of Columbia and vicinity.

2590 ————. Suter's Tavern. Columbia Historical Society. Records, 26:189–93, 1924.
Georgetown, ca. 1800.

2591 COX, WILLIAM V. Celebration of the one-hundredth anniversary of the establishment of the seat of government in the District of Columbia. Washington, D. C., Government Printing Office, 1901. 343p. illus.
Fifty-sixth Congress, second session, House Document 552.

2592 CUNNINGHAM, HARRY FRANCIS. The old City Hall, Washington, D. C. Architectural Record, 37:268–73, Mar. 1915. illus.
1820. George Hadfield, architect.

2593 CUNNINGHAM, HARRY FRANCIS; YOUNGER, JOSEPH A.; AND SMITH, J. WILMER. Measured drawings of Georgian architecture in the District of Columbia, 1750–1820. N. Y., Architectural Book Publishing Co., 1914. 66 illus.

2594 DALEY, JOHN M. Georgetown University: origin and early years. Washington, D. C., Georgetown University Press, 1957. 324p. illus.
Covers 1787–1842.

2595 DAVIS, DEERING; DORSEY, STEPHEN P.; AND HALL, RALPH COLE. Georgetown houses of the Federal period, Washington, D. C., 1780–1830. N. Y., Architectural Book Publishing Co., 1944. 130p. illus.

2596 [Department of State Building. Contemporary description.] Atkinson's Casket, no. 1:25–26, Jan. 1832.

2597 DRAPER, ELIZABETH K. Only a few of the many fine historic places and people on Old Capitol Hill, Southeast. Washington, D. C., Metropolis Building Association, 1953. 12p.

2598 EBERLEIN, HAROLD DONALDSON, AND HUBBARD, CORTLANDT VAN DYKE. Historic houses of George-town and Washington City. Richmond, Va., Dietz Press, 1958. 480p. illus.

2599 EICHLER, ALFRED W., AND HUOT, L. L. Entrance detail and mantle [sic], Hood residence, Washington, D. C. Architecture, v. 40, no. 4, Oct. 1919. illus. only.

2600 ERB, ALBERT P. Early architecture of the District of Columbia. Architecture, v. 46–47, Oct. 1922–July 1923. illus. only.

2601 Famous Octagon house in Washington. House Beautiful, 44:244–45, Oct. 1918. illus.

2602 FEDERAL WRITERS' PROJECT. Our Washington: a comprehensive album of the nation's capital in words and pictures. Chicago, A. C. McClurg and Co., 1939. 178p. illus.

2603 ———. Washington, city and capital. Washington, D. C., Government Printing Office, 1937. 1141p. illus.

2604 FORNEY, R. W. Historic Octagon house. National Republic, 20:23, July 1932. illus.

2605 FRYE, VIRGINIA KING. St. Patrick's — first Catholic church of the Federal city. Columbia Historical Society. Records, 23:26–51, 1920.
First building, 1810.

2606 GORDON, WILLIAM A. Old homes on Georgetown Heights. Columbia Historical Society. Records, 18:70–91, 1915.

2607 GRANT, ULYSSES S., III. Development of the plan of Washington. Americana, 24:370–85, July 1930.

2608 ———. The L'Enfant plan and its evolution. Columbia Historical Society. Records, 33–34:1–25, 1932.

2609 GREENOUGH, HORATIO. Aesthetics at Washington, no. 1. Washington, D. C., John T. Towers, 1851. 22p.

2610 GUTHEIM, FREDERICK. Who designed the Washington Monument? American Institute of Architects. Journal, 15:136–42, Mar. 1951. illus.

Misconceptions concerning the plans of Robert Mills and others, 1836–80.

2611 HALE, WILLIAM HARLAN. The grandeur that is Washington. Harper's, 168:560–69, 1934.

Discussion starts with 1792.

2612 HALL, LOUISE. The design of the old Patent Office. Society of Architectural Historians. Journal, 15:27–30, Mar. 1956. illus.

Designed by Robert Mills and William P. Elliot, 1834–36.

2613 HAMLIN, TALBOT. Federal architecture in Washington: the first fifty years. Magazine of Art, 43:223–29, Oct. 1950. illus.

1790–1840.

2614 HARVEY, FREDERICK L. (comp.). History of the Washington National Monument Society. Washington, D. C., Government Printing Office, 1903. 362p.

Fifty-seventh Congress, second session, Senate Document 224. Cornerstone 1848. Robert Mills, architect.

2615 HOLMES, OLIVER WENDELL. The Colonial taverns of Georgetown. Columbia Historical Society. Records, 51–52:1–18.

1747–83.

2616 HUOT, L. L. Entrance detail, house at Georgetown, D. C. Architecture, v. 40, no. 6, Dec. 1919. illus. only.

2617 ———. Mantle [sic] in house at Georgetown, D. C. Architecture, v. 40, no. 4, Oct. 1919. illus. only.

2618 HUTCHINS, FRANK, AND HUTCHINS, CORTELLE. Washington's Washington. Washington, D. C., Historical Research Service, 1925. 12p. illus.

2619 HUXTABLE, A. L. The Washington Monument, 1836–84. Progressive Architecture, 38:141–44, Aug. 1957. illus.

2620 JACKSON, CORDELIA. People and places in old Georgetown. Columbia Historical Society. Records, 33–34:133–62, 1932.

2621 ———. Tudor Place. Columbia Historical Society. Records, 25:68–86, 1923.

Between 1794 and 1814. Dr. William Thornton, architect.

2622 JACOBSEN, HUGH NEWELL. A guide to the architecture of Washington, D. C. N. Y., Frederick A. Praeger, 1965. 211p. illus.

Published for the Washington-Metropolitan Chapter, American Institute of Architects.

2623 JELLIFEE, L. C. The Octagon, headquarters of the American Institute of Architects. Architects and Builders Magazine, 3:440–42, Sept. 1902. illus.

2624 JUSSERAND, J. J. With Americans of past and present days. N. Y., Charles Scribner's Sons, 1916. 350p. illus.

Pp. 135–95 on "Major L'Enfant and the Federal city."

2625 KIMBALL, SIDNEY FISKE. Origin of the plan of Washington. Architectural Review, 7:41–45, Sept. 1918. illus.

2626 KIMBALL, SIDNEY FISKE, AND BENNETT, WELLS. Competition for the Federal buildings, 1792–93. American Institute of Architects. Journal, 7:8–12, 98–102, 202–11, 355–61, 521, 527, Jan., Mar., May, Aug., Dec. 1919; 8:117–24, Mar. 1920. illus.

2627 KOCHKA, J. L. Photographing historic Washington landmarks. Photo-era, 63:121–24, Sept. 1929. illus.

2628 LATROBE, JOHN H. B. Construction of the public buildings in Washington. Maryland Historical Magazine, 4:221–28, Sept. 1909.
Read before Maryland Historical Society in 1865.

2629 LOCKWOOD, MARY S. Historic homes in Washington. . . . N. Y., ca. 1889. 304p. illus.

2630 MCCLURE, STANLEY N. The Lincoln Museum and the house where Lincoln died. Washington, D. C., 1949. 42p. illus.
National Park Service. Historical Handbook Series, no. 3.

2631 MACFARLAND, HENRY B. F. George Washington's plan for the capital city. American Architect, 93:112–13, Apr. 1908.

2632 MILLS, ROBERT. Water-works for the metropolitan city of Washington. Washington, D. C., L. Towers, 1853. 36p.

2633 MOORE, CHARLES. Personalities in Washington architecture. Columbia Historical Society. Records, 37–38:1–15, 1937.

2634 ———. Washington, past and present. N. Y., Century Co., 1929. 340p. illus.

2635 MORRIS, MAUD BURR. An old Washington mansion (2017 I Street, Northwest). Columbia Historical Society. Records, 21:114–28, 1918.

2636 MOSES, LIONEL. The Octagon, Washington, D. C. Art World, 2:293–96, June 1917.

2637 NEWELL, FREDERICK HAYNES (ed.). Planning and building the city of Washington. Washington, D. C., Ransdell, 1932. 258p. illus.
Published by the Washington Society of Engineers. George Washington as a city planner.

2638 NEWTON, ROGER HALE. Bulfinch's designs for the Library of Congress. Art Bulletin, 23:221–22, Sept. 1941. illus.

2639 NOEL, F. REGIS, AND DOWNING, MARGARET BRENT. The Court-house of the District of Columbia. Washington, D. C., Judd and Detweiler, 1919. 105p. illus.

2640 The Octagon, Number 1741 New York Avenue, Washington, D. C. Art and Progress, 6:129–33, Feb. 1915.

2641 OLSZEWSKI, GEORGE J. Restoration of Ford's Theater, Washington, D. C. Washington, D. C., Department of the Interior, 1963.

2642 OWEN, ROBERT DALE. Hints on public architecture, containing, among illustrations, views and plans of the Smithsonian Institution: together with an appendix relative to building materials. N. Y., G. P. Putnam, 1849. 119p. illus.

2643 PADOVER, SAUL. Thomas Jefferson and the national capital. Washington, D. C., Government Printing Office, 1946. 522p. illus.
Correspondence with Hallet, Thornton, Latrobe, etc.

2644 [Patent Office. Contemporary description.] Robert Merry's Museum, 1:89–90, Apr. 1841. illus.

2645 PAXTON, ANNABEL BETTS. Washington doorways. Richmond, Va., Dietz Press, 1940. 144p. illus.

2646 PEETS, ELBERT. Genealogy of L'Enfant's Washington. American Institute of Architects. Journal, 15:115, 151, 187, 1927.

2647 ———. The genealogy of the plan of Washington. Society of Architectural Historians. Journal, 10:3–4, May 1951. illus.
Foreign and American precedents for L'Enfant's plan.

2648 ———. L'Enfant's Washington; notes on redrafting of the autograph plan. Architectural Record, 72:158–60, 1932.
Examination of the central part of L'Enfant's plan, with notes.

2649 PETER, GRACE GLASGOW ECKER. A portrait of Old George Town. Richmond, Va., Dietz Press, 1951. 324p. illus.
Street-by-street history of the city and its houses, 1703———.

2650 The planners of the city of Washington — L'Enfant, the French Catholic, and Dermott, the Irish Catholic — "The Tin Case map of the city 1797–1798" as drawn by Dermott, and from which the city has been built. American Catholic Historical Researches, n.s. 2:64–78, Jan. 1906.

2651 [Post Office. Contemporary description.] National Era, 11:198, Dec. 10, 1857.

2652 [Public buildings.] Niles' Weekly Register, 25:349–50, Jan. 31, 1824.
Reports of Charles Bulfinch and James Hoban on the progress of the Capitol and the White House.

2653 RAINEY, ADA. The charm of old Washington. Washington, D. C., F. E. Sheiry, 1932. 62p. illus.
Early Republican houses.

2654 ROBERTS, CHALMERS MCGEAGH. The Washington Monument: the story of a national shrine. Washington, D. C., lithographed by Litho Process Co., 1948. 58p. illus.
Covers 1848–1948.

2655 RUSK, WILLIAM SENER. The story of Washington. Americana, 28:498–505, 1934.

2656 SHIPLEY, RUTH B. The historic Winder Building. Columbia Historical Society. Records, 50:235–44.
1849———.

2657 SIMON, L. A. Threat to the old Patent Office. American Institute of Architects. Journal, 21:160–63, Apr. 1954. illus.

2658 SMITH, DARRELL HEVENOR. The Office of the Supervising Architect of the Treasury; its history, activities and organization. Baltimore, Johns Hopkins Press, 1923. 138p.

Institute for Government Research. Service Monograph of the United States Government, no. 23.

2659 SMITH, DELOS H. A forgotten mansion — Tusculum. Columbia Historical Society. Records, 50:159–65, illus.

Ca. 1816, in ruins in 1934. One mile outside the District of Columbia.

2660 SMITH, HAL H. Historic Washington homes. Columbia Historical Society. Records, 11:243–67, 1908.

2661 [Smithsonian Institution. Contemporary description.] National Era, 1:3, Apr. 1, 1847.

2662 [Stephen A. Douglas house. Announcement of contract for building.] National Era, 11:75, May 7, 1857.

2663 THAYER, R. H. History, organization and functions of the Office of Supervising Architect of the Treasury Department. Washington, D. C., Government Printing Office, 1886. 55p.

2664 TINDALL, WILLIAM. District buildings. Columbia Historical Society. Records, 26:146–56, 1924.

2665 TOPHAM, WASHINGTON. The Benning-McGuire house, E Street and neighborhood. Columbia Historical Society. Records, 33–34:87–131, 1932.

Covers other houses.

2666 TORBERT, MRS. ALICE COYLE. Doorways and dormers of old Georgetown. Washington, D. C., 1932. 31p. illus.

A guide. First edition, 1930.

2667 WALTER, THOMAS USTICK. Report on the new Treasury buildings and Patent Office at Washington. . . . Philadelphia, L. R. Bailey, 1838. 18p.

2668 [Washington. Contemporary descriptions.] Gazette of the United States, 3:185, Oct. 8, 1791. New Yorker, 6:332, Feb. 9, 1839. Portfolio, 2:154, Sept. 13, 1806.

2669 Washington, the Federal city. House and Garden, 78:sec. 1, 1–62, July 1940. illus.

2670 Washington homes. House and Garden, 78:sec. 2, 1–46, July 1940. illus.

2671 [Washington Monument. Contemporary description.] Literary World, 2:540, Jan. 1, 1848.

2672 WENTZELL, VOLKMAR. The nation's capital by night. National Geographic Magazine, 77:514–30, Apr. 1940. illus.

2673 WIGHT, P. B. Government architecture and government architects. American Architect and Building News, 1:75–77, 83–85, 91–93, Mar. 18, 1876.

2674 WILCOX, U. V. Octagon house. Mentor, 17:23–28, July 1929. illus.

2675 WILLIAMS, EDWIN MELVIN. Building the Federal city, the first decade (1791–1801) of Washington, D. C. Americana, 22:174–226, 1928.

2676 YOUNGER, JOSEPH. Brentwood, Benjamin Latrobe, architect, Washington, 1818. Architecture, 37:55–56, Mar. 1918. illus.

2677 ZEVELY, DOUGLAS. Old residences and family history in the City Hall neighborhood. Columbia Historical Society. Records, 6:104–22, 1903.

Washington — Capitol

Charles Bulfinch, Benjamin Latrobe, T. U. Walter, and others, architects.

2678 ANDERSON, MARY FRANCIS. The old brick Capitol, Washington, D. C. Americana, 23:162–68, Apr. 1929.

1812.

2679 ASHTON, EUGENE. The Latrobe corn-stalk columns. Magazine of American History, 18:128–29, Aug. 1887. illus.

2680 BANNISTER, TURPIN C. The genealogy of the dome of the United States Capitol. Society of Architectural Historians. Journal, 7:1–31, Jan.–June 1948. illus.

Planning and erection of the dome by Thomas Ustick Walter, 1851–64.

2681 BENNETT, WELLS. Stephen Hallet and his designs for the national Capitol, 1791–1794. American Institute of Architects. Journal, 4:290–95, 324–30, 376–83, 411–18, July–Oct. 1916. illus.

2682 [Bronze balustrade of the Capitol. Contemporary information.] Peterson's Magazine, 35:87, Jan. 1859.

2683 BROWN, GLENN. History of the United States Capitol. Washington, D. C., Government Printing Office, 1899–1904. 2v. illus.

Fifty-sixth Congress, first session, Senate Document 60.

2684 ———. United States Capitol in 1800. Columbia Historical Society. Records, 4:128–34, 1901.

2685 BRYAN, WILHELMUS BOGART. History of the national Capitol from its foundation through the period of the adoption of the Organic Act. N. Y., Macmillan Co., 1914–16. 2v. illus.

2686 CAEMMERER, HANS PAUL. Architects of the United States Capitol. Columbia Historical Society. Records, 48–49:1–28. illus.

1793–1939.

2687 [Capitol.] *See* United States Architect of the Capitol, *Annual Report*, for various years. Washington, D. C., Government Printing Office.

2688 [Capitol. Contemporary descriptions.] American Register, 1809, pp. 372–73. Atkinson's Casket, 1:25, 7:314–15, Jan., July 1832. Monthly Repository and Library of Entertaining Knowledge, 3:229–32, Dec. 1832. National Era, 6:103, June 25, 1852; 11:127, Aug. 6, 1857; 13:88, June 2, 1859. National Register, 8:130–31, Aug. 28, 1819. New York Mirror, 3:308–9, Aug. 17, 1844. Niles' Weekly Register, 10:382–83, Aug. 1816. Parley's Magazine, 4:222–23, July 1836. Sartain's Union Magazine of Literature and Art, 10:193, Feb. 1852. Western Miscellany, 1:98, Oct. 1848.

2689 CLUSS, ADOLF. Architecture and architects at the Capital of the United States from its foundation until 1875. Proceedings of the 10th Annual Convention of the American Institute of Architects . . . 1876. Washington, D. C., 1877. pp. 38–44.

2690 Documentary history of the construction and development of the United States Capitol, building and grounds. Washington, D. C., Government Printing Office, 1904. 1312p. illus.

Fifty-eighth Congress, second session, House Reports 646, v. 9.

2691 ERB, ALBERT P. Original posts and fence from the United States Capitol. Architecture, v. 52, no. 3, Sept. 1925. illus. only.

2692 FAIRMAN, CHARLES EDWIN. Art and artists of the Capitol of the United States of America. Washington, D. C., Government Printing Office, 1927. 526p. illus.

Sixty-ninth Congress, first session, Senate Document 95.

2693 FRARY, IHNA THAYER. They built the Capitol. Richmond, Va., Garrett and Massie, 1940. 324p. illus.

2694 GROSVENOR, GILBERT. The Capitol, wonder building of the world. National Geographic Magazine, 43:603–16, June 1923. illus.

2695 HAMLIN, TALBOT FAULKNER. Birth of American architecture. Parnassus, 10:8–12, Nov. 1938. illus.

Concerning the architects.

2696 ———. A previously unpublished perspective of the United States Capitol by B. H. Latrobe. Society of Architectural Historians. Journal, 15:26–27, May 1956. illus.

Description of colored drawing submitted to President Jefferson in 1806.

2697 HAZELTON, GEORGE COCHRANE, JR. The national Capitol, its architecture, art and history. N. Y., J. F. Taylor and Co., 1897. 301p. illus.

2698 HOWARD, JAMES Q. The architects of the American Capitol. International Review, 1:736–53, Nov. 1874.

2699 KIMBALL, SIDNEY FISKE, AND BENNETT, WELLS. William Thornton and his design for the national Capitol. Art Studies, v. 1. 1923. illus.

Subsequently issued as an extra number of *American Journal of Archaeology*.

2700 LATROBE, BENJAMIN HENRY. A private letter to the individual members of Congress on the subject of the public buildings of the United States at Washington. Washington, D. C., S. H. Smith, 1806. 32p.

2701 LATROBE, JOHN HAZLEHURST BONNEVAL. The Capitol and Washington at the beginning of the present century. Baltimore, W. K. Boyle, 1881. 30p. illus.

An address delivered before the American Institute of Architects, 1881.

2702 MILLS, ROBERT. Guide to the Capitol of the United States. Washington, D. C., J. C. Greer, 1854. 82p. illus.

First edition, 1834.

2703 NORTON, PAUL FOOTE. Latrobe, Jefferson, and the national Capitol. Doctoral Dissertation, Princeton University, 1952. [442 leaves.]

1801–17.

2704 ———. Latrobe's ceiling for the Hall of Representatives. Society of Architectural Historians. Journal, 10:5–10, May 1951. illus.
1804–7.

2705 PAGE, WILLIAM TYLER. The story of the nation's Capitol. Alexandria, Va., Washington — Mt. Vernon Memorial Book Corp., 1932. 184p. illus.
History and description.

2706 ROSENBERGER, HOMER T. Thomas Ustick Walter and the completion of the United States Capitol. Columbia Historical Society. Records, 50:273–322. illus.
1851–65.

2707 WALTER, THOMAS USTICK. Letter to the Committee of the United States Senate on Public Buildings, in reference to an enlargement of the Capitol. . . . Washington, D. C., L. Towers, 1850. 7p.

2708 ———. Report of the architect of the United States Capitol extension and the new dome. . . . Washington, D. C., Government Printing Office, 1864. 10p.

2709 Who was the architect of the United States Capitol extension? Architecture, 36:138–39, July 1917.

Washington — White House
James Hoban and Benjamin Latrobe, architects.

2710 BAKER, ABBY GUNN. The erection of the White House. Columbia Historical Society. Records, 16:120–29, 1913.

2711 BIBB, A. BURNLEY. Restoration of the White House. House and Garden, 3:127–39, Mar. 1903. illus.

2712 BRYAN, WILHELMUS BOGART. The name White House. Columbia Historical Society. Records, 1932, pp. 33–34, 306–7.

2713 CAEMMERER, HANS PAUL. The White House. South Atlantic Quarterly, 47:501–21, Oct. 1948.
Covers 1791–1946.

2714 CHITTENDEN, CECIL ROSS. The White House and its yesterdays; a narrative of an American home. Alexandria, Va., Washington–Mt. Vernon Memorial Book Corp., 1932. 155p. illus.

2715 GRIFFIN, M. I. J. Irish builders of the White House. American-Irish Historical Society. Journal, v. 7, 1907.

2716 ———. James Hoban, the architect and builder of the White House. American Catholic Historical Researches, Jan. 1907.

2717 GUTHEIM, F. Rebuilding the White House. Architectural Record, 105:116–19ff., June 1949. illus.

2718 KIMBALL, SIDNEY FISKE. The genesis of the White House. Century, 95:523–28, Feb. 1918.

2719 LEWIS, ETHEL. The White House, an informal history of its architecture, interiors and gardens. N. Y., Dodd, Mead and Co., 1937. 330p. illus.

2720 MEHAFFEY, JOSEPH C. Early history of the White House. Military Engineer, 20:201–6, May–June 1928.

2721 MOORE, CHARLES. The restoration of the White House. Century Magazine, 65:807–31, Apr. 1903.

2722 ———. The restoration of the White House. D. A. R. Magazine, 57:513–44, Sept. 1923.

2723 NEWLANDS, FRANCIS GRIFFITH. White House restoration. Washington, D. C., Government Printing Office, 1904. 31p.

2724 ORR, DOUGLAS WILLIAM. The renovation of the White House. American Institute of Architects. Journal, 13:111–18, 160–67, Mar.–Apr. 1950. illus.
Repairs and additions since 1807.

2725 The restoration of the White House. American Architect, 79:67–70, Feb. 28, 1903.

2726 The restoration of the White House. Message of the President of the United States, transmitting the report of the architects. Washington, D. C., Government Printing Office, 1903. 51p. illus.
Fifty-seventh Congress, second session, Senate Document 197.

2727 SCHUYLER, MONTGOMERY. The new White House. Architectural Record, 13:358–88, Apr. 1903. illus.

2728 SINGLETON, ESTHER. The story of the White House. N. Y., S. S. McClure Co., 1907. 2v. illus.

2729 SMALLEY, E. V. The White House. Century Magazine, 27:805–15, Apr. 1884. illus.

2730 TRUETT, RANDLE BOND. The White House, home of the Presidents. N. Y., Hastings House, 1949. 81p. illus.
1792———.

2731 [White House. Contemporary descriptions.] American Penny Magazine, 2:333–34, June 27, 1846. Atkinson's Casket, 9:409, Sept. 1831. Robert Merry's Museum, 9:183, June 1845. National Register, 4:176, Sept. 13, 1817.

2732 [White House. 1823.] Niles' Weekly Register, 25:349–50, Jan. 31, 1824.
Copy of a letter from Charles Bulfinch to Joseph Elgar, Commissioner of Public Buildings, enclosing report on progress on the President's house.

FLORIDA

2733 CONNOR, JEANNETTE THURBER. Nine old wooden forts of St. Augustine. Florida Historical Society. Quarterly, 4:103–11, 171–80, Jan., Apr. 1926.

2734 FEDERAL WRITERS' PROJECT. Florida: a guide to the southernmost state. N. Y., Oxford University Press, 1939. 600p. illus.

2735 ———. A guide to Key West. N. Y., Hastings House, 1949. 122p. illus.

1513———. American Guide Series. First published, 1941.

2736 ———. Seeing Saint Augustine. Saint Augustine, Fla., The Record Press, 1937. 73p. illus.

2737 Gregory House being restored in Torreya State Park. Museum News, 18:1, 5, May 15, 1940.

2738 GRIFFIN, JOHN W. The Addison Blockhouse. Florida Historical Quarterly, 30:276–93, Jan. 1952. illus.

1836. Volusia County.

2739 ———. An archeologist at Fort Gadsen. Florida Historical Quarterly, 28:254–61, Apr. 1950.

1818. Franklin County.

2740 HARRIGAN, ANTHONY, AND DAVIS, MARY LAMAR. Two plantation houses in Florida. Antiques, 64:46–47, July 1953. illus.

The Grove, 1827, and Goodwood, 1840's, near Tallahassee.

2741 JONES, E. ALFRED. A drawing of the Governor's house at St. Augustine in east Florida in 1764. Art in America, 10:82–85, Feb. 1922. illus.

2742 MATSCHAT, CECILE HULSE. Suwannee River. N. Y., Farrar and Rinehart, 1938. 296p. illus.

Rivers of America series.

2743 PHINNEY, A. H. Florida's Spanish missions. Florida Historical Society. Quarterly, 4:15–21, July 1925.

2744 REYNOLDS, CHARLES B. The oldest house in the United States, St. Augustine, Florida. N. Y., Foster and Reynolds Co., 1921. 31p.

An examination of the St. Augustine Historical Society's claim that its house on St. Francis Street was built in the year 1565 by the Franciscan monks.

2745 THOMAS, DAVID Y. Report upon the historic buildings, monuments and local archives of St. Augustine, Florida. American Historical Association. Reports, 1:339–52, 1905.

2746 UNITED STATES. NATIONAL PARK SERVICE. Fort Marion and Fort Matanzas National Monuments. Washington, D. C., Government Printing Office, 1940. 16p. illus.

St. Augustine.

2747 VOLLBRECHT, JOHN L. The dramatic story of Spain's great 17th century fortress in Saint Augustine. St. Augustine, Fla., The Record Press, 1948. 32p. illus.

Castillo de San Marlos.

GEORGIA

2748 BANDY, MRS. B. J. The old Vann house in Georgia. Chronicles of Oklahoma, 32:94–98, Spring 1954.

Spring Place, Ga., *ca.* 1720———, and plans to restore it.

2749 BEESON, LEOLA SELMAN. The old state capitol in Milledgeville and its cost. Georgia Historical Quarterly, 34:195–202, Sept. 1950.
1805–11.

2750 BROOKS, ROBERT PRESTON. Wormsloe house and its masters. Georgia Historical Quarterly, 40:144–51, June 1956.
Near Savannah, 1736–1956.

2751 BUSH-BROWN, HAROLD. Architecture in Atlanta. Atlanta Historical Bulletin, 5:278–83, 1940.

2752 ———. Historic architecture in Georgia. College Art Journal, 6:133–39, 1946.

2753 CORRY, JOHN P. Houses of Colonial Georgia. Georgia Historical Quarterly, 14:181–201, Sept. 1930.
Savannah.

2754 DE BAILLOU, CLEMENS. The White House in Augusta. Early Georgia, 1:10–12, Fall 1954.
Ca. 1747. Report of an archeological investigation.

2755 FEDERAL WRITERS' PROJECT. Atlanta, capital of the South. N. Y., O. Durrell, 1949. 318p. illus.
First published in 1942 with title, *Atlanta, City of the Modern South.* American Guide Series.

2756 ———. Augusta. Augusta, Ga., Tidwell Printing Supply Co., 1938. 218p. illus.

2757 ———. Georgia: a guide to its towns and countryside. Athens, University of Georgia Press, 1940. 559p. illus.

2758 ———. Mulberry Grove in Colonial times. Georgia Historical Quarterly, 23:237–52, 315–36, 1939.
Near Savannah.

2759 ———. Richmond Oak Grove Plantation. Georgia Historical Quarterly, 24:22–42, 124–44, 1940.
Near Savannah.

2760 ———. Savannah. Savannah, Ga., Review Printing Co., 1937. 208p. illus.

2761 HINES, NELLE WOMACK. Treasure album of Milledgeville and Baldwin County, Georgia. Milledgeville, Ga., J. W. Burke Co., 1936. 52p. illus.

2762 HOLLINGSWORTH, CLYDE DIXON. Birdsville. Georgia Historical Quarterly, 41:42–47, Mar. 1957.
Jenkins County, 1764–1956.

2763 HOWARD, MRS. ANNIE HORNADY (ed.). Georgia homes and landmarks. Atlanta, Ga., Southern Features Syndicate, 1929. 186p. illus.

2764 LANNING, JOHN TATE. Spanish missions of Georgia. Chapel Hill, University of North Carolina Press, 1935. 321p. illus.

2765 LATTIMORE, RALSTON B. Fort Pulaski, National Monument, Georgia. Washington, D. C., 1954. 56p. illus.
Built 1829–47. National Park Service. Historical Handbook Series, no. 18.

2766 McDonough, James Vernon. William Jay — Regency architect in Georgia and South Carolina. Doctoral Dissertation, Princeton University, 1950. 301 leaves.

Activities in Savannah, 1817–25.

2767 Mahan, Joseph B. The Chief Joseph Vann house. Early Georgia, 1:6–9, Fall 1954.

Spring Place, before 1804.

2768 Marsh, Kenneth Frederick, and Marsh, Blanche. Athens, Georgia's columned city. Asheville, N. C., Biltmore Press, 1964. 84p. illus.

2769 Master detail series. Historic American buildings: Westover, Milledgeville, Baldwin County; Davenport house, Savannah, Chatham County. Architectural Forum, 64:499–508, June 1936. illus.

2770 New England in Georgia. House and Garden, 42:50–51, July 1922. illus.

2771 Nichols, Frederick D. Bibliography of architecture in Georgia to 1865. American Association of Architectural Bibliographers, University of Virginia, March 1957.

2772 Nichols, Frederick Doveton, and Johnston, Frances Benjamin. The early architecture of Georgia. Chapel Hill, University of North Carolina Press, 1957. 292p. illus.

2773 Perkerson, Medora Field. White columns in Georgia. N. Y., Rinehart, 1952. 367p. illus.

1756—ca. 1890.

2774 Ross, Mary. Restoration of the Spanish missions in Georgia — 1598–1606. Georgia Historical Quarterly, 10:171–99, 1926.

2775 Southern romanticism. House and Garden, 77:16–26, Mar. 1940. illus.

Savannah.

2776 Thompson, M. T. The grist mill in Georgia. Georgia Review, 6:332–46, Fall 1953.

2777 Zelinsky, Wilbur. The Greek Revival house in Georgia. Society of Architectural Historians. Journal, 13:9–12, May 1954. illus.

1800–60.

2778 ———. The log house in Georgia. Georgia Review, 43:173–93, Apr. 1953. illus.

Construction, distribution, and chronology, 1780———.

KENTUCKY

GENERAL REFERENCES

2779 Andrews, Alfred. Gideon Shryock, Kentucky architect. Antiques, 48:35–37, July 1945. illus.

2780 ———. Greek Revival houses in Kentucky. Master's Thesis, Columbia University, 1942.

2781 ANTIQUES. Kentucky issue. Antiques, 52:293–388, Nov. 1947. illus.
Contents include: Clay Lancaster, "Kentucky's Architectural Firsts," pp. 331–34; J. Winston Coleman Jr., "Kentucky Landmarks," pp. 344–45.

2782 COLEMAN, J. WINSTON, JR. Stage coach inns in Kentucky. Kentucky Progress Magazine, 7:144–48, 1936.

2783 [Doorways. Illustrations.] Kentucky Progress Magazine, 6:74–77, Winter 1934. illus. only.

2784 EMBRY, JACQUELINE. Romantic houses in the gallant Bluegrass. Kentucky Progress Magazine, 6:22–24, Fall 1933. illus.
Review of 1850.

2785 FARRELL, JOSEPHINE. Some old Kentucky homes. Country Life in America, 49:49–51, Apr. 1926. illus.

2786 FEDERAL WRITERS' PROJECT. Kentucky: a guide to the Blue-grass State. N. Y., Harcourt, Brace and Co., 1939. 489p. illus.

2787 GARRISON, RICHARD. Old homes of the Blue Grass: a photographic review. Lexington, Ky., 1950. 84p. illus.
Kentucky homes built 1779–1851.

2788 HAMLIN, TALBOT F. The A. I. A. meets in Kentucky. Pencil Points, 21:279–93, May 1940. illus.

2789 HOWE, AMANDA. Some historic Kentucky inns. Kentucky Progress Magazine, 6:25–27, 45, Fall 1933. illus.
Reprinted from the *Automobile Bulletin*, November 1932.

2790 LAFFERTY, MAUDE WARD. The lure of Kentucky, a historical guide book. Louisville, Ky., Standard Printing Co., 1939. 369p.

2791 LANCASTER, CLAY. Adaptations from Greek Revival builders' guides in Kentucky. Art Bulletin, 32:62–70, Mar. 1950. illus.
1835–60.

2792 ———. Back streets and pine trees: the work of John McMurtry, nineteenth century architect-builder of Kentucky. Lexington, Ky., Bur Press, 1956. 122p. illus.
Active 1833–90, born 1812. Kentucky Monographs, 4.

2793 ———. Early ironwork of central Kentucky and its role in the architectural development. Antiques, 53:354–58, May 1948. illus.
1792–1877.

2794 ———. Gideon Shryock and John McMurtry, architect and builder of Kentucky. Art Quarterly, 6:257–75, 1943. illus.

2795 ———. Major Thomas Lewinski: emigré architect in Kentucky. Society of Architectural Historians. Journal, 11:13–20, Dec. 1952. illus.

2796 ———. Through half a century: Palladianism in the Bluegrass. Gazette des Beaux Arts, s.6 25:347–70, June 1944. illus.

2797 LEWIS, GEORGE A. Old Innes Fort on Elkhorn Creek. Kentucky State Historical Society. Register, 19:29–31, Jan. 1921.

2798 McDonald, Josephine Farrell. Some old Kentucky homes. Kentucky Progress Magazine, 6:15–18, 44, Fall 1933. illus.

2799 Morgan, Frederic L. Public buildings of old Kentucky. Kentucky Progress Magazine, 6:18–22, Fall 1933. illus.
Classic revival.

2800 Newcomb, Rexford. Architecture in Kentucky. Kentucky Progress Magazine, 6:4–13, 42, 43, Fall 1933. illus.

2801 ———. Architecture in old Kentucky. Urbana, University of Illinois Press, 1953. 185p. illus.
1775–1900.

2802 ———. Architecture of old Kentucky. Kentucky State Historical Society. Register, 31:185–200, July 1933. illus.

2803 ———. Old Kentucky architecture. N. Y., William Helburn, 1940. 13p. of text. 223 illus.
Colonial, Early Republican, Greek Revival, Gothic, and other styles, erected prior to the War between the States.

2804 ———. Small houses of old Kentucky. Kentucky Progress Magazine, 6:112–17, Spring 1934. illus.

2805 Old Kentucky homes. House and Garden, 78:34–37, Sept. 1940. illus.

2806 Pirtle, Alfred. Some early engineers and architects in Kentucky. Kentucky Historical Society. Register, 12:37–53, Sept. 1914.

2807 Reid, Kenneth. Background in old Kentucky. Pencil Points, 21:262–78, May 1940. illus.

2808 Simpson, Elizabeth. Bluegrass houses and their traditions. Lexington, Ky., Transylvania Press, 1933. 408p. illus.
History of the ownerships and descriptions of the physical characteristics of about fifty-two Kentucky houses and one college.

2809 Stratton, H. O. Kentucky doorways. House Beautiful, 77:80–81, Mar. 1935. illus.

2810 Thomas, Mrs. Elizabeth Patterson. Old Kentucky homes and gardens. Louisville, Ky., Standard Printing Co., 1939. 180p. illus.

2811 Williams, Mary Ida. Living in Kentucky; the story of old Kentucky homes from log cabin to Greek Revival. n.p., 1962. 95p. illus.

LOCATIONS

Bardstown

2812 Jillson, Willard Rouse. House of J. Rowan where "My Old Kentucky Home" was written. Kentucky State Historical Society. Register, 19:1–8, May 1921.
Reprinted in pamphlet form at Frankfort, Ky.

2813 Sherlock, Chelsa C. My old Kentucky home. Better Homes and Gardens, 2:14, 15, 40, 41, Mar. 1924. illus.
Federal Hill, 1795 and later. *Better Homes and Gardens* was published under the name of *Fruit, Garden and Home* in March, 1924.

Campbell County

2814 SIMPSON, ADA HUTCHINSON. Some old homes in Campbell County. Christopher Gist Historical Society. Papers for 1950–51, leaves 74–82.
Newport and Alexandria, Ky., *ca.* 1800——.

Clark County

2815 DAVIS, PEARL BLAIR. The old stone meeting house. D. A. R. Magazine, 85:913–14, 916, Nov. 1951. illus.
Before 1793.

Covington

2816 BULLOCK, WILLIAM T. Sketches of a journey. London, John Miller, 1827.
Includes a plan by J. B. Papworth of a projected town to be named Hygeia.

2817 MCKENNA, ELEANOR C. Covington's art treasure. Christopher Gist Historical Society. Papers for 1952–53, leaves 98–102.
St. Mary's Cathedral, Catholic, 1853. Present structure, 1895.

2818 ROTH, GEORGE F., JR. Early Covington architecture. Christopher Gist Historical Society. Papers for 1955–56, leaves 12–18.
Ca. 1817—*ca.* 1900.

Crab Orchard

2819 BURCH, ESTHER WHITLEY. First brick house in Kentucky. D. A. R. Magazine, 51:214–17, Oct. 1917. illus.
Whitley house, 1783, near Crab Orchard.

2820 HERRING, ELIZA A. Whitley mansion. Kentucky Historical Society. Register, 15:25–26, 1917. illus.
1786–87, restored. (1783?)

Frankfort

2821 FEDERAL WRITERS' PROJECT. Old capitol and Frankfort guide. [Frankfort, Ky.], N. McChesney, [1939]. 98p. illus.

2822 Georgian mansion built in 1796: designed by Thomas Jefferson. Pencil Points, 16:109–10, Mar. 1935. illus. only.
Liberty Hall.

2823 JILLSON, WILLARD ROUSE. Frankfort, capital of Kentucky, about 1860. Kentucky State Historical Society. Register, 38:277–79, 1940.

2824 KIMBALL, FISKE. Jefferson's designs for two Kentucky houses. Society of Architectural Historians. Journal, 9:14–16, Oct. 1950. illus.
Farmington, *ca.* 1810, Louisville; John Brown house, Frankfort, 1796.

2825 Liberty Hall. Kentucky State Historical Society. Register, 34:392–94, Oct. 1936. illus.

2826 Master detail series. Historic American buildings: Liberty Hall, Frankfort; Thomas Jefferson, architect. Architectural Forum, 61:205–9, Sept. 1934. illus.

Harrodsburg

2827 Harrodsburg number. Kentucky Progress Magazine, Fall 1934. illus.

2828 MATHERLY, JESTA BELL A. Interesting old homes found in Harrodsburg. In Kentucky, 12:18–19, 40, 42–43, Spring 1948. illus.

Around 1774.

2829 Old mud meeting house. Harrodsburg Herald, 1900. 40p.

2830 Replica of Fort Harrod, Harrodsburg, 1923–28. Historical Quarterly, 3:19–22, Oct. 1928.

2831 STEPHENSON, W. W. Historic homes of Harrodsburg, Kentucky. Kentucky State Historical Society. Register, 10:9–14, Sept. 1912.

2832 WINTERMUTE, H. OGDEN. Harrodsburg, Kentucky: the Jamestown of the West. Antiques Journal, 4:22–25, Nov. 1949. illus.

1774——.

Jefferson County

2833 ELLWANGER, ELLA HUTCHINSON. Oxmoor, its builder and its historian. Kentucky State Historical Society. Register, 17:8–21, Jan. 1919. illus.

2834 LANCASTER, CLAY. The homes of Francis Hunt. Antiques, 57:42–44, Jan. 1950. illus.

John Hunt house, 1814; Francis Hunt house, 1843; Loudoun, 1849.

Lexington and *Fayette County*

2835 CAPEN, OLIVER BRONSON. Country homes of famous Americans, part 7. Henry Clay. Country Life in America, 6:158–62, June 1904. illus.

Contains illustration of Ashland as built by Henry Clay.

2836 FEDERAL WRITERS' PROJECT. Lexington and the Blue Grass country. Lexington, Ky., E. M. Glass. 149p. illus.

2837 GOODE, CLARA. Chaumière des Prairies [*sic*], Lexington, Kentucky. Journal of American History, 16:325–31, Oct.–Dec. 1922.

Little on the building.

2838 HARRISON, MRS. IDA WITHERS. Chaumière du Prairie, home of David Meade. Journal of American History, 9:563–73, Oct.–Dec. 1915.

Little on the building.

2839 LANCASTER, CLAY. Ante bellum suburban villas and rural residences of Fayette County, Kentucky, and some outstanding homes of Lexington. [Lexington? Kentucky, 1955.] [19p.] illus.

1780–1857.

2840 ———. Three Gothic Revival houses at Lexington: Ingleside, Loudoun, and Aylesford. Society of Architectural Historians. Journal, 6:13–21, Jan. 1947. illus.

2841 Master detail series. Historic American buildings: Rose Hill, Mulberry Lane, Lexington, Kentucky. Architectural Forum, 62:567–68, June 1935.

1818.

2842 NEWCOMB, REXFORD. Transylvania College and her century-old Greek Revival building, Gideon Shryock, architect. Art and Archaeology, 29:250–55, 285, June 1930. illus.

1833.

2843 SHERLOCK, CHELSA C. Ashland. Better Homes and Gardens, 2:13, 35–36, May 1924. illus.

Design credited to Latrobe, 1806. Reconstructed 1857.

2844 Transylvania College, 1780–1948. Antiques Journal, 3:6–18, Sept. 1948. illus.

Logan County

2845 VICK, MRS. J. WELLS. Elmwood. D. A. R. Magazine, 90:951–52, 958, 1046, Dec. 1956.

Before 1820.

Louisville

2846 ANDERSON, KITTY. Soldiers' Retreat, a historical house and its famous people. Kentucky State Historical Society. Register, 17:67–77, Sept. 1919.

Near Louisville.

2847 BROWN, THEODORE M. Introduction to Louisville architecture. Louisville, Ky., Louisville Free Public Library, 1960. 38p. illus.

2848 FEDERAL WRITERS' PROJECT. Centennial history of the University of Louisville. Louisville, Ky., University of Louisville, 1939. 301p. illus.

2849 HUTCHINGS, E. T. Louisville. Pencil Points, 21:295–308, May 1940. illus.

2850 Old Louisville. Louisville, Ky., University of Louisville, 1961. 68p. illus.

2851 PIRTLE, ALFRED. Mulberry Hill; the first home of George Rogers Clark in Kentucky. Kentucky State Historical Society. Register, 15:49–54, Sept. 1917.

Destroyed, near Louisville.

Madison County

2852 Castlewood, Madison County, Kentucky, Gideon Shryock, architect. Architectural Forum, 61:210–16, Sept. 1934. illus.

Ca. 1820 at Richmond.

Mason County

2853 LEE, LUCY C. Historic homes in Mason County, Kentucky. Kentucky State Historical Society. Register, 7:43–47, Sept. 1909.

Nelson County

2854 ADAMS, EVELYN CRADY. Goodin's Fort in Nelson County, Kentucky. Filson Club Historical Quarterly, 27:3–28, Jan. 1953. illus.

1780.

2855 WICKLIFFE, JOHN D. Pioneer stations in Nelson County. Historical Quarterly, 2:129–33, Apr. 1928.

Forts. *Historical Quarterly* published by Filson Club, Louisville, Ky.

New Haven

2856 Abbey of Our Lady of Gethsemani, Order of Reformed Cistercians, commonly called Trappists. 1924. 39p.

1851–66.

Oldham County

2857 TRABUE, ALICE ELIZABETH. Spring Hill, Oldham County, Kentucky, home of Major W. Berry Taylor. Kentucky State Historical Society. Register, 18:23–29, May 1920.
Ca. 1800.

Pleasant Hill

2858 WOOD, HENRY CLEVELAND. Pleasant Hill and the Shaker folk. Kentucky Progress Magazine, 6:234–37, Fall 1934. illus.

Shelbyville

2859 [C. B.] Historic home. Kentucky State Historical Society. Register, p. 38, Jan. 1909.
Nineteenth-century home of Mark Hardin.

Washington County

2860 RANDOLPH, COLEMAN. The old house on the hill; a brief historical sketch issued as a souvenir. Morristown, N. J., 1921. 23p. illus.
Thomas Marshall house, after 1780.

LOUISIANA

GENERAL REFERENCES

2861 FEDERAL WRITERS' PROJECT. Louisiana: a guide to the state. N. Y., Hastings House, 1941. 746p. illus.

2862 KANE, HARNETT THOMAS. Plantation parade; the grand manner in Louisiana. N. Y., W. Morrow and Co., 1945. 342p. illus.

2863 KNIFFEN, FRED B. Louisiana house types. American Association of Geographers. Annals, 26:179–93, Dec. 1936.

2864 KOCH, RICHARD. Ceramic materials of old Louisiana buildings. American Ceramic Society. Bulletin, 17:329–31, Aug. 1938.
Technical description from Historic American Buildings Survey.

2865 LAUGHLIN, CLARENCE JOHN. Ghosts along the Mississippi; an essay in the poetic interpretation of Louisiana's plantation architecture. N. Y., Charles Scribner's Sons, 1948. illus.
Also: Bonanza Books, 1961.

2866 ——. Louisiana plantation houses. Magazine of Art, 41:210–13, Oct. 1948. illus.
Ca. 1700——.

2867 ——. Plantation architecture in Louisiana. Architectural Review, 101:215–21, June 1947. illus.
Correction: 102:212, Dec. 1947.

2868 ——. The river houses: along the Mississippi the spirit of a vanished culture lingers in the ruined columns of the great plantations. American Heritage, 7:54–63, June 1956. illus.

Louisiana, 1820–60.

2869 LOUISIANA. DEPT. OF COMMERCE AND INDUSTRY. Louisiana plantation homes. Special tour ed. Baton Rouge, 1962. 83p. illus.

2870 MURPHY, HELEN S. Souls of old houses. Louisiana Historical Quarterly, 13:59–63, Jan. 1930.

Five plantation houses.

2871 Old Louisiana buildings. Photographs by the Historic American Buildings Survey in Louisiana. Richard Koch, photographer. Southwest Review, 20:169–83, 1935. illus.

2872 OVERDYKE, W. DARRELL. Louisiana plantation homes: Colonial and antebellum. N. Y., Architectural Book Publishing Co., distributed by Hastings House, 1965. 206p. illus.

2873 PICKENS, BUFORD L. Regional aspects of early Louisiana architecture. Society of Architectural Historians. Journal, 7:33–36, Jan. 1948. illus.

2874 Portfolio of old plantation houses reflecting the glory that was Louisiana's. Country Life in America, 58:51–54, Oct. 1930. illus.

2875 Revival from ruin. Louisiana's great plantations are being lived in once more. Life, 32:72–83ff., June 9, 1952. illus.

2876 REYNOLDS, JAMES. Plantations on the bayous. House Beautiful, 82:34–35, July–Aug. 1940. illus.

Octave, Domingo, Praline, Rosewood. 1780—ca. 1850.

2877 RIES, MAURICE. Mississippi Fort, called Fort-de-la Boulaye (1700–1715): first French settlement in present day Louisiana; a report by Gordon W. Callender, Prescott H. F. Follett, Albert Lieutaud and Maurice Ries. Reprinted from the Louisiana Historical Quarterly, 19:829–99, Oct. 1936. illus.

2878 SAXON, LYLE. Old Louisiana. N. Y., Century Co., 1929. 388p. illus.

2879 ——. Vanished paradise — The Shadows, 1830; Madewood, 1848; Belle Grove; Three Oaks; Uncle Sam Plantation; Oak Lawn Manor, 1827. Country Life in America, 67:34–41, Nov. 1934. illus.

2880 SMITH, ADDE G. Louisiana plantations. American Heritage, 4:26–31, Winter 1953. illus.

1812——.

2881 SPRATLING, WILLIAM P. Old plantation architecture in Louisiana. Architectural Forum, 44:217–24, 301–6, April–May 1926. illus.

2882 SPRATLING, WILLIAM P., AND SCOTT, NATALIE. Old plantation houses in Louisiana. N. Y., William Helburn, 1927. 162p. illus.

2883 TEBBS, ROBERT W. Louisiana plantations. Pencil Points, 19:249–64, Apr. 1938. illus.

2884 WILSON, SAMUEL, JR. Louisiana drawings by Alexandre de Batz. Society of Architectural Historians. Journal, 22:75–89, May 1963. illus.

Eighteenth century.

LOCATIONS

Baton Rouge

2885 NOLL, ARTHUR HOWARD. Some southern capitols — part 2. Louisiana's capitol. American Architect and Building News, 30:145–46, Dec. 6, 1890. illus.

1847. Burned in 1862, rebuilt in 1882. Supposedly a reconstruction of the 1847 building.

New Iberia

2886 LAIST, THEODORE F. The architecture of the Bayou Teche country. Western Architect, 37:51–56, Mar. 1928. illus.

Covers: Oaklawn, Franklin; Weeks house, New Iberia; Dabney plantation house, near New Iberia; and others.

2887 PAGE, MARIAN. Historic restorations: Shadows-on-the-Teche. Interiors, 122:86–93, Feb. 1963. illus.

New Iberia.

New Orleans

2888 ARTHUR, STANLEY CLISBY. A history of the United States Custom House, New Orleans. New Orleans, Survey of Federal Archives in Louisiana, 1940.

2889 ———. New Orleans: history of the Vieux Carré, its ancient and historical buildings. New Orleans, H. Harmanson, 1936. 246p. illus.

2890 BARNETT, CARA CHASTANG. Fascinating New Orleans and its iron lace-work: romance, history. [New Orleans? n.p., 1953.] [35p.] illus.

2891 [Cathedrals, new and old. Contemporary description.] Debow's Review, 10:366–67, Mar. 1851.

2892 COHN, DAVID LEWIS, AND LAUGHLIN, CLARENCE JOHN. New Orleans and its living past. Boston, Houghton Mifflin Co., 1941. illus.

2893 COLEMAN, JOHN P. Old New Orleans homes. Clippings in the New Orleans State Scrapbooks at Howard Library, New Orleans.

2894 CURTIS, NATHANIEL CORTLANDT. Creole architecture of old New Orleans. Architectural Record, 43:435–46, May 1918. illus.

Illustrations of wrought and cast iron from the collection of photographs at Newcomb College.

2895 ———. Dome of the old St. Louis Hotel, New Orleans. Architectural Record, 39:355–58, Apr. 1916. illus.

1840.

2896 ———. Early small dwellings and shops in the French Quarter of New Orleans. American Institute of Architects. Journal, 16:27–31, Jan. 1928. illus.

2897 ———. New Orleans, its old houses, shops and public buildings. Philadelphia, J. B. Lippincott Co., 1933. 367p. illus.

2898 CURTIS, NATHANIEL CORTLANDT, AND SPRATLING, W. P. Architectural tradition in New Orleans. American Institute of Architects. Journal, 13:279–96, Aug. 1925. illus.

2899 DELCROIX, EUGENE A. Map of old New Orleans, showing locations of old houses. Pencil Points, 19:203–4, Apr. 1938. illus.

With sixteen photographs, pp. 204–20.

2900 ———. Patios, stairways and iron-lace balconies of old New Orleans: a series of photographs. New Orleans, H. Harmanson, 1938. 92p. illus.

2901 DUFOUR, C. L. Henry Howard: forgotten architect. Society of Architectural Historians. Journal, 11:21–24, Dec. 1952. illus.

d. 1884.

2902 EMBURY, AYMAR, II. Old New Orleans, the picturesque buildings of the French and Spanish regime. Architectural Record, 30:85–98, July 1911. illus.

2903 [Exchange Hotel. Contemporary description.] Niles' Weekly Register, 52:224, June 3, 1837.

2904 FAVROT, CHARLES A. Historical sketch on the construction of the Custom House of the city of New Orleans. Louisiana Historical Quarterly, 3:467–74, Oct. 1920. illus.

2905 FEDERAL WRITERS' PROJECT. New Orleans city guide. Boston, Houghton Mifflin Co., 1938. 430p. illus.

2906 FEITEL, ARTHUR. New Orleans beckons you. Pencil Points, 19:221–23, Apr. 1938. illus.

2907 FORTIER, JAMES J. A. The Pontalba historic house. Antiques Journal, 5:17–18, Feb. 1950. illus.

2908 GENTHE, ARNOLD. Impressions of old New Orleans — a book of pictures. N. Y., George H. Doran Co., 1926. 250p. illus.

2909 GOLDSTEIN, MOISE H. The architecture of old New Orleans. New Orleans, Tulane University Press, 1902. 17p. illus.

Prize Senior Essay, Class of 1902, Tulane University.

2910 Historic New Orleans. American Ceramic Society. Bulletin, 16:306–9, July 1937. illus.

Brief discussion of the sights.

2911 IRELAND, IRMA THOMPSON. Arabesque: ornamental iron work of the French Quarter in New Orleans. Design, 36:3–11, Feb. 1935. illus.

2912 JOOR, HARRIET. New Orleans, the city of iron lace. Craftsman, 11:172–80, Nov. 1906. illus.

2913 KANE, HARNETT THOMAS. Queen New Orleans, city by the river. N. Y., William Morrow and Co., 1949. 374p. illus.

2914 KENDALL, JOHN S. Old houses of New Orleans. Louisiana Historical Quarterly, 17:680–705, Oct. 1934. illus.

2915 ———. Old New Orleans houses and some of the people who lived in them. Louisiana Historical Quarterly, 20:794–820, July 1937.

2916 ———. The Pontalba buildings. Louisiana Historical Quarterly, 19:119–49, Jan. 1936.

1846.

2917 KING, GRACE. New Orleans, the place and the people. N. Y., Macmillan Co., 1902. 404p. illus.
First edition, 1895.

2918 KOCH, RICHARD. Architectural highlights of the Vieux Carré. Pencil Points, 19:231–46, Apr. 1938. illus.

2919 LAUGHLIN, CLARENCE JOHN. Architecture of New Orleans. Architectural Review, 100:35–40, Aug. 1946. illus.

2920 ———. Galleries of old New Orleans. Craft Horizons, 12:8–13, May 1952. illus.

2921 LYNN, STUART M. New Orleans. N. Y., Hastings House, 1949. 168p. illus.
1728——.

2922 Master detail series. Historic American buildings: Beauregard house, 1113 Chartres Street, New Orleans. Architectural Forum, 63:495–506, Nov. 1935. illus.

2923 Old New Orleans. American Architect, 146:49–56, June 1935. illus.

2924 OWEN, ALLISON. Architectural charm of old New Orleans. American Institute of Architects. Journal, 1:426–35, Oct. 1913. illus.

2925 RICCIUTI, ITALO WILLIAM. New Orleans and its environs, the domestic architecture — 1727–1870. N. Y., William Helburn, 1938. 160p. illus.

2926 SAUER, LILLIAN BREWSTER. Sidelights on the haunted house. New Orleans, 1930. 30p. illus.
Warrington house.

2927 SHUEY, MARY WILLIS. Ironwork of old New Orleans. Antiques, 18:224–27, Sept. 1930. illus.
Ca. 1795–1860.

2928 SPAULDING, SUMNER. New Orleans and the Vieux Carré. California Arts and Architecture, 53:7–39, June 1938.

2929 SPRATLING, WILLIAM P. Picturesque New Orleans. New Orleans, Tulane University Press, 1923. 4p. illus.

2930 STEIN, JOSEPH A. New Orleans. Pencil Points, 19:195–202, Apr. 1938. illus.
The plan of the city.

2931 SUYDAM, EDWARD HOWARD. Portfolio of old plantation houses reflecting the glory that was Louisiana's. Country Life in America, 58:51–54, Oct. 1930. illus. only.
Pencil sketches.

2932 TUNNELL, BARBARA MADISON. Aristocrat of the Vieux Carré: Grima house, a beautiful example of Georgian architecture. House Beautiful, 66:68–69, July 1929. illus.
1823.

2933 Il Vieux Carré di New Orleans. English trans. by M. Petrignani. Zodiac, n.s. 10:18–51, 190–94, 1962. illus.

2934 WILSON, SAMUEL. An architectural history of the Royal Hospital and the Ursuline Convent of New Orleans. Louisiana Historical Quarterly, 29:559–659, July 1946.

First convent, 1734.

2935 ———. Benjamin Henry Boneval Latrobe: impressions respecting New Orleans . . . diary and sketches, 1818–1820. N. Y., Columbia University Press, 1951. 196p. illus.

2936 ———. The De La Ronde Plantation house. Society of Architectural Historians. Journal, 13:24–26, Mar. 1954. illus.

On Versailles, house built on Mississippi below New Orleans, *ca.* 1805.

2937 ———. A guide to architecture of New Orleans, 1699–1959. N. Y., Reinhold Publishing Corp., 1959. 76p. illus.

Sponsored by the American Institute of Architects, New Orleans Chapter, Guide Book Committee.

2938 ———. Latrobe's Custom House, New Orleans, 1807–09. Society of Architectural Historians. Journal, 14:30–31, Oct. 1955. illus.

2939 ———. New Orleans ironwork. Magazine of Art, 41:214–17, Oct. 1948. illus.

2940 WOOD, MINTER. Life in New Orleans in the Spanish period. Louisiana Historical Society. Publications, 22:642–47, July 1939. illus.

Saint Francisville

2941 LEWIS, ADDIE L. Afton Villa. St. Francisville, La., 1935. 13p.

2942 Rosedown, built in 1835 at Saint Francisville, La. Arts and Decoration, 39:12–13, Oct. 1933. illus.

2943 YOUNG, STARK. Deep South notes — part 2. New Republic, 71:343–44, Aug. 10, 1932.

Rosedown Plantation, 1835.

Saint James Parish

2944 YOUNG, STARK. Deep South notes — part 1. New Republic, 71:315–16, Aug. 3, 1932.

Uncle Sam's Plantation.

MARYLAND

GENERAL REFERENCES

2945 ANTIQUES. Maryland issue. Antiques, 65:282–326, Apr. 1954. illus.

Contents include: "Open House in Maryland"; Aaron G. Fryer, "Odessa, Delaware"; Harold Donaldson Eberlein and Courtlandt Van Dyke Hubbard, "Holly Hill in Anne Arundel County, Maryland."

2946 BERKLEY, HENRY J. Colonial ruins, Colonial architecture and brickwork of the Chesapeake Bay section. Maryland Historical Magazine, 19:1–10, Mar. 1924.

2947 [Colonial architecture of Maryland.] Architectural Record, 3:337–46, 1894. illus. only.

2948 EARLE, SWEPSON. The Chesapeake Bay country. Baltimore, Thomsen-Ellis and Co., 1924. 519p. illus.

2949 EARLE, SWEPSON, AND SKIRVEN, PERCY G. (eds.). Maryland's Colonial eastern shore. Baltimore, Munder, Thomsen Press, 1916. 203p. illus.

2950 ERB, ALBERT P. Early architecture of Maryland. Architecture, v. 48–50, Sept. 1923—Sept. 1924. illus. only.

2951 FEDERAL WRITERS' PROJECT. Maryland: a guide to the Old Line State. N. Y., Oxford University Press, 1940. 561p. illus.

2952 FORMAN, HENRY CHANDLEE. Early manor and plantation houses of Maryland — 1634–1800. Easton, Md., The Author, 1934. 271p. illus.

2953 ———. The Maryland Cross Dwelling. Maryland Historical Magazine, 43:22–27, Mar. 1948. illus.
1676–1700.

2954 ———. Tidewater Maryland, architecture and gardens. N. Y., Architectural Book Publishing Co., 1956. 208p. illus.
Covers 1634–1850. Sequel to *Early Manor and Plantation Houses of Maryland*, 1934.

2955 ———. The transition in Maryland architecture. Maryland Historical Magazine, 44:275–81, Dec. 1949. illus.
1680–1720.

2956 KEISTER, J. L.; MUNSON, O. J.; SALOMONSKY, EDGAR; AND SALOMONSKY, VERNA COOK. Early architecture of Maryland. Architecture, v. 36–40, Nov. 1917—July 1919. illus. only.

2957 McGROARTY, WILLIAM BUCKNER. Four Virginia "Blenheims" and somewhat of those who built them. Tyler's Quarterly Historical and Genealogical Magazine, 29:241–48, Apr. 1948. illus.
About estates named "Blenheim" in Caroline, Albemarle, Westmoreland, and Accomac counties, Maryland, built around 1705.

2958 RALEY, ROBERT L. Early Maryland plasterwork and stuccowork. Society of Architectural Historians. Journal, 20:131–35, Oct. 1961. illus.

2959 RUSK, WILLIAM SENER. Early Maryland architects. Americana, 35:265–75, Apr. 1941.
Extracts from architects' advertisements in Colonial newspapers.

2960 SCARBOROUGH, KATHERINE. Homes of the Cavaliers. N. Y., Macmillan Co., 1930. 392p. illus.
Covers 1740–90.

2961 SCARFF, JOHN H. Some houses of Colonial Maryland. Monograph Series, 16:253–77, Aug. 1930. illus.

2962 SILL, HOWARD. Some old Maryland houses. American Institute of Architects. Journal, 13:5–7, Jan. 1925. illus. only.
Covers Baltimore, Ellicott City, and Prince Georges County.

2963 SMITH, DELOS HAMILTON. Old Maryland churches. D. A. R. Magazine, 59:5–14, Jan. 1925.

2964 SWANN, DON. Colonial and historic homes of Maryland. Baltimore, Etch-crafters Art Guild, 1939. 2v. illus.
One hundred original etchings.

2965 WILSON, EVERETT B. Maryland's Colonial mansions and other early houses. N. Y., A. S. Barnes, 1965. 249p. illus.

2966 WILSTACH, PAUL. Tidewater Maryland. Indianapolis, Bobbs-Merrill Co., 1931. 383p. illus.

2967 WORTHINGTON, ADDISON F. Twelve old houses west of the Chesapeake Bay. Boston, Rogers and Manson Co., 1918. 51p. illus.
Some Virginia examples included.

2968 ZIEGLER, CHARLES A. An architectural ramble through Maryland. American Architecture and Architectural Review, 125:237–44, Mar. 1, 1924. illus.

2969 ———. Colonial architecture of the eastern shore of Maryland. White Pine Series of Architectural Monographs, v. 2, no. 6, Dec. 1916. 15p. illus.

LOCATIONS

Annapolis

2970 BEIRNE, ROSAMOND RANDALL. The Chase house in Annapolis. Maryland Historical Magazine, 49:177–95, Sept. 1954. illus.
1769–72.

2971 BORDLEY, JAMES, JR. New light on William Buckland. Maryland Historical Magazine, 46:153–54, June 1951.
Work in Annapolis, 1771–74.

2972 CAVANAGH, CATHERINE FRANCES. Ancient abodes of Annapolis. Americana, 4:819–28, Nov. 1909.

2973 DAVIS, DEERING. Annapolis houses 1700–1775. N. Y., Architectural Book Publishing Co., 1947. 124p. illus.

2974 DESMOND, EFFINGHAM C. Pre-Revolutionary Annapolis house, designed by Matthew Buckland for Matthias Hammond, Esquire — in two parts. Monograph Series, part 1, v. 15, no. 4, 1929, 24p.; part 2, v. 15, no. 5, 1929, 25p. illus.
Part 2 by R. T. H. Halsey. Now credited to William, not Matthew, Buckland.

2975 EBERLEIN, HAROLD DONALDSON. The Harwood house, Annapolis. Architectural Forum, 37:159–70, Oct. 1922. illus.
Commonly called the Hammond-Harwood house (1770–74).

2976 FLYNN, GEORGE J. A miracle in wood. Southern Lumberman, 187:303–6, Dec. 15, 1953. illus.
Wooden dome, 1775–89, of State House.

2977 HOPKINS, HENRY POWELL. Colonial houses of Annapolis, Maryland and their architectural details. Baltimore, 1963. 14p. illus.

2978 KEY, REBECCA. A notice of some of the first buildings. . . . Maryland Historical Magazine, 14:258–71, Sept. 1919.

2979 MAGRUDER, P. H. Colonial Government House of Maryland. U. S. Naval Institute. Proceedings, 61:1405–11, 1935.

2980 MARSH, J. H. America's finest Georgian architecture; Hammond house, Annapolis. Arts and Decoration, 30:84, Nov. 1928. illus.

2981 RAMSBURGH, EDITH ROBERTS. Annapolis and its Early American homes. D. A. R. Magazine, 61:652–59, 735–42, Sept., Oct. 1927.

2982 RANDALL, T. HENRY. Colonial Annapolis. Architectural Record, 1:309–43, Jan. 1891. illus.

2983 SCARLETT, CHARLES, JR. Governor Horatio Sharpe's Whitehall. Maryland Historical Magazine, 46:8–26, Mar. 1951. illus.
Ca. 1764.

2984 SMITH, DELOS HAMILTON. Annapolis on the Severn. Monograph Series, 15:141–68, 1929. illus.

2985 ———. Colonial houses at Annapolis. Architectural Review, 10:69–72, 91, 96, Mar. 1920. illus.

2986 SOCIETY OF COLONIAL WARS. Maryland State House, memorial to John Appleton Wilson. Baltimore, Society of Colonial Wars in the State of Maryland, 1931. 59p. illus.
History of Maryland's capitols.

2987 STEPHENS, M. WATTS. The Colonial Council House. Patriotic Marylander, 1:7–10, June 1915.

2988 STURDY, HENRY FRANCIS, AND TRADER, ARTHUR. Seeing Annapolis and the Naval Academy. . . . Baltimore, Thomsen-Ellis-Hutton Co., 1949. 48p. illus.
First published 1937. Buildings erected around 1700——.

2989 THOM, DECOURCY W. The old Senate chamber. Maryland Historical Magazine, 25:365–84, Dec. 1930.

2990 ———. The restoration of the old Senate chamber in Annapolis. Maryland Historical Magazine, 2:326–35, Dec. 1907.

2991 TILGHMAN, J. DONNELL. Bill for the construction of the Chase house. Maryland Historical Magazine, 33:23–26, 1938.
Detailed bill of costs.

2992 TILGHMAN, OSWALD. Annapolis, history of ye ancient city and its public buildings. Annapolis, Md., Capital Press, 1925. 47p. illus.
First edition, 1914.

2993 WERNER, C. W. Architectural research in the Annapolis Dock Space. Society of Architectural Historians. Journal, 21:140–45, Oct. 1962. illus.

2994 WHITE, MRS. MILES, JR. Museum by chance, the Hammond-Harwood house in Annapolis. Antiques, 63:338–41, Apr. 1953. illus.
1770–74.

2995 WILSON, J. APPLETON. Restoration of the Senate chamber. Maryland Historical Magazine, 22:54–62, Mar. 1927.

2996 WRIGHT, ST. C., AND GARY, JOY. Historic Annapolis. Pictures by M. E. Warren and by courtesy of the Annapolis Camera Club. Annapolis, 1960. illus.

Anne Arundel County

2997 HOLDEN, ARTHUR C. Domestic architecture of Anne Arundel County, Maryland. Monograph Series, v. 17, no. 5, 1931. 26p. illus.

Baltimore and *Baltimore County*

2998 [Battle Monument. Contemporary description.] Atkinson's Casket, 9:385, Sept. 1825.

1815. Maximilian Godefroy, architect. First Egyptian Revival attempt in United States.

2999 BEVAN, EDITH ROSSITER. Perry Hall: country seat of the Gough and Carroll families. Maryland Historical Magazine, 45:33–46, Mar. 1950. illus.

Ca. 1774, restored 1926.

3000 ———. Willow Brook, country seat of John Donnell. Maryland Historical Magazine, 44:33–41, Mar. 1949. illus.

West Baltimore, 1799.

3001 BUCKLER, RIGGIN. Colonial doorways of Baltimore, Maryland. Brickbuilder, 23:140–43, June 1914. illus.

3002 ———. Early American details. Architectural Forum, 41:199–202, Oct. 1924. illus.

Mantels.

3003 ———. Mantel at Evergreen, Baltimore. Brickbuilder, 24:37–38, Feb. 1915. illus.

3004 ———. Spring house, Goodloe-Harper estate, Roland Park, Baltimore. Architectural Forum, 45:61–62, July 1926. illus.

3005 ECKELS, CLAIRE W. Baltimore's earliest architects. Doctoral Dissertation, Johns Hopkins University, 1950.

3006 ERB, ALBERT P. Mount Clare, home of Charles Carroll, Baltimore, Maryland. Architecture, v. 51, no. 2, Feb. 1925. illus. only.

3007 First National Bank of Baltimore. A bank and its times . . . 1806–1956. Baltimore, [1956]. [72p.] illus.

Maritime and industrial development of Baltimore and Maryland.

3008 HALL, B. F. Adventure with an old house: Atamasco, Green Spring Valley. House Beautiful, 77:91–92, May 1935. illus.

1750 and later, near Baltimore.

3009 HAMMOND, JOHN MARTIN. Homewood, Baltimore, Maryland — in two parts. Architectural Record, 41:435–47, 525–35, May, June 1917. illus.

Variously dated 1798–1809. William Edwards, builder.

3010 HOWARD, McHENRY. The Washington Monument and Squares. Maryland Historical Magazine, 13:179–82, June 1918.

3011 HOWLAND, RICHARD HUBBARD, AND SPENSER, ELEANOR P. The architecture of Baltimore, a pictorial history. Baltimore, Johns Hopkins Press, 1953. 149p. illus.

3012 HOYT, WILLIAM D., JR. Bill for the carpenter work on Hampton. Maryland Historical Magazine, 33:352–71, 1938.

Itemized bill.

3013 ———. "Hampton," home of the Ridgelys. Garden Club of America. Bulletin, 11:33–36, Nov. 1948. illus.

1783–90.

3014 ———. (ed.). Robert Mills and the Washington Monument in Baltimore. Maryland Historical Magazine, 34:144–60, 177–89, 1939.

Texts of related documents (1813).

3015 HUNTER, WILBUR HARVEY, AND ELAM, CHARLES H. Century of Baltimore architecture; an illustrated guide . . . including an index to Baltimore architecture. Baltimore, Peale Museum, 1957. 48p. illus.

3016 HUNTER, WILBUR HARVEY, JR. Robert Cary Long, Jr. and the battle of the styles. Society of Architectural Historians. Journal, 16:28–30, Mar. 1957. illus.

On his church architecture in Baltimore, 1834–49.

3017 ———. Salvage of 1810 sculpture. Society of Architectural Historians. Journal, 14:27–28, Dec. 1955. illus.

Entrance arch and sculptured relief of the Commercial and Farmers Bank, Baltimore.

3018 HYDE, BRYDEN BORDLEY. Evesham, a Baltimore villa. Maryland Historical Magazine, 52:202–9, Sept. 1957. illus.

Neo-Gothic house built or remodeled in 1857.

3019 KIMBALL, SIDNEY FISKE. Latrobe's designs for the Cathedral of Baltimore. Architectural Record, 42:541–50, Dec. 1917; 43:37–45, Jan. 1918. illus.

1806.

3020 LESSEM, HAROLD I., AND MACKENZIE, GEORGE C. Fort McHenry National Monument and historic shrine. Washington, 1950. 38p. illus.

1794———. National Park Service. Historical Handbook Series, no. 5.

3021 LEWIS, ROBERT ERSKINE. Brooklandwood, Baltimore County. Maryland Historical Magazine, 43:280–93, Dec. 1948. illus.

Covers estate from 1788–1916.

3022 LUCKETT, MRS. EDMOND B. The history of the Washington Monument in Baltimore. Patriotic Marylander, 1:55–61, June 1915.

1815–29. Robert Mills, architect.

3023 MARYLAND HISTORICAL SOCIETY. The re-creation of Grey Rock, Baltimore County. Maryland Historical Magazine, 50:82–92, June 1955. illus.

House near Pikesville, built ca. 1858.

3024 MUNICIPAL MUSEUM OF THE CITY OF BALTIMORE. Baltimore housing — past, present and future. Baltimore, Peale Museum, 1948. 20p. illus.

1830——. Peale Museum Historical Series, 3, Apr. 1948.

3025 NELSON, LEE H. An architectural study of Fort McHenry; Fort McHenry National Monument and historic shrine, Baltimore, Maryland. Philadelphia, Department of the Interior, National Park Service, 1961. 113 leaves. illus.

3026 Opening of the Homewood house. Johns Hopkins Alumni Magazine, 21:127–51, 1933.

3027 PAUL, J. GILMAN D'ARCY. A Baltimore estate: Guilford and its three owners. Maryland Historical Magazine, 51:14–26, Mar. 1956. illus.

1822–1913.

3028 PERLMAN, BERNARD B. The construction and cost of Homewood. Society of Architectural Historians. Journal, 14:26–28, Mar. 1955. illus.

Baltimore, built for Charles Carroll, Jr., 1801–3.

3029 Robert Mills and the Washington Monument in Baltimore. Maryland Historical Magazine, 34:144–60, June 1939; 35:178–89, June 1940.

Documents.

3030 RUSK, WILLIAM S. Godefroy and St. Mary's Chapel, Baltimore. Liturgical Arts, 2:140–45, June–Sept. 1933.

3031 ——. Some buildings of old Baltimore. Americana, 27:300–305, July 1933.

3032 SCARFF, JOHN H. "Hampton," Baltimore County, Maryland. Maryland Historical Magazine, 43:96–107, June 1948. illus.

Begun 1783. Given to National Park Service, 1948.

3033 [Shot tower. Contemporary description.] Ariel, 2:159, Jan. 24, 1829.

3034 SIOUSSAT, ANNIE LEAKIN. The old Carroll homestead, Mount Clare — Maryland Colonial Dames Headquarters. Antiquarian, 2:24–25, July 1924.

1754.

3035 STEFFENS, D. H. Colonial doorways and doorsteps in Baltimore. House Beautiful, 46:72–73, 110–11, Aug. 1919. illus.

3036 STURGES, WALTER KNIGHT. A bishop and his architect: the story of the building of Baltimore Cathedral. Liturgical Arts, 17:53–57, 63–64, Feb. 1949. illus.

Cathedral of the Assumption of the Blessed Virgin Mary by Benjamin Henry Latrobe, 1805–21.

3037 UNITED STATES. NATIONAL PARK SERVICE. Fort McHenry National Monument and historic shrine, Maryland. [Washington, D. C., 1940.] 15p.

3038 WHITE, FRANK F., JR. (ed.). Edward Thornton looks at Baltimore. Maryland Historical Magazine, 50:66–72, Mar. 1955.

Description from 1793.

Bladensburg

3039 ERB, ALBERT P. House in Bladensburg, Md., built by Christopher Lownes in 1746. Architecture, v. 51, no. 4, Apr. 1925. illus. only.

3040 ———. House in Bladensburg, Md., on the Annapolis Road, built *ca.* 1750. Architecture, v. 52, no. 1, July 1925. illus. only.

3041 KEMPTON, CHRISTINE. Colonial homes of old Bladensburg, Md. House Beautiful, 48:105–7, Aug. 1920. illus.

Calvert County

3042 FOOTNER, HULBERT. Charles' gift. Saturday Evening Post, 212:23, 80–83, July 1, 1939. illus.

1650.

3043 ———. Charles' gift; salute to a Maryland home of 1650. N. Y., Harper, 1939. 290p. illus.

Preston House called Preston-at-Patuxent.

Cambridge

3044 MORRIS, E. B., SR. Trinity Church on Church Creek. American Institute of Architects. Journal, 29:182–83, Apr. 1958. illus.

Ca. 1680.

Carroll County

3045 KLEIN, FREDERIC SHRIVER. Union Mills, the Shriver homestead. Maryland Historical Magazine, 52:290–306, Dec. 1957. illus.

House and mill north of Westminster, built by Andrew and David Shriver in 1797.

Chestertown

3046 CLARK, RAYMOND B., JR. The Abbey, or Ringgold house, at Chestertown, Maryland. Maryland Historical Magazine, 46:81–92, June 1951. illus.

Ca. 1740.

3047 SKIRVEN, PERCY G. Old Court House, Chestertown, built before 1698. Patriotic Marylander, 3:51–54, Sept. 1916.

Dorchester

3048 DOWNING, MARGARET B. First church in Maryland. Commonweal, 5:402–4, Feb. 16, 1927.

St. Mary's Church, known as Queen's Chapel, 1769.

Easton

3049 Oldest frame building in America. Current Opinion, 71:381–82, Sept. 1921.

Meeting house, 1683. (Is it?)

Frederick

3050 BOWIE, LUCY LEIGH. The ancient barracks at Fredericktown, where Hessian prisoners were quartered during the Revolutionary War. Frederick, Md., Maryland State School for the Deaf, 1939. 31p. illus.

3051 DELAPLAINE, E. S. Historic shrine in Maryland: Taney home at Frederick. National Republic, 22:12–13, Oct. 1934. illus.

1815.

3052 ———. Visiting the Taney home. National Republic, 18:20–21, Sept. 1930. illus.

1799.

Howard County

3053 HABER, FRANCIS C. Burleigh Manor in Howard County. Maryland Historical Magazine, 51:212–23, Sept. 1956. illus.
Ca. 1805.

3054 SCARFF, JOHN HENRY. Belmont, Howard County. Maryland Historical Magazine, 48:37–52, Mar. 1953. illus.
By Caleb Dorsey, ca. 1732–38.

Leonardtown

3055 POOLE, MARTHA SPRIGG. Tudor Hall and those who lived there. Maryland Historical Magazine, 46:257–77, Dec. 1951. illus.
1744——.

Montgomery County

3056 DUNLOP, GEORGE THOMAS; DUNLOP, ALEXANDER McCOOK; AND LEISENRING, L. MORRIS. Hayes, a Montgomery County house. Maryland Historical Magazine, 49:89–115, June 1954. illus.
1760's.

3057 FARQUHAR, ROGER BROOKE. Historic Montgomery County, Maryland, old homes and history. Silver Spring, Md., 1952. 373p. illus.
Ca. 1775——. Includes Georgetown, D. C.

Prince Georges County

3058 BROWN, WARD. Montpelier, the Snowden-Long house, Prince Georges County, Maryland. Monograph Series, 16:169–96, 1930. illus.
Before 1751, near Laurel.

3059 CRENSHAW, MARY MAYO. Dower house, Calvert family mansion, Maryland. St. Nicholas, 52:496–99, Mar. 1925.
Near Rosaryville. Once known as Mt. Airy.

3060 ERB, ALBERT P. Mantels in Tavern, the Marlboro house, in Upper Marlboro, Prince Georges County, Maryland, built ca. 1712. Architecture, v. 52, no. 5, Nov. 1925. illus. only.

3061 FERGUSON, ALICE L. Susquehannock Fort on Piscataway Creek. Maryland Historical Magazine, 36:1–9, Mar. 1941. illus.

3062 Mount Airy, the provincial home of the Calverts of Maryland. D. A. R. Magazine, 56:715–22, Dec. 1922.
1660 and later.

3063 THURMAN, FRANCIS LEE. Litte known and unfrequented haunts of Washington. Virginia Magazine of History, 43:139–43, 1935.
Material on Thornton and Montpelier.

Queen Anne's County

3064 CLARK, SARA SETH, AND CLARK, RAYMOND B., JR. Bloomingdale, or Mount Mill, Queen Anne's County. Maryland Historical Magazine, 50:203–18, Sept. 1955. illus.
Connected houses built 1695, 1792.

3065 Morse, Edward C. Blakeford, Queen Anne's County. Maryland Historical Magazine, 50:291–304, Dec. 1955. illus.
Built 1834–39.

3066 Waterman, Thomas Tileston. Readbourne, Queen Anne's County. Maryland Historical Magazine, 45:95–103, June 1950. illus.
Ca. 1735, recently restored.

Riverdale

3067 Holland, Eugenia Calvert. Riverdale, the Stier-Calvert home. Maryland Historical Magazine, 45:271–93, Dec. 1950. illus.
1800–1801.

3068 Holland, Eugenia Calvert, and Tuemmley, Fred W. The Calvert mansion, "Riversdale." National Capital Park and Planning Commission, Prince Georges County Regional Office, 1950. 45p. illus.
1802.

Saint Mary's County

3069 Forman, Henry Chandlee. The "Kent Fort Manor" and "St. Peter's Key" myths. Maryland Historical Magazine, 49:171–74, June 1954.
On confusion and misinformation on their identity and age.

3070 ———. The Rose Croft in old St. Mary's. Maryland Historical Magazine, 35:26–31, 1940.
Plantation house in city of St. Mary's.

3071 McKenna, Marian. Sotterly, St. Mary's County. Maryland Historical Magazine, 46:173–87, Sept. 1951. illus.
Before 1727.

3072 Nairn, Fraser. Mr. Satterlee of Sotterley in St. Mary's County, Maryland. Country Life in America, 65:56–58, Mar. 1934. illus.
1730.

3073 Smith, Delos Hamilton. Old landmarks in Maryland's oldest county, Saint Mary's County. Art and Archaeology, 33:243–51, 265, Sept. 1932. illus.

Talbot County

3074 Arensberg, Charles F. C., and Arensberg, James M. Compton, Talbot County. Maryland Historical Magazine, 48:215–26, Sept. 1953. illus.
Before 1700.

3075 Bourne, M. Florence. Thomas Kemp, shipbuilder, and his home, Wades Point. Maryland Historical Magazine, 49:271–89, Dec. 1954. illus.
1820——.

3076 Chisling, Elliott L. Wye house, home of the Lloyd's, Talbot County, Maryland. Monograph Series, v. 16, no. 5, 1930. 23p. illus.
Ca. 1782.

3077 Howard, McHenry. Wye house. Talbot County, Maryland. Maryland Historical Magazine, 18:293–99, Dec. 1923.

3078 Isaac, Erich. Kent Island. Maryland Historical Magazine, 52:93–119, 210–32, June, Sept. 1957. illus.

Based on Master's Thesis, Johns Hopkins University. Includes account of Kent Fort Manor, 1639–1919.

3079 Merritt, Elizabeth. Old Wye Church, Talbot County, Maryland, 1694–1949: a history of St. Luke's at Nye Mills. . . . Baltimore, Maryland Historical Society, 1949. 42p.

3080 Tilghman, J. Donnell. Wye house. Maryland Historical Magazine, 48:89–108, June 1953. illus.

Ca. 1663.

Washington County

3081 Mish, Mary Vernon. Park Head Church and the Reverend Jeremiah Mason. Maryland Historical Magazine, 51:39–49, Mar. 1956.

Methodist Episcopal Church, near Pecktonville, Md., 1833.

MISSISSIPPI

GENERAL REFERENCES

3082 Deupree, Mrs. N. D. Some historic homes in Mississippi. Mississippi Historical Society. Publications, 6:245–64, 1902; 7:325–47, 1903. illus.

Brief sketches of twenty-one houses.

3083 Federal Writers' Project. Mississippi: a guide to the Magnolia State. N. Y., Hastings House, 1949. 545p. illus.

First published 1938. American Guide Series.

3084 Oliver, Nola Nance. The Gulf Coast of Mississippi. N. Y., Hastings House, 1941.

Photographs with brief descriptions.

3085 Sutton, Cantey Venable (ed.). History of art in Mississippi. Gulfport, Miss., Dixie Press, 1929. 177p. illus.

LOCATIONS

Biloxi

3086 Evans, W. A. Jefferson Davis shrine — Beauvoir house. Journal of Mississippi History, 2:206–11, 1940.

3087 Ragusin, Anthony V. The centennial of the Biloxi Lighthouse. Journal of Mississippi History, 11:204–6, July 1949.

1847–1949.

3088 Smith, Katherine Louise. Home of Jefferson Davis. House Beautiful, 15:272–74, Apr. 1904. illus.

Beauvoir, 1852–54.

Jackson

3089 HOLCOMB, GENE. The Mississippi Governor's Mansion. Journal of Mississippi History, 2:3–21, 1940.

3090 NOLL, ARTHUR HOWARD. Some southern capitols — part 1, Mississippi's Capitol. American Architect and Building News, 29:84–86, Aug. 9, 1890. illus.
1836–39. William Nichols, architect.

3091 TAYLOR, J. R. Capitol buildings of Mississippi. Mississippi Department of Archives and History. Register, pp. 567–77, 1904.

Natchez

3092 COOPER, J. WESLEY. Natchez: a treasure of ante-bellum homes. Philadelphia, E. Stern, [for Southern Historical Publications, 1957]. 159p. illus.
Thirty-five houses in and near Natchez, 1780–1861.

3093 CUTTS, ANSON BAILEY. America preserved. Architectural Review, 83:183–86, Apr. 1938. illus.
Colonial and Classic Revival, in and near Natchez.

3094 DUPEE, FREDERICK. Colonnades in the deep South: Natchez, the Versailles of a vanished empire of cotton. Travel, 66:13–14, 51, Feb. 1936. illus.
Monteigne, Longwood, Magnolia Hall, Revena, Greenleaves.

3095 FAUST, M. E. Some historic houses of Natchez. House Beautiful, 67:310–12, Mar. 1930. illus.

3096 HERING, OSWALD. Plantation homes of the Mississippi: princely mansions of Natchez — what they stand for in American tradition — the origin of their architecture. Arts and Decoration, 43:10–13, Oct. 1935. illus.
Classic Revival.

3097 MARSHALL, THEODORA BRITTON, AND EVANS, GLADYS CRAIL. They found it in Natchez. New Orleans, Pelican Publishing Co., [1939]. 236p. illus.

3098 Melrose — symbolic of the South — built in 1845. Country Life in America, 66:58–63, Oct. 1934.
1840's.

3099 Natchez. House Beautiful, 81:62–63, Mar. 1939. illus.
Ca. 1780—*ca.* 1850.

3100 Natchez pilgrimage. Antiques, 37:140–41, Mar. 1940. illus.

3101 NEWELL, MRS. GEORGIA (WILLSON), AND COMPTON, CHARLES CROMARTIE. Natchez and the pilgrimage. Kingsport, Tenn., Southern Publishers, 1935. 39p. illus.

3102 OLIVER, NOLA NANCE. Natchez — symbol of the old South. N. Y., Hastings House, 1940. 101p. illus.

3103 ———. This too is Natchez. N. Y., Hastings House, 1953. 71p. illus.
Historic houses built *ca.* 1776——.

3104 PETERSON, CHARLES. Notes on Natchez. Society of Architectural Historians. Journal, 14:30–31, Mar.; 28–30, Dec. 1955. illus.

On Mount Locust (*ca.* 1785), Longwood (*ca.* 1861), and the prefabricated frame of a house (1790).

3105 PISHEL, ROBERT GORDON. Natchez, museum city of the old South. Tulsa, Okla., Magnolia Publishing Co., 1959. 128p. illus.

1775——.

3106 RONIM, E. E. Quaint houses of the South — Colonial homes of Natchez. House and Garden, 11:59–64, Feb. 1907. illus.

3107 TYREE, IRENE S. Natchez ante-bellum homes. Natchez, Miss., T. L. Ketchings Co., 1964. 128p. illus.

3108 VAN COURT, CATHARINE. The old house. Richmond, Va., Dietz Press, 1950. 137p. illus.

1816. Courtland plantation near Natchez now in Homochitto National Forest.

3109 WEEKS, LEVI. Levi Weeks on Natchez, 1812. Society of Architectural Historians. Journal, 15:27–28, May 1956. illus.

A letter to Ep. Hoyt, dated Natchez, 27 Sept. 1812, on the architecture of the town.

3110 WILLINK, CECILE. Historic houses of old Natchez. Country Life in America, 47:51–54, Dec. 1924. illus.

NORTH CAROLINA

GENERAL REFERENCES

3111 ALLCOTT, JOHN V. Colonial homes in North Carolina. Raleigh, Carolina Charter Tercentenary Commission, 1963. 103p. illus.

3112 FEDERAL WRITERS' PROJECT. North Carolina: a guide to the Old North State. Chapel Hill, University of North Carolina Press, 1939. 600p. illus.

3113 HENDERSON, ARCHIBALD, AND WOOTTEN, BAYARD. Old homes and gardens of North Carolina. Chapel Hill, University of North Carolina Press, 1939. 250p. illus.

3114 HINSHAW, CLIFFORD REGINALD, JR. North Carolina canals before 1860. North Carolina Historical Review, 25:1–56, Jan. 1948.

1787–1860.

3115 Historic homes in North Carolina. North Carolina Booklet, v. 2, Jan. 1903. 25p.

Covers The Groves, Wakefield, houses in the Cape Fear country.

3116 Historic homes in North Carolina. North Carolina Booklet, v. 3, Oct. 1903. 37p.

Covers Fort Defiance, Panther Creek, Clay Hill.

3117 [cancelled]

3118 MARSH, BLANCHE, AND MARSH, KENNETH F. Plantation heritages in Up-country, South Carolina. Asheville, N. C., Biltmore Press, 1962. 189p. illus.

3119 North Carolina number. Southern Magazine, v. 2, no. 5, 1935.
Material on the restoration of Fort Raleigh.

3120 WATERMAN, THOMAS TILESTON, AND JOHNSTON, FRANCES BENJAMIN. The early architecture of North Carolina; a pictorial survey. Chapel Hill, University of North Carolina Press, 1941. 290p. illus.

3121 WHITEHOUSE, FRANK E. Cape Hatteras Lighthouse; sentinel of the Atlantic graveyard. Regional Review, 3:11–16, 1939.

LOCATIONS

Bath

3122 RODMAN, LIDA TUNSTALL. Historic homes and people of old Bath town. North Carolina Booklet, 2:3–13, 1902.

Beaufort Harbor

3123 BARRY, RICHARD SHRIVER. Fort Macon: its history. North Carolina Historical Review, 27:163–77, Apr. 1950. illus.
1826–1924.

Brunswick County

3124 CURTIS, N. C. Saint Philip's Church, Brunswick County, North Carolina. Architectural Record, 47:181–82, Feb. 1920. illus.
Colonial.

Chapel Hill

3125 JONES, BARCLAY. Space, time and Chapel Hill. Carolina Quarterly, 6:7–14, Dec. 1953.
University of North Carolina, 1793——.

Davie County

3126 MARTIN, THOMAS L. Churches of Davie County, North Carolina: a photographic study. [Charlotte, N. C., 1957.] 68p. illus.

Durham

3127 Open to visitors: Johnston house, Durham, North Carolina. Christian Science Monitor, p. 13, Jan. 18, 1939.

Edenton

3128 CHAPPELL, MACK. The Cupola house and its associations. North Carolina Booklet, 15:203–17, Apr. 1916.
1758.

Granville County

3129 CALDWELL, JAMES ROY, JR. The churches of Granville County, North Carolina, in the eighteenth century. Joseph Carlyle Sitterson (ed.). Studies in Southern History. Chapel Hill, University of North Carolina Press, 1957. pp. 1–22.

Greensboro

3130 BROOKS, AUBREY LEE. David Caldwell and his log college. North Carolina Historical Review, 28:399–407, Oct. 1951.
Near Greensboro, N. C., 1766–1806.

Hillsboro

3131 GATLING, E. I. John Berry of Hillsboro. Society of Architectural Historians. Journal, 10:18–22, Mar. 1951. illus.

Lincolnton

3132 HINTON, MARY HILLIARD. Ingleside, home of Colonel John Ingles. North Carolina Booklet, 15:158–65, Jan. 1916.

New Bern

3133 BYRD, CLARA BOOTH. The Maude Moore Latham Tryon Palace collection. D. A. R. Magazine, 85:693–701, Sept. 1951. illus.

Includes account of the original structure, 1767–70.

3134 CARRAWAY, GERTRUDE S. "A waterfront Williamsburg and a miniature Charleston"; a sketch of the old buildings in New Bern, North Carolina. National Historical Magazine, 76, no. 3:4–15, 1940.

3135 CLARK, KENNETH. Eastern North Carolina town house, the Smallwood-Jones residence. White Pine Series of Architectural Monographs, v. 13, no. 3, 1927. 19p. illus.

3136 HANNIGAN, CHARLES FRANCIS. New Bern, the Athens of North Carolina — in two parts. White Pine Series of Architectural Monographs, part 1, v. 13, no. 1, 1927, 19p.; part 2, v. 13, no. 2, 1927. illus.

Colonial.

3137 KIMBALL, SIDNEY FISKE, AND CARRAWAY, GERTRUDE S. Tryon's Palace. New York Historical Society. Quarterly Bulletin, 24:13–22, Jan. 1940. illus.

1767. John Hawks, architect.

3138 ROBINSON, LINA H. Tryon's Palace. D. A. R. Magazine, 82:1752–53, Oct. 1948.

Buildings erected by John Hawks, 1767–70.

3139 VAUGHAN, M. Tryon Palace restoration. Connoisseur, 144:135–36, Nov. 1959. illus.

1767.

Raleigh and *Wake County*

3140 [Capitol. Contemporary description.] Niles' Weekly Register, 44:114, Apr. 20, 1833.

1833–40. Ithiel Town and David Patton, architects.

3141 DEVEREUX, ANNIE LANE. Historic homes. Part 5 — Welcome. North Carolina Booklet, 11:115–16, Oct. 1911.

3142 Home of a president: cottage in which Andrew Johnson was born, in Raleigh, North Carolina. Christian Science Monitor, p. 15, Jan. 12, 1938.

3143 PAULSON, J. D. Jewel of the Greek Revival style. Art and Archaeology, 35:69–75, Mar.–Apr. 1934. illus.

Capitol.

3144 STEARNS, WALTER M. Haywood Hall. Raleigh, N. C., Wake County Committee of the North Carolina Society of the Colonial Dames of America, 1948. 12p. illus.

1792.

Statesville

3145 CLARK, ROSAMOND. A sketch of Fort Dobbs. North Carolina Booklet, 19:133–38, Apr. 1920.

   1755. Destroyed.

3146 HARRILL, FANNIE GERTRUDE. Old Fort Dobbs. D. A. R. Magazine, 45:299–303, Dec. 1914.

Wilmington

3147 HUNT, H. L., JR. Orton Plantation. Country Life in America, 71:31–33, Jan. 1937. illus.

   1725.

Winston-Salem

3148 CARTER, JANE LEWIS. A picture book of old Salem, a Moravian Congregation town settled in 1766. Winston-Salem, N. C., Collins Co., [1956]. [31p.] illus.

3149 CREWS, HALL. Old Salem, now a part of Winston-Salem, North Carolina. Monograph Series, v. 15, no. 2, 1929. 21p. illus.

SOUTH CAROLINA

GENERAL REFERENCES

3150 BAUM, DWIGHT JAMES, AND SALOMONSKY, VERNA COOK. Early architecture of South Carolina. Architecture, v. 43–44, Feb.–Sept. 1921. illus. only.

3151 COHEN, HENNIG. Robert Mills, architect of South Carolina. Antiques, 55:198–200, Mar. 1949. illus.

   1802–30.

3152 FEDERAL WRITERS' PROJECT. South Carolina: a guide to the Palmetto State. N. Y., Oxford University Press, 1941. 514p. illus.

3153 HARRIS, ESTELLE. First homes in Carolina. D. A. R. Magazine, 62:613–24, 1929.

3154 LEIDING, HARRIETTE KERSHAW. Historic houses of South Carolina. Philadelphia, J. B. Lippincott Co., 1921. 318p. illus.

3155 RUTLEDGE, ARCHIBALD HAMILTON. Home by the river. Indianapolis, Bobbs-Merrill Co., [1955]. 175p. illus.

   First edition, 1941. Hampton Plantation buildings, 40 miles northeast of Charleston, since 1730 and their restoration since 1937.

3156 SALLEY, ALEXANDER S., JR. The State Houses of South Carolina, 1751–1936. Columbia, S. C., Cary Printing Co., 1936. 39p. illus.

3157 South Carolina number. Southern Magazine, v. 1, no. 1, 1934. 60p. illus.

   Some material on Colonial churches in Charleston.

3158 STONEY, SAMUEL GAILLARD. Colonial church architecture. Charleston, 1954. 9 leaves. illus.

   Sixteen Episcopal church buildings in South Carolina, since 1796. Publications of the Dalcho Historical Society of the Diocese of South Carolina, 5.

3159 ———. Plantations of the Carolina low country. . . . Charleston, S. C. Carolina Art Association, [1955]. 247p. illus.

First edition, 1938. Discusses fifty-five houses, 1686–1878.

3160 [cancelled]

3161 TODD, JOHN R., AND HUTSON, FRANCIS M. Prince William's Parish and plantations. Richmond, Va., Garrett and Massie, 1935. 266p. illus.

More material on the lands than the buildings.

3162 WILLIS, BESSIE H. Colonial and Revolutionary homes in South Carolina. D. A. R. Magazine, 43:377–79, July 1913.

3163 WILSON, CHARLES C. A history of the practice of architecture in the state of South Carolina. South Carolina Chapter, American Institute of Architects, 1938. 45p.

LOCATIONS

Beaufort

3164 FEDERAL WRITERS' PROJECT. Beaufort and the sea islands. Savannah, Ga., Review Printing Co., 1938. 47p. illus.

3165 HARRILL, SOPHIE C. Beaufort, South Carolina; the second oldest town in the United States. House Beautiful, 49:299–300, Apr. 1921. illus.

Colonial houses.

3166 SALOMONSKY, VERNA COOK. Two Colonial interiors from Beaufort, South Carolina. Architectural Record, 49:267–71, Mar. 1921. illus.

Charleston

3167 Antiques in Charleston. Antiques, 53:202–7, Mar. 1948. illus.

Colonial William Washington house (1768) and the Heyward-Washington house (1749).

3168 CASEY, WILLIAM. Charleston doorways, entrance motives from a South Carolina city. White Pine Series of Architectural Monographs, 14:241–64, 1928. illus.

Covers 1706–72.

3169 CHAMBERLAIN, SAMUEL, AND CHAMBERLAIN, NARCISSA. Southern interiors of Charleston, South Carolina. N. Y., Hastings House, 1956. 172p. illus.

3170 CHANDLER, JOSEPH EVERETT. Some Charleston mansions. White Pine Series of Architectural Monographs, v. 14, no. 4, 1928. 19p. illus.

Covers 1757–1811.

3171 Charleston houses. House and Garden, 49:198–200, May 1926. illus.

3172 Charleston opens historic playhouse with historic play. Architectural Record, 83:20–25, Jan. 1938. illus.

In Planters' Hotel, 1806.

3173 Charm of old Charleston, new world city of old world memories. White Pine Series of Architectural Monographs, v. 14, no. 2, 1928. 19p. illus.

3174 CURTIS, MRS. ELIZABETH (GIBBON). Gateways and doorways of Charleston, South Carolina, in the eighteenth and nineteenth centuries. N. Y., Architectural Book Publishing Co., 1926. 68p. illus.

3175 DAWSON, C. STUART. Gateways of old Charleston. Country Life in America, 39:48–49, Jan. 1921. illus.

3176 DEAS, ALSTON. Early ironwork of Charleston. Columbia, S. C., Bostick and Thornley, 1941. 111p. illus.

3177 Fort Sumter, National Monument, South Carolina. Washington, D. C., 1952. 48p. illus.
National Park Service. Historical Handbook Series, no. 12.

3178 FRASER, CHARLES. A Charleston sketchbook, 1796–1806. Charleston, S. C., Carolina Art Association, ca. 1940. 40p. illus.

3179 FURMAN, SARA. Harrietta, an old plantation house on the Santee River. House Beautiful, 70:475–80, Dec. 1931. illus.
Eighteenth century. Forty miles from Charleston.

3180 GUTHEIM, F. Old architecture and new plans for Charleston, S. C. Magazine of Art, 40:198ff., May 1947. illus.

3181 HEYWARD, D. Dock Street Theatre, Charleston, an artistic and intellectual center. Magazine of Art, 31:10–15, Jan. 1938. illus.
1735–36.

3182 The Heyward Washington House. Charleston, S. C., Charleston Museum, 1949. 13p. illus.
Built after 1770. Charleston Museum Leaflet, 23.

3183 Historic Charleston Foundation. Charleston's historic houses; Ninth Annual Tours, sponsored by Historic Charleston Foundation. Charleston, S. C., 1956. 52p. illus.

3184 HORTON, CORINNE. Old Charleston gateways. House and Garden, 8:245–50, Dec. 1905. illus.

3185 JOHNSON, GEORGE, AND MELCHERS, SAINT JOHN. Glimpses of old residences in Charleston. House Beautiful, 46:96–97, Aug. 1919. illus.
Covers 1767–1830.

3186 KENNEDY, J. ROBIE, JR. Examples of Georgian work in Charleston, South Carolina. Architectural Record, 19:283–94, Apr. 1906. illus.

3187 LAPHAM, SAMUEL, JR. Architectural significance of the rice mills of Charleston, S. C. Architectural Record, 56:178–84, Aug. 1924. illus.
Ante-bellum.

3188 LAPHAM, SAMUEL, JR., AND SIMONDS, ALBERT. Development of Charleston architecture — in three parts. Architectural Forum, part 2, 39:299–306, Dec. 1923; part 3, 40:33–40, Jan. 1924. illus.
Part 1: A Simonds. 39:153–60, Oct. 1923.

3189 LEIDING, HARRIETTE KERSHAW. Charleston, historic and romantic. Philadelphia, J. B. Lippincott Co., 1931. 293p. illus.

3190 McCORMACK, HELEN G. An architectural inventory for Charleston. American Society of Architectural Historians. Journal, 1, no. 3–4:21–23, July–Oct. 1941.

3191 MacELWEE, R. S. Preservation and restoration of Charleston's fine old architecture. American City, 42:134–35, Feb. 19, 1930.

3192 MacFARLANE, W. G. Quaint old Charleston, America's most historic city. Charleston, S. C., Legerton, 1951. 64p. illus.
1670——.

3193 MARVIN, ROY. Town House of Charleston, South Carolina. William Gibbes residence. White Pine Series of Architectural Monographs, v. 14, no. 3, 1928. 20p. illus.
Before 1776.

3194 MECHLIN, LEILA. Glimpse of old Charleston and the nearby rice plantations. American Magazine of Art, 14:475–85, Sept. 1923. illus.

3195 MURPHY, CHRISTOPHER, JR. Memories of the old South: plantation homes. Country Life in America, 57:60–61, Jan. 1930. illus.
Harrietta. Forty miles from Charleston.

3196 NAFE, PAUL O. Middleton Place: where history was made and beauty endures. [Cambridge, Mass., Teknitone Publications, 195–?] 32p. illus.
Estate on Ashley River above Charleston, S. C.

3197 Old slave quarters. Charleston. House and Garden, 75:70, Mar. 1939. illus.

3198 Old town houses and famous landmarks. House and Garden, 75:40–44, 48–49, Mar. 1939. illus.
1750–1850.

3199 Oldest theatre: opening of the restored Dock Street Theatre. Time, 30:41–42, Dec. 6, 1937.

3200 Plantation houses; saga of Charleston's glory told in these great river estates. House and Garden, 75:28–33, Mar. 1939. illus.

3201 RAVENEL, BEATRICE ST. JULIEN. Architects of Charleston. Charleston, S. C., Carolina Arts Association, 1945. 329p. illus.

3202 RAVENEL, HARRIOTT H. (MRS. ST. JULIEN). Charleston, the place and the people. N. Y., Macmillan Co., 1931. 528p. illus.

3203 RILEY, EDWARD M. Historic Fort Moultrie in Charleston Harbor. South Carolina Historical and Genealogical Magazine, 51:63–74, Apr. 1950.
1776——.

3204 ROBERTS, D. M. Dock Street Theatre rebuilt; federal project restores first real theatre in our country. Scholastic, 31:10–11, Jan. 15, 1938. illus.

3205 ROBIE, VIRGINIA. Bull-Pringle house (Miles Brewton), Charleston, South Carolina. Antiques, 5:168–71, Apr. 1924. illus.
Ca. 1765.

3206 SIMONDS, ALBERT. Development of Charleston architecture — part 1. Architectural Forum, 39:153–60, Oct. 1923. illus.

3207 ——. Edwards-Smyth house, Charleston, South Carolina. White Pine Series of Architectural Monographs, 14:265–87, 1928. illus.

3208 ——. Forty years of preservation. American Institute of Architects. Journal, 34:26–29, Dec. 1960. illus.

3209 ——. Some minor Charleston houses. Architectural Forum, 42:81–88, Feb. 1925. illus.

3210 SIMONDS, ALBERT, AND LAPHAM, SAMUEL. Charleston, South Carolina. N. Y., American Institute of Architects, 1927. 200p. illus.
Octagon Library of Early American architecture.

3211 SMITH, ALICE RAVENEL HUGER. Twenty drawings of the Pringle house on King Street, Charleston, South Carolina. Charleston, S. C., Lanneau's Art Store, 1914. 24p. illus.
Ca. 1765. Includes article, "Colonial House of Miles Brewton with Some Account of Their Owners," by Daniel Elliott Huger Smith.

3212 SMITH, ALICE RAVENEL HUGER, AND SMITH, DANIEL ELLIOTT HUGER. Dwelling houses of Charleston, South Carolina. Philadelphia, J. B. Lippincott Co., 1917. 386p. illus.

3213 STEVENSON, FREDERIC R. Charleston and Savannah. Society of Architectural Historians. Journal, 10:3–9, Dec. 1951. illus.
1730——.

3213A STONEY, SAMUEL GAILLARD. This is Charleston; a survey of the architectural heritage of a unique American city. Charleston, S. C., Carolina Art Association, 1960. 137p. illus.
First edition, 1944.

3214 Vanderhorst Row, Charleston, South Carolina; a prototype of the modern apartment house. Architectural Forum, 39:59–61, Aug. 1923. illus.
1800.

3215 WAY, WILLIAM. The history of Grace Church, Charleston, South Carolina: the first hundred years. Charleston, S. C., 1948. 206p. illus.
Episcopal, 1845.

3216 WILLIAMS, GEORGE WALTON. St. Michael's, Charleston, 1751–1951. Columbia, University of South Carolina Press, 1951. 375p. illus.

3217 WILLIS, E. Two historic restorations enshrining the beauty of Charleston. Country Life in America, 55:41–42, Apr. 1929. illus.

3218 WOOTTEN, MRS. BAYARD (MORGAN), AND STONEY, SAMUEL GAILLARD. Charleston, azaleas and old bricks. Boston, Houghton Mifflin Co., 1937. 24p. illus.

3219 WRIGHT, RICHARDSON. Charles-town [*sic*] houses. House and Garden, 75:27–44, Mar. 1939. illus.

Clemson

3220 COOK, HARRIET HEFNER. Fort Hill, John C. Calhoun Shrine, Clemson College, South Carolina. Clemson, S. C., 1948. 35p. illus.

House built 1802–3, recently restored.

Colleton

3221 GLOVER, BEULAH. Temple of Sports in Colleton. South Carolina History, 11:8, 20, Feb. 1948.

Col. Barnard Elliott, *ca.* 1768.

Columbia

3222 GREEN, EDWIN LUTHER. History of the buildings of the University of South Carolina. Columbia, S. C., R. L. Bryon, 1909.

3223 MASSEY, JAMES CARLTON. Robert Mills documents, 1823: a house for Ainsley Hall in Columbia, S. C. Society of Architectural Historians. Journal, 22:228–32, Dec. 1963. illus.

Reply: C. Feiss. 23:113, May 1964.

John's Island

3224 LAPHAM, SAMUEL, JR. Architectural specifications of a century ago, being a copy, with commentary, of documents and drawings for a church on John's Island, South Carolina, by Robert Mills, architect (1781–1855). Architectural Record, 53:239–44, Mar. 1923. illus.

Sumter County

3225 SAUNDERS, ANN CATHERINE ANDERSON. Hill Crest, the old Anderson homestead in Sumter County, South Carolina. D. A. R. Magazine, 45:3–6, July 1914.

TENNESSEE

GENERAL REFERENCES

3226 BRANDAU, ROBERTA SEAWELL (ed.). History of homes and gardens of Tennessee. Nashville, Tenn., Garden Study Club of Tennessee, 1935. 503p. illus.

3227 COCHRAN, GIFFORD ALEXANDER, AND HOFFMAN, F. BURRAL. Grandeur in Tennessee, Classical Revival architecture in a pioneer state. N. Y., J. J. Augustin, 1946. 132p. illus.

3228 FEDERAL WRITERS' PROJECT. Tennessee: a guide to the state. N. Y., Hastings House, 1949. 558p. illus.

First published 1939. American Guide Series.

3229 MATHEWS, MAXINE. Old inns of east Tennessee. East Tennessee Historical Society. Publications, 2:22–33, 1930.

3230 PATTEN, Z. CARTTER. A history of the mansion on the Tellico River. Tennessee Historical Quarterly, 10:366–69, Dec. 1951.
1846——.

3231 SCOFIELD, EDNA. Evolution and development of Tennessee houses. Tennessee Academy of Science. Journal, 11:229–39, 1936.

Starts with one-room log houses.

LOCATIONS

Chattanooga

3232 ALLEN, PENELOPE JOHNSON (comp.). Guide book of Chattanooga and vicinity. Chattanooga, Tenn., 1935. 27p.

Published under the auspices of Volunteer Chapter United States Daughters of 1812.

Franklin

3233 McGANN, WILL SPENCER. Old Carter house at Franklin, Tennessee. Tennessee Historical Magazine, ser. 2, 3:40–44, Oct. 1932. illus.

Greeneville

3234 CONNALLY, ERNEST ALLEN. The Andrew Johnson Homestead at Greeneville, Tennessee. East Tennessee Historical Society. Publications, 29:118–40. illus.

Occupied by Johnson from 1851 to 1875, recently restored.

Hartsville

3235 YOUNG, S. M. Old Rock House. Tennessee Historical Magazine, ser. 2, 3:59–64, Oct. 1932. illus.

Late eighteenth century, between Hartsville and Dixon Springs.

Knoxville

3236 CATES, ALICE SMITH. Blount Mansion — the cradle of Tennessee. D. A. R. Magazine, 69:344–49, 1935.

1792.

3237 PORTER, MATILDE A. Swan Pond, the Ramsey home. Tennessee Historical Magazine, ser. 2, 3:283–86, 1932. illus.

1797.

Maury County

3238 POLK, GEORGE W. St. John's Church. Tennessee Historical Magazine, 7:147–53, Oct. 1921. illus.

Near Columbia. Gothic, 1839–41.

3239 YEATMAN, TREZEVANT PLAYER, JR. St. John's — a plantation church of the Old South. Tennessee Historical Quarterly, 10:334–43, Dec. 1951.

Episcopal, 1839–89.

Memphis

3240 ROBISON, JAMES TROY. Fort Assumption: the first recorded history of white man's activity on the present site of Memphis. West Tennessee Historical Society. Papers, 5:62–78.

1540–1740.

Nashville

3241 ANDERSON, MARY F. Jackson's Hermitage — an intimate record of its builder. Americana, 26:502–15, 1932. illus.

Begun 1819.

3242 The architecture of Nashville. American Institute of Architects. Journal, 7:159–70, 251–58, June 1919. illus.

3243 BEARD, WILLIAM EWING. Nashville, the home of history makers. Nashville, Tenn., Civitan Club, 1929. 93p.

3244 BEARD, MRS. WILLIAM EWING. The Capitol, Nashville, Tennessee. Nashville, Tenn., Davie Printing Co., 1912.
Finished 1855. William Strickland, architect.

3245 CALDWELL, MRS. JAMES E. (comp.). Historic and beautiful homes near Nashville. Nashville, Tenn., 1911.

3246 CALDWELL, MRS. MARY FRENCH. Andrew Jackson's Hermitage. Nashville, Tenn., Ladies' Hermitage Association, 1933. 106p. illus.

3247 DAVENPORT, F. G. Cultural life in Nashville, 1825–1860. Chapel Hill, University of North Carolina Press, 1941. 246p. illus.
Some material on architects.

3248 Hermitage. Antiques, 22:96–97, 1932. illus.

3249 HORN, STANLEY FITZGERALD. The Hermitage, home of Old Hickory. N. Y., Greenburg, 1950. 226p. illus.
First published 1938.

3250 McRAVEN, WILLIAM HENRY. Nashville: "Athens of the South." Chapel Hill, N. C., Scheer and Jervis for the Tennessee Book Co., 1949. 303p. illus.

3251 ORR, MARY T. John Overton and Traveler's Rest. Tennessee Historical Quarterly, 15:216–23, Sept. 1956.
1799——.

3252 PARRENT, H. CLINTON, JR. Adolphus Heiman and the building methods of two centuries. Tennessee Historical Quarterly, 12:204–12, Sept. 1953.
His work in Nashville, 1846–61.

Shelby County

3253 CHANDLER, WALTER. The court houses of Shelby County. West Tennessee Historical Society. Papers, 7:72–78.
1820——.

TEXAS

GENERAL REFERENCES

3254 AMERICAN INSTITUTE OF ARCHITECTS. DALLAS CHAPTER. The prairie's yield; forces shaping Dallas architecture from 1840 to 1962. N. Y., Reinhold Publishing Corp., 1962. 72p. illus.

3255 ANTIQUES. Texas issue. Antiques, 53:385–480, June 1948. illus.
Includes photographs and some information on architecture.

3256 BRACKEN, DOROTHY KENDALL, AND REDWAY, MAURINE WHORTON. Early Texas homes. Dallas, Southern Methodist University Press, 1956. 188p. illus.
1745–1865.

3257 BYWATERS, JERRY. More about Southwestern architecture. Southwest Review, 18:234–64, Spring 1933. illus.

Includes discussion of the development of Texas architecture to U. S. architecture.

3258 CARROLL, H. BAILEY. Texas collection. Southwestern Historical Quarterly, 63:137–38, July 1959.

Descriptions of ten houses opened for the Jefferson Historical Pilgrimage, 1959.

3259 ———. Texas county histories: a bibliography. Austin, Tex., Texas State Historical Association, 1943.

3260 CLARK, MARY WHATLEY. Historical stone ranch houses along the Clear Fork of the Brazos. Cattleman, 33:19–21, Jan. 1947. illus.

3261 CONNALLY, ERNEST ALLEN. Architecture at the end of the South: central Texas. Society of Architectural Historians. Journal, 11:8–12, Dec. 1952. illus.

Discussion of geographic inflences. Several examples from Austin and the Vance House in San Antonio.

3262 ———. The ecclesiastical and military architecture of the Spanish province of Texas. Doctoral Dissertation, Harvard University, 1955. 594p. illus.

1691–1823. Abstract: *Hispanic American Historical Review*, 36:360–61, Aug. 1956.

3263 CONNOR, SEYMOUR V. Log cabins in Texas. Southwestern Historical Quarterly, 53:105–16, Oct. 1949. illus.

Construction practices, *ca.* 1835.

3264 DAGGETT, ELLA K. Early Texas architecture. Southern Home and Garden, May 1941, p. 10. illus.

French, Spanish, and Greek Revival influences on the Vance Hotel in Castroville and the Cos House in San Antonio.

3265 EVANS, ELLIOT A. P. The East Texas house. Society of Architectural Historians. Journal, 11:1–7, Dec. 1952. illus.

1820–90.

3266 FEDERAL WRITERS' PROJECT. Texas; a guide to the Lone Star State. N. Y., Hastings House, 1940. 718p. illus.

3267 GARWOOD, ELLEN. Early Texas inns. Southwestern Historical Quarterly, 60:219–44, Oct. 1956. illus.

1827–42.

3268 HART, KATHERINE. Preserving old homes in Texas. Southwestern Historical Quarterly, 63:181–89, Oct. 1959.

3269 HUMBLE OIL AND REFINING CO. A map of historical homes and buildings throughout Texas. [1957?]

Published in cooperation with the Texas Historical Foundation.

3270 JEFFRIES, C. Early Texas architecture. Bunker's Monthly, pp. 907–14, June 1928.

Methods of wood and fireplace construction and other fixtures.

3271 McADAMS, NANCY R. 19th century Texas architecture, a bibliography. Arranged for the Texas Architecture Survey, a joint project of the School of

Architecture, University of Texas and the Amon Carter Museum of Western Art, May 1964. Mimeographed.

3272 MORGAN, RUTH. Texas looks to its heritage. Antiques, 65:469–71, June 1954. illus.

Preservation and restoration.

3273 MORRISS, ANNIE MAE. Historic ranches and plantations of Texas. Cattleman, 36:27–28, 30, 32, Feb. 1950.

1718——.

3274 NATIONAL COUNCIL FOR HISTORIC SITES AND BUILDINGS. Preliminary inventory of historic sites and buildings open to the public. The Southwest: Texas. Southwestern Historical Quarterly, 56:139–44, July 1952.

3275 The oldest house in Texas. Frontier Times, 27:14–16, Oct. 1949.

Reprinted from St. Louis Globe Democrat, Nov. 1898. Log house in the Guadalupe Mountains, 1714(?).

3276 SANFORD, TRENT ELWOOD. The architecture of the Southwest: Indian, Spanish, American. N. Y., W. W. Norton and Co., 1950. 312p. illus.

Texas: pp. 151–71, 244–45, 284–87.

LOCATIONS

Austin

3277 EMERSON, SALLY. Woodlawn house. Texas State Historical Society. Junior Historian, 17:18–20, 30, Nov. 1956. illus.

1853.

3278 HARRIS, AUGUST WATKINS. Minor and major mansions in early Austin. Austin, Tex., 1958. 116p. illus.

Consolidation of two earlier works published separately in Austin in 1955 and 1958.

Beaumont

3279 FEDERAL WRITERS' PROJECT. Beaumont. Houston, Tex., Anson Jones Press, [1939]. 167p. illus.

1835——.

Brazoria County

3280 STROBEL, ABNER J. The old plantations and their owners of Brazoria County, Texas. Houston, 1930. 46p.

Denison

3281 FEDERAL WRITERS' PROJECT. The Denison guide. Denison, Texas, Denison Chamber of Commerce, 1939. 29p. illus.

DeWitt County

3282 CARRERRA, NORA. Pioneer homes of DeWitt County. Texas State Historical Society. Junior Historian, 13:27–29, Sept. 1952.

Near Cuero, 1826——.

3283 KUCHLER, MARY MARGIE. Early homes in DeWitt County. Texas State Historical Society. Junior Historian, 11:5–6, 12, May 1951. illus.

1826–48.

Fredericksburg

3284 EICKENROHT, MARVIN. The Kaffee-Kirche at Fredericksburg, Texas, 1846. Society of Architectural Historians. Journal, 25:60–63, Mar. 1966.

Galveston

3285 BARNESTONE, HOWARD. The Galveston that was. N. Y., Macmillan Co., 1965.

3286 CARROLL, H. BAILEY. Texas collection. Southwestern Historical Quarterly, 63:150–52, July 1959. illus.

Restoration of the Williams-Tucker house, 1838–40.

3287 GALVESTON HISTORICAL SOCIETY. Historic Galveston homes. [Galveston, Tex., 1951.] 48p. illus.

1840–94, covers twenty-seven houses.

3288 WODEHOUSE, LAWRENCE. The Custom House, Galveston, Texas, 1857–61, by Ammi Burnham Young. Society of Architectural Historians. Journal, 25:64–67, Mar. 1966.

Guadalupe County

3289 TUTTLE, RITA. The Humphrey house. Texas State Historical Society. Junior Historian, 13:17–18, Sept. 1952.

1855, construction details, near Sequin.

Henderson

3290 ROGERS, MARTHA PAUL. The old Howard home. Texas State Historical Society. Junior Historian, 12:13–14, Dec. 1951.

1850.

Houston

3291 FUERMANN, GEORGE. The face of Houston. Houston, Premier Printing Co., 1963. 61p. illus.

Primarily photographs, a few old buildings.

3292 ———. Houston: the feast years, an illustrated essay. Houston, Tex., 1962. 51p. illus.

Includes several old photographs and early maps.

3293 MOORE, MARVIN C. Restoration of the Nichols-Rice house. American Institute of Architects. Journal, 37:25–28, Jan. 1962.

1850, now in Sam Houston Park in Houston.

Huntsville

3294 FERGUSON, DAN. Austin College in Huntsville. Southwestern Historical Quarterly, 53:386–403, Apr. 1950. illus.

1851——.

McLennon County

3295 CONGER, ROGER NORMAN. Historic log cabins of McLennon County. Waco, Tex., Bone-Crow Co., 1954. 14p. illus.

Heritage Society of Waco, Bulletin no. 1. Discusses seventeen buildings.

Marion County

3296 Texas frontier home: Blue Bonnet Farm. Antiques, 42:242–43, Nov. 1942. illus.

1847, enlarged 1867, near Jefferson.

Nacogdoches

3297 BLAKE, R. B. Historic Nacogdoches. Nacogdoches Historic Society, 1939. 28p. illus.

Palestine

3298 NEYLAND, JAMES. Anderson County and its court houses. Texas State Historical Society. Junior Historian, 17:16–17, 30, Jan. 1957. illus.

Five courthouses, 1847–1956.

3299 ———. Old homes of Palestine. Texas State Historical Society. Junior Historian, 18:21–25, Sept. 1957. illus.

Houses built between 1846 and 1910.

Parker County

3300 COTTEN, FRED R. Log cabins of the Parker County region. West Texas Historical Association. Yearbook, 29:96–104, Oct. 1953. illus.

Details of construction, 1855–66.

Port Isabel

3301 MCKENNA, VERNA JACKSON. Old Point Isabel Lighthouse: beacon of Brazos Santiago. Port Isabel, Tex., Port Isabel Press, 1952. 24p. illus.

1852——.

San Antonio

3302 DALTON, INEZ STRICKLAND. The Menger Hotel: San Antonio's Civic and Social Center, 1859–1877. West Texas Historical Association. Yearbook, 15:85–102, Oct. 1956.

3303 FEDERAL WRITERS' PROJECT. Old Villita. San Antonio, Tex., City of San Antonio, 1939. 22p. illus.

3304 RAMSDELL, CHARLES. San Antonio: a historical and pictorial guide. Austin, University of Texas Press, 1959. 308p. illus.

Shackelford County

3305 RISTER, CARL COKE. Fort Griffin on the Texas frontier. Norman, University of Oklahoma Press, [1956]. 216p. illus.

1854–81.

Smith County

3306 SMITH COUNTY HISTORICAL SOCIETY AND HISTORICAL SURVEY COMMITTEE. [Historic houses] . . . chronicles of Smith County, v. 3, no. 1, Spring 1964. 25p. illus.

Entire issue on twenty historic houses.

Waco

3307 BARNES, LAVONIA JENKINS. Old homes of Waco and the people who lived in them. Waco, Tex., Heritage Society of Waco, 1955. illus.

Ante-bellum and 1860's.

VIRGINIA

GENERAL REFERENCES

3308 ALLEN, EDWARD B. Chimneys of Colonial days. International Studio, 77:156–59, May 1923. illus.

3309 ANDREWS, MARIETTA MINNIGERODE. George Washington's country. N. Y., E. P. Dutton Co., 1930. 318p. illus.

3310 Architecture in Virginia. Virginia Historical Register, 6:37–42, Jan. 1853.
The progress of architecture in Virginia.

3311 [Architecture in Virginia from preservation standpoint.] *See* Association for Preservation of Virginia Antiquities. *Yearbook*, 1896———.

3312 ARTHUR, ROBERT. Tidewater forts of Colonial Virginia. Coast Artillery Journal, 57:3–20, July 1922.

3313 CARSON, WILLIAM E. Historic shrines of Virginia. Richmond, Va., State Commission on Conservation and Development, 1933. 76p. illus.

3314 CHANDLER, J. A. C., AND THAMES, T. B. Colonial Virginia. Richmond, Va., Times-Dispatch Co., 1907. 388p. illus.

3315 CLAIBORNE, HERBERT AUGUSTINE. Comments on Virginia brickwork before 1800. [Boston], Walpole Society, 1957. 47 [43]p. illus.
Covers 1611–1800.

3316 CLARK, KENNETH. Architectural inspiration from northern Virginia. Monograph Series, v. 17, no. 3, 1931. 26p. illus.
Covers 1757–1805 in Fairfax and Stafford counties.

3317 DONOVAN, JERRY. John Jordan, Virginia builder. Society of Architectural Historians. Journal, 9:17–19, 1950. illus.
1777–1854. Activities of 1802–54.

3318 FEDERAL WRITERS' PROJECT. Virginia: a guide to the Old Dominion. N. Y., Oxford University Press, 1940. 699p. illus.

3319 FISHWICK, MARSHALL WILLIAM. John Jordan: Virginia builder. Commonwealth: The Magazine of Virginia, 17:13–14, 39, Oct. 1950.
Architectural activities, 1810———.

3320 ———. The Virginia tradition in architecture. American Institute of Architects. Journal, 22:99–105, Sept. 1954.

3321 FORMAN, HENRY CHANDLEE. Virginia architecture in the seventeenth century. Williamsburg, Va., Virginia 350th Anniversary Celebration Corporation, 1957. 79p. illus.
1607–1730. Jamestown 350th Anniversary Historical Booklet, 11.

3322 FRARY, IHNA THAYER. Thomas Jefferson, architect and builder. Richmond, Va., Garrett and Massie, 1950. 154p. illus.
Extant buildings in Virginia, 1768———.

3323 GAINES, WILLIAM H., JR. Inns, churches, and other statehouses: the capitols of the colony, 1641–1780. Virginia Cavalcade, 1:12–16, Autumn 1951. illus.

3324 GOODWIN, RUTHERFOORD. Brief history of and guide book to Jamestown, Williamsburg and Yorktown. Richmond, Va., Cottrell Cooke, 1930. 63p. illus.

3325 GREGORY, THURLOW GATES. Iron of America was first made in Virginia. [Cleveland? 1957.] 57 leaves. illus.
1619–22.

3326 HEMPHILL, WILLIAM EDWIN. An album for the nostalgic: covered bridges in Virginia. Virginia Cavalcade, 1:17–19, Autumn 1951. illus.
Photographs from 1939 of twelve bridges, 1822——.

3327 HEMPHILL, WILLIAM EDWIN; SCHLEGEL, MARVIN WILSON; AND ENGELBERG, SADIE ETHEL. Cavalier commonwealth: history and government of Virginia. N. Y., McGraw-Hill Book Co., [1957]. 686p. illus.

3328 Houses of the Old South. American Architect, 147:57–64, Sept. 1935. illus.

3329 HUMPHREY, HENRY B., JR. Homes of our presidents. Country Life in America, 49:53–55, 60–62, Mar.–Apr. 1926; 50:37–39, 65–66, 70–76, May–Aug. 1926. illus.
Mount Vernon and Monticello.

3330 JAMES RIVER GARDEN CLUB, RICHMOND. Historic gardens of Virginia. Richmond, Va., William Byrd Press, 1923. 355p. illus.
E. T. Sale (ed.).

3331 KEISTER, J. L.; MUNSON, O. J.; AND WEBER, J. A. Early architecture of Virginia. Architecture, 34:262–64, 266, Dec. 1916; 35:34, 35, 88, 89, Mar. 1917; 36:90, 91, 161, 179, July–Oct. 1917. illus. only.

3332 KIBLER, JAMES LUTHER. Colonial Virginia shrines. Richmond, Va., Garrett and Massie, 1936. 98p. illus.
Guidebook to Jamestown, Williamsburg, and Yorktown.

3333 ——. Historic Virginia landmarks from Cape Henry to Richmond. Richmond, Va., Garrett and Massie, 1929. 141p. illus.

3334 KOCHER, ALFRED LAWRENCE, AND DEARSTYNE, HOWARD. Shadows in silver; a record of Virginia, 1850–1900, in contemporary photographs taken by George and Huestis Cook, with additions from the Cook Collection. N. Y., Charles Scribner's Sons, 1954. 264p. illus.

3335 LANCASTER, ROBERT A., JR. Historic Virginia homes and churches. Philadelphia, J. B. Lippincott Co., 1915. 527p. illus.

3336 MASON, GEORGE CARRINGTON. The courthouses of Princess Anne and Norfolk counties. Virginia Magazine of History and Biography, 57:405–15, Oct. 1949. illus.
1640–1846.

3337 NASH, MRS. SUSAN HIGGINSON. Paints, furniture and furnishings. Architectural Record, 78:447–58, Dec. 1935. illus.
Concerning Colonial use of color in Virginia.

3338 [Negro cabin. Contemporary description.] Dollar Magazine, 1:129–31, May 1841.

3339 NICHOLS, FREDERICK DOVETON. The early architecture of Virginia: journals. American Association of Architectural Bibliographers. Papers, 2:83–113, 1966.
Comprehensive bibliography.

3340 ———. The early architecture of Virginia: original sources and books. American Association of Architectural Bibliographers. Papers, 1:81–124, 1965.
Comprehensive bibliography.

3341 NICHOLS, FREDERICK DOVETON, AND O'NEAL, WILLIAM B. Architecture in Virginia, 1776–1958: the Old Dominion's twelve best buildings. Richmond, Virginia Museum of Fine Arts, 1958. unpaged. illus.

3342 NILES, BLAIR. The James. N. Y., Farrar and Rinehart, 1939. 359p. illus.
Rivers of America series.

3343 PATTERSON, BRUCE V. Guide book of the Virginia Peninsula. Newport News, Va., Franklin Printing Co., 1935. 94p. illus.

3344 ROTHERY, AGNES. New roads in Old Virginia. N. Y., Houghton Mifflin Co., 1929. 223p. illus.

3345 ROUSE, PARKE SHEPHERD, JR. A James River road to historic estates. Commonwealth: The Magazine of Virginia, 21:24–26, Mar. 1954. illus.
1726——.

3346 SALE, EDITH TUNIS. Manors of Virginia in Colonial times. Philadelphia, J. B. Lippincott Co., 1909. 310p. illus.

3347 SMITH, ALAN WILLIAM (ed.). Virginia, 1584–1607, the first English settlement in North America: a brief history with a selection of contemporary narratives. London, T. Brun, [1957]. 117p. illus.

3348 SQUIRES, W. H. T. Days of yesteryear in colony and commonwealth. Portsmouth, Va., Printcraft Press, 1928. 301p. illus.

3349 SWEM, E. G. Virginia historical index. Roanoke, Va., Stone Printing Co., 1934–36. 2v.

3350 TYLER, LYON G. Colonial brick buildings. Tyler's Quarterly Historical and Genealogical Magazine, 17:69–70, 1935.

3351 Virginia number. Southern Magazine, v. 2, no. 3, 1935.
Material on the capitols and Stratford.

3352 Wales, Dinwiddie County, Virginia and Dr. Hugh Mercer's Apothecary Shop, Fredericksburg, Va. American Architect, 143:69–72, May 1933. illus.

3353 WALKER, H. History keeps house in Virginia. National Geographic Magazine, 109:441–84, Apr. 1956. illus.

3354 WATERMAN, THOMAS TILESTON. The bay system in Colonial Virginia building. William and Mary Quarterly, 2nd ser. 15:117–22, 1935.

3355 WHIFFEN, M. Early county courthouses of Virginia. Society of Architectural Historians. Journal, 18:2–10, Mar. 1959. illus.

3356 WILSTACH, PAUL. Potomac landings. N. Y., Tudor Publishing Co., 1937. 378p. illus.

Appeared serially in *Country Life in America*, v. 39, 1920–21.

3357 ———. Tidewater, Virginia. Indianapolis, Bobbs-Merrill Co., 1929. 326p. illus.

3358 WRIGHT, LOUIS BOOKER (ed.). Virginia heritage. Washington, D. C., Public Affairs Press, [1957]. 50p. illus.

Originally a supplement to the *Washington Post and Times Herald*, Mar. 31, 1957.

3359 ZIEGLER, CARL A. An architectural ramble through Virginia — in two parts. American Architecture and Architectural Review, part 1, 123:531–34, June 1923; part 2, 124:141–51, Aug. 1923. illus.

DOMESTIC

3360 BALDWIN, FRANK CONGER. Early architecture of the Rappahannock Valley. American Institute of Architects. Journal, 3:113–18, 234–40, 329–36, Mar., June, Aug. 1915.

Covers Kenmore (begun 1752), Fredericksburg; Cleve Manor (*ca.* 1754); Gaymont (1725), Caroline County; and Belle Grove (1830), Frederick County.

3361 CHRISTIAN, FRANCES A., AND MASSIE, SUZANNA W. Homes and gardens in Old Virginia. Richmond, Va., Garrett and Massie, 1962. 544p. illus.

For the Garden Club of America. First edition, 1930.

3362 DIETZ, FRIEDA MEREDITH. Photographic studies of old Virginia homes and gardens. 3rd ed. Richmond, Va., Dietz Press, 1953. 67p. illus.

3363 FARRAR, EMMIE FERGUSON. Old Virginia houses along the James. N. Y., Hastings House, [1957]. 231p. illus.

1632———.

3364 KOCHER, ALFRED LAWRENCE. Plantation houses of Virginia. Antiques, 60:186–89, Sept. 1951. illus.

1700———.

3365 LANCASTER, R. A., JR. Historic houses and homes of Virginia. Richmond, Va., Bell Book and Stationery Co., 1912. 450p. illus.

3366 LYNE, CASSIE MONCURE. Lee homes in Virginia. Confederate Veteran, 36:288–89, Aug. 1928.

Covers Stratford, Ditchley, and Arlington.

3367 Master detail series. Historic American buildings. Architectural Forum, 66:53–60, Jan. 1937. illus.

Covers Mary Washington house, Fredericksburg; Folly Farms, Folly Mills; Greenway, Charles City County.

3368 Measured drawings of Early American architecture. Architectural Record, 67:587–90, June 1930. illus.

Covers Martha Washington's kitchen and Galt house.

3369 Old Virginia houses. American Architect, 148:51–58, May 1936. illus.

3370 ROTHERY, AGNES EDWARDS. Houses Virginians have loved. N. Y., Rinehart, [1954]. 319p. illus.

3371 SALE, EDITH TUNIS. Interiors of Virginia houses of Colonial times, from the beginnings of Virginia to the Revolution. Richmond, Va., William Byrd Press, 1927. 503p. illus.

3372 ———. Manors of Virginia in Colonial times. Philadelphia, J. B. Lippincott Co., 1909. 309p. illus.

3373 STONE, MARY C. YOUNGER. Virginia presidents and their homes. National Historical Magazine, 73, no. 5:46–50, 1939.

3374 WATERMAN, THOMAS TILESTON. English antecedents of Virginia architecture. American Philosophical Society. Proceedings, 80:57–63, 1939. illus.

3375 ———. Mansions of Virginia, 1706–1776. Chapel Hill, University of North Carolina Press, 1946. 456p. illus.

3376 WATERMAN, THOMAS TILESTON, AND BARROWS, JOHN A. Domestic Colonial architecture of Tidewater Virginia. N. Y., Charles Scribner's Sons, 1947. 191p. illus.

Earlier printing, 1932.

3377 WHIFFEN, M. Some Virginian house plans reconsidered. Society of Architectural Historians. Journal, 16:17–19, May 1957.

3378 WHITE, GODDARD M. Details of early Southern architecture; two famous mansions of Virginia. Architectural Forum, 34:139–42, Apr. 1921; 35:67–70, Aug. 1921. illus.

Covers Sabine Hall, Westover, and Shirley.

RELIGIOUS

3379 ANDERSON, MARY F. Old parish churches in Virginia. Americana, 24:151–58, Apr. 1930.

3380 BROCK, HENRY IRVING. Colonial churches in Virginia. Richmond, Va., Dale Press, 1930. 94p. illus.

3381 Colonial churches in Virginia; a series of sketches. Richmond, Va., Southern Churchman Co., 1907. 319p. illus.

3382 DANIEL, JAMES RANDOLPH VIVIAN. These still stand: some early Virginia Colonial churches. Virginia Cavalcade, 1:4–8, Autumn 1951. illus.

Ca. 1632–1723.

3383 DAVIS, MARGARET. Tidewater churches. South Atlantic Quarterly, 35:86–97, 1936.

3384 JOHNSTON, MRS. S. LACEY. Historic churches of Virginia. American Monthly Magazine, 39:49–54, Aug. 1911.

3385 MASON, GEORGE CARRINGTON. The Colonial churches of Spotsylvania and Caroline counties, Virginia. Virginia Magazine of History and Biography, 58:442–72, Oct. 1950. illus.

1714–1817.

3386 ———. Colonial churches of Tidewater Virginia. Richmond, Va., Whittet and Shepperson, 1945.

3387 ———. The Colonial churches of Westmoreland and King George counties, Virginia. Virginia Magazine of History and Biography, 56:154–72, 280–93, Apr.–July 1948. illus.

3388 MEADE, WILLIAM. Old churches, ministers and families of Virginia. Philadelphia, J. B. Lippincott Co., 1857. 2v. illus.

Other editions to 1897.

3389 RAWLINGS, JAMES SCOTT. Virginia's Colonial churches, an architectural guide: together with their surviving books, silver, and furnishings. Richmond, Va., Garrett and Massie, 1963. 286p. illus.

3390 WHIFFEN, M. Colonial churches of Virginia. Royal Institute of British Architects. Journal, s.3 66:430–33, Oct. 1959. illus.

3391 WIGMORE, FRANCIS MARION. Old parish churches of Virginia. Washington, D. C., Government Printing Office, 1929. 46p. illus.

A pictorial historic exhibition of photographs in color, lent to the Library of Congress by Francis M. Wigmore.

LOCATIONS

Albemarle County

3392 ADAMS, HERBERT BAXTER. Thomas Jefferson and the University of Virginia. . . . Washington, D. C., Government Printing Office, 1888. 308p. illus.

3393 ALBEMARLE CLUB OF COLONIAL DAMES. Historical guide to Albemarle County. Charlottesville, Va., Albemarle Club of Colonial Dames, 1924. 64p. illus.

3394 BROWN, GLENN. Letters from Thomas Jefferson and William Thornton, architect, relating to the University of Virginia. American Institute of Architects. Journal, 1:21–27, Jan. 1913. illus.

3395 [CARLTON, MABEL MASON.] Thomas Jefferson; an outline of his life and service with the story of Monticello, the home he reared and loved. N. Y., Thomas Jefferson Memorial Foundation, 1924. 21p. illus.

The Monticello Papers, no. 1.

3396 FRARY, IHNA THAYER. Salvation of a Virginia mansion: Glen Echo, near Charlottesville. Arts and Decoration, 53:29–31, 44, Feb. 1941. illus.

3397 GAINES, WILLIAM HARRIS, JR. Under a Jeffersonian dome: the rotunda of the University of Virginia, hub of an "academical village." Virginia Cavalcade, 5:20–25, Summer 1955. illus.

1823.

3398 GLENN, GARRARD. University of Virginia. Geographical Magazine, 3:58–72, 1936.

Influence of Jefferson.

3399 GRAYSON, JENNIE THORNLEY. Old Christ Church, Charlottesville, Virginia, 1826–1895. Albemarle County Historical Society. Papers, 8:27–53, illus.

3400 GREENLEAF, MARGARET. Castle Hill, Virginia. Country Life in America, 26:41–43, Oct. 1914. illus.
Colonial.

3401 HARNIT, FANNY. Monticello. D. A. R. Magazine, 50:158–62, Feb. 1917.

3402 KIMBALL, MARIE G. Jefferson's furniture comes home to Monticello. House Beautiful, 66:164, 165, 186, 188, 190, Aug. 1929. illus.

3403 KIMBALL, SIDNEY FISKE. Church designed by Jefferson. Architectural Record, 53:184–86, Feb. 1923. illus.
Episcopal church, Charlottesville, 1824.

3404 ———. Genesis of Jefferson's plan for the University of Virginia. Architecture, 48:397–99, Dec. 1923. illus.

3405 ———. Monticello, the home of Jefferson. American Institute of Architects. Journal, 12:174–81, Apr. 1, 1924. illus.

3406 ———. Thomas Jefferson as architect of Monticello and Shadwell. Harvard Architectural Quarterly, 2:89–137, June 1914. illus.

3407 MUIRHEAD, JAMES F. Jefferson's Virginian home. Landmark, 4:103–7, Feb. 1922.

3408 NICHOLS, FREDERICK DOVETON. The two Viewmonts. Magazine of Albemarle County History, 13:23–27, 1954. illus.
Ca. 1744 by Joshua Fry, and later house of early nineteenth century.

3409 PATTON, JOHN SHELTON. Jefferson, Cabell and the University of Virginia. N. Y. and Washington, D. C., Neale Publishing Co., 1906. 380p. illus.

3410 ———. Monticello. University of Virginia Alumni Bulletin, ser. 3, 7:633–46, Oct. 1914.

3411 PATTON, JOHN SHELTON, AND CRENSHAW, LEWIS D. (eds.). Glimpses of the past and present of the University of Virginia. Charlottesville, Va., Michie Co., 1915. 97p. illus.

3412 PATTON, JOHN SHELTON, AND DOSWELL, SALLIE J. Monticello and its master. Charlottesville, Va., Michie Co., 1925. 78p. illus.

3413 ———. University of Virginia: glimpses of its past and present. Lynchburg, Va., J. P. Bell and Co., 1900. 96p. illus.

3414 RHODES, THOMAS L. Story of Monticello. Washington, D. C., American Publishing Co., 1928. 94p. illus.

3415 SADLER, MRS. ELIZABETH HATCHER. Bloom of Monticello. Richmond, Va., Whittet and Shepperson, 1925. 20p. illus.

3416 ST. CLAIRE, EMILY ENTWISLE. Beautiful and historic Albemarle. Richmond, Va., Appeals Press, 1932. 110p. illus.

3417 WILSTACH, PAUL. Jefferson and Monticello. Garden City, N. Y., Doubleday, Page and Co., 1925. 258p. illus.
Limited edition same as first edition. Second revised edition: Doubleday, Doran and Co., 1931. 262p. illus.

3418 ———. Jefferson's little mountain. National Geographic Magazine, 55:481–503, Apr. 1929. illus.

Amelia County

3419 TURNER, W. R. The Hillsman house. William and Mary Quarterly, 2nd ser. 19:79–81, 1939.
 Ca. 1770.

Appomattox County

3420 SMITH, ETHEL MARION. Clover Hill: early history of an old Appomattox landmark. Virginia Magazine of History and Biography, 57:269–73, July 1949. illus.
 Ca. 1790.

Augusta County

3421 DAY, HORACE, AND DAY, ELIZABETH NOTTINGHAM. Some examples of architecture in Augusta County and Staunton, Virginia. Staunton, Va., McClure Printing Co., 1947. 8p. illus.

3422 VAN DEVANTER, JAMES NICHOLS. History of the Augusta Church, from 1737 to 1900. Staunton, Va., Rose Printing Co., 1900. 71p. illus.

Bedford County

3423 GAINES, WILLIAM HARRIS, JR. Thomas Jefferson's favorite hideaway. Virginia Cavalcade, 5:36–39, Summer 1955. illus.
 "Poplar Forest," 1806–22.

3424 GLASS, ANNE CLEGHORNE. Poplar Forest, home of Thomas Jefferson. D. A. R. Magazine, 85:761–62, Oct. 1951. illus.
 1806.

3425 PARKER, LULA EASTMAN JETER. The history of Bedford County, Virginia . . . bicentennial edition, 1754–1954. [Bedford, Va., Bedford Democrat, 1954.] 135p.
 Chapter on "Stately Homes."

3426 WATSON, LUCILLE MCWANE. Thomas Jefferson's other home. Antiques, 71:342–46, Apr. 1957. illus.
 Poplar Forest Plantation, 1806–19.

3427 WILSTACH, PAUL. Thomas Jefferson's secret home; Poplar Forest, Bedford County, Virginia. Country Life in America, 53:41–43, Apr. 1928. illus. Also: St. Nicholas, 55:699–700, July 1928.
 Near Lynchburg (1806).

Campbell County

3428 CHRISTIAN, WILLIAM ASBURY. Lynchburg and its people. Lynchburg, Va., J. P. Bell and Co., 1900. 463p. illus.

3429 HADLEY, RICHARD H. The theatre in Lynchburg, Virginia, from its beginnings in 1822 to the outbreak of the Civil War. Doctoral Dissertation, University of Michigan, 1947. 292p.

Charles City County

3430 BROWN, B. T. Shirley on the Royal James. Arts and Decoration, 38:36–37, Feb. 1933. illus.

Between 1720 and 1740.

3431 Details of early Southern architecture. Architectural Forum, 35:67–70, Aug. 1921. illus.

Shirley.

3432 DOWDEY, CLIFFORD SHIRLEY. The great plantation: a profile of Berkeley Hundred and Plantation Virginia from Jamestown to Appomattox. N. Y., Rinehart, [1957]. 320p. illus.

Patented 1618. Summarized by the author: "The Harrisons of Berkeley Hundred," *American Heritage*, 8:58–70, Apr. 1957. illus.

3433 TYLER, LYON GARDINER. Weyanoke, the oldest church plate and the first wind mill. Tyler's Quarterly Historical and Genealogical Magazine, 16:85–88, 1934.

Description of an early windmill.

3434 Westover restored. Country Life in America, 30:25–27, Aug. 1916. illus.

3435 WILLEY, DAY ALLEN. Westover. House and Garden, 11:231–35, June 1907. illus.

Ca. 1730 and later.

Charlotte County

3436 Government to purchase Patrick Henry's estate. Museum News, 17:1, Feb. 15, 1940.

Red Hill.

Clarke County

3437 HUGHES, CHARLES RANDOLPH. Old Chapel, Clarke County, Virginia. Berryville, Va., Blue Ridge Press, 1906. 74p. illus.

Culpeper County

3438 HANES, BLANCHE FITZHUGH. Salubria, the Colonial home of Mrs. Thompson (Lady Spottswood), and the stopping place of Thomas Jefferson and other notables. Journal of American History, 11:252–56, Apr. 1917.

1739.

Dinwiddie County

3439 DAVIS, MARGARET. Doorways to yesterday. Catholic World, 142:74–79, 1935.

Seventeenth- and eighteenth-century houses.

3440 LANCASTER, ROBERT A., JR. Wales, Dinwiddie County, Virginia. Virginia Magazine of History, 44:232–37, 1936.

Late eighteenth century.

3441 Story of old Petersburg and southside Virginia. Petersburg, Va., J. T. Morriss and Sons, *ca.* 1940. 34p. illus.

3442 WYATT, EDWARD AVERY, IV. Old Blanford Church. Commonwealth: The Magazine of Virginia, 21:28, 78–85, June 1954. illus.

Petersburg, *ca.* 1737.

3443 ———. Plantation houses around Petersburg, in the counties of Prince George, Chesterfield, and Dinwiddie, Virginia. Petersburg, Va., 1955. 52p. illus.
Ca. 1616.

Essex County

3444 Bathurst, home of the Jones family of Virginia and Kentucky. Kentucky Historical Society. Register, 14:53–55, Sept. 1916. illus.
Near Tappahannock. Colonial.

Fairfax County

3445 ANDERSON, MARY F. Restoration of Arlington Mansion. Americana, 28:449–77, 1934.
Remodeled 1820 by George Hadfield.

3446 BAILEY, WORTH. General Washington's new room. Society of Architectural Historians. Journal, 10:16–18, May 1951. illus.
Banquet Hall at Mount Vernon, 1776–87.

3447 BALL, EMMA R. [MRS. C. B. BALL]. Washington's home and the story of the Mount Vernon Ladies' Association of the Union. Richmond, Va., Whittet and Shepperson, 1912. 18p. illus.

3448 Bill for acquisition by Federal Government of Mount Vernon. National Republic, 18:11, May 1930.

3449 BROWN, B. T. Restoration in Alexandria, Virginia; C. B. Moore home. House Beautiful, 71:205–8, Mar. 1932. illus.

3450 BRUSH, WARREN D. The building of Mount Vernon mansion. House Beautiful, 51:130–31, 162–64, Feb. 1922. illus.

3451 ———. George Washington — the house builder. American Forests, 54:69–71, 91, Feb. 1948. illus.
Mt. Vernon, remodeled 1773–78.

3452 CAPEN, OLIVER BRONSON. Country homes of famous Americans. Part 5. George Washington. Country Life in America, 5:499–504, Apr. 1904. illus.

3453 CHASE, ENOCH AQUILA. History of Arlington. Washington, D. C., National Art Service Co., 1929. 22p. illus.

3454 ———. Restoration of Arlington House. Columbia Historical Society. Records, 33–34:239–65, 1932.

3455 CLAIBORNE, H. A. Restoration in progress, Gunston Hall in Virginia. Antiques, 63:334–37, Apr. 1953. illus.
1755–59.

3456 COLEMAN, ELIZABETH DABNEY. Mary Curtis Lee's "Arlington." American Heritage, 5:25–31, Spring 1954. illus.
1802–16.

3457 CONNOR, HARRY R. Gunston Hall, Fairfax County. Monograph Series, v. 16, no. 3, 1930. 27p. illus.
Ca. 1758.

3458 CRAWFORD, M. D. C. Alexandria: an old Virginia classic. Arts and Decoration, 15:108–9, June 1921. illus.

3459 CRENSHAW, MARY MAYO. Gunston Hall. St. Nicholas, 52:938–42, July 1925. illus.

3460 ———. Stately Woodlawn Mansion. Antiquarian, 7:41–44, Sept. 1926.
Built by Lawrence Lewis (1805). Dr. William Thornton, architect.

3461 DAVIS, DEERING, AND OTHERS. Alexandria houses, 1750–1830. N. Y., Architectural Book Publishing Co., 1946. 128p. illus.

3462 DODGE, HARRISON HOWELL. Mount Vernon, its owner and its story. Philadelphia, J. B. Lippincott Co., 1932. 232p. illus.

3463 DUHAMEL, JAMES F. Belvoir. Columbia Historical Society. Records, 35–36:146–53, 1935.

3464 DUKE, JANE TAYLOR. Gunston Hall. House Beautiful, 83:50–52, 127–31, May 1941. illus.

3465 FEDERAL WRITERS' PROJECT. Alexandria. Alexandria, Va., [Williams Printing Co.], 1939. 27p. illus.

3466 FLOURNOY, MRS. WILLIAM CABELL. Arlington. Confederate Veteran, 31:134–36, Apr. 1923.

3467 Gadsby's Tavern. D. A. R. Magazine, 67:71–74, 1933.
Alexandria (1752).

3468 GAHN, BESSIE WILMARTH. Mystery house in Alexandria. D. A. R. Magazine, 66:412–14, 1932.
Describes a sketch similar to Washington Headquarters house in Georgetown.

3469 George Washington, country gentleman; an account of a visit to Mount Vernon from the diary of Benjamin Latrobe. Country Life in America, 41:34–41, Dec. 1921. illus.
Sketches by Latrobe.

3470 GORDON, JOHN B. Alexandria's old meeting house. D. A. R. Magazine, 63:538–41, Sept. 1929.
Presbyterian meetinghouse, 1774.

3471 GRIFFITHS, FREDERICK S., and JOHNSON, MEREDITH. The Kesters at Woodlawn and Gunston Hall. Alexandria Association. Year Book, pp. 47–63, 1957. illus.
The purchase and restoration of the two plantations 1890–1912.

3472 Gunston Hall. Life, 11:118–21, Dec. 15, 1941. illus.

3473 HAMILTON, J. G. DEROULHAC. Arlington; a national memorial. Current History, 24:720–23, Aug. 1926.

3474 HARCOURT, HELEN. Mount Vernon, the American Mecca. New Age, 6:319–24, Apr. 1907.

3475 HAYES, FRANCIS W., JR. Colonial churches in Fairfax County, Virginia. Historical Society of Fairfax County, Virginia. Yearbook, 2:18–22.
1732–76.

3476 [cancelled]

3477 KABLER, DOROTHY HOLCOMBE. The story of Gadsby's Tavern. Alexandria, Va., Newell-Cole Co., 1952. 71p. illus.
1752——.

3478 KIMBALL, FISKE. Gunston Hall. Society of Architectural Historians. Journal, 13:3–8, May 1954. illus.

3479 KOPP, C. B. Salona, historic refuge of Dolly Madison. National Republic, 20:6–7, July 1932. illus.
1801, near McLean.

3480 LEE, CUSTIS. Arlington House and its associations. Washington, D. C., U. S. Quartermaster Corps, 1932. 45p. illus.

3481 LINDSEY, MARY. Historic homes and landmarks of Alexandria, Virginia. Alexandria, Va., Newell-Cole Co., 1931. 52p. illus.

3482 LOSSING, BENSON. Home of Washington; or, Mount Vernon and its associations. . . . N. Y., Virtue and Yorston, 1871. 446p. illus.
First edition, 1870; also published Hartford, Conn., G. W. Rogers, 1870. A revision of his *Home of Washington and Its Associations.* . . . N. Y., W. A. Townsend, 1865 and 1866.

3483 LOWTHER, MINNIE KENDALL. Mount Vernon, Arlington and Woodlawn; history of these national shrines from the earliest titles of ownership to the present, with biographical sketches, portraits, and interesting reminiscences of the families who founded them. Washington, D. C., C. H. Potter and Co., 1922. 83p. illus.

3484 ——. Mount Vernon; its children, its romances, its allied families and mansions. Philadelphia, John C. Winston Co., 1930. 282p. illus.
Second edition, 1932. 302p. illus.

3485 LYNE, MRS. WILLIAM H. Gunston Hall — famous estate of George Mason. Confederate Veteran, 36:210–12, June 1928.

3486 McGROARTY, WILLIAM BUCKNER. The old Presbyterian Meeting House at Alexandria, Virginia, 1774–1874. Richmond, Va., William Byrd Press, 1940. 81p. illus.

3487 MATHEWS, JAMES T., JR. Romance of Old Christ Church, Alexandria, Virginia. Washington, D. C., Park Press, 1926. 31p. illus.

3488 MILLER, WILHELM. Mount Vernon as Washington would have had it. Country Life in America, 26, no. 2:49–52; no. 3:48–49, 80, 82; no. 4:43–45, 82, 84; no. 6:58–59, June–Oct. 1914. illus.

3489 MOORE, CHARLES. Gunston Hall. D. A. R. Magazine, 61:678–80, Sept. 1927.

3490 MOORE, GAY MONTAGUE. Seaport in Virginia: George Washington's Alexandria. Richmond, Va., Garrett and Massie, 1949. 274p. illus.
1730–1865.

3491 Mount Vernon, Arlington House, Dumbarton House. House and Garden, 78:supp. 20–26, July 1940. illus.

3492 [Mount Vernon. Contemporary descriptions.] Atkinson's Casket, 11:505, Nov. 1829. Dollar Magazine, 1:147–48, May 1841. Ladies' Companion, 12:101, Jan. 1840. New World, 3:322, Nov. 20, 1841. Southern Literary Messenger, 18:53–57, Jan. 1852. Western Miscellany, 1:74–76, Sept. 1848. Yale Literary Magazine, 23:354–57, Aug. 1858; 24:19–20, Oct. 1858.

3493 Mount Vernon: the garden, the home, the builders. Garden and Home Builder, 45:456–80, July 1927. illus.

3494 NELLIGAN, MURRY H. The building of Arlington House. Society of Architectural Historians. Journal, 10:11–15, May 1951. illus.
1802——.

3495 ——. Lee Mansion, national memorial. 2nd ed. Washington, D. C., 1956. 47p. illus.
National Park Service. Historical Handbook Series, no. 6.

3496 PAGE, THOMAS NELSON. Mount Vernon and its preservation, 1858–1910; the acquisition, restoration and care of the home of Washington by the Mount Vernon Ladies' Association of the Union for over half a century. N. Y., Knickerbocker Press, 1910. 84p. illus.

3497 Rededication exercises of restored Virginia landmark; old church built in 1774 abounds in associations with George Washington and his contemporaries. Minute Man, 23:114–18, June 1928.
Presbyterian meetinghouse, Alexandria.

3498 Robert E. Lee's home at Arlington. Antiques, 27:26–27, Jan. 1935. illus.
1803, portico 1826.

3499 ROBERTSON, THOMAS B. Ruins of old church at Old Arlington Gate. William and Mary Quarterly, 21:67–70, July 1912.

3500 ROBINSON, BERTHA LOUISE. Old Southern mansion of Gunston Hall. Journal of American History, 4:94–100, 1910.

3501 ROGERS, ALLA HARMAN. History of Mount Vernon, America's patriotic shrine. Washington, D. C., National Art Service Co., 1932. 27p. illus.

3502 ROSENBERGER, FRANCIS COLEMAN. An old fortress of the Lord. Commonwealth: The Magazine of Virginia, 19:30–31, Apr. 1952. illus.
Presbyterian meetinghouse, 1774. Alexandria.

3503 SAYLOR, HENRY H. Alexandria, Virginia. White Pine Series of Architectural Monographs, v. 12, no. 4, 1926. 19p. illus.

3504 SCHULZ, EDWARD HUGH. Belvoir on the Potomac. . . . Fort Humphreys, Va., 1933. 14p. illus.

3505 SHERMAN, CAROLINE BALDWIN. Old Virginia landmark. William and Mary Quarterly, 2nd ser. 7:87–91, Apr. 1927.
Ash Grove (1790 and later).

3506 SHOULTS, W. E. Home of the first farmer of America. National Geographic Magazine, 53:602–28, May 1928. illus.
Mount Vernon.

3507 SINCLAIR, LOUISA SWANN. Gadsby's Ballroom. National Historical Magazine, 74, no. 12:6–9, 1940.
In Gadsby's Tavern, Alexandria.

3508 SLOAN, SAMUEL. How to restore Mount Vernon. Society of Architectural Historians. Journal, 10:33–34, Dec. 1951.
Reprinted from *Architectural Review and Builder's Journal*, Aug. 1868.

3509 SMITH, DELOS. Abington of Fairfax County. D. A. R. Magazine, 63:325–30, June 1929.

3510 SMOOT, MRS. BETTY CARTER. Days in an old town. Alexandria, Va., 1934. 189p. illus.
Notes on Alexandria houses.

3511 SPENCER, RICHARD HENRY. The Carlyle house and its associations — Braddock's headquarters — here the Colonial governors met in council, April, 1755. William and Mary Quarterly, 18:1–17, July 1909.
Alexandria (1752).

3512 STAPLEY, MILDRED. The house of George Washington. Country Life in America, 26:39–44, May 1914. illus.

3513 STEPHENSON, JEAN. Mount Vernon: a monument to American idealism. D. A. R. Magazine, 62:85–92, Feb. 1928.

3514 STRICKLAND, WILLIAM. The tomb of Washington at Mt. Vernon. Philadelphia, Carey and Hart, 1940. 76p. illus.

3515 STUNTZ, S. C. The Carlyle house, Alexandria, Virginia. D. A. R. Magazine, 50:4–9, Jan. 1917.

3516 Through Virginia to Mount Vernon; extracts from the journal of Benjamin Henry Latrobe, friend of Washington and architect of the Capitol. Appleton's Booklovers' Magazine, 6:3–17, July 1905.

3517 [Tomb of Washington. Contemporary descriptions.] Cabinet of Religion, New York, 2:479–80, Oct. 24, 1829. Rural Repository, 25:137–38, May 1849.

3518 WATERMAN, THOMAS TILESTON. Architecture of Alexandria. Antiques, 47:89–92, Feb. 1945. illus.

3519 WILSTACH, PAUL. Country home of George Washington. Country Life in America, 29:23–26, Apr. 1916. illus.

3520 ———. Mount Vernon, Washington's home and the nation's shrine. N. Y., Doubleday, Page and Co., 1916. 301p. illus.

Fauquier County

3521 COMSTOCK, HELEN. North Wales: a Georgian country house in Virginia. Antiques, 60:303–7, Oct. 1951. illus.
1716——.

3522 PEAK, MAYME OBER. Oak Hill, the Fauquier home of Chief Justice Marshall. House Beautiful, 49:288–89, 330, Apr. 1921. illus.
1818.

Fluvanna County

3523 Bremo, designed and built by Thomas Jefferson in 1815. Arts and Decoration, 39:10–11, Oct. 1933. illus.

3524 GAINES, WILLIAM HARRIS, JR. A home dedicated to service. Virginia Cavalcade, 6:20–29, Autumn 1956. illus.
"Bremo," 1818–20.

3525 KIMBALL, SIDNEY FISKE. The building of Bremo. Virginia Magazine of History and Biography, 57:3–13, Jan. 1949. illus.
1802–20.

Frederick County

3526 VIRGINIA STATE CHAMBER OF COMMERCE. Old Stone Church in Winchester. Commonwealth: The Magazine of Virginia, 21:8–9, Apr. 1954. illus.
Presbyterian, 1790.

Giles County

3527 GAINES, WILLIAM HARRIS, JR. The most delicious and comfortable of resorts. Virginia Cavalcade, 6:22–27, Summer 1956. illus.
"Eggleston's Springs," 1830's—1909.

Gloucester County

3528 CATES, ALICE SMITH. Rosewell, the ancestral home of the Pages of Virginia. D. A. R. Magazine, 57:451–59, Aug. 1923.
Begun 1725, destroyed 1916.

3529 CROWDER, R. T. First manor-houses in America and estates of the first Americans; a journey to the historic mansions along the York River in Gloucester County, Virginia. Journal of American History, 3:283–95, 1909.

3530 FARRAR, EMMIE FERGUSON. Old Virginia houses: the Mobjack Bay country. N. Y., Hastings House, [1955]. 175p. illus.
1658——.

3531 JAMES, MRS. E. STEWART. Cappahosic house. D. A. R. Magazine, 85:199–200, Mar. 1951. illus.
Ca. 1712.

3532 [Rosewell. Contemporary description.] Southern Literary Messenger, 10:41–42, Jan. 1844.

3533 WATERMAN, THOMAS TILESTON. Rosewell, Gloucester County. Architectural Forum, 52:17–20, Jan. 1930. illus.

Henrico County

3534 ALBRIGHT, C. LEONARD. Historic Mason's Hall at Richmond, Virginia. Grand Lodge Bulletin, 31:404–5, Jan. 1930.
Called oldest Masonic Hall in the United States.

3535 BRAGG, L. M. Virginia house in the Regency style, Wickham-Valentine house in Richmond. International Studio, 97:21–24, Sept. 1930. illus.
1812. Robert Mills, architect.

3536 BUCHANAN, JAMES, AND HAY, WILLIAM. Copy of letter to Thomas Jefferson relocating Virginia capitol buildings. Virginia Magazine of History, 41:158–59, 1933.

3537 CHRISTIAN, WILLIAM ASBURY. Richmond, her past and present. Richmond, Va., L. H. Jenkins, 1912. 618p. illus.

3538 DUMBAULD, EDWARD. Jefferson's residence in Richmond. Virginia Magazine of History and Biography, 60:323–26, Apr. 1952. illus.
1780.

3539 KIMBALL, SIDNEY FISKE. Thomas Jefferson and the first monument of the Classic Revival in America — in three parts. American Institute of Architects. Journal, part 1, 3:371–81, Sept. 1915; part 2, 3:421–33, Oct. 1915; part 3, 3:473–91, Nov. 1915.
The capitol, begun 1785.

3540 LANCASTER, ROBERT A., JR. Wilton. Virginia Magazine of History, 41:310–17, 1933.
1747–53.

3541 Letters to Jefferson relative to the Virginia capitol. William and Mary Quarterly, 2nd ser. 5:95–98, Apr. 1925.
1785.

3542 [Monumental Church. Contemporary discussion and illustration.] American Pioneer, 1:371, Nov. 1842. illus.
Richmond, 1813–14. Robert Mills, architect.

3543 ROBINS, SALLY NELSON. Oldest house in Richmond, Virginia, now called the Edgar Allen Poe Shrine. House Beautiful, 54:488, 544, Nov. 1923. illus.
Ca. 1686.

3544 RYAN, EDWARD L. The old villa that stood on French Garden Hill. Virginia Magazine of History, 47:356–59, 1939.
Richmond, demolished.

3545 ———. "Poplar Vale." Virginia Magazine of History, 48:202–6, 1940.
In Richmond, demolished 1920.

3546 ———. Singleton House. Virginia Magazine of History, 41:102–8, 1933.
Late eighteenth century.

3547 ———. State Court House. Virginia Magazine of History, 41:280–88, 1933.

3548 ———. Warsaw. Virginia Magazine of History, 40:347–54, 1932.
Richmond, John Harmer Gilmer house. Nineteenth century.

3549 SCOTT, MARY WINGFIELD. Houses of old Richmond. Richmond, Va., Valentine Museum, 1941. 332p. illus.

3550 ———. Old Richmond neighborhoods. Richmond, Va., 1950. 322p. illus.
1783–1873.

3551 Scraps from a note book — the capitol, Virginia. Historical Register, 1:169, Oct. 1848.
A letter from Jefferson to Madison in 1788 from Paris, describing the model for the capitol.

3552 WEDDELL, ALEXANDER WILBOURNE. Richmond, Virginia, in old prints, 1737–1887. Richmond, Va., Johnson Publishing Co., 1932. 254p. illus.

Isle of Wight County

3553 VAN DERPOOL, JAMES GROTE. The restoration of old St. Luke's. Commonwealth: The Magazine of Virginia, 22:13–15, 46, Sept. 1955. illus.

1632, near Smithfield, Va.

3554 ——. Restoration of St. Luke's, Smithfield, Va. Society of Architectural Historians. Journal, 17:12–18, Mar. 1958. illus.

3555 VAN DERPOOL, JAMES GROTE, AND MALONE, DUMAS. Historic St. Luke's. . . . N. Y., 1957. 21p. illus.

James City County

3556 BATH, GERALD HORTON. America's Williamsburg. Williamsburg, Va., Colonial Williamsburg, Inc., 1946. 48p. illus.

3557 BROWN, BARBARA TRIGG. Restoration of Colonial Williamsburg. Good Housekeeping, 99:70–71, 125, Nov. 1934. illus.

Carter-Saunders house, before 1761.

3558 ——. Restoring historic Williamsburg. Good Housekeeping, 99:74–75, 152, July 1934. illus.

St. George Tucker house, 1790 and earlier.

3559 ——. A small house restored in old Williamsburg. Good Housekeeping, 99:78, Dec. 1934. illus.

73 Francis Street.

3560 ——. Williamsburg, a shrine for American patriots. American Home, 12:349–51, Nov. 1934. illus.

3561 BROWN, GLENN. Jamestown. Architectural Record, 63:78–79, Jan. 1928. illus.

Church, *ca.* 1637.

3562 CAYWOOD, LOUIS RICHARD. Green Spring Plantation. Virginia Magazine of History and Biography, 65:67–83, Jan. 1957. illus.

House built for Sir William Berkeley in 1643 and associated buildings. Torn down in 1796, new house by Latrobe in 1796.

3563 CHAMBERLAIN, SAMUEL. Behold Williamsburg, a pictorial tour of Virginia's Colonial capital. N. Y., Hastings House, 1947. 176p. illus.

3564 CHORLEY, KENNETH. Progress in the restoration of Colonial Williamsburg. Architectural Record, v. 80, Nov. 1936. illus.

Photographs of details.

3565 COLEMAN, CHARLES WASHINGTON. The Wythe house, Williamsburg, Virginia. Magazine of American History, 7:270–75, Oct. 1881. illus.

3566 Colonial capitol of Virginia. American Architect and Building News, 16:198–99, Oct. 25, 1884. illus.

3567 COLONIAL WILLIAMSBURG, INC. An album of Williamsburg restoration photographs. Williamsburg, Va., Colonial Williamsburg, Inc., 1933. illus.

Mounted photographs showing stages of restoration.

3568 ————. A brief and true report for the traveller concerning Williamsburg in Virginia. . . . Richmond, Va., Dietz Press, 1935. 192p. illus.

3569 ————. The capitol. . . . Williamsburg, Va., Colonial Williamsburg, Inc., 1934. 43p. illus.

1751, destroyed 1832.

3570 ————. The Governor's Palace. Williamsburg, Va., Colonial Williamsburg, Inc., 1934. 14p. illus.

Destroyed 1781.

3571 ————. Guide book for Williamsburg, Virginia. Williamsburg, Va., Colonial Williamsburg, Inc., 1935. 47p. illus.

3572 ————. The official guidebook of Colonial Williamsburg. . . . Williamsburg, Va., 1951. 96p. illus.

History, 1633————, of over 100 buildings with guide map.

3573 ————. The Raleigh Tavern. Williamsburg, Va., Colonial Williamsburg, Inc., 1934. 30p. illus.

Before 1742.

3574 ————. Travis house. Williamsburg, Va., Colonial Williamsburg, Inc., 1933. 15p. illus.

3575 ————. Williamsburg restoration; a brief review of the plan, purpose, and policy of the Williamsburg restoration. Williamsburg, Va., Colonial Williamsburg, Inc., 1933. 24p. illus.

3576 Colonial Williamsburg, Va.; the historical background and restoration. Museum Journal, 42:157–60, Oct. 1942.

3577 COTTER, JOHN L. Excavations at Jamestown, Va. Antiquity, 31:19–24, Mar. 1957. illus.

3578 ————. Jamestown: treasure in the earth. Antiques, 71:44–46, Jan. 1957. illus.

Archaeological excavations.

3579 ————. Rediscovering Jamestown. Archaeology, 10:25–30, Mar. 1957. illus.

3580 DUELL, PRENTICE. Excavations at Williamsburg. Architectural Record, 69:16–17, Jan. 1931. illus.

3581 FORMAN, HENRY CHANDLEE. Jamestown and St. Mary's: buried cities of romance. Baltimore, Johns Hopkins Press, 1938. 355p. illus.

Doctoral Dissertation, University of Pennsylvania.

3582 GAINES, WILLIAM HARRIS, JR. "Green Spring" — a tale of three mansions. Virginia Cavalcade, 6:30–37, Spring 1957. illus.

Houses on a site near Jamestown, 1649–83.

3583 GOODWIN, WILLIAM ARCHER RUTHERFOORD. Bruton Parish Church restored, and its historic environment. Petersburg, Va., Franklin Press, 1907. 205p. illus.

3584 Governor's Palace, Colonial Williamsburg; measured drawings and views — in four parts. Architectural Record. part 1, 78:378–81; part 2, 78:395–409; part 3, 80:354–63, 368; part 4, 80:370–71, Dec. 1935–Nov. 1936. illus.

3585 GRAF, DON. Origin of present-day architecture; characteristics of the Colonial style. American Home, 11:338–39, May 1934. illus.

3586 GREGORY, GEORGE C. Jamestown first brick State House. Virginia Magazine of History, 43:193–99, 1935.
1631–96.

3587 ——. Log houses at Jamestown, 1607. Virginia Magazine of History, 44:287–95, 1936.

3588 HATCH, CHARLES E., JR. America's oldest legislative assembly and its Jamestown statehouses. Revised ed. Washington, 1956. 46p. illus.
1614–98. National Park Service. Interpretive Series in History, no. 2.

3589 ——. Jamestown, Virginia; the town site and its story. Washington, D. C., 1949. 52p. illus.
National Park Service. Historical Handbook Series, no. 2.

3590 HEATWOLE, C. J. Historic Williamsburg to be the national museum of '76. Virginia Journal of Education, 21:439–43, June 1928.

3591 HEMPHILL, WILLIAM EDWIN. "Hallowed be the place." Virginia Cavalcade, 6:22–29, Spring 1957. illus.
Church tower at Jamestown, ca. 1647.

3592 Historic residences in Williamsburg. Tyler's Quarterly Historical and Genealogical Magazine, 11:73–84, Oct. 1929.
Tucker house, Blair house, and Peyton Randolph house.

3593 HUDSON, J. P. Jamestown artisans and craftsmen. Antiques, 71:46–50, Jan. 1957. illus.
Tools found in archaeological excavations.

3594 KOCHER, ALFRED LAWRENCE, AND DEARSTYNE, HOWARD. Colonial Williamsburg, its buildings and gardens. Williamsburg, Va., Colonial Williamsburg, Inc., distributed by Holt, Rinehart and Winston, 1961. 104p. illus.
First published 1949.

3595 LEE, W. D. Renascence of Carter's Grove on the James River, now the home of A. M. McCrea. Architecture, 67:185–94, Apr. 1933. illus.
1751.

3596 Measured drawings of Early American architecture: Galt house, Williamsburg. Architectural Record, 67:587–90, June 1930. illus.

3597 MEEKS, CARROLL L. V. Lynx and Phoenix: Litchfield and Williamsburg. Society of Architectural Historians. Journal, 10:18–23, Dec. 1951. illus.
Architectural resemblances.

3598 MOOREHEAD, S. P. Problems in architectural restoration, Colonial Williamsburg. Art in America, 43:23–29ff., May 1955. illus.

3599 ——. Tazewell Hall. Society of Architectural Historians. Journal, 14:14–17, Mar. 1955. illus.
Williamsburg, Va., built 1775 or before.

3600 MORPURGO, J. E. Williamsburg, Virginia. Transatlantic, no. 41:25–31, Spring 1948. illus.

3601 The Old Raleigh Tavern. Hobbies, 54:39, 58, Oct. 1949. 1769–76.

3602 OLDS, NATHANIEL S. Williamsburg and its restoration. Philadelphia, privately printed, 1929. 11p. illus.

3603 OSBORNE, JOSEPH ALEXANDER. Williamsburg in Colonial times. Richmond, Va., Dietz Press, 1935. 166p. illus.

3604 PARK, EMILY HARDEE. Old Williamsburg. American Monthly Magazine, 31:527–32, Sept. 1907.

3605 PERRY, W. G. Notes on the architecture of Colonial Williamsburg. Architectural Record, 78:363–77, Dec. 1935. illus.

3606 POWER, ETHEL B. Colonial stage reset for action. House Beautiful, 76:54–57, July 1934. illus.

3607 REEVE, E. A. Inside a Virginia Colonial house in Williamsburg. House and Garden, 64:28–29, Nov. 1933. illus.

3608 Restoration at Williamsburg; Perry, Shaw and Hepburn, architects. Pencil Points, 17:224–46, May 1936. illus.
Measured drawings and photographs.

3609 Restoration of Colonial Williamsburg in Virginia; Perry, Shaw and Hepburn, architects, with portfolio of buildings, maps and plans, measured drawings and working details— in two parts. Architectural Record, part 1, 78:359–458, Dec. 1935; part 2, 80:337–84, Nov. 1936. illus.

3610 Restoration of Williamsburg, Virginia; Perry, Shaw and Hepburn, architects. American Architect, 147:10, 36–52, Dec. 1935. illus.

3611 ROSÉ, GRACE N., AND ROSÉ, J. M. Williamsburg today and yesterday. N. Y., G. P. Putnam's Sons, 1940. 77p. illus.

3612 SCRIBNER, ROBERT LESLIE. Fort St. George. Virginia Cavalcade, 5:20–25, Autumn 1955. illus.
St. George Tucker house, 1788, Williamsburg.

3613 Some notes on Green Spring. Virginia Magazine of History, 37:289–300, Oct. 1929.
Home of Sir William Berkeley, the Ludwells, and the Lees. Destroyed.

3614 STANSBURY, CHARLES FREDERICK. The Jamestown Tower. Eclectic Magazine, 146:470–75, June 1906.

3615 TYLER, LYON GARDINER. Williamsburg, the old Colonial capital. William and Mary Quarterly, 16:1–65, July 1907.

3616 ———. Williamsburg, the old Colonial capital. Richmond, Va., Whittet and Shepperson, 1907. 285p. illus.

3617 WALL, ALEXANDER J. Restoration of Williamsburg, Va. New York Historical Society. Quarterly Bulletin, 16:3–9, 1932.

3618 WELLS, J. W. Hazard of Colonial Williamsburg. American Institute of Architects. Journal, 20:193–95, Oct. 1953.

3619 WERTENBAKER, THOMAS JEFFERSON. Jamestown, 1607–1957. American Philosophical Society. Proceedings, 101:369–74, Aug. 1957. illus.

3620 WHIFFEN, MARCUS. The eighteenth-century houses of Williamsburg; a study of architecture and building in the Colonial capital of Virginia. Williamsburg, Va., Colonial Williamsburg, Inc., distributed by Holt, Rinehart and Winston, 1960. 223p. illus.

3621 ———. The public buildings of Williamsburg, Colonial capital of Virginia; an architectural history. Williamsburg, Va., Colonial Williamsburg, Inc., 1958. 269p. illus.
Williamsburg Architectural Studies, v. 1.

3622 [William and Mary College. Contemporary description.] Southern Literary Messenger, 30:382–83, May 1860.

3623 Williamsburg — what it means to architecture, to gardening, to decoration. House and Garden, 72:37–67, Nov. 1937. illus.

3624 WILLIAMSBURG ARCHITECTURAL STUDIES. v. 1———. Williamsburg, Va., Colonial Williamsburg, Inc., 1958———. illus.

3625 WILLIAMSBURG GARDEN CLUB. Williamsburg scrap book. Richmond, Va., Dietz Press, 1932. 97p. illus.

3626 WILLIAMSBURG HOLDING CORPORATION. Williamsburg restoration; a brief review of the plan, purpose and policy of the Williamsburg restoration; an authoritative statement issued by those in charge of the undertaking. Williamsburg, Va., Williamsburg Holding Corp., 1931. 31p. illus.

3627 WYLLIE, JOHN C. George Tucker's description of Williamsburg in 1796. William and Mary Quarterly, 2nd ser. 19:192–96, 1939.
Reprint from George Tucker, *The Valley of Shenandoah* . . . , N. Y., 1824, 2v.

King George County

3628 BALDWIN, FRANK CONGER. Early architecture of the Rappahannock Valley, Marmion, 1750. American Institute of Architects. Journal, 4:87–95, Mar. 1916. illus.

3629 LEWIS, CHARLES WILLIAM, JR. St. Paul's Church, King George County. Northern Neck of Virginia Historical Magazine, 3:213–20, Dec. 1953.
Episcopal, 1766.

King William County

3630 [Augustine Moor house. Contemporary description.] American Penny Magazine, 1:772, Jan. 10, 1846.

3631 CLARKE, PEYTON NEALE. Old King William homes and families. Louisville, Ky., J. P. Morton Co., 1897. 211p. illus.

3632 LANCASTER, ROBERT A., JR. Pampatike and Winton. Virginia Magazine of History, 41:223–30, 1933.

Lancaster County

3633 MORRIS, EDWIN BATEMAN. Vicarious loafing; Christ Church, Lancaster County, Va., built in 1732, by R. Carter. American Institute of Architects. Journal, 13:34–37, Jan. 1950. illus.

3634 PEIRCE, ELIZABETH COMBS. Courthouses of Lancaster County, 1656–1950. Northern Neck of Virginia Historical Magazine, 1:23–35, Dec. 1951.
1652——.

3635 ——. Saint Mary's White Chappell, Parish Church of Saint Mary's White Chappel Parish, Lancaster County. Northern Neck of Virginia Historical Magazine, 5:384–88, Dec. 1955.
1740, restored 1830.

3636 SADTLER, OTIS K. Post offices in Lancaster County. Northern Neck of Virginia Historical Magazine, 2:134–39, Dec. 1952.
1793——.

Loudoun County

3637 HERTZ, SOLANGE STRONG. Old stone houses of Loudoun County, Virginia; an illustrated tour. Leesburg, Va., 1950. 38p. illus.

3638 LAMB, MRS. MARTHA J. Oak Hill, the house of President Monroe. Magazine of American History, 21:381–85, May 1889. illus.
1820–23. James Hoban.

3639 STRONG, SOLANGE. Quaker houses of Loudoun County, Virginia. Antiques, 54:333–35, Nov. 1948. illus.
1733–80.

Montgomery County

3640 LAMB, JANIE P. B. "Smithfield," home of the Prestons, in Montgomery County, Virginia. Virginia Magazine of History, 47:109–25, 1939.
1773.

Nansemond County

3641 MASON, GEORGE C. Colonial churches of Nansemond County. William and Mary Quarterly, 2nd ser. 21:37–54, Jan. 1941.

New Kent County

3642 BLACK, ROBERT E. The restoration of St. Peter's in New Kent. Commonwealth: The Magazine of Virginia, 20:20–21, 37, Aug. 1953. illus.
Episcopal.

3643 COLEMAN, ELIZABETH DABNEY. Liberty is its name; a Baptist church in New Kent County. Virginia Cavalcade, 5:43–47, Autumn 1955.
Liberty Baptist Church, organized 1830.

3644 PRATT, HARDEN DE V., III. The restoration of Christ's Cross, New Kent County, Virginia. Virginia Magazine of History and Biography, 65:328–31, July 1957. illus.
Seventeenth century.

Norfolk County

3645 House of F. K. Barbour built about 1750, moved thirty miles, re-erected in 1935; R. M. Carrere, architect. American Architect and Architecture, 148:71–74, Jan. 1936. illus.

3646 Myers house in Norfolk, Va. Antiques, 54:180–82, Sept. 1948. illus.
1791.

Northampton County

3647 ROBERTSON, T. B. Court houses of Northampton County. William and Mary Quarterly, 23:51–58, July 1914.

Northumberland County

3648 BEALE, GEORGE WILLIAM. Old "Mantua" in Northumberland County, Virginia. Edited by Lucy Brown Beale. Northern Neck of Virginia Historical Magazine, 1:19–22, Dec. 1951.
Ca. 1816.

Page County

3649 KERKHOFF, JENNIE ANN. Old homes of Page County, Virginia. Luray, Va., Lauck, 1962. 212p. illus.

Powhatan County

3650 RYAN, EDWARD L. "Keswick" — in Powhatan. Virginia Magazine of History, 48:57–60, 1940.
James River plantation in Powhatan and Chesterfield counties.

Prince George County

3651 LUTZ, EARLE. Appomattox Manor. Mentor, 17:34–35, July 1929. illus.
1651, near Hopewell.

3652 ROBBINS, A., JR. Historic Merchant's Hope Church. Commonwealth: The Magazine of Virginia, 24:15–17, Sept. 1957. illus.
1655——.

3653 ROBERTS, MARY FANTON. Brandon, with its memories of perukes and farthingales. Arts and Decoration, 43:6–9, 43, Jan. 1936. illus.
First half eighteenth century, with additions.

3654 SCRIBNER, ROBERT LESLIE. Martin as Merchant, plus Hope. Virginia Cavalcade, 6:44–47, Spring 1957. illus.
Merchant's Hope Church, built possibly in 1657.

Prince William County

3655 HARRISON, FAIRFAX. Landmarks of old Prince William; a study of origins in northern Virginia. Richmond, Va., privately printed, Old Dominion Press, 1924. 2v. illus.

3656 SALE, MRS. EDITH DABNEY (TUNIS). Upper Brandon; James River home of F. O. Byrd. House Beautiful, 68:50–52, July 1930. illus.
Early nineteenth century.

Princess Anne County

3657 KELLAM, SADIE SCOTT, AND KELLAM, V. HOPE. Old houses in Princess Anne. Portsmouth, Va., Printcraft Press, 1931. 235p. illus.

3658 KYLE, LOUISE VENABLE. The old Thoroughgood house. Commonwealth: The Magazine of Virginia, 24:15–17, 36, Mar. 1957. illus.
Built by Adam Thoroughgood (1604–40) as early as 1637.

3659 MIDDLETON, ARTHUR PIERCE. The struggle for the Cape Henry Lighthouse, 1721–1791. American Neptune, 8:26–36, Jan. 1948. illus.

3660 RACHAL, WILLIAM M. E. Walled fortress and resort hotels. Virginia Cavalcade, 2:20–27, Summer 1952. illus.
Old Point Comfort and Fortress Monroe, 1819–1930.

Richmond County

3661 BALDWIN, F. C. Early architecture of the Rappahannock Valley; Mount Airy. American Institute of Architects. Journal, 4:448–54, Nov. 1916. illus.
1758.

3662 BROOKE, ARTHUR. Colonial mansion of Virginia. Architectural Record, 1:91–95, Aug. 1899.
Mount Airy.

3663 DABNEY, EDITH. Historic mansions of the Rappahannock — Sabine Hall. American Homes and Gardens, 6:197–200, May 1909. illus.
1730.

3664 GHEQUIERE, T. BUCKLER. Richmond County Court House, Virginia. American Architect and Building News, 2:199, June 28, 1877. illus.
1748 at Warsaw.

Rockbridge County

3665 THURMAN, FRANCIS LEE. Red House, Rockbridge County, Virginia, present home of James Patton Alexander. Virginia Magazine of History, 47:244–47, 1939.
Early eighteenth century by John McDowell.

3666 VIRGINIA STATE CHAMBER OF COMMERCE. Home is bought for Jackson Memorial. Commonwealth: The Magazine of Virginia, 21:26–43, Apr. 1954. illus.
Gen. Thomas Jonathan Jackson, 1851–61.

Spotsylvania County

3667 AVIS, A. The saving of Kenmore. Woman Citizen, n.s. 9:12, Jan. 24, 1925. illus.

3668 BALDWIN, FRANK CONGER. Early architecture of the Rappahannock Valley — Kenmore (1753–1777). American Institute of Architects. Journal, 3:113–18, Mar. 1915. illus.

3669 BERRYMAN, FLORENCE SEVILLE. Kenmore, Fredericksburg, Va., an example of Early American art. American Magazine of Art, 16:301–6, June 1925. illus.

3670 CRENSHAW, MARY MAYO. Saving the Fielding Lewis home. Antiquarian. 9:56–59, Sept. 1927.
Kenmore, Fredericksburg.

3671 DUKE, JANE TAYLOR. Kenmore and the Lewises. Garden City, N. Y., Double-day and Co., 1949. 268p. illus.

Fredericksburg around 1752, restored.

3672 ———. Kenmore, the home of George Washington's sister and her husband, Fielding Lewis, patriot. House Beautiful, 81:24–27, 81–82, Feb. 1939. illus.

3673 FLEMING, MRS. VIVIAN MINOR. Kenmore Mansion, built 1752, home of Colonel Fielding Lewis and his wife, Betty Washington. Fredericksburg, Va., Kenmore Association, 1924. 23p. illus.

3674 GOOLRICK, JOHN T. Old homes and history around Fredericksburg. . . . Richmond, Va., Garrett and Massie, 1929. 105p. illus.

3675 Kenmore in Fredericksburg, Virginia. Antiques, 53:293–96, Apr. 1948. illus.

Ca. 1752.

3676 MILLER, ROGER. Six old Virginia houses. American Institute of Architects. Journal, 13:61–66, Feb. 1925. illus. only.

Braxton house, Rising Sun Tavern, bank building, Mary Washington house, and the sentry box in Fredericksburg, and Weaver Tree in Albemarle County.

3677 PIPER, ADALINE D. Charm of Chatham, an historic mansion of the South, recently restored. House Beautiful, 59:437–41, Apr. 1926. illus.

1721.

3678 ———. A famous Virginia house opens its doors. Arts and Decoration, 52:10–12, 44, Aug. 1940. illus.

Doggett house, 1780.

3679 POWELL, D. V. M. Colonial churches in Spotsylvania County. William and Mary Quarterly, 2nd ser. 11:3–6, 1931.

3680 STERN, PHILIP N. Ornamental stuccowork at Kenmore. Antiques, 27:16–18, Jan. 1935. illus.

Stuccowork, 1775.

Stafford County

3681 WATERMAN, THOMAS TILESTON. Old court house buildings, Stafford Court House, Virginia. William and Mary Quarterly, 2nd ser. 16:247, 587–88, 1936.

Surry County

3682 BOHANNON, A. W. Old Surry: thumb-nail sketches of places of historic interest in Surry County, Virginia. Petersburg, Va., Plummer Printing Co., 1927. 74p. illus.

3683 ———. The old town of Cobham. Virginia Magazine of History and Biography, 57:252–68, July 1949. illus.

1680–1905.

3684 HAMMOND, JOHN MARTIN. Claremont Manor on the James: an historic brick house of Queen Anne type. House Beautiful, 51:564–65, June 1922.

Seventeenth century and later.

3685 MILLAR, DONALD. Jacobean house in Virginia. . . . Architectural Record, 57:220, 285–88, Mar. 1925. illus.

Bacon's castle, Smithfield (*ca.* 1655).

3686 MOOREHEAD, SINGLETON P., AND KENDREW, A. EDWIN. Restoration work at the Warren house. Virginia Magazine of History, 43:204–8, 1935.

3687 SCRIBNER, ROBERT LESLIE. The "Old Brick Church." Virginia Cavalcade, 6:16–21, Spring 1957. illus.

St. Luke's Church, near Smithfield, built *ca.* 1632.

Talbot County

3688 BORDLEY, JAMES, JR. Ratcliffe Manor. Maryland Historical Magazine, 45:73–74, Mar. 1950.

1755–56.

Warwick County

3689 MASON, GEORGE CARRINGTON. The first Colonial church of Denbigh Parish, Warwick County, Virginia. Virginia Magazine of History and Biography, 57:286–91, July 1949. illus.

Around 1636–86.

Westmoreland County

3690 ALEXANDER, FREDERICK WARREN. Stratford Hall and the Lees connected with its history. Oak Grove, Va., The Author, 1912. 332p. illus.

Ca. 1729.

3691 ARMES, ETHEL. Stratford on the Potomac. Greenwich, Conn., United Daughters of the Confederacy, 1928. 40p. illus.

3692 ———. Stratford on the Potomac. Antiques, 23:175–77, 1933.

3693 CAPEN, OLIVER BRONSON. Country homes of famous Americans. Part 10. Robert E. Lee. Country Life in America, 6:432–34, Sept. 1904. illus.

3694 CUMMIN, HAZEL E. Home of the Westmoreland Lees. Stratford Hall, Va. Country Life in America, 77:28–31, Apr. 1940. illus.

3695 ———. Stratford Hall, seat of the Westmoreland Lees, restored. American Home, 22:15–17, Sept. 1939. illus.

3696 HOPPIN, CHARLES ARTHUR. Origin of Wakefield, Washington's birthplace. Tyler's Quarterly Historical and Genealogical Magazine, 8:217–41, Apr. 1927.

3697 ———. Seven old houses on the Wakefield estate. Tyler's Quarterly Historical and Genealogical Magazine, 11:85–93, Oct. 1929.

3698 ———. The simple glory that was Wakefield to be restored. Tyler's Quarterly Historical and Genealogical Magazine, 9:219–24, Apr. 1928.

3698A HUDSON, J. PAUL. George Washington birthplace, national monument, Virginia. Washington, D. C., 1956. 44p. illus.

National Park Service. Historical Handbook Series, no. 26.

3699 KENNEDY, MRS. S. D. Stratford, Westmoreland County, Virginia. Journal of American History, 17:333–36, 1923.

3700 PERRY, ARMSTRONG. Stratford, Va., birthplace of the Lees. D. A. R. Magazine, 59:27–30, 64–69, Jan. 1925.

3701 ROBERT E. LEE MEMORIAL FOUNDATION, INC. Stratford, Colonial home and plantation, Westmoreland County, Virginia. [Washington, D. C., B. S. Adams, 1940.] [16p.] illus.

3702 [Stratford Hall. Contemporary description.] Southern Literary Messenger, 6:800–803, Dec. 1840.

Wythe County

3703 COLEMAN, ELIZABETH DABNEY. Showers of shot. Virginia Cavalcade, 5:33–35, Autumn 1955. illus.

Shot tower in Wythe County, at Jackson's Ferry, 1796–1831.

York County

3704 HATCH, CHARLES E., JR. Yorktown and the siege of 1781. Washington, D. C., 1952. 58p. illus.

National Park Service. Historical Handbook Series, no. 14.

3705 KENNEDY, WILL P. Restoring Yorktown shrines. D. A. R. Magazine, 61:799–809, 887–95, Nov., Dec. 1927.

3706 Restoration of a southern Colonial estate, York Hall, the residence of Captain George P. Blow, Yorktown, Va. Architectural Forum, 35:211–20, Dec. 1921. 1740–41.

3707 TRUDELL, CLYDE F. Colonial Yorktown. Richmond, Va., Dietz Press, 1938. 206p. illus.

"Being a brief historie of the place; together with something of its houses and publick buildings. With manie illustrations in pen and ink by ye author."

3708 UNITED STATES. NATIONAL PARK SERVICE. Colonial National Historical Park. Washington, D. C., Government Printing Office, 1940. 16p. illus.

Jamestown excavations and Yorktown houses.

3709 York Hall restored. Country Life in America, 40:52–55, Oct. 1921. illus.

Also known as the Nelson house.

WEST VIRGINIA

3710 Album of historic homes. Jefferson County Historical Society. Magazine, 15:4–29, 1949. illus.

Contents: Elmwood and Cold Spring (near Shepherdstown, 1797——); Leeland (Shepherdstown, 1823——); Rion Hall (1836——); Claymont Court (near Charles Town, 1820——).

3711 Album of historic homes, VII. Jefferson County Historical Society. Magazine, 21:10–20, Dec. 1955. illus.

On Retirement, Rose Hill Farm, and Belmont.

3712 Album of historic homes, VIII. Jefferson County Historical Society. Magazine, 22:5–15, Dec. 1956. illus.

On Head Spring, built 1774, and Prospect Hall, built 1804.

3713 BROOKS, A. B. Story of Fort Henry. West Virginia History, 1:110–18, 1940.
Originally named Fort Fincastle, Wheeling, 1774.

3714 BUSHONG, LEE. Restorations of Washington family homes, Jefferson County,
West Virginia. D. A. R. Magazine, 85:95–100, Feb. 1951. illus.
Homes associated with the Washington family, 1770——.

3715 CARNES, EVA MARGARET. Centennial history of the Philippi covered bridge,
1852–1952. Philippi, W. Va., Barbour County Historical Society, 1952. 101p.
illus.

3716 CARPENTER, CHARLES. Story of historic Harewood. National Republic, 21:15–
16, Aug. 1933. illus.
Near Charles Town, *ca.* 1770.

3717 COOK, ROY BIRD. Virginia frontier defenses, 1719–1795. West Virginia History,
1:119–30, 1940.
List of forts, stockades, and block houses, Virginia and West Virginia. (Mostly in
West Virginia now.)

3718 DAYTON, RUTH NEESON. Lewisburg landmarks. Charleston, W. Va., Education Foundation, 1957. 62p. illus.
1774——.

3719 DISCIPLES OF CHRIST HISTORICAL SOCIETY. The Campbell home: its growth,
importance, and present status. Harbinger and Discipliana, 14:96–98, July
1954. illus.
Bethany, built in 1792 or later.

3720 FAIRBAIRN, CHARLOTTE JUDD. George Washington's lost plantation in Jefferson County, West Virginia. Berryville, Va., Blue Ridge Press, [1954]. 19p.
illus.
Bullskin Plantation, bought in 1750, and Rock Hall, burned in 1906.

3721 FEDERAL WRITERS' PROJECT. Historic Romney, 1762–1937. Romney, W. Va.,
1937. 67p. illus.

3722 ——. West Virginia: a guide to the Mountain State. N. Y., Oxford University Press, 1941. 559p. illus.

3723 HARMER, HARVEY WALKER. Covered bridges of Harrison County, West Virginia. Charleston, W. Va., Education Foundation, [1956]. 146p. illus.

3724 ——. Old grist mills of Harrison County. [Charleston, W. Va., Charleston
Printing Co., 1940.] 260p. illus.

3725 HUNTER, KATHERINE M., AND HUNTER, BERNARD C. Some notes on Berkeley
Springs, West Virginia. William and Mary Quarterly, 2nd ser. 16:347–51,
July 1936. illus.
Ca. 1780 and Classic Revival.

3726 HUYETT, S. BURNS. The Tiffin house and its builder — Dr. Edward Tiffin. Jefferson County Historical Society. Magazine, 20:5–9, Dec. 1954. illus.
Charles Town, *ca.* 1780.

3727 KEMP, LOUISE SINGLETON. Old mills. Jefferson County Historical Society. Magazine, 21:21–28, Dec. 1955. illus.

Grist mills in Jefferson County, 1788–1938.

3728 LANGDON, LOUISE GARDNER. Shannon Hill. Jefferson County Historical Society. Magazine, 20:13–18, Dec. 1954. illus.

Near Charles Town, 1840.

3729 MINGHINI, LORRAINE, AND VAN METRE, THOMAS EARLE. History of Trinity Episcopal Church and Norborne Parish, Martinsburg, Berkeley County, West Virginia . . . 1771–1956. [Martinsburg? W. Va., 1956?] 204p. illus.

3730 SANDERS, J. C. Old Fort Ashby. West Virginia History, 1:104–9, 1940.

1755, an account of its restoration, near Frankfort.

3731 THURSTON, MYNNR. The Washingtons and their Colonial homes in West Virginia. Charles Town, W. Va., 1936. 29p. illus.

3732 [West Virginia.] Some West Virginia material included in Virginia entries.

3733 West Virginia number. Southern Magazine, v. 2, no. 9, 1936. 48p.

North Central States

GENERAL REFERENCES

3734 BUSHNELL, DAVID I. Villages of the Algonquian, Siouan, and Caddoan tribes west of the Mississippi. Washington, D. C., Government Printing Office, 1922. 211p. illus.

United States. Bureau of American Ethnology, Bulletin 77.

3735 COLE, HARRY ELLSWORTH. Stage coach and tavern tales of the Old Northwest. Cleveland, Ohio, Arthur H. Clark Co., 1930. 376p. illus.

3736 DRURY, JOHN. Historic Midwest houses. Minneapolis, University of Minnesota Press, 1947. 246p. illus.

3737 HAVINGHURST, WALTER. Upper Mississippi. N. Y., Farrar and Rinehart, 1937. 258p. illus.

Rivers of America series.

3738 NEWCOMB, REXFORD. Architecture of the Old Northwest Territory: a study of early architecture in Ohio, Indiana, Illinois, Michigan, Wisconsin and part of Minnesota. Chicago, University of Chicago Press, 1950. 175p. illus.

1785–1860, includes some structures in Iowa and Kentucky.

3739 ——. Studies in regional architecture. College Art Journal, 5:93–99, Jan. 1946.

3740 SWANSON, LESLIE CHARLES. Covered bridges in Illinois, Iowa, and Wisconsin. Moline, Ill., 1960. 40p. illus.

3741 THWAITES, REUBEN GOLD. Early western travels, 1748–1846. Cleveland, Ohio, Arthur H. Clark Co., 1904–7. 32v.

Reprints from early travel books, indexed. Many houses mentioned.

3742 WERTENBAKER, THOMAS JEFFERSON. The molding of the Middle West. American Historical Review, 53:223–34, Jan. 1948.

ILLINOIS

GENERAL REFERENCES

3743 CHAMBERLIN, DANN. Covered bridges in Illinois. Covered Bridge Topics, 13:1, 6, Spring 1955. illus.

1848–1939.

3744 COLBY, LYDIA. An elastic sod house. Illinois State Historical Society. Journal, 18:1035–38, Jan. 1926.
1855.

3745 CUSTER, MILO (ed.). Some pioneer buildings of Central Illinois. Bloomington, Ill., Central Illinois Historical Society, Publication no. 2, 1924. 21 illus.

3746 DRURY, JOHN. Old Illinois houses. Springfield, Ill., 1948. 220p. illus.
Occasional publications of the Illinois State Historical Society, no. 51. Originally series of weekly articles in Chicago Daily News, 1941——.

3747 ELDER, PAUL WILSON. Early taverns and inns in Illinois. Illinois State Historical Society. Journal, 20:578–83, Jan. 1928.

3748 FEDERAL WRITERS' PROJECT. Illinois: descriptive and historical guide. Chicago, A. C. McClurg and Co., 1939. 687p. illus.

3749 HURIE, ANNA KATHRYN. Early mills in Illinois. Illinois State Historical Society. Journal, 22:593–600, Jan. 1930. illus.

3750 MONAGHAN, JAY. This is Illinois: a pictorial history. Chicago, University of Chicago Press, 1949. 211p. illus.
1673–1949.

3751 NEWCOMB, REXFORD. Beginnings of architecture in Illinois. Illinois State Historical Society. Journal, 39:303–22.

3752 O'DONNELL, THOMAS EDWARD. Outline of the history of architecture in Illinois. Illinois State Historical Society. Transactions, pp. 124–43, 1931.

3753 ———. A proposed survey of the architectural development in Illinois. Illinois State Historical Society. Transactions, 38:75–79, 1926.

3754 ———. Recording the early architecture of Illinois in the Historic American Buildings Survey. Illinois State Historical Society. Transactions, pp. 185–213, 1934.

3755 REED, EARL H. Historic American Buildings Survey; Northern Illinois, 1716–1867. Chicago, 1934. 50 illus.
Another set of plates issued 1937.

3756 SCHNAPP, MARGARET KATHERINE. Historic churches in Illinois. Illinois State Historical Society. Journal, 21:525–33, Jan. 1929.

LOCATIONS

Addison

3757 POELLOT, DANIEL E. The old church at Addison. Concordia Historical Institute. Quarterly, 21:14–26, Apr. 1948. illus.
Lutheran church, 1837–1946.

Albion

3758 BOEWE, CHARLES E. Prairie Albion: an English settlement in pioneer Illinois. Carbondale, Southern Illinois University Press, 1962. 317p. illus.

3759 O'DONNELL, THOMAS EDWARD. Albion, an early English settlement in Southern Illinois. Western Architect, 35:123–26, Oct. 1926. illus.
Ca. 1820—ca. 1860.

Batavia

3760 GUSTAFSON, JOHN A. Historical Batavia. Batavia, Ill., Batavia Historical Society, 1962. 140p. illus.

Cahokia

3761 BABB, MARGARET E. Mansion house of Cahokia and its builder — Nicholas Jarrot. Illinois State Historical Society. Transactions for the year 1924, pp. 78–93.

3762 Cahokia, 250th Anniversary Celebration Association, 1699–1949; the birthplace of the Midwest, Cahokia, Illinois. . . . East St. Louis, Ill., Geiger Printing Co., 1949. 48p. illus.

3763 PETERSON, CHARLES E. Notes on Old Cahokia. French American Review, 1:184–225, July–Sept. 1948.

3764 ———. Notes on Old Cahokia. Illinois State Historical Society. Journal, 42:193–208.

3765 STUDY, GUY. Oliver Parks restores the Jarrot Mansion at Cahokia. Illinois State Historical Society. Journal, 38:351–53.

1799–1806, claimed to be the oldest brick house in the state.

3766 ———. The restoration of the Holy Family Church, Cahokia, Illinois. Missouri Historical Society. Bulletin, 5:257–65, July 1949.

1787–99.

Cairo

3767 FEDERAL WRITERS' PROJECT. Cairo guide. Nappanee, Ind., E. V. Publishing House, 1938. 62p. illus.

Carlinville

3768 BROWN, WILLIAM BARRICK. The history of a famous court house located at Carlinville, Illinois. Carlinville, Ill., Press of the Carlinville Democrat, 1934. 54p. illus.

Chicago

3769 ANDREAS, ALFRED THEODORE. History of Chicago. Chicago, Ill., A. T. Andreas Co., 1884–86. 3v. illus.

See especially: 1:504–6; 2:562–67; 3:62–74.

3770 CURREY, JOSIAH SEYMOUR. Story of old Fort Dearborn. Chicago, A. C. McClurg and Co., 1912. 173p. illus.

3771 DRURY, JOHN. Old Chicago houses. Chicago, University of Chicago Press, 1941. 518p. illus.

3772 FEDERAL WRITERS' PROJECT. Selected bibliography; Illinois, Chicago and its environs. Chicago, 1937. 58p.

3773 RANDALL, FRANK ALFRED. History of the development of building construction in Chicago. Urbana, University of Illinois Press, 1949. 388p. illus.

3774 SIEGEL, ARTHUR S. Chicago's famous buildings; a photographic guide to the city's architectural landmarks and other notable buildings. Chicago, University of Chicago Press, 1965. 230p. illus.

3775 SPARKS, EDWIN E. The beginnings of Chicago. American Architect, 81:101–4, Sept. 26, 1903.

3776 ———. The beginnings of Chicago. Western Society of Engineers. Journal, pp. 357–72, 1903. illus.

3777 TALLMADGE, THOMAS EDDY. Architecture in old Chicago. Chicago, University of Chicago Press, 1941. 218p. illus.

Coles County

3778 BALCH, ALFRED B. Pioneer log church, Coles County, Illinois. Illinois State Historical Society. Journal, 13:85–86, Apr. 1921.

Evanston

3779 TALLMADGE, THOMAS E. Architectural history of a western town. American Architect, 115:443–51, Mar. 26, 1919. illus.

Covers *ca.* 1840–1919.

Galena

3780 BALE, FLORENCE GRATIOT. The Branton Tavern. Illinois State Historical Society. Journal, 29:151–60, 1936.

Mid-nineteenth century, near Galena.

3781 CARROLL, VIRGINIA D. The Galena Market House, oldest in the Midwest. Illinois State Historical Society. Journal, 45:50–54, Spring 1952. illus.

1846–1947.

3782 FEDERAL WRITERS' PROJECT. Galena guide. Chicago? 1937. 79p. illus.

3783 ILLINOIS STATE HISTORICAL LIBRARY. De Soto house: hundred-year-old Galena Hotel. Illinois State Historical Society. Journal, 47:315–21, Autumn 1954. illus.

1855——.

Galesburg

3784 Log city days. Galesburg, Ill., Knox College Centenary Publications, 1937. 79p. illus.

Lebanon

3785 LESTER, W. A. Historic college of Egypt. Egyptian Key: Opens the Doors of Southern Illinois, 3:55–59, Apr. 1948. illus.

McKendree College, 1827–1948.

3786 St. Clair County Historical Society presents a Lebanon tour, June 22, 1963. . . . Belleville, Ill., 1963. 18p. illus.

Metamora

3787 IRVING, J. C., AND OTHERS. Old court house at Metamora presented to the state of Illinois. Illinois State Historical Society. Journal, 14:365–81, Oct. 1921, Jan. 1922.

Nauvoo

3788 BURGESS, SAMUEL A. The story of the Mansion house. Nauvoo, Ill., 1940. 8p.

3789 FEDERAL WRITERS' PROJECT. Nauvoo guide. Chicago, A. C. McClurg and Co., 1939. 49p. illus.

3790 FLANDERS, ROBERT BRUCE. Nauvoo: kingdom on the Mississippi. Urbana, University of Illinois Press, 1965. 364p. illus.

3791 LILLIBRIDGE, ROBERT M. Architectural currents on the Mississippi River frontier: Nauvoo, Illinois. Society of Architectural Historians. Journal, 19:109–14, 1960.

3792 McGAVIN, ELMER CECIL. The Nauvoo Temple. Salt Lake City, Deseret Book Co., 1962. 185p. illus.

3793 VESTAL, PEARL. Nauvoo's Mormon decade: the 1840's and current views of the Latter Day Saints and their shrines. Hamilton, Ill. 4v. illus.

New Salem

3794 BOOTON, JOSEPH F. Record of the restoration of New Salem: New Salem State Park near Petersburg, Illinois, 1932–1933. State of Illinois, Department of Public Works and Buildings. 88p. illus.

3795 POND, FERN NANCE. New Salem memorial. D. A. R. Magazine, 69:101–2, 1935.

Prairie du Rocher

3796 SUESS, ADOLPH B. Glimpses of Prairie du Rocher. . . . Belleville, Ill., Buechler Printing Co., 1942. 14p. illus.

Princeton

3797 FEDERAL WRITERS' PROJECT. Princeton guide. Princeton, Ill., Republican Printing Co., 1939. 48p. illus.

Rock Island

3798 AUGUSTANA EVANGELICAL LUTHERAN CHURCH. A century of life and growth: Augustana, 1848–1948. Rock Island, Ill., Augustana Book Concern, 1948. 158p. illus.

Sangamon County

3799 SALE, MRS. ANTHONY W. Old mills of Sangamon County. Illinois State Historical Society. Journal, 18:1056–58, Jan. 1926.

Springfield

3800 BUNN, ALICE EDWARDS. The story of the house. Springfield, Ill., 1945. 17p.

3801 The Governor's Mansion a century ago. Illinois State Historical Society. Journal, 38:330–38, 1945.
1853–57.

3802 HICKEY, JAMES T. The Lincoln's Globe Tavern. Illinois State Historical Society. Journal, 56:629–53, 1963.
Destroyed.

3803 ILLINOIS. GENERAL ASSEMBLY. Information on Illinois State House. In five parts: 1:347–75, 1869; 1:731–66, 1871; 1:407–27, 1873; 1:479–500, 1875; 2:doc. F, 1879.

3804 ILLINOIS. SECRETARY OF STATE. Guide to Illinois capitol and other buildings at Springfield. Springfield, Ill., 1938. illus.

3805 ILLINOIS STATE HISTORICAL LIBRARY. The Governor's Mansion a century ago. Illinois State Historical Society. Journal, 48:330–37, Autumn 1955. illus.

Documents from the construction of the Executive Mansion, 1853–56.

3806 PRATT, HARRY EDWARD. Lincoln's Springfield. Springfield, Ill., Illinois State Historical Society, 1955. 32p. illus.

Virginia

3807 MARTIN, LORENE. Allendale, an old adobe house. Illinois State Historical Society. Journal, 28:110–14, July 1935.

1852, near Virginia.

Warrenville

3808 NATZKE, BARBARA. The living past of Warrenville, Ill. Peter Piper Press, 1965. 20p. illus.

INDIANA

GENERAL REFERENCES

3809 BOCK, EUGENE R. The covered bridge in Indiana. Indiana Historical Bulletin, 31:56–63, 76–83, Mar.–Apr. 1954.

Includes table of covered bridges.

3810 BURNS, LEE. Early architects and builders of Indiana. Indiana Historical Society. Publications, 11:179–215, 1935. illus.

Contains a number of biographies and documentary information.

3811 CHAMBERLIN, DANN. Covered bridges of Parke and Putnam counties, Indiana. Covered Bridge Topics, 12:1–2, Spring 1954.

1859–1915.

3812 COTTMAN, GEORGE STREIBY. Centennial history and handbook of Indiana. Indianapolis, Max R. Hyman, 1915. 464p. illus.

Illustrations of many public buildings, pp. 203–464.

3813 DUNN, JACOB PIATT. Indiana and Indianans, a history of aboriginal and territorial Indiana and the century of statehood. Chicago and N. Y., American Historical Society, 1919. 5v. illus.

Illustrates early statehouses. Old Capitol, 1832–36, Ithiel Town, architect.

3814 ELLSWORTH, HENRY WILLIAM. Valley of the Upper Wabash, Indiana, with hints on its agricultural advantages: plan of a dwelling. . . . N. Y., Pratt, Robinson and Co., 1838. 175p. illus.

Plan, materials, probable cost.

3815 FEDERAL WRITERS' PROJECT. Indiana: a guide to the Hoosier State. N. Y., Oxford University Press, 1941. 548p. illus.

3816 FRITSCH, WILLIAM AUGUST. German settlers and German settlements in Indiana. Evansville, Ind., 1915. 61p. illus.

3817 HARVEY, MAX. The covered bridges of Parke County, Indiana. Montezuma, Ind., 1959. Unpaged. illus.

Parke County has thirty-eight covered bridges still standing (1966), of which thirty-one are still in use.

3818 Homes along the Ohio. House and Garden, 78:55, Sept. 1940. illus.

Lanier house, 1844, and Shrewsbury house, Madison; Starks house, Aurora.

3819 Illustrated historical atlas of the state of Indiana. Chicago, Baskin, Forster and Co., 1876. 462p. illus.

3820 INDIANA FEDERATION OF ART CLUBS. Art guide to Indiana. Extension Division, Indiana University. Bulletin, v. 16, no. 8, Apr. 1931. 184p. illus.

3821 Indiana gazetteer, or topographical dictionary of the state of Indiana. Indianapolis, E. Chamberlain, 1849. 440p. illus.

Contemporary illustrations of buildings.

3822 KETCHAM, BRYAN E. Covered bridges on the byways of Indiana. [Lockland? Ohio, by author, 1949.] 216p. illus.

1834–1922.

3823 KNOX, JULIA LeCLERC. Pioneer homesteads. Indiana Magazine of History, 18:371–80, Dec. 1922.

3824 LOUCKS, KENNETH. John Elder: pioneer builder. Indiana Magazine of History, 26:25–33, Mar. 1930.

3825 PEAT, WILBUR DAVID. Indiana houses of the nineteenth century. Indianapolis, Indiana Historical Society, 1962. 195p. illus.

3826 PECKHAM, HOWARD H. Indiana. Antiques, 58:377–86, Nov. 1950. illus.

3827 RIFNER, BEN. Early architecture of Indiana. Master's Thesis, Ohio State University, 1942.

3828 SIMPICH, FREDERICK. Indiana journey. National Geographic Magazine, 70:267–320, Sept. 1936. illus.

LOCATIONS

Bedford

3829 EVANS, NORMAN C. Spring Mill: the story of southern Indiana's pioneer village. [Indianapolis? 1953.] 148p. illus.

Hidden Valley village settled ca. 1814, abandoned ca. 1893, restored 1927.

Carroll County

3830 MAYHILL, MRS. B. B. Old inns and taverns of Carroll County. Indiana Historical Bulletin, 28:178–82, Nov. 1951.

1838——.

Corydon

3831 CLELAND, ETHEL. New facts about the Corydon State House. Indiana Magazine of History, 9:14–19, Mar. 1913.

1811–12.

3832 COLEMAN, CHRISTOPHER B. Restoration of the capitol at Corydon. Indiana Magazine of History, 30:255–58, Sept. 1934.

3833 COTTMAN, GEORGE STREIBY. Corydon State House: Hoosier shrine. . . . Department of Conservation, State of Indiana, Division of Lands and Waters, Publication no. 94, 1930. 53p. illus.

3834 Indiana's first state capitol at Corydon. Indiana Historical Bulletin, 7:6–7, Oct. 1929.
Account of the restoration of the capitol. 1825.

3835 MOORES, CHARLES. Old Corydon. Indiana Magazine of History, 13:20–41, Mar. 1917.

Crawfordsville

3836 FORBES, JOHN D. Crawfordsville, U. S. A.: the American small town as an architectural microcosm. College Art Journal, 7:286–96, Summer 1948. illus.
1836–1936.

3837 KNOX, JULIA LeCLERC. Some interesting Crawfordsville people and their homes. Indiana Magazine of History, 22:285–96, Sept. 1926.

Evansville

3838 WOODEN, HOWARD E. Public museum. Architectural heritage of Evansville; an interpretive review of the nineteenth century. Evansville, Ind., Evansville Museum of Arts and Sciences, 1962. 78p. illus.

Franklin County

3839 BOSSERT, MICHAEL. Early schools of Franklin County. Indiana Magazine of History, 26:218–36, Sept. 1930.

Goshen

3840 BARTHOLOMEW, H. S. K. Old landmarks of Goshen. Indiana Magazine of History, 29:198–202, Sept. 1933.

Indianapolis

3841 BURNS, LEE. Indianapolis: the old town and the new. Indianapolis, Cornelius Printing Co., 1923. 44p. illus.

3842 LILLY, ELI. History of the Little Church on the Circle: Christ Church Parish, Indianapolis, 1837–1955. Indianapolis, The Rector, Wardens, and Vestrymen of Christ Protestant Episcopal Church, 1957. 376p. illus.

3843 LOUCKS, KENNETH. Hoosier hostelry a hundred years ago. Indiana Historical Bulletin, 8:313–15, 1931.
Union Inn, 1824–36.

Jackson County

3844 BURGE, WARREN. An historic cabin. Knightstown, Ind., The Thornwood Printery, 1914. 31p. illus.
1807. Claimed to be oldest log cabin in Indiana.

Lafayette

3845 HARLAN, MABEL LOUISE WHITEHEAD. The old Junction house, Pearl River, and other papers about Lafayette's yesteryears. Lafayette, Ind., Tippecanoe County Historical Assoc., 1954. 20p. illus.

Historical essays, 1825–1949.

Madison

3846 COTTMAN, GEORGE STREIBY. James F. D. Lanier home. Department of Conservation, State of Indiana, Division of Lands and Waters, Publication no. 64, 1927. 43p. illus.

1843. Francis Costigan, architect.

3847 ———. James F. D. Lanier house, an Indiana memorial, Madison, Indiana. Department of Conservation, State of Indiana, Division of Lands and Waters, Publication no. 59, 1927. 11p.

3848 GARBER, BLANCHE GOODE. Lanier family and Lanier home. Indiana Magazine of History, 22:277–84, Sept. 1926.

3849 KNOX, JULIA LeCLERC. Old Sullivan home, Madison, Indiana. Indiana Magazine of History, 31:109–11, June 1935.

1816.

3850 ———. Quaint little old Indiana city. Indiana Magazine of History, 28:88–95, June 1932.

Michigan Hill (near Madison)

3851 KNOX, JULIA LeCLERC. Cravenhurst. Indiana Magazine of History, 29:339–42, Dec. 1933.

New Albany

3852 KNOX, JULIA LeCLERC. Old Phineas Kent mansion of New Albany. Indiana Historical Bulletin, 9:405–7, Apr. 1932.

Ca. 1852.

New Harmony

3853 FRETAGOET, NORA C. Historic New Harmony: a guide. Mount Vernon, Ind., The Western Star, 1923. 66p. illus.

First edition, 1914.

3854 KNOX, JULIA LeCLERC. Unique little town of New Harmony. Indiana Magazine of History, 32:52–58, Mar. 1935.

3855 LOCKRIDGE, ROSS F. Old Fauntleroy home. New Harmony, New Harmony Memorial Commission, 1939. 219p. illus.

1815.

North Manchester

3856 BILLINGS, W. E. Historic homes of North Manchester. North Manchester, Ind., Dr. Manasseh Cutler Chapter, Daughters of the American Revolution, 1949. 15p.

1834——.

Paoli

3857 NEWCOMB, REXFORD. Greek Revival courthouse in Southern Indiana. Architectural Forum, 48:177–80, Feb. 1928. illus.

1850.

Rush County

3858 DOGGETT, DENZIL. Water-powered mills of Flat Rock River. Indiana Magazine of History, 32:319–59, 1936.

Ca. 1820.

Salem

3859 HOBBS, MARTHA SAYLES. Historic homes of Salem, Indiana, and vicinity. Indiana Magazine of History, 21:33–59, Mar. 1925.

1814–60.

Switzerland County

3860 DUFOUR, PERRET. Swiss settlement of Switzerland County, Indiana. Indianapolis, Indiana Historical Society, 1925. 446p.

3861 KNOX, JULIA LeCLERC. Two pioneer homesteads of Switzerland County. Indiana Magazine of History, 28:247–50, Dec. 1932.

John David Dufour house and David Blunk house.

Vevay

3862 KNOX, JULIA LeCLERC. Century old Wright home. Indiana Magazine of History, 32:380–83, 1936.

3863 ———. The old ferryhouse at Vevay, Indiana. Indiana Magazine of History, 45:171–72, June 1949.

3864 ———. Old Jean Daniel Morerod home, Vevay, Ind. Indiana Magazine of History, 27:125–28, June 1931.

3865 ———. Some interesting pioneer homesteads in and around Vevay, Indiana. Vevay? 1948. 53p. illus.

First published 1927. On houses built around 1811.

Vincennes

3866 BURNS, LEE. Life in old Vincennes. Indiana Historical Society. Publications, 8:437–60.

Description and history.

3867 GAVISK, FRANCIS H. Old Vincennes Cathedral. Vincennes, Indiana, 1934. 7p.

1825. George Rogers Clark National Memorial Leaflets, no. 3.

3868 McQUAID, JAMES D., AND McQUAID, MARIE LUCIER. A guide book to historic Vincennes. Vincennes, Ind., 1965. 112p. illus.

3869 O'DONNELL, THOMAS EDWARD. Historic cathedral and library, Vincennes, Ind. Architectural Forum, 45:81–84, Aug. 1926. illus.

3870 VAN NATTER, FRANCIS MARION. Cathedral of old Vincennes. National Republic, 20:6–7, Apr. 1933.

3871 VINCENNES FORTNIGHTLY CLUB. Historic Vincennes: tourists' guide. Vincennes, Ind., 1956. 40p. illus.

Many earlier editions.

3872 WHITTON, M. O. Grouseland and its early builders. American Collector, 12:8–9ff., Feb. 1943. illus.

IOWA

GENERAL REFERENCES

3873 DUBELL, SUSAN I. Pioneer home. Palimpsest, 12:445–54, Dec. 1931.
General discussion of pioneer log construction.

3874 DUFFIELD, GEORGE C. An Iowa settler's homestead. Annals of Iowa, ser. 3, 6:206–15, Oct. 1903.

3875 FEDERAL WRITERS' PROJECT. Iowa: a guide to the Hawkeye State. N. Y., Hastings House, 1949. 583p. illus.
1673———. American Guide Series. First published 1938.

3876 HOFFMAN, M. M. John Francis Rague (1799–1877) pioneer architect of Iowa. Annals of Iowa, ser. 3, 19:444–48, 1934.

3877 SHARP, MILDRED J. Early cabins in Iowa. Palimpsest, 2:16–29, Jan. 1921.
Discussion of pioneer log structures.

3878 SWISHER, JACOB A. Iowa, land of many mills. Iowa City, Iowa, State Historical Society of Iowa, 1940. 317p. illus.
History and preservation.

3879 ZOOK, NANCY GIBBONS. Mills that turned with a right good will. Iowan, 4:25–33, 48, Apr.–May 1956. illus.
On some surviving water-powered mills, 1830–80.

LOCATIONS

Bentonsport

3880 SAYRE, LOIS. Historic Bentonsport. Iowan, 3:24–33, 48–49, 51–52, Aug.–Sept. 1955. illus.
1836–1955.

Bloomington

3881 MAHAN, BRUCE E. Three early taverns. Palimpsest, 3:250–60, Aug. 1922.

Burlington

3882 FEDERAL WRITERS' PROJECT. Guide to Burlington, Iowa. Burlington, Iowa, Acres-Blackmar Co., 1938. 72p. illus.

Cedar Rapids

3883 FEDERAL WRITERS' PROJECT. Guide to Cedar Rapids and northeast Iowa. Cedar Rapids, Iowa, Laurence Press, 1937. 79p. illus.

Davenport

3884 MESCHER, SHIRLEY. Davenport house. Annals of Iowa, 31:368–71, July 1952.
1852–53.

Des Moines

3885 ADAMS, GORDON. Terrace Hill. Iowan, 3:24–29, 43–44, Feb.–Mar. 1955. illus.
1857.

3886 SWISHER, JACOB A. Capitols at Des Moines. Iowa Journal of History and Politics, 39:52–87, Jan. 1941. illus.

Covers 1857 building and present building, 1888.

Dubuque

3887 BEASLEY, ROBERT. Restoration in Dubuque. Iowan, 5:32–35, Apr.–May 1957. illus.

On a stone house built by John McMahon in 1835 and restored since 1947.

3888 FEDERAL WRITERS' PROJECT. Guide to Dubuque. Dubuque, Iowa, Hoermann Press, 1937. 32p. illus.

3889 GALLAHER, RUTH A. First church in Iowa. Palimpsest, 7:1–10, Jan. 1926. illus.

Log church, 1834.

3890 SULLIVAN, ROGER, AND SWISHER, J. A. The Dubuque Shot Tower. Palimpsest, 30:377–88, Dec. 1949. illus.

1856.

Estherville

3891 FEDERAL WRITERS' PROJECT. Guide to Estherville, Iowa, Emmet County and Iowa Great Lakes Region. Estherville, Iowa, Estherville Enterprise Print, 1939. 36p. illus.

Iowa City

3892 BATES, KATHERINE V. Old South Hall. Palimpsest, 29:97–110, Apr. 1948. illus.

University of Iowa campus, 1858, burned 1901.

3893 KEYES, MARGARET N. Nineteenth-century home architecture of Iowa City. Doctoral Dissertation, Florida State University, 1965.

3894 Old capitol. Iowa City, State University of Iowa, 1928. 16p.

3895 PETERSEN, WILLIAM JOHN. Butler's capitol. Palimpsest, v. 36, no. 12, Dec. 1955. illus.

1841——. By Walter Butler, 1800–44.

3896 SHAMBAUGH, BENJAMIN FRANKLIN. Founding of Iowa City. Palimpsest, 20:137–76, May 1939. illus.

Contains an account of the building of the Iowa State Capitol (cornerstone, 1840) and its architect, John Francis Rague.

3897 ——. The old stone capitol remembers. Iowa City, State Historical Society of Iowa, 1939. 435p.

Material on Father Mazzuchelli, John Francis Rague, and the capitol.

3898 VAN TASSEL, VALENTINE. When Friendly Lucas went to Iowa. Antiques Journal, 11:14–15, 30, June 1956. illus.

Plum Grove, 1844——.

Keokuk

3899 BICKEL, R. J. "Rat Row" in Keokuk. Annals of Iowa, 34:450–53, Oct. 1956.

On the buildings of the American Fur Company, 1828–33.

Keosauqua

3900 SAYRE, LOIS. Keosauqua. Iowan, 10:12–17, 28–29, Spring 1962. illus.

McGregor

3901 FEDERAL WRITERS' PROJECT. Guide to McGregor. McGregor, Iowa, J. F. Widman and Sons Co., 1938. 24p. illus.

Madison County

3902 HARTSOOK, MRS. F. P. Covered bridges in Madison County, Iowa. Covered Bridge Topics, v. 13–14, Fall 1955—Spring 1956. illus.

Muscatine

3903 FISHBURN, JESSE J. Octagon Place. Palimpsest, 29:33–38, Feb. 1948. illus.
1855. Samuel Sinnett, architect.

Nora Springs

3904 HICKS, DWIGHT B. Log cabin remnant of Iowa history. Annals of Iowa, 32:146–48, Oct. 1953.
1853. By Edson Gaylord.

Story City

3905 TJERNAGEL, NEHEMIAS. Pioneer Iowa homes. Annals of Iowa, 31:146–51, Oct. 1951.
Near Story City, 1855——.

Wapello County

3906 HARKNESS, PEARL RUPE. Mars Hill log church. Annals of Iowa, 32:530–34, Jan. 1955.
Missionary Baptist Church, Mars Hall (or Hill), 1857–1954.

West Branch

3907 STRATTON, MAUD BRANSON. Herbert Hoover's home town: the story of West Branch. West Branch, Iowa, 1948. 175p. illus.
Ca. 1851——.

KANSAS

3908 ASBURY, ROBERT F. Kansas architecture; a survey of development from the pre-territorial period to the present. Master's Thesis, Kansas University, 1961.

3909 CALDWELL, MARTHA B. Annals of Shawnee Methodist Mission and Indian Manual Labor School. Topeka, Kan., Kansas State Historical Society, 1939. 120p. illus.

3910 ——. The Eldridge house. Kansas Historical Quarterly, 9:347–70, 1940.
Hotel, Lawrence, Kan.

3911 DE ZURKO, EDWARD R. Early Kansas churches. Society of Architectural Historians. Journal, 6:22–29, Jan. 1947. illus.

3912 ———. Early Kansas churches. Manhattan, Kansas State College, 1949. 71p. illus.

1830–76.

3913 DICK, EVERETT NEWTON. Sod-house frontier, 1854–1890; a social history of the northern plains from the creation of Kansas and Nebraska to the admission of the Dakotas. N. Y., D. Appleton-Century Co., 1937. 550p. illus.

3914 DOYLE, W. E. Indian forts and dwellings. Annual Report of the Board of Regents of the Smithsonian Institution for the year 1876, pp. 460–65.

Wichita.

3915 FEDERAL WRITERS' PROJECT. Kansas: a guide to the Sunflower State. N. Y., Hastings House, 1949. 538p. illus.

1540———. American Guide Series. First published 1939.

3916 HEINTZELMAN, JOHN CRANSTON. A century of Kansas architecture. Kansas Magazine, pp. 63–72, 1957. illus.

1855–1946.

3917 ISELY, BLISS. Grass wigwam at Wichita. Kansas Historical Quarterly, 2:66–71, 1933.

3918 KANSAS STATE HISTORICAL SOCIETY. Old Pawnee Capitol, an account of the first capitol building of Kansas, the town of Pawnee, initial sessions of the First Territorial Legislature, destruction of the town of Pawnee, ruins of the capitol building. Topeka, Kan., Kansas State Printing Plant, 1928. 38p. illus.

3919 MALIN, JAMES CLAUDE. Housing experiments in the Lawrence community, 1855. Kansas Historical Quarterly, 21:95–121, Summer 1954.

3920 ROSS, MRS. EDITH CONNELLEY. Old Shawnee Mission. Topeka, Kan., Kansas State Printing Plant, 1928. 28p. illus.

3921 SHERLOCK, CHELSA CLELLA. Old John Brown's cabin, Osawatomie, Kansas. Better Homes and Gardens, Dec. 1926. illus.

3922 TAFT, ROBERT. Photographic history of early Kansas. Kansas Historical Quarterly, 3:3–14, Feb. 1934.

Photographs by Alexander Gardener of buildings standing in Kansas in 1868.

3923 WHITTEMORE, MARGARET. Sketchbook of Kansas landmarks. Topeka, Kan., College Press, 1936. 125p. illus.

Second edition, 1937.

MICHIGAN

3924 American home pilgrimages — part 5 — Michigan. American Home, 20:29–30, 101–3, Oct. 1938. illus.

3925 BROWN, HENRY D., AND MARRIOTT, MRS. W. D. City and county buildings in Detroit. Detroit Historical Society. Bulletin, 10:6–10, Mar. 1954. illus.

1828———.

3926 BURTON, CLARENCE MONROE. Detroit in earlier days; a few notes on some of the old buildings in the city. Detroit, Mich., Burton Abstract and Title Co. 36p. illus.

3927 CAMPAU, M. WOOLSEY. Two distinguished old Jefferson Avenue houses. Detroit Historical Society. Bulletin, 4:5–9, May 1948. illus.

Trowbridge house, 1830's; Sibley house, 1848.

3928 CLARK, E. M. Restoration of old Fort Holmes on Mackinac Island. Michigan Historical Magazine, 20:295–300, 1936.

3929 DUNBAR, WILLIS F. Glimpses of Michigan, 1840–60. Michigan History, 32:225–37, Sept. 1948.

Mostly Kalamazoo, 1840–50.

3930 FARMER, SILAS. The history of Detroit and Michigan. Detroit, Mich., S. Farmer and Co., 1884.

Part 7, architectural.

3931 FEDERAL WRITERS' PROJECT. Michigan: a guide to the Wolverine State. N. Y., Oxford University Press, 1941. 682p. illus.

3932 FERRY, HAWKINS. Gothic and Tuscan revivals in Detroit, 1828–1875. Art Quarterly, 9:234–56, 1946. illus.

3933 ———. Representative Detroit buildings. Detroit Institute of Art. Bulletin, 21:46–63, Mar. 1943.

1823———.

3934 GOODRICH, CALVIN. An outland post called Detroit. Michigan Alumnus. Quarterly Review, 45:311–18, 1939.

On the fort (1763) and early town.

3935 HAIGH, HENRY A. Henry Ford's typical American village at Dearborn. Michigan Historical Magazine, 13:506–43, 1929.

3936 ———. Old Ten Eyck Tavern. Michigan Historical Magazine, 15:441–45, 1931. Detroit.

3937 KIMBALL, SIDNEY FISKE. Old houses of Michigan. Architectural Record, 52:227–40, Sept. 1922. illus.

3938 [LORCH, EMIL.] Report of the Committee on Michigan Architecture of the Michigan Society of Architects. American Society of Architectural Historians. Journal, 2:34–35, Apr. 1942.

3939 McKEE, HARLEY J. Glimpses of architecture in Michigan. Michigan History, 50:1–27, Mar. 1966.

Based on data in the archives of the Historic American Buildings Survey.

3940 ——— (comp.). Records of buildings in the state of Michigan. Michigan History, 50:28–49, Mar. 1966.

List compiled to update and expand entries in the Historic American Buildings Survey 1941 catalogue and 1959 supplement.

3941 MITCHELL, EDWIN VALENTINE. American village. N. Y., Stackpole Sons, 1938. 261p. illus.

Henry Ford's Greenfield Village at Dearborn.

3942 Old Fort Michilimackinac. Ann Arbor, University of Michigan Press, 1939. 12p. illus.

3943 POOLE, S. ALICIA. Historic community house. Michigan Historical Magazine, 15:438–40, 1931.

John Jacob Astor house, Mackinac Island.

3944 QUAIFE, M. M. Mansion of St. Martin. Burton Historical Collections, 3:33–48, Jan. 1925.

Detroit, late eighteenth century.

3945 SAGENDORPH, KENT. Michigan: the story of the university. N. Y., E. P. Dutton and Co., 1948. 348p. illus.

American College and University Series, v. 2.

3946 STOKSTAD, MARILYN. Michigan pioneer architecture: the Greek Revival style. Michigan History, 36:48–54, Mar. 1952.

1830–60.

3947 STRATTON, WILLIAM B. The growth of Detroit. Western Architect, 24:126–28, Oct. 1916. illus.

Nineteenth century.

3948 TAYLOR, HOWELL. Historic houses of Southwest Michigan. Series in Sunday Detroit News, 1931–1932.

3949 ———. Michigan's pioneer architecture. Michigan History, 37:19–26, Mar. 1953. illus.

1825–55.

3950 VAN FLEET, JAMES ALVIN. Old and New Mackinac. Ann Arbor, Mich., Courier Steam Printing-House, 1870. 176p. illus.

MINNESOTA

3951 BURRIS, EVADENE A. Building the frontier home. Minnesota History, 15:43–55, Mar. 1924. illus.

3952 Chippewa Mission. St. Paul, Minn., Minnesota Historical Records Survey Project, 1941. 42p. illus. Mimeographed.

Near Watson. Report of the Chippewa Mission Archaeological Investigation.

3953 DEAN, WILLIAM BLAKE. History of the capitol buildings of Minnesota. Minnesota Historical Society. Collections, 12:1–42, Dec. 1908. illus.

First capitol, 1853.

3954 Early historic structures: Faribault house; Afton octagonal house. Northwest Architect, 4:4–5, Jan.–Feb. 1940.

Faribault house, 1837, St. Paul; Afton octagonal house, 1860's.

3955 FEDERAL WRITERS' PROJECT. Minnesota: a state guide. N. Y., Viking Press, 1938. 523p. illus.

3956 LEACH, MRS. PAUL J. Haunted windmill. Minnesota History, 12:65–67, 1931.

Faribault County.

3957 McClure, Harlan Ewart. Twin cities architecture; Minneapolis and St. Paul, 1820–1955. N. Y., Reinhold Publishing Corp., 1955. 44p. illus.

3958 Marin, William A. Sod houses and prairie schooners. Minnesota History, 12:135–56, June 1931.

Describes the typical sod house.

3959 Nonnweiler, Mary H. Sibley House Association of the Minnesota D. A. R. D. A. R. Magazine, 83:37–38, Jan. 1949. illus.

Built 1835. Acquired by D. A. R. in 1910.

3960 Torbert, Donald R. A century of art and architecture in Minnesota. Minneapolis, University of Minnesota Press, 1958. 62p. illus.

A History of the Arts in Minnesota Series.

3961 ———. A century of Minnesota architecture. Minneapolis, Minneapolis Society of Fine Arts, 1958. unpaged. illus.

3962 ———. Minneapolis — architecture and architects, 1848–1908; a study of style trends in architecture in a midwestern city together with a catalogue of representative buildings.

Doctoral Dissertation, University of Minnesota, 1951.

MISSOURI

GENERAL REFERENCES

3963 Ankeney, J. S. Century of Missouri art. Columbia, Mo., 1922. 20p. illus.

Reprinted from the *Missouri Historical Review*, 16:481–501, July 1922. illus.

3964 Bryan, John Albury (ed.). Missouri's contribution to American architecture. St. Louis, St. Louis Architectural Club, 1928. 286p. illus.

3965 Federal Writers' Project. Missouri: a guide to the "Show me" State. N. Y., Duell, Sloan and Pearce, 1941. 611p. illus.

3966 ———. The Oregon Trail; the Missouri River to the Pacific Ocean. N. Y., Hastings House, *ca.* 1939. 244p. illus.

3967 Peterson, Charles E. French houses of the Illinois country. Missouriana, 10:4–7, Aug.–Sept. 1938. illus.

3968 Roach, Cornelius. Missouri's eleven state capitols. Missouri Historical Review, 7:224–31, July 1913.

1820–1912.

3969 Stevens, Walter B. The Missouri tavern. Missouri Historical Review, 15:241–76, Jan. 1921. illus.

The tavern as an institution. *Ca.* 1820—*ca.* 1860.

3970 Van Ravenswaay, Charles. Architecture in the Boon's Lick country. Missouri Historical Society. Bulletin, 6:491–502, July 1950. illus.

Cooper and Howard counties, 1819–70.

3971 ——. Boon's Lick country. 1940. 21p. illus. Mimeographed.

Historical and architectural guide for Cooper, Howard, and Saline counties.

3972 ——. Three Missouri houses in the American tradition. Antiques, 45:134–39, Mar. 1944. illus.

Woods-Holman house, 1818, Caledonia; Burckhardtt Parlor, 1832, now in City Art Museum of St. Louis; Robert Campbell house, 1851, St. Louis.

3973 VILES, JONAS. The capitals and capitols of Missouri. Missouri Historical Review, 13:135–56, 232–50, Jan.–Apr. 1919.

3974 WILLIAMS, WALTER. The tavern on the Boon's Lick Road. Overland, 2nd ser., 58:417–20, Nov. 1911.

LOCATIONS

Arrow Rock (Saline County)

3975 GRAVES, MRS. W. W. Old tavern at Arrow Rock. Missouri Historical Review, 19:256–61, Jan. 1925.

3976 GUITAR, SARAH. Arrow Rock Tavern. Missouri Historical Review, 20:499–503, July 1926.

1830.

3977 TODHUNTER, MRS. RYLAND. Historic Arrow Rock Tavern. D. A. R. Magazine, 59:477–82, Aug. 1925.

Booneville

3978 Brief history of the Thespian Hall, Booneville, Missouri. Thespian Hall Preservation Committee, 1937. 16p. illus.

1855–57.

Franklin County

3979 HILDNER, GEORGE J. One hundred years for God and country, St. John's, the church and the community, 1839–1940, historical sketches. Washington, Mo., Washington Missourian, 1940. 128p. illus.

Catholic, Franklin County, Mo.

Fulton

3980 PAYNE, DAVID. Missouri family album: story of the James Robnett house near Fulton. House and Garden, 79:48–49, Apr. 1941.

1858.

Herculaneum

3981 SHOEMAKER, FLOYD C. Herculaneum shot tower. Missouri Historical Review, 20:214–16, Jan. 1926.

1809.

Hermann

3982 SCHMIDT, MILDRED, AND SCHMIDT, JOSEPH. German influence on Hermann houses. American-German Review, 20:13–17, Apr.–May 1954. illus.

Buildings. By the German Settlement Society of Philadelphia in Hermann, Mo., *ca.* 1836.

Kansas City

3983 The United States Trading House or factory at Fort Osage, 1808–1827, a documentary history. Commission for the Restoration of Ft. Osage, 1941. 16p. illus. Mimeographed.

St. Charles County

3984 MISSOURI HISTORICAL SOCIETY. The Nathan Boone house. Missouri Historical Society. Bulletin, 13:332–36, Apr. 1957.

Stone house built by a son of Daniel Boone in St. Charles County, *ca.* 1818–19.

St. Louis

3985 The Berthold Mansion. Missouri Historical Society. Collections, 4:290–94, 1914. illus.

3986 BRYAN, JOHN ALBURY. Outstanding architects in St. Louis between 1804 and 1904. Missouri Historical Review, 28:83–90, Jan. 1934.

Biographical sketches of nineteen architects with partial list of their works.

3987 COYLE, ELINOR MARTINEAU. Old Saint Louis homes, 1790–1865; the stories they tell. St. Louis, Folkestone Press, 1964. 167p. illus.

3988 DRUMM, STELLA M., AND VAN RAVENSWAAY, CHARLES. The old Court House. Missouri Historical Society. Glimpses of the Past, v. 7, no. 1–6, Jan.–June 1940.

1839–62.

3989 LeBAUME, LOUIS. Early architecture of St. Louis, 1764–1900. American Architect, 133:713–18, June 5, 1928. illus.

3990 McCUE, GEORGE. The building art in St. Louis: two centuries; a guide to the architecture of the city and its environs. St. Louis, sponsored and published by the St. Louis Chapter, American Institute of Architects, 1964. 96p. illus.

3991 McCUE, GEORGE R., AND KRAMER, GERHARDT THEODORE. Landmark for the living. American Institute of Architects. Journal, 43:43–45, Apr. 1965. illus.

St. Louis, old Post Office.

3992 PETERSON, CHARLES E. Colonial St. Louis: building a Creole capital. St. Louis, Missouri Historical Society, 1949. 69p. illus.

Reprinted from Missouri Historical Society. *Bulletin*, Apr.–Oct. 1947, with corrections and additions.

3993 ———. The Museum of American Architecture: a progress report. American Society of Architectural Historians. Journal, 1, no. 3–4:24–26, July–Oct. 1941.

The Jefferson National Expansion Memorial on the St. Louis riverfront.

3994 ———. Old St. Louis riverfront. St. Louis Public Library. Bulletin, Apr. 11–30, 1938. 19p. illus.

Contains a short bibliography.

3995 POWELL, MARY. Public art: sculpture, mural decorations, stained glass and noteworthy buildings in St. Louis. St. Louis Public Library. Bulletin, Jan. 1921. 32p.

3996 St. Louis — new and old. Western Architect, 23:49–50, June 1916. illus.

Ste. Genevieve

3997 CHILDS, M. W. Two centuries look down upon this home; Valle house, Ste. Genevieve, Missouri. Better Homes and Gardens, 12:34–35, Mar. 1934. illus.

3998 PETERSON, CHARLES E. Early Ste. Genevieve, Missouri and its architecture. Missouri Historical Review, 35:207–32, Jan. 1941. illus.

3999 ———. Guide to Ste. Genevieve with notes on its architecture. St. Louis, 1940. 21p. illus.

4000 ———. Old Ste. Genevieve and its architecture. Missouri Historical Review, 35:207–32, Jan. 1941.

Washington

4001 McCLURE, MRS. ELEANOR B. Early history of Washington, Missouri. Washington, Mo., Washington Missourian, 1939. 48p. illus.

NEBRASKA

4002 ABBOTT, N. C. That Cass County Court House — an informal history. Nebraska History, 29:339–50, Dec. 1948. illus.

4003 BARNES, CASE G. Sod house (1862–97). Lincoln, Nebraska, 1930. 287p. illus.

4004 DORSEY, JAMES O. Omaha dwellings, furniture and implements. U. S. Bureau of American Ethnology, 13th Annual Report, 1891–92. Washington, D. C., 1896. pp. 263–88. illus.
Aboriginal.

4005 FEDERAL WRITERS' PROJECT. Nebraska: a guide to the Cornhusker State. N. Y., Viking Press, 1939. 424p. illus.

OHIO

GENERAL REFERENCES

4006 American home pilgrimages — Ohio. American Home, part 1, the Lakeshore, 19:25–36, Jan. 1938; part 2, Marietta, Zanesville, Columbus, 19:41–44, Feb. 1938; part 3, Scioto Valley and Cincinnati, 19:43–45, Mar. 1938. illus.

4007 BAREIS, GEORGE F. Pioneer cabin in the history of Madison Township. Ohio State Archaelogical and Historical Society. Quarterly, 11:259–61.

4008 CLARK, EDNA MARIA. Ohio art and artists. Richmond, Va., Garrett and Massie, 1932. illus.
Chapters 3 and 14 briefly cover Ohio architecture.

4009 DIEHL, JOHN A. Covered bridges in Ohio. Historical and Philosophical Society of Ohio. Bulletin, 7:123–25, Apr. 1949. illus.

4010 Famous houses of Ohio. D. A. R. Magazine, 70:1113–15, 1936.

4011 FEDERAL WRITERS' PROJECT. The Ohio guide. N. Y., Oxford University Press, 1940. 634p. illus.

4012 ———. Ohio's capitals. Columbus, Ohio, Secretary of State, 1937. 12p. illus.

4013 FRARY, IHNA THAYER. Early domestic architecture in Ohio. American Architect, 123:307–12, Apr. 11, 1923. illus.

4014 ———. Early homes of Ohio. Richmond, Va., Garrett and Massie, 1936. 336p. illus.

4015 ———. Old wall stencils of Ohio. Antiques, 38:169, 1940. illus.

4016 HAMLIN, TALBOT FAULKNER. Ohio architecture — yesterday and today. American Institute of Architects. Journal, 20:255–61, Oct. 1953; 21:31–35, Jan. 1954.
Since 1788.

4017 HATCHER, HARLAN HENTHORNE. The Buckeye country; a pageant of Ohio. N. Y., H. C. Kinsey and Co., 1940. 325p. illus.
Chapters on Ohio architecture.

4018 Historic American Buildings Inventory for Ohio. Washington, D. C., National Park Service, Division of Architecture, 1962. 6p.

4019 INGRAM, PATRICIA SMITH. Hudson: early 19th century domestic architecture. Society of Architectural Historians. Journal, 12:9–14, May 1953. illus.
1820–40's.

4020 KING, I. F. Typical log cabin. Ohio State Archaeological and Historical Society. Quarterly, 10:175–77.

4021 KNITTLE, RHEA MANSFIELD. Early Ohio taverns: tavern-sign, barge, banner, chair and settee painters. Ashland, Ohio, privately printed, 1937. 39p.

4022 O'DONNELL, THOMAS EDWARD. Influence of the Carpenters' Handbooks in the early architecture of Ohio. Architecture, 55:169–71, Mar. 1927. illus.

4023 ———. Mantel designs in the early architecture of Ohio. Architecture, 56:11–14, July 1927. illus.

4024 ———. Ornamental ironwork; Early American examples in Ohio show New England influence. House Beautiful, 64:694–95, 730, Dec. 1928. illus.

4025 ———. Ornamental ironwork in early Ohio architecture. Architecture, 54:299–302, Oct. 1926. illus.

4026 ———. Some Greek Revival doorways in Ohio. Architectural Forum, 49:649–52, Nov. 1928. illus.

4027 OHIO STATE ARCHAEOLOGICAL AND HISTORICAL SOCIETY. [Historic houses in Ohio.] Museum Echoes, 23:1–6, 9–13, 17–22, 25–29, 33–38, 41–45, 49–53, 57–61, 65–69, 73–77, 81–85, 89–90, 92–94, Jan.–Dec. 1950. illus.
Discusses twelve houses.

4028 ORIANS, GEORGE HARRISON. My life in a log-house. Northwest Ohio Quarterly, 27:146–59, Autumn 1955.
On the structure, furnishings, and facilities of log houses surviving in Ohio after 1900.

4029 OVERMAN, WILLIAM D. Index to materials for the study of Ohio history. Ohio State Archaeological and Historical Society. Quarterly, 44:138–55, 1935.

4030 ———. Select list of materials on Ohio history in serial publications. Ohio State Archaeological and Historical Society. Quarterly, 50:137–70, 1941.

4031 ROBBINS, CARLE. Concerning the improver and front porch builder. Cleveland, Ohio, The Bystander, pp. 8–11, Dec. 8, 1928. illus.

Early Ohio houses, with and without porches.

4032 ———. On a neglected heritage. Cleveland, Ohio, The Bystander, pp. 21–23, Nov. 24, 1928. illus.

Early doorways.

4033 RODABAUGH, JAMES HOWARD. From mounds to mansions: Ohio architecture in history. Historical and Philosophical Society of Ohio. Bulletin, 13:3–24, Jan. 1955. illus.

4034 ROOS, FRANK JOHN, JR. An investigation of the sources of early architectural design in Ohio. Doctoral Dissertation, Ohio State University, 1938. illus.

Condensed in *Abstracts of Doctoral Dissertations*, no. 26, Columbus, Ohio State University Press, 1938.

4035 ———. Ohio: architectural cross-road. Society of Architectural Historians. Journal, 12:3–8, May 1953. illus.

1772–1850's.

4036 ———. Ohio's early architecture. Antiques, 49:28–31, Jan. 1946. illus.

4037 ———. Reflections of New England's architecture in Ohio. Old-Time New England, 28:40–48, Oct. 1937. illus.

4038 SMITH, S. WINIFRED. Campuses and buildings of Ohio colleges and universities. Museum Echoes, 22:17–22, 25–29, 33–38, 41–45, 49–53, 57–61, 65–69, 73–79, 81–85, 89–94, Mar.–Dec. 1949. illus.

Ten colleges and universities.

4039 WEINY, DANIEL W. Early Colonial architecture of the Ohio Valley. Architecture, 41:pl.53, May 1920; 43:pl.65, May 1921; 45:pl.94, June 1922; 47:pl.95, June 1923; 51:pl.39, 40, Mar. 1925. illus. only.

LOCATIONS

Brecksville

4040 Master detail series. Historic American Buildings Survey: the Congregational Church, Brecksville, Cuyahoga County, Ohio. Architectural Forum, 64:187–88, Mar. 1936. illus.

1844.

4041 SMITH, S. WINIFRED. Brecksville Congregational Church. Museum Echoes, 21:41–45, June 1948. illus.

1844.

Carrollton

4042 McCook Home dedicated. Museum Echoes, 21:85–87, Nov. 1948.

Built in early 1840's.

Chillicothe

4043 FEDERAL WRITERS' PROJECT. Chillicothe, Ohio's first capital. Chillicothe, Ohio, Chillicothe Civic Association, 1941. 32p. illus.

4044 ———. Chillicothe and Ross County. Columbus, Ohio, F. J. Heer Printing Co., *ca.* 1938. 91p. illus.

4045 O'DONNELL, THOMAS EDWARD. The Greek Revival in Chillicothe — Ohio's old capital city. Architecture, 52:355–60, Oct. 1925. illus.

4046 RODABAUGH, JAMES HOWARD. Adena — a restored Ohio home. Antiques, 64:477–79, Dec. 1953. illus.

1806.

Cincinnati

4047 BECKER, CARL M., AND DAILY, WILLIAM H. Some architectural aspects of German-American life in nineteenth century Cincinnati. Historical and Philosophical Society of Ohio. Bulletin, 20:[75]–88, 1962.

4048 CINCINNATI CITY PLANNING COMMISSION. Inventory and appraisal of historical sites, buildings and areas. Cincinnati, Ohio, 1960. 101p.

4049 FEDERAL WRITERS' PROJECT. They built a city; 150 years of industrial Cincinnati. Cincinnati, Ohio, Cincinnati Post, 1938. 402p. illus.

4050 Harriet Beecher Stowe house to be dedicated. Museum Echoes, 22:45–46, June 1949.

1832–1949.

4051 KIMBALL, SIDNEY FISKE. Masterpieces of Early American art — part 1 — a notable old house in Cincinnati. Art and Archaeology, 8:297, Sept.–Oct. 1919. illus.

The Taft house, *ca.* 1820.

4052 KING, ARTHUR G. The exact site of Fort Washington and Daniel Drake's error. Historical and Philosophical Society of Ohio. Bulletin, 11:128–46, Apr. 1953. illus.

1789.

4053 KNOPF, RICHARD C.; BABY, RAYMOND S.; AND SMITH, DWIGHT LA VERNE. The re-discovery of Fort Washington. Historical and Philosophical Society of Ohio. Bulletin, 11:2–12, Jan. 1953. illus.

Occupied 1789–1804, remains discovered fifteen feet underground in 1952.

4054 LANCASTER, CLAY. The Egyptian Hall and Mrs. Trollope's Bazaar. Magazine of Art, 43:94–99, 112, Mar. 1950. illus.

1828–31.

4055 MONTGOMERY, HENRY C. St. Peter in Chains, Cincinnati. Museum Echoes, 21:9–14, Feb. 1948. illus.

Catholic cathedral, 1840.

4056 POTTER, R. S., AND MONTGOMERY, H. C. Classic Revival architecture in Cincinnati. Society of Architectural Historians. Journal, 6:18–21, July 1947. illus.

4057 ROOS, FRANK JOHN, JR. Cincinnati's Taft house. American Magazine of Art, 29:440–45, July 1936. illus.

4058 SCHUYLER, MONTGOMERY. The building of Cincinnati. Architectural Record, 23:337–66, May 1908. illus.

4059 SIPLE, WALTER H. Taft Museum. Cincinnati Art Museum. Bulletin, 14:1–21, Jan. 1933. illus.

4060 SMITH, S. WINIFRED. Plum Street Temple, Cincinnati. Museum Echoes, 21:65–70, Sept. 1948. illus.

B'Nai Yeshurun erected 1866 and predecessor building, 1848–66.

Cleveland

4061 AMERICAN INSTITUTE OF ARCHITECTS. CLEVELAND CHAPTER. Cleveland architecture, 1796–1958. N. Y., Reinhold Publishing Corp., 1958. 64p. illus.

4062 ———. Project Inventory of Buildings of Architectural Significance. 3rd ed. Cleveland, Ohio, 1959. 5p.

List of buildings warranting preservation.

4063 CHAPMAN, EDMUND H. The development of the city of Cleveland, Ohio, to 1860. Doctoral Dissertation, New York University, 1951.

4064 DIX, WILLIAM S., JR. The theater in Cleveland, Ohio, 1854–1875. Doctoral Dissertation, University of Chicago, 1946. 496p.

4065 Dunham Tavern in Cleveland, Ohio. Antiques, 35:76–77, Feb. 1939. illus.

Ca. 1830.

4066 FRARY, IHNA THAYER. Dunham Tavern: its story. Antiques Journal, 3:4–7, Apr. 1948. illus.

Rufus Dunham, 1824.

Columbus

4067 Capitol, Columbus, Ohio. American Architect, 46:26–27, Oct. 1894. illus.

4068 CUMMINGS, ABBOTT LOWELL. The Alfred Kelley house of Columbus, Ohio: the home of a pioneer statesman. Columbus, Ohio, Franklin County Historical Society, 1953. 52p. illus.

1836–38.

4069 ———. The Ohio state capitol competition. Society of Architectural Historians. Journal, 12:15–18, May 1953. illus.

1838.

4070 O'DONNELL, THOMAS EDWARD. Greek Revival capitol at Columbus, Ohio. Architectural Forum, 42:5–8, Jan. 1925.

1839–61. Henry Walter and others, architects.

4071 SMITH, S. WINIFRED. First Congregational Church, Columbus. Museum Echoes, 21:57–61, Aug. 1948.

1852———.

Dayton

4072 FITZGERALD, ROY G. An interesting old court house. Historical and Philosophical Society of Ohio. Bulletin, 6:112–15, July 1948. illus.

1848.

4073 GUNDERSON, ROBERT GRAY. The Dayton Log Cabin Convention of 1840. Historical and Philosophical Society of Ohio. Bulletin, 7:203–10, Oct. 1949. illus.

4074 SMITH, S. WINIFRED. Grace Methodist Church, Dayton. Museum Echoes, 21:49–53, July 1948. illus.

> 1812–1921.

Findlay

4075 FEDERAL WRITERS' PROJECT. Findlay and Hancock County centennial, 1937. Findlay, Ohio, 1937. 52p. illus.

Fremont

4076 O'DONNELL, THOMAS EDWARD. Old Greek Revival courthouse, Fremont, Ohio. Architectural Forum, 45:221–24, Oct. 1926. illus.

> *Ca.* 1840.

Gambier

4077 CHALMERS, GORDON KEITH. The college in the forest, 1835. N. Y., American Branch, Newcomen Society of England, 1948. 24p. illus.

> Kenyon College.

Gates Mills

4078 WILKINSON, HELEN ALVINA. Gates Mills and a history of its village church. Gates Mills, Ohio, privately printed for St. Christopher's-by-the-River, [1955]. 123p. illus.

> 1845——.

Granville

4079 St. Luke's Episcopal Church, Granville. Museum Echoes, 21:1–4, Jan. 1948. illus.

> 1837–1947.

4080 SPENCER, EMA. New England town in Ohio. Ohio Magazine, 1:215–24, Sept. 1906.

> Classic Revival.

Hudson

4081 COMMITTEE ON HISTORICAL BUILDINGS. Record of old houses of Hudson, Ohio: a brief history of 115 of Hudson's oldest houses. [Hudson, Ohio], 1950. 22p.

> 1806–78.

4082 FRARY, IHNA THAYER. Ohio town of New England traditions. The home of the "Yale of the West." House Beautiful, 52:36–37, 75–77, July 1922. illus.

> Classic Revival.

4083 ———. Old Western Reserve College. Architectural Record, 44:575–76, Dec. 1918. illus.

4084 O'DONNELL, THOMAS EDWARD. Early architecture in the state of Ohio: Hudson, a town of New England traditions. Western Architect, 38:138–40, Aug. 1929. illus.

4085 SMITH, S. WINIFRED. Christ Protestant Episcopal Church, Hudson. Museum Echoes, 21:73–76, Oct. 1948. illus.

> 1846——.

Kirtland

4086 Master detail series. Historic American buildings: Kirtland Temple. Architectural Forum, 64:177–83, Mar. 1936. illus.

1833–36.

4087 SMITH, S. WINIFRED. The Temple at Kirtland. Museum Echoes, 21:33–38, May 1948. illus.

Temple of the Reorganized Church of the Latter-Day Saints, 1833.

Lancaster

4088 Effinger house, Lancaster, Ohio, 1823. Society of Architectural Historians. Journal, 16:31–32, Dec. 1957. illus.

4089 ENT, DOROTHY MAE. Architectural development in early Lancaster, Ohio. Master's Thesis, Ohio State University, 1945. 187p.

4090 MacCRACKEN, BESS W. St. John's Church, Lancaster, Ohio, 1848–1948. Antiques Journal, 3:12–13, May 1948. illus.

Lebanon

4091 TOWNSLEY, GARDNER H. Historic Lebanon — beginning with Beedle's Station in 1795. [Lebanon, Ohio], Western Star, [1940]. 48p. illus.

1795——.

Lima

4092 FEDERAL WRITERS' PROJECT. Guide to Lima and Allen County. Lima, Ohio, 1938. 64p. illus.

Manchester

4093 CARLISLE, MORTEN. Buckeye Station, built by Nathaniel Massie in 1797. Ohio State Archaeological and Historical Society. Quarterly, 40:1–22, 1931.

Marietta

4094 BUELL, ROWENA. House of seven porches, Allen-Buell house, Marietta. Your Garden and Home, p. 16, Jan. 1933.

1836.

4095 First Congregational Church of Marietta, Ohio. Architectural Record, 20:116–20, Aug. 1906. illus.

1807.

4096 HAWES, E. M. Ohio's Campus Martius. Art and Archaeology, 33:309–15, Nov. 1932. illus.

1788.

4097 HILDRETH, SAMUEL P. The old court house and jail of Washington County, Ohio. American Pioneer, 1:163–64, May 1842. illus.

1798. Griffin Green, architect.

4098 NYE, MINNA TUPPER. Campus Martius, Marietta, Ohio. American Monthly Magazine, 39:5–7, July 1911.

4099 O'DONNELL, THOMAS EDWARD. Early architecture of Marietta, the oldest city in Ohio. Architecture, 51:1–4, Jan. 1925. illus.

4100 SCHNEIDER, NORRIS FRANZ. Campus Martius State Memorial Museum. Marietta, Ohio, MacDonald Printing Co., 1932.
Covers 1787–95.

4101 [WATERS, HARRIET.] Old Marietta. Privately printed, 1934.
Photographs from an album owned by Miss Harriet Waters, taken between 1870 and 1890.

Milan

4102 O'DONNELL, THOMAS EDWARD. Early architecture of the state of Ohio: early houses in Milan. Western Architect, 36:159–63, Oct. 1927. illus.
Ca. 1830–40.

Mount Pleasant

4103 Mt. Pleasant Meeting House. Museum Echoes, 22:22–23, Mar. 1949.
Quaker meetinghouse, 1800——.

Mount Vernon

4104 IZANT, GRACE GOULDER. Mount Vernon, Ohio — a study in architecture. Your Garden and Home, pp. 14, 22, 28, Apr. 1934. illus.

Newark

4105 HUNTER, ROBBINS, JR. The Davidson house, Newark, Ohio. Antiques Journal, 3:19–20, Feb. 1948. illus.
Ca. 1815.

4106 WEINY, DANIEL W. Colonial architecture of Ohio: the Buckingham residence, Newark, Ohio. Architecture, 51:pl. 39, 40, Mar. 1925. illus.
1842–43.

Schoenbrunn (near *New Philadelphia*)

4107 Ohio's first free schoolhouse to be restored. School Life, 11:143, Apr. 1926.
1772.

4108 WEINLAND, JOSEPH E. Romantic story of Schoenbrunn, the first town in Ohio, a brief account of the town, its destruction and finding of the lost town after 146 years. Dover, Ohio, Seibert Printing Co., 1928. 36p. illus.

Springfield

4109 Old tavern to be preserved: Pennsylvania House, Springfield, Ohio. Hobbies, 45:43, Sept. 1940.

Tallmadge (near *Akron*)

4110 Master detail series. Historic American Buildings Survey: Church of the Congregational Society, Tallmadge, Summit County, Ohio. Architectural Forum, 64:184–86, Mar. 1936. illus.
1822.

4111 SMITH, S. WINIFRED. First Congregational Church, Tallmadge. Museum Echoes, 21:19–21, Mar. 1948. illus.
1821.

Troy

4112 The Overfield Tavern. Historical and Philosophical Society of Ohio. Bulletin, 7:23–26, Jan. 1949.

1808.

Tuscarawas County

4113 FEDERAL WRITERS' PROJECT. Guide to Tuscarawas County. New Philadelphia, Ohio, Tucker Printing Co., 1939. 119p. illus.

Unionville

4114 CANTERBURY, BEULAH. Tavern by the side of the road. American Cookery, 38:267–73, 1933.

1810.

4115 WHITE, MRS. FRANK R. Shandy Hall. Cleveland, Ohio, Western Reserve Historical Society, 1954. [4p.] illus.

1815. Reprinted from the *Historical Society News*, v. 9, no. 7, July 1954.

Vermilion

4116 O'DONNELL, THOMAS EDWARD. Early architecture of the state of Ohio. The Joseph Swift house, near Vermilion, Ohio. Western Architect, 38:40–44, Mar. 1929. illus.

4117 ———. Early architecture of the state of Ohio, part 4. Joseph Swift house, an example of Greek Revival architecture. Western Architect, 33:109–13, Oct. 1924. illus.

1840.

Warren

4118 FEDERAL WRITERS' PROJECT. Warren and Trumbull County. Warren? Ohio, 1938. 60p. illus.

Western Reserve (see also towns)

4119 CHERRY, MARJORIE LOOMIS. Blockhouses and military posts of the Firelands. Shippensburg, Pa., 1934. 94p.

4120 FRANCE, JEAN REITSMAN. Early church architecture in the Western Reserve. Society of Architectural Historians. Journal, 7:31–32, July–Dec. 1948.

Abstract of Master's Thesis, Oberlin College, 1948.

4121 FRARY, IHNA THAYER. Group of early northern Ohio churches. American Architect and the Architectural Review, 126:49–50, July 16, 1924. illus.

4122 ———. Two early Ohio churches. Architectural Record, 56:286–88, Sept. 1924. illus.

Brief account of the Tallmadge Congregational Church and the Claridon Church.

4123 O'DONNELL, THOMAS EDWARD. Early architecture in the state of Ohio. Part 1, the Western Reserve. Western Architect, 31:112–15, Oct. 1922. illus.

Covers Carpenter house, near North Olmstead, and describes organization of Western Reserve.

4124 ———. Early architecture of the state of Ohio. Part 2, some old farmhouses of the Western Reserve. Western Architect, 31:127–29, Nov. 1922. illus.

Covers Coe house, near North Olmstead, and Goodrich Tavern, near Vermilion.

4125 ———. The early architecture in the state of Ohio. Part 3. Post-Colonial houses of the Western Reserve. Western Architect, 32:103–5, Sept. 1923. illus.

Worthington

4126 SMITH, S. WINIFRED, AND SMITH, VANCE W. The First Presbyterian Church, Worthington. Museum Echoes, 21:25–29, Apr. 1948. illus.

1830——.

Zanesville

4127 FEDERAL WRITERS' PROJECT. Zanesville and Muskingum County. Zanesville, Ohio, 1937. 38p. illus.

WISCONSIN

GENERAL REFERENCES

4128 BAUCHLE, MAY L. Wisconsin's rival houses. Wisconsin Magazine, 2:14, 32, Nov. 1924.

Brisbois house, Prairie du Chien (1815 or later); Porlier house, Green Bay, oldest frame house? (1780 and later).

4129 COMMITTEE OF WISCONSIN WOMEN. Wisconsin's historic sites. Kohler, Wis., 1948. 87p. illus.

Guide book to historic houses, 1634–1948.

4130 FEDERAL WRITERS' PROJECT. Wisconsin: a guide to the Badger State. N. Y., Duell, Sloan and Pearce, 1941. 651p. illus.

4131 GUTH, ALEXANDER CARL. Early day architects in Wisconsin. Wisconsin Magazine of History, 18:141–45, Dec. 1934.

1830's–50's, Greek Revival.

4132 HARRIS, W. J. Greek Revival in Wisconsin; Benjamin Church built Milwaukee's oldest house. House and Garden, 78:59, Sept. 1940. illus.

4133 HINTZ, NORMAN CLARE. Nineteenth century Wisconsin churches. Urbana, Ill., Department of Architecture, University of Illinois, 1962. 20 leaves. illus. Typescript.

4134 LANGSDORF, FRANCIS. Architect and builder . . . Father Mazzuchelli. Badger History, 2, no. 8:14–17, 1949. illus.

1831–52.

4135 LARCHER, J. H. A. The taverns and stages of early Wisconsin. Wisconsin Historical Society. Proceedings, 62:117–67, 1915.

4136 PERRIN, RICHARD W. E. Historic Wisconsin architecture. Milwaukee, Wis., Wisconsin Chapter, American Institute of Architects, 1960. 35p. illus.

4137 ———. Historic Wisconsin buildings; a survey of pioneer architecture, 1835–1870. Milwaukee, Wis., Milwaukee Public Museum Press, 1962. 91p. illus.

4138 ———. Wisconsin architecture; a catalogue of buildings represented in the Library of Congress . . . 1965. Washington, D. C., Historic American Buildings Survey, Department of the Interior, National Park Service, [1966]. 80p. illus.

4139 SIVESIND, RAYMOND S. Historic sites in our State Park Program. Wisconsin Magazine of History, 32:436–44, June 1949.

Contemplated restoration of historic sites.

4140 TITUS, W. A. Helena shot tower. Wisconsin Magazine of History, 11:320–27, Apr. 1928.

1831. Illustrated, *Wisconsin Magazine of History*, 8:68, Sept. 1924.

4141 ———. Three pioneer taverns. Wisconsin Magazine of History, 17:179–86, 1933.

On the Sheboygan—Fond du Lac trail. Wade Tavern, Greenbush, 1850.

4142 WHYTE, BERTHA KITCHELL. Four old Wisconsin mills. Wisconsin Magazine of History, 34:101–4, Winter 1950. illus.

1850's.

4143 ———. Octagonal houses and barns. Wisconsin Magazine of History, 34:42–46, Autumn 1950. illus.

Sixteen houses and ten barns. 1839———.

4144 ———. Wisconsin heritage. Boston, C. T. Branford Co., [1954]. 327p. illus.

LOCATIONS

Appleton

4145 RANEY, WILLIAM F. Appleton. Wisconsin Magazine of History, 33:135–51, Dec. 1949. illus.

1831———.

Baraboo

4146 COLE, HARRY ELLSWORTH. Stage coach and tavern days in the Baraboo region. Baraboo, Wis., Baraboo News Publishing Co., 1923. 72p. illus.

Also in: Wisconsin Academy of Sciences, Arts and Letters. *Transactions*, 22:1–8, 1926.

Belmont

4147 LASS, WILLIAM E. Belmont. Wisconsin Magazine of History, 40:179–83, Spring 1957. illus.

Town founded in 1836, abandoned after 1884; restoration of the Wisconsin Territorial Capitol and Supreme Court Building as constructed in 1836.

Green Bay

4148 TYLER, K. Captain John Winslow Cotton house, Green Bay, Wis. Hobbies, 45:44–45, July 1940.

Greenbush

4149 Wade house. Badger History, 4:14–18, Oct. 1950. illus.

By Sylvanus Wade, 1848–50, being restored.

Iowa County

4150 BARTON, A. O. Wisconsin's oldest courthouse. Wisconsin Magazine of History, 2:332–34, Mar. 1919.
1859.

Kaukauna

4151 The Grignon house at Kaukauna. Badger History, 1:10–13, May 1948.
1838–39.

Madison

4152 BAUHS, A. J. The renovation of Saint Raphael Cathedral. Wisconsin Magazine of History, 39:171–77, Spring 1956. illus.
Catholic, 1854–1955.

Milton

4153 TITUS, W. A. First concrete building in the United States, architect, Joseph Goodrich. Wisconsin Magazine of History, 24:183–88, Dec. 1940. illus.
1844.

Milwaukee

4154 GUTH, ALEXANDER CARL. Early day architects in Milwaukee. Wisconsin Magazine of History, 10:17–28, Sept. 1926.
Ca. 1848—*ca.* 1900.

Okauchee

4155 WHELAN, LINCOLN F. The Okauchee house. Wisconsin Magazine of History, 33:7–14, Sept. 1949.
Inn, 1840——.

Portage

4156 Preservation of the old Indian Agency house as an historical monument. Wisconsin Archaeologist, n.s. 10:77–79, Jan. 1931.
1832.

Prairie du Chien

4157 HEGEMAN, JEANNETTE. Frontier home. National Historical Magazine, 73, no. 5:25–28, 1939.
Restoration of "Villa Louis," *ca.* 1837, built by Hercules Louis Dousman.

4158 KINGSLEY, I. T. Villa Louis, now known as Dousman Municipal Park, Prairie du Chien, Wisconsin. Country Life in America, 72:35–37, Oct. 1937. illus.

4159 Villa Louis: the Dousman Mansion. Badger History, 2:14–17, Jan. 1949. illus.

Racine

4160 PATTON, HELEN FRANCES. Public school architecture in Racine, Wisconsin, and vicinity from the time of settlement to 1900. Doctoral Dissertation, University of Wisconsin, 1965. 675p.
1833——.

Watertown

4161 CARSON, I. LEIGHTON. Octagon house. American Antiques Journal, 3:16–18, Jan. 1948. illus.

Ca. 1855. John Richards, architect.

4162 IVEY, ZIDA C. The famous octagon house at Watertown. Wisconsin Magazine of History, 24:167–73, Dec. 1940. illus.

1853–56.

Williams Bay

4163 JENKINS, PAUL B. A stove-wood house. Wisconsin Magazine of History, 7:189–93, Dec. 1923. illus.

1848–49, near Williams Bay.

Architects

GENERAL REFERENCES

All titles including architects' names and locations are listed under locations. See Index for complete references. This list of architects obviously makes no pretension of completeness.

4164 Architectural education in 1847. American Institute of Architects. Journal, 8:195–202, Nov. 1947.

4165 Architectural profession in the past, present, and future. American Institute of Architects. Journal, 7:41–46, Jan. 1947.

[Biographical sketches of American architects.] See standard biographical dictionaries: e.g., *Appleton's Cyclopaedia of American Biography*; *Dictionary of American Biography*; *National Cyclopaedia of American Biography*, indexed in *White's Conspectus of American Biography*; Thieme-Becker, *Allgemeines kunsterlexicon*; also such sources as *Proceedings of the American Institute of Architects*. The *Dictionary of American Biography*, with articles by Talbot F. Hamlin, Fiske Kimball, and others, mentions the locations of numerous manuscript collections concerning the architects.

4166 BORNEMANN, RICH. Some Ledoux-inspired buildings in America. Society of Architectural Historians. Journal, 13:15–17, Mar. 1954. illus.

Influence of Claude-Nicolas Ledoux, 1799–1816.

4167 CLARK, ELIOT CANDEE. History of the National Academy of Design, 1825–1953. N. Y., Columbia University Press, 1954. 296p. illus.

4168 DELAND, W. A. Memoirs of centurian architects. American Institute of Architects. Journal, 10:3–9, 81–87, 130–36, 180–84, July–Oct. 1948.

Architects who were members of the Century Club. Mostly late nineteenth century.

4169 EBERLEIN, HAROLD DONALDSON. Early American architects. Country Life in America, 48:70–72, Oct. 1925. illus.

Brief survey, mentioning many men.

4170 HADDON, RAWSON W. First architectural society in America. Architectural Record, 38:287–88, Aug. 1915.

4171 KERVICK, FRANCIS WILLIAM WYNN. Architects in America of Catholic tradition. Rutland, Vt., C. E. Tuttle Co., 1962. 140p. illus.

Biographical dictionary with illustrations.

4172 NOFFSINGER, JAMES PHILIP. The influence of the École des Beaux-Arts on the architects of the United States. Washington, D. C., Catholic University of America Press, 1955. 123p.

1846–1954. Thesis, Catholic University of America, 1955.

4173 ROOS, FRANK J., JR. Concerning several American architectural leaders. Design, 37:3–5, 40, Dec. 1935. illus.

4174 RUSK, WILLIAM SENER. William Thornton, Benjamin H. Latrobe, Thomas U. Walter and the classical influence in their works. Baltimore, 1929. 77p. illus.

Doctoral Dissertation, Johns Hopkins University, 1933. Bibliography, including references to newspaper items and manuscript collections.

4175 UPJOHN, H. Architect and client a century ago. Architectural Record, 74:377–82, Nov. 1933.

ARCHITECTS

Barnett, George I. (b. 1815)

4176 BARNETT, TOM P. George I. Barnett, pioneer architect of the West. Western Architect, 18:13–14, 23–24, Feb. 1912. illus.

Benjamin, Asher (1773–1845)

4177 BACH, RICHARD FRANZ. Asher Benjamin revived. American Architect, 112:449–50, Dec. 19, 1917.

4178 Bible of Classicism, the influence on today's decoration, of Asher Benjamin's *Builders' Companion.* House and Garden, 77:46–49, June 1940. illus.

Builders' Companion, 1827.

4179 CUMMINGS, ABBOTT L. An investigation of the sources, stylistic evolution, and influence of Asher Benjamin's *Builder's Guides.* Doctoral Dissertation, Ohio State University, 1951.

On seven publications for architects and carpenters, 1797–1843.

4180 EMBURY, AYMAR, II. Asher Benjamin. N. Y., Architectural Book Publishing Co., 1917. 169p. illus.

Selected plates from five of the Benjamin handbooks.

4181 HADDON, RAWSON W. Mr. Embury's Asher Benjamin. Architectural Record, 42:181–84, Aug. 1917.

4182 O'DONNELL, THOMAS EDWARD. Asher Benjamin. Architecture, 54:375–78, Dec. 1926. illus.

Bogardus, James (1800–1874)

4183 BANNISTER, TURPIN CHAMBERS. Bogardus revisited. Part 1: the iron fronts. Part 2: the iron towers. Society of Architectural Historians. Journal, 15:12–22, Dec. 1956; 16:11–19, Mar. 1957. illus.

His later influence and the vogue of cast-iron buildings (ferromania), 1842–90.

Buckland, William (1734–74)

4184 BEIRNE, ROSAMOND RANDALL, AND SCARFF, JOHN HENRY. William Buckland, 1734–1774; architect of Virginia and Maryland. Baltimore, Maryland Historical Society, 1958. 175p. illus.

4185 PAGE, MARIAN. Makers of tradition, U. S. A.: the personal style of William Buckland. Interiors, 125:70–81ff., Feb. 1966. illus.

Bulfinch, Charles (1763–1844)

4186 BULFINCH, ELLEN SUSAN. Life and letters of Charles Bulfinch. Boston, Houghton Mifflin Co., 1896. 323p. illus.

4187 Charles Bulfinch, architect. Brochure Series of Architectural Illustration, 9:123–33, July 1903. illus.

4188 HOWELLS, JOHN MEAD. Charles Bulfinch, architect. American Architect, 93:195–200, June 1908. illus.

4189 KIRKER, HAROLD CLARK, AND KIRKER, JAMES. Charles Bulfinch: architect as administrator. Society of Architectural Historians. Journal, 22:29–35, Mar. 1963. illus.

4190 NEWCOMB, REXFORD. Charles Bulfinch, first American-born architect of distinction. Architect, 9:289–93, Dec. 1927. illus.

4191 PLACE, CHARLES A. Charles Bulfinch, architect and citizen. Boston, Houghton Mifflin Co., 1925. 294p. illus.

4192 ROTHSCHILD, LINCOLN. A triumphal arch by Charles Bulfinch. Old-Time New England, 29:161–62, Apr. 1939.

4193 SHANNON, MARTHA A. S. Architecture of Charles Bulfinch. American Magazine of Art, 17:431–37, Aug. 1925. illus.

4194 ———. Charles Bulfinch, the first American architect. Architecture, 52:431–36, Dec. 1925. illus.

4195 WILLARD, ASHTON R. Charles Bulfinch, the architect. New England Magazine, 3:273–99, Nov. 1890. illus.

Dake, Thomas Reynolds (1785–1852)

4196 CONGDON, HERBERT WHEATON. Dake of Castleton: house-joiner extraordinary. Vermont Quarterly, 17:39–72, Apr.–July 1949. illus.
Activities of 1810–33 in Windsor and Castleton, Vt.

Davis, Alexander Jackson (1803–92)

4197 ANDREWS, W. Alexander Jackson Davis; commentary with some hitherto unpublished buildings. Architectural Review, 109:307–12, May 1951. illus.

4198 CARD, MARIAN. A. J. Davis and the printed specification. College Art Journal, 12:354–59, Summer 1953.
1854.

4199 ———. A house plan of 1854. University of Rochester Library. Bulletin, 8:9–15, Autumn 1952. illus.

4200 DONNELL, EDNA. A. J. Davis and the Gothic Revival. Metropolitan Museum. Studies, 5:183–233, Sept. 1936. illus.

Includes a list of source books of Gothic Revival ornament.

4201 PRATT, RICHARD H. Architect of the romantic era. House and Garden, 52:122–23, 154–56, Oct. 1927. illus.

Downing, Andrew Jackson (1815–52)

4202 [Obituary.] Mrs. Monell. Knickerbocker, Oct. 1852.

4203 PRATT, RICHARD H. In the days of Downing. House and Garden, 52:102–3, 134, 136, Dec. 1927. illus.

4204 TATUM, GEORGE BISHOP. Andrew Jackson Downing: arbiter of American taste, 1815–1852. Doctoral Dissertation, Princeton University, 1950. 383p.

Fowler, Orson Squire (1809–87)

4205 CREESE, WALTER. Fowler and the domestic octagon. Art Bulletin, 28:89ff., 1946.

4206 [O. S. Fowler.] Harbinger, 8:14, Nov. 11, 1848.

Godefroy, Maximilian (1765—ca. 1840)

4207 ALEXANDER, ROBERT LESTER. The art and architecture of Maximilian Godefroy. Doctoral Dissertation, New York University, 1961. 442p.

4208 DAVISON, CAROLINE V. (ed.). Maximilian Godefroy. . . . Maryland Historical Magazine, 29:1–20, 175–212, Sept. 1934.

4209 QUYNN, DOROTHY LOUISE. Maximilian and Eliza Godefroy. Maryland Historical Magazine, 52:1–34, Mar. 1957. illus.

Green, John Holden (1777–1850)

4210 SWAN, MABEL M. John Holden Green, architect. Antiques, 52:24–27, July 1947. illus.

Active 1809–30, Providence, R. I.

Hadfield, George (ca. 1764–1826)

4211 HUNSBERGER, GEORGE S. The architectural career of George Hadfield. Columbia Historical Society. Records, 51–52:46–65. illus.

4212 [Obituary.] National Journal, Washington, D. C., Feb. 6, 1826.

Hamilton, Andrew (d. 1741)

4213 NEWCOMB, REXFORD. Architect of Independence Hall. Western Architect, 35:82–85, July 1926. illus.

4214 ———. Honorable Andrew Hamilton, barrister-gentleman-architect. Architect, 10:45–50, Apr. 1928. illus.

Harrison, Peter (1716–75)

4215 BACH, RICHARD FRANZ. Peter Harrison: pioneer American architect. Architectural Record, 43:580–81, June 1918. illus.

4216 BATCHELDER, SAMUEL FRANCIS. Peter Harrison. Old-Time New England, 6:12–19, Jan. 1916. illus.

4217 BRIDENBAUGH, CARL. Peter Harrison, first American architect. Chapel Hill, University of North Carolina Press, 1949. 195p. illus.

4218 HART, CHARLES HENRY. Peter Harrison, 1716–1775, first professional architect in America. Massachusetts Historical Society. Proceedings, pp. 261–68, Mar. 1916.
Also issued as a reprint.

4219 KIMBALL, SIDNEY FISKE. Colonial amateurs and their models: Peter Harrison — in two parts. Architecture, part 1, 53:155–60, June 1926; part 2, 54:185–90, July 1926. illus.

4220 NEWCOMB, REXFORD. Peter Harrison, Early American classicist. Architect, 10:315–18, June 1928. illus.

Haviland, John (1792–1852)

4221 BAIGELL, MATTHEW ELI. John Haviland. Doctoral Dissertation, University of Pennsylvania, 1965. 433p.

4222 NEWCOMB, REXFORD. John Haviland, Early American architectural specialist. Architect, 11:285–88, Dec. 1928. illus.

4223 [Obituary.] Daily National Intelligencer, Washington, D. C., Apr. 16, 1852.

4224 Obituary notice of John Haviland. Philadelphia, Isaac Ashmead, 1852. 14p. illus.
From the Journal of Prison Discipline, v. 7, July 1852.

Hoadley, David (1774–1839)
4225 David Hoadley, architect. Art and Progress, 3:545–46, Apr. 1912. illus.

Hoban, James (ca. 1762–1831)
4226 OWEN, FREDERICK D. First government architect, James Hoban of Charleston, S. C. Architectural Record, 11:581–89, Oct. 1901. illus.

Hooker, Philip (1766–1836)
4227 ROOT, EDWARD WALES. Philip Hooker. N. Y., Charles Scribner's Sons, 1929. 242p. illus.

Hunt, William Morris (1824–79)
4228 DANES, GIBSON A. A biographical and critical study of William Morris Hunt, 1824–1879. Doctoral Dissertation, Yale University, 1949.

Jefferson, Thomas (1743–1826)
4229 BERMAN, ELEANOR DAVIDSON. Thomas Jefferson among the arts, an essay in Early American aesthetics. N. Y., Philosophical Library, 1947. 305p. illus.

4230 FRARY, IHNA THAYER. Thomas Jefferson, architect and builder. Richmond, Va., Garrett and Massie, 1931. 139p. illus.

4231 HEATWOLE, C. J. Thomas Jefferson as an architect. Virginia Journal of Education, 19:361–63, May 1926.

4232 ISHAM, NORMAN MORRISON. Jefferson's place in our architectural history. American Institute of Architects. Journal, 2:230–35, May 1941.

4233 KIMBALL, FISKE. Form and function in the architecture of Jefferson. Magazine of Art, 40:150–53, Apr. 1947. illus.

4234 ———. Jefferson and the public buildings of Virginia. Huntington Library. Quarterly, 12:115–20, 303–10, Feb., May 1949. illus.

His manuscript drawings for buildings in Williamsburg, 1770–76, and Richmond, 1779–80.

4235 ———. Jefferson the architect. Forum, 75:926–31, June 1926.

4236 ———. Jefferson's place in our architectural history. American Institute of Architects. Journal, 2:329–30, July 1914.

4237 ———. Thomas Jefferson and the origins of the Classic Revival in America. Art and Archaeology, 1:219–27, May 1915. illus.

4238 ———. Thomas Jefferson, architect: original designs in the possession of Thomas Jefferson Coolidge, Jr. Cambridge, Mass., Riverside Press, 1916. 205p. illus.

4239 LAMBETH, WILLIAM ALEXANDER. Thomas Jefferson and the arts. American Institute of Architects. Journal, 12:454–55, Oct. 1924. illus.

A letter concerning the hiring of two Italian sculptors.

4240 LAMBETH, WILLIAM ALEXANDER, AND MANNING, WARREN H. Thomas Jefferson as an architect and a designer of landscapes. Boston, Houghton Mifflin Co., 1913. 121p. illus.

4241 LANCASTER, CLAY. Jefferson's architectural indebtedness to Robert Morris. Society of Architectural Historians. Journal, 10:3–10, Mar. 1951. illus.

His use of designs from Morris' *Select Architecture*, 1775.

4242 LEHMANN, KARL. Thomas Jefferson, American humanist. N. Y., Macmillan Co., 1947. 273p. illus.

Reprint: University of Chicago Press, 1965.

4243 LERSKI, HANNA. The British antecedents of Thomas Jefferson's architecture. Doctoral Dissertation, Johns Hopkins University, 1957–58.

4244 MAYOR, A. HYATT. Jefferson's enjoyment of the arts. Metropolitan Museum. Bulletin, n.s. 2:140–66, Dec. 1943. illus.

4245 NEWCOMB, REXFORD. Thomas Jefferson, the architect. Architect, 9:429–32, Jan. 1928. illus.

4246 O'NEAL, WILLIAM BAINTER. A checklist of writings on Thomas Jefferson as an architect. Charlottesville, Va., University of Virginia Press, 1959. 18p.

American Association of Architectural Bibliographers, Pub. 15.

4247 PRATT, RICHARD H. Jefferson and his fellow architects. House and Garden, 51:74–75, 126, 148, July 1927. illus.

4248 REPS, JOHN W. Thomas Jefferson's checkerboard towns. Society of Architectural Historians. Journal, 20:108–14, Oct. 1961.

4249 RICE, HOWARD CROSBY, JR. A French source of Jefferson's plan for the prison at Richmond. Society of Architectural Historians. Journal, 12:28–30, Dec. 1953. illus.

1785, influence of Pierre Gabriez Bugniet of Lyons.

4250 RODMAN, W. S. Lighting schemes of Thomas Jefferson. Illuminating Engineering Society. Transactions, 12:105–21, 1917.

4251 SCHOULER, JAMES. Thomas Jefferson. N. Y., Dodd, Mead and Co., 1919. 252p. illus.

4252 STAPLEY, MILDRED. Thomas Jefferson, the architect, a tribute. Architectural Record, 29:178–85, Jan. 1911.

4253 WATERMAN, THOMAS TILESTON. Thomas Jefferson; his early works in architecture. Gazette des Beaux Arts, s.6 24:89–106, Aug. 1943.

Kearsley, Dr. John (1684–1772)

4254 NEWCOMB, REXFORD. Dr. John Kearsley, physician-architect of Philadelphia. Architect, 10:177–81, May 1928. illus.

Latrobe, Benjamin Henry (1764–1820)

4255 Benjamin H. Latrobe. American Architect and Building News, 1:36–37, Jan. 29, 1876.

4256 HAMLIN, TALBOT FAULKNER. Benjamin Henry Latrobe. N. Y., Oxford University Press, 1955. 633p. illus.

4257 ———. Benjamin Henry Latrobe: the man and the architect. 1942. illus.

4258 KIMBALL, SIDNEY FISKE. Benjamin Henry Latrobe and the beginnings of architectural and engineering practice in America. Michigan Technic, 30:218–23, 1917. illus.

4259 LATROBE, BENJAMIN HENRY. Journal of Latrobe. N. Y., D. Appleton and Co., 1905. 269p. illus.

"Being the notes and sketches of an architect, naturalist and traveler in the United States from 1796 to 1820 . . . with an introduction by J. H. B. Latrobe."

4260 ———. Oration before the Society of Artists of the United States. Portfolio, v. 5, 1811.

4261 LATROBE, FERDINAND C., II. Benjamin Henry Latrobe: descent and works. Maryland Historical Magazine, 33:247–61, 1938.

List of works, dated.

4262 Memoir of Benjamin Henry Latrobe. Ackermann's Repository, Jan. 1821.

4263 NEWCOMB, REXFORD. Benjamin Henry Latrobe, Early American architect. Architect, 9:173–77, Nov. 1927. illus.

4264 RUSK, WILLIAM SENER. Benjamin H. Latrobe and the Classical influence in his work. Maryland Historical Magazine, 31:126–54, 1936.

4265 SEMMES, JOHN EDWARD. Latrobe and his times, 1803–1891. Baltimore, Norman, Remington Co., 1917. 601p. illus.

Refers to J. H. B. Latrobe, with some information on B. H. Latrobe.

L'Enfant, Pierre Charles (1734–1825)

4266 KITE, ELIZABETH S. L'Enfant and Washington . . . 1791–1792. Baltimore, Johns Hopkins University Press, 1929. 182p. illus.

4267 The story of L'Enfant. Western Architect, 14:14–16, Aug. 1909.

Lienau, Detlef (1818–87)

4268 KRAMER, ELLEN W. Detlef Lienau, an architect of the brown decades. Society of Architectural Historians. Journal, 14:18–25, Mar. 1955. illus.

Buildings designed 1848–83.

4269 ———. The domestic architecture of Detlef Lienau, a conservative Victorian. Doctoral Dissertation, New York University, 1958.

1850–57, New York.

McComb, John, Jr. (1763–1853)

4270 McCOMB, JOHN, JR. Diary of John McComb, Jr. American Architect, 93:15, Jan. 11, 1908.

4271 WILDE, EDWARD S. John McComb, Jr., architect. American Architect, 94:49–53, 57–63, Aug. 1908.

McIntire, Samuel (1757–1811)

4272 DYER, WALTER A. Samuel McIntire, master carpenter. House Beautiful, 37:65–69, Feb. 1915. illus.

4273 KIMBALL, SIDNEY FISKE. Estimate of McIntire. Antiques, 21:23–25, 1932. illus.

4274 NEWCOMB, REXFORD. Samuel McIntire, Early American architect. Architect, 9:37–43, Oct. 1927. illus.

4275 PRATT, RICHARD H. McIntire, the Colonial carpenter. House and Garden, 51:108, 158, 162, 164, Feb. 1927. illus.

4276 SWAN, MABEL M. Revised estimate of McIntire. Antiques, 20:338–43, Dec. 1931. illus.

Mazzuchelli, Father Samuel C. (b. 1806)

4277 Sister of Santa Clara College. An Iowa pioneer. Annals of Iowa, ser. 3, 6:282–88. illus.

Mills, Robert (1718–1855)

4278 CLARK, ALLEN C. Robert Mills architect and engineer. Columbia Historical Society. Records, 40–41:1–32, 1940.

4279 EVANS, RICHARD XAVIER (ed.). Daily journal of Robert Mills, Baltimore, 1816. Maryland Historical Magazine, 30:257–71, 1935.

Excerpts from the MS in the Library of Congress.

4280 GALL, MARGARET. Mills, the master builder. South Carolina Magazine, 13:12–13, 60–61, Jan. 1950. illus.

Architectural activities in South Carolina and the District of Columbia, 1800–1855.

4281 GALLAGHER, MRS. H. M. PIERCE. Robert Mills, America's first native architect. Architectural Record, 65:387–93, 478–84, Apr., May 1929; 66:67–72, July 1929. illus.

4282 ———. Robert Mills, architect and engineer. Architectural Record, 40:584–86, Dec. 1916. illus.

4283 ———. Robert Mills, architect of the Washington Monument, 1781–1855. N. Y., Columbia University Press, 1935. 233p. illus.

4284 HALL, L. Mills, Strickland, and Walter: their adventures in a world of science. Magazine of Art, 40:266–71, Nov. 1947. illus.

4285 NEWCOMB, REXFORD. Robert Mills, American Greek Revivalist. Architect, 9:697–99, Mar. 1928. illus.

4286 WILSON, CHARLES C. Robert Mills, architect. Columbia, University of South Carolina, Bulletin 77, Feb. 1919.

Renwick, James (1818–95)

4287 MCKENNA, ROSALIE THORNE. James Renwick, Jr., and the Second Empire style in the United States. Magazine of Art, 44:97–101, Mar. 1951. illus. Work of 1858–69.

Rhoads, Samuel (1711–84)

4288 KOCHER, A. LAWRENCE. Handbooks of Samuel Rhoads, carpenter-builder. Architectural Record, 50:507–9, Dec. 1921.

Shryock, Gideon (1802–80)

4289 NEWCOMB, REXFORD. Gideon Shryock — pioneer Greek Revivalist of the Middle West. Kentucky State Historical Society. Register, 26:221–35, Sept. 1928. illus.

4290 ———. Gideon Shryock — pioneer Greek Revivalist of the West. Architect, 11:41–46, Oct. 1928. illus.

Sloan, Samuel (1815–84)

4291 COOLIDGE, HAROLD NORMAN, JR. Samuel Sloan (1815–1884), architect. Doctoral Dissertation, University of Pennsylvania, 1963.

Strickland, William (ca. 1787–1854)

4292 ADDISON, AGNES. Latrobe vs. Strickland. American Society of Architectural Historians. Journal, 2:26–29, July 1942.

4293 ———. Progress of studies on William Strickland, architect. American Society of Architectural Historians. Journal, 2:33–34, Apr. 1942.

4294 GILCHRIST, AGNES ADDISON. William Strickland, architect and engineer, 1788–1854. Philadelphia, University of Pennsylvania Press, 1950. 145p. illus.

4295 ———. William Strickland: architect of the university, 1829. General Magazine and Historical Chronicle, 54:50–59, Autumn 1951.

4296 GILLIAMS, E. LESLIE. A pioneer American architect. Architectural Record, 23:123–35, Feb. 1908. illus.

4297 NEWCOMB, REXFORD. William Strickland, American Greek Revivalist. Architect, 10:453–58, July 1928. illus.

4298 [Obituary.] American Philosophical Society. Proceedings, 6:28–32, 1859.

Tefft, Thomas Alexander (1826–59)

4299 WRISTON, BARBARA. The architecture of Thomas Tefft. Rhode Island School of Design. Bulletin, 28:37–45, Nov. 1940. illus.

4300 ———. Thomas Tefft, progressive Rhode Islander. Rhode Island Historical Society. Collections, 34:60–61, Apr. 1941. illus.

Thornton, William (1759–1828)

4301 BROWN, GLENN. DR. William Thornton, architect. Architectural Record, 6:53–70, July–Sept. 1896. illus.

4302 CLARK, ALLEN C. Dr. and Mrs. William Thornton. Columbia Historical Society. Records, 18:144–208, 1915.

4303 HUNT, G. H. William Thornton and John Fitch. Nation, 98:602–3, May 21, 1914.

4304 NEWCOMB, REXFORD. Doctor William Thornton, Early American amateur architect. Architect, 9:559–63, Feb. 1928. illus.

4305 RUSK, WILLIAM SENER. William Thornton, architect. Pennsylvania History, 2:86–98, 1935.

Town, Ithiel (1784–1844)

4306 KELLY, JOHN FREDERICK. Forgotten incident in the life of Ithiel Town. Old-Time New England, 31:62–71, Jan. 1941. illus.

4307 NEWCOMB, REXFORD. Ithiel Town of New Haven and New York. Architect, 11:519–23, Feb. 1929. illus.

4308 NEWTON, ROGER HALE. Town and Davis, architects. N. Y., Columbia University Press, 1942. 315p. illus.

4309 SEYMOUR, GEORGE DUDLEY. Ithiel Town — architect. Art and Progress. 3:714–16, Sept. 1912. illus.

Trumbull, John (1756–1843)

4310 SIZER, THEODORE. John Trumbull, amateur architect. Society of Architectural Historians. Journal, 8:1–6, July–Dec. 1949. illus.

Upjohn, Richard (1802–78)

4311 [Obituary.] American Architect and Building News, Aug. 24, 1878.

4312 UPJOHN, EVERARD MILLER. Richard Upjohn, architect and churchman. N. Y., Columbia University Press, 1939. 243p. illus.

Walter, Thomas Ustick (1804–87)

4313 MASON, C. G., JR. Memoir of the late Thomas Ustick Walter. American Institute of Architects. Proceedings, 1889.

4314 NEWCOMB, REXFORD. Thomas Ustick Walter. Architect, 10:585–89, Aug. 1928. illus.

4315 RUSK, WILLIAM SENER. Thomas U. Walter and his works. Americana, 33:151–79, Apr. 1939. illus.
Includes bibliography.

Willard, Soloman (1783–1861)

4316 WHEILDEN, WILLIAM WILLDER. Memoir of Soloman Willard, architect and superintendent of the Bunker Hill Monument. Boston, Bunker Hill Monument Association, 1865. 272p. illus.

Young, Ammi B. (1799–1874)

4317 MORRIS, EDWIN BATEMAN. Ammi B. Young. American Institute of Architects. Journal, 1:69–71, Feb. 1944. illus.

4318 OVERBY, O. R. Ammi B. Young in the Connecticut Valley. Society of Architectural Historians. Journal, 19:119–23, Oct. 1960. illus.

Bibliographies

In addition to those listed below extensive bibliographies appear in many of the titles listed by location. See also the standard indices: e.g., Art Index, Industrial Arts Index, Poole's Index to Periodical Literature, Readers' Guide to Periodical Literature, *and* Subject Index to Periodicals.

4319 AMERICAN ASSOCIATION OF ARCHITECTURAL BIBLIOGRAPHERS. Papers, 1965. v. 1——.
William B. O'Neal, ed., University of Virginia Press.

4320 AMERICAN LIBRARY ASSOCIATION. Sources for reproductions of works of art. American Library Association. Bulletin, 30:287–99, Apr. 1936.
Compiled by A. L. A. Visual Methods Committee.

4321 ANDREWS, CHARLES M. Guide to the manuscript materials for the history of the United States to 1783, in the British Museum, in minor London archives, and in the libraries of Oxford and Cambridge. Washington, D. C., Carnegie Institute, 1908.

4322 ——. Guide to the materials for American history, to 1783, in the Public Record Office of Great Britain. Washington, D. C., Carnegie Institute, 1912, 1914.

4323 ARCHITECTURAL BOOKS 1760. Society of Architectural Historians. Journal, 12:28, Oct. 1953.

4324 BACH, RICHARD FRANZ. Bibliography of the literature of Colonial architecture. Architectural Record, 38:382, Sept. 1915; 39:92–93, 388–89, Jan., Apr. 1916; 40:188–89, 582–83, Aug., Dec. 1916; 41:189, 472–74, Feb., May 1917; 42:89–91, 185–88, 283–84, July, Aug., Sept. 1917; Addenda for 1917, 44:177–80, Aug. 1918.

4325 ——. Books on Colonial architecture. Architectural Record, 38:281–86, 379–82, 592–94, 690–93, Aug., Sept., Nov., Dec. 1915; 39:89–93, 186–90, 292–94, 384–89, 568–74, Jan., Feb., Mar., Apr., June 1916; 40:89–92, 185–89, 279–81, 493–94, 578–83, July, Aug., Sept., Nov., Dec. 1916; 41:84–87, 187–89, 279–85, 373–74, 470–74, 566–71, Jan., Feb., Mar., Apr., May, June 1917; 42:88–91, 185–88, 283–84, 486–91, July, Aug., Sept., Nov. 1917; Addenda for 1917, 44:85–90, 175–80, July, Aug. 1918

4326 ———. Early American architecture and the allied arts. Architectural Record, 59:265–73, 328–34, 483–88, 525–32, Mar., Apr., May, June 1926; 60:65–70, July 1926; 63:577–80, June 1928; 64:70–72, 150–52, 190–92, July, Aug., Sept. 1928.

The allied arts here include glassware, metalwork, pottery, textiles, and furniture.

4327 BEERS, HENRY PUTNEY. Bibliographies in American history. N. Y., H. W. Wilson, 1942. 487p.

4328 [Bibliography of New England.] New England Quarterly, v. 1, Jan. 1928———.

Published in at least one issue a year, covers all topics concerning New England.

4329 BOSSERMAN, J. NORWOOD; NICHOLS, F. D.; AND O'NEAL, W. B. Index of American architectural drawings before 1900. Charlottesville, Va., American Association of Architectural Bibliographers, University of Virginia Press, 1957. 24p.

Supplement, 1958.

4330 BOSTON. PUBLIC LIBRARY. Catalogue of books referring to architecture, construction and decoration. Boston, The Trustees, 1894. 150p.

4331 BOYD, J. P. A new guide to the indispensable sources of Virginia history. William and Mary Quarterly, 3rd ser. 15:3–13, 1958.

An account of the Virginia Colonial Records Project.

4332 BRADFORD, THOMAS LINDSLEY. The bibliographer's manual of American history, containing an account of all state, territory, town and county histories relating to the United States of North America, with verbatim copies of their titles, and useful bibliographical notes . . . and with an exhaustive index by titles, and an index by states. Philadelphia, Henkels, 1907. 2v.

4333 BROWN, GLENN (comp.). American Institute of Architects. Quarterly Bulletin, v. 1–13, 1900–1912.

Contains an index of literature from the publications of architectural societies and periodicals on architecture and allied subjects.

4334 CHARLES, B. Accession of architectural library of Herbert Browne by the Society for the Preservation of New England Antiquities. Old-Time New England, 38:6–12, July 1947. illus.

4335 CHICAGO. ART INSTITUTE . . . RYERSON LIBRARY. Index to art periodicals, compiled in Ryerson Library, Art Institute of Chicago. Boston, G. K. Hall, 1962. 11v.

4336 COLUMBIA UNIVERSITY. AVERY ARCHITECTURAL LIBRARY. Catalogue of the Avery Architectural Library. N. Y., Library of Columbia College, 1895. 1139p.

4337 COOK, RUTH V. Current bibliography in architectural history. American Society of Architectural Historians. Journal, v. 1, no. 1, Jan. 1941 and succeeding numbers.

An invaluable list including all important items, European and American. Cross-indexed geographically and chronologically.

4338 CRICK, B. R., AND ALMAN, MIRIAM (eds.) ; BEALES, H. L. (general supervisor). A guide to manuscripts relating to America in Great Britain and Ireland. London, Oxford University Press, 1961. 667p.

Published for the British Association for American Studies. Gives location and brief description of manuscripts in Great Britain and Ireland on the history and literature of the American Colonies and the United States.

4339 FOWLER, LAWRENCE HALL, AND BAER, ELIZABETH. Fowler Architectural Collection of the Johns Hopkins University; catalogue. Baltimore, Evergreen House Foundation, 1961. 383p.

4340 Glossary of architectural and antiquarian terms. House Beautiful, 55:676; 56:52, 144, 240, 356, 484, 600; 57:52, 148, 264, 396, 564, 602, 604, June 1924— May 1925. illus.

4341 GREENE, STEPHEN. An annotated list of 50 bridge books relating primarily to covered bridges. Brattleboro, Vt., Book Cellar, 1960. 7p.

4342 GRIFFIN, GRACE GARDNER. Guide to manuscripts relating to American history in British depositories reproduced for the Division of Manuscripts of the Library of Congress. Washington, D. C., Library of Congress, 1946.

4343 ―――― (ed.). Writings on American history. American Historical Association. Annual Report, 1902, 1903, 1906–37.

The basic listing in this field. Appears about five years late.

4344 Guide to the items relating to American history in the Reports of the English Historical Manuscripts Commission and their Appendices. Annual Report of the American Historical Association, 1899. Washington, D. C., Government Printing Office, 1899. pp. 611–700.

4345 Guide to the material in the National Archives. Washington, D. C., Government Printing Office, 1940. 303p.

4346 HALE, RICHARD W., JR. Guide to photocopied historical material in the United States and Canada. Ithaca, N. Y., Cornell University Press for the American Historical Association, 1961. 241p.

4347 HAMLIN, SARAH H. J. Some articles of architectural interest published in American periodicals prior to 1851. Appendix B in Talbot Hamlin's *Greek Revival Architecture in America*, London, Oxford University Press, 1944, pp. 356–82.

4348 HAMLIN, TALBOT FAULKNER. Architectural research in America. Art in America, 33:182–92, Oct. 1945. illus.

4349 ――――. Bibliography of American architecture. N. Y., Avery Library, *ca.* 1935.

4350 HISTORIC AMERICAN BUILDINGS SURVEY. Catalog of the measured drawings and photographs of the Survey in the Library of Congress, comprising additions since March 1, 1941. Washington, D. C., Government Printing Office, 1959. illus.

First edition, 1938, later edition, 1941.

4351 ————. Chicago and nearby Illinois areas; list of measured drawings, photographs and written documentation in the Survey, 1966. Park Forest, Ill., Prairie School Press, 1966.

4352 HISTORICAL RECORDS SURVEY, DIVISION OF PROFESSIONAL AND SERVICE PROJECTS ADMINISTRATION. Guide to manuscript depositories in:

Florida	New Hampshire
Illinois	New Jersey
Iowa	New York (City and State)
Louisiana	Rhode Island
Massachusetts	Tennessee
Michigan	United States
Minnesota	Wisconsin
Missouri	Worcester (Mass.) Historical
Nebraska	Society

4353 HITCHCOCK, HENRY-RUSSELL. American architectural books; a list of books, portfolios, and pamphlets on architecture and related subjects published in America before 1895. Minneapolis, University of Minnesota Press, 1962. 130p.
Reprint. Other editions, 1938–40, 1946.

4354 HUTH, HANS. Preservationism: a selected bibliography. American Society of Architectural Historians. Journal, 1, no. 3–4:33–45, July–Oct. 1941.
For all countries.

4355 ILLINOIS, UNIVERSITY OF. LIBRARY. Printed books on architecture, 1485–1805; an exhibition of selected works held May 10—June 10, 1960 in the University of Illinois Library at Urbana, arranged by Helen Margaret Reynolds. A brief history and a catalog of the exhibition by Ernest Allen Connally. Urbana, Ill., Adah Patton Memorial Fund, 1960. 39p. illus.

4356 Interior architecture and decoration; a selected list of references. New York Public Library. Bulletin, 43:87–112, 396–404, Feb., May 1939.
Also issued as a separate publication by American Institute of Decorators.

4357 KAPLAN, MILTON (comp.). Pictorial Americana; a select list of photographic negatives in the Prints and Photographs Division of the Library of Congress. Washington, D. C., Library of Congress, Prints and Photographs Division, 1945. 38 leaves.

4358 KAUFFMAN, HENRY J. Literature on log architecture. Dutchman, 7:30–34, Fall 1955. illus.
Review of publications since ca. 1920.

4359 KOCHER, A. LAWRENCE. Library of the architect. Architectural Record, 56:123–28, 218–24, 316–20, 517–20, Aug., Sept., Oct., Dec. 1924; 57:29–32, 125–28, 221–24, 317–20, Jan., Feb., Mar., Apr. 1925.

4360 LANCASTER, CLAY. Builders' guide and plan books and American architecture. Magazine of Art, 41:17–22, Jan. 1948. illus.

4361 MEEKS, C. L. V. Books and buildings, 1449–1949: one hundred great architectural books most influential in shaping the architecture of the Western world. Society of Architectural Historians. Journal, 8:55–67, Jan. 1949. Also: Progressive Architecture, 30:114ff., Sept. 1949.

4362 ———. Current research in architectural history; report. Society of Architectural Historians. Journal, 8:86–89, Jan. 1949.

4363 METROPOLITAN MUSEUM OF ART. Photographs of American architecture, painting, sculpture and decorative arts; a list of photographers and dealers from whom the museum has purchased photographs. N. Y., Metropolitan Museum of Art, 1937. 28p.

A list of dealers in photographs also appeared in Richard F. Bach, *Books on Colonial Architecture*, part 7 — photographs. Architectural Record, 42:283–84, Sept. 1917.

4364 MUMFORD, LEWIS. Architecture. Chicago, American Library Association, 1926. 34p.

Reading with a Purpose series, no. 23.

4365 PARK, H. List of architectural books available in America before the Revolution. Society of Architectural Historians. Journal, 20:115–30, Oct. 1961. illus.

4366 PAULLIN, CHARLES O., AND PAXSON, FREDERIC L. Guide to the materials in London Archives for the history of the United States since 1783. Washington, D. C., Carnegie Institute, 1914.

4367 PETERSON, CHARLES E. List of published writings of special interest in the study of historic architecture of the Mississippi Valley. St. Louis, Mo., U. S. Department of the Interior, National Park Service, Historic American Buildings Survey, Central Unit, 1940. 29p. Mimeographed.

4368 ROOS, FRANK JOHN, JR. Writings on Early American architecture. Columbus, Ohio State University Press, 1943. 271p.

Current volume is a revised and enlarged edition of this title.

4369 SOCIETY OF ARCHITECTURAL HISTORIANS. Preliminary report and listings of special works; compiled by J. C. Van Derpool. Society of Architectural Historians. Journal, 8:68–85, Jan. 1949.

4370 UNITED STATES. LIBRARY OF CONGRESS. DIVISION OF MANUSCRIPTS. List of manuscript collections in the Library of Congress to July 1931, by Curtis Wiswell Garrison. . . . Washington, D. C., Government Printing Office, 1932.

Reprinted from *Annual Report of American Historical Association*, for 1930, pp. 123–249.

4371 ———. Manuscripts in public and private collections in the United States. Washington, D. C., Government Printing Office, 1924. 98p.

4372 UNITED STATES. NATIONAL PARK SERVICE. Historic American Buildings Survey: catalogue of the measured drawings and photographs of the Survey in the Library of Congress, Mar. 1, 1941. Washington, D. C., Government Printing Office, 1941. 470p. illus.

4373 ———. Park and recreation progress. Washington, D. C., Department of the Interior, 1938——.

Yearbook, includes bibliography.

4374 WALL, ALEXANDER J. Books on architecture printed in America, 1775–1830. In bibliographical essays, a tribute to Wilberforce Eames. Cambridge, Mass., Harvard University Press, 1924. pp. 299–311.

4375 WATKINS, E. W. 156 Early American books on architecture and allied subjects in bequest of W. Gedney Beatty. New York Historical Society. Quarterly Bulletin, 26:11, Jan. 1942.

4376 WITHEY, HENRY F., AND WITHEY, ELSIE RATHBURN. Biographical dictionary of American architects (deceased). Los Angeles, New Age Publishing Co., [1956]. 678p.

4377 YOUTZ, PHILIP N. American life in architecture. Chicago, American Library Association, 1932. 47p.
Reading with a Purpose series, no. 55.

Index

Page numbers are in italics.

Harrison, Peter, p. *12*; 722, 990, 994, 1523, 1525, 1544, 4215–20
Harrodsburg, Ky., 2827–32
Hart, Charles Henry, 4218
Hart, Katherine, 3268
Hartford, Conn., 266, 284, 606, 635, 642, 701–5
Hartsook, Mrs. F. P., 3902
Hartsville, Tenn., 3235
Harvard University, 953, 1013, 1021, 1029, 1036, 1041, 1045
Harvey, Evangeline Lukena, 2257
Harvey, Frederick L., 2614
Harvey, Max, 3817
Harwood house. *See* Hammond-Harwood house
Hasbrouck house, New Paltz, N. Y., 2141
Hasbrouck house, Newburgh, N. Y., 2044, 2046
Haskell, Arthur C., p. *7*; 518
Haskell, Daniel C., 169
Haskell house, West Gloucester, Mass., 1116
Hastings, Helen M., 1826, 2135
Hatch, Charles E., Jr., 3588, 3589, 3704
Hatcher, Harlan Henthorne, 4017
Hatfield, Mass., 1124
Hathaway house, Salem, Mass., 1273
Haven house, Framingham, Mass., 1114
Haven house, Portsmouth, N. H., 1464
Haverford College, 2214
Haverhill, Mass., 1125–27
Haverhill, N. H., 1433
Haverstick, Horace, 2375
Haverstraw, N. Y., 1842
Haviland, John, p. *13*; 2423, 2428, 4221–24
Havinghurst, Walter, 3737
Hawes, E. M., 4096
Hawkes, Nathan Mortimer, 1150
Hawks, John, 3137, 3138
Hawthorne house. *See* Wayside, Concord, Mass.
Hay, William, 3536
Hayden, Barbara E., 1277
Hayes, Francis W., Jr., 3475
Hayes, John Russell, 1629
Hayes, Lyman Simpson, 1609

Hayes, Marian, 519
Hayes, William Danforth, 1609
Hayes house, Chester County, Pa., 2259
Hayes house, Montgomery County, Md., 3056
Hayward, Arthur H., 381
Haywood Hall, Raleigh, N. C., 3144
Hazard house, Newport, R. I., 1541, 1542
Hazelton, George Cochrane, Jr., 2697
Head Spring, Jefferson County, W. Va., 3712
Head Tide, Me., 803
Heatwole, C. J., 3590, 4231
Hegeman, Jeannette, 4157
Heidgerd, William, 2136
Heiman, Adolphus, 3252
Heintzelman, John Cranston, 3916
Hemphill, William Edwin, 3326, 3327, 3591
Hempstead, N. Y., 1843
Henderson, Archibald, 3113
Henderson, Tex., 3290
Hennessy, William G., 1408, 1470
Henrico County, Va., 284, 385, 2445, 2539, 3534–52, 4249
Henry, Patrick, 3436
Hensel, William Uhler, 2280, 2281
Herculaneum, Mo., 3981
Hering, Oswald, 3096
Hermann, Mo., 3982
Hermitage, Nashville, Tenn., 2511, 3241, 3246, 3248, 3249
Herring, Eliza A., 2820
Hersey, Carl K., 2071
Hersey, G. L., 148
Hersey, Horatio Brooks, 908
Hertel, Fredrika W., 2034
Hertz, Solange Strong, 3637
Hetfield house, Elizabeth, N. J., 1709
Hewitt, Edward Shepard, 203
Heydinger, Earl J., 2229
Heyward, D., 3181
Heyward-Washington house, Charleston, S. C., 3167, 3182
Hibbard house, Concord, Vt., 1601
Hickey, James T., 3802
Hicks, Dwight B., 3904
Hicks house, Cambridge, Mass., 1030–32

Perley, Sidney, 1083, 1298, 1363
Perlman, Bernard B., 3028
Perrin, Richard W. E., 4136–38
Perry, Armstrong, 3700
Perry, Arthur Latham, 1382
Perry, Matilda Hardendorf, 1686
Perry, W. G., 3605
Perry Hall, Baltimore, Md., 2999
Perth Amboy, N. J., 1737, 1738
Peter, Grace Glasgow Ecker, 2649
Peterboro, N. H., 1443
Peterich, Gerda, 1771
Peters, Richard, Jr., 2398
Petersburg, Va. See Dinwiddie County
Petersen, Hegen, 268
Petersen, William John, 3895
Petersham, Mass., 1230
Peterson, Arthur Everett, 1941
Peterson, Charles E., 110–12, 161–63, 2206, 2258, 2443–45, 2529, 2530, 3104, 3763, 3764, 3967, 3992–94, 3998–4000, 4367
Pettee, Julia, 744
Pevsner, N., 490
Philadelphia, Pa., 219, 255, 385, 394, 2207, 2214, 2302–2468
Philbrick, Julia A., 1084
Philbrick house, Weare, N. H., 1474
Philippi, W. Va., 3715
Philipse Castle, Tarrytown, N. Y., 2115, 2117, 2118, 2153
Philipse manor house, Yonkers, N. Y., 385, 2153, 2165–71
Phillips, J. H., 537
Phillips, James Duncan, 1299, 1300
Phillips, Julia Bowles, 1328
Philosophical Hall, Philadelphia, 2434
Phinney, A. H., 2743
Phippsburg, Me., 814
Pickens, Buford L., 2873
Pickering, Ernest, 231
Pickwick, Hazel, 1437
Pierce, Mrs. Melusina Fay, 2012
Pierce-Nichols house, Salem, Mass., 1295
Pierson, William Harvey, 62, 889
Pigeon Cove, Mass., 1231
Pike-Haven-Foster house, Framingham, Mass., 1114

Pike house, Little Rock, Ark., 2564
Pike-Streeter Tavern, Waterford, Vt., 1615
Pilkington, Walter, 1812
Pindar, Peter Augustus, 397, 661, 662
Pineapple house, Salem, Mass., 1301
Pingree house, Salem, Mass., 1316
Pinkham, Charles E., 834
Pinkowski, Edward, 2485
Pintard, Mrs., 1976
Piper, Adaline D., 3677, 3678
Piper, Fred Smith, 1146
Pirtle, Alfred, 2806, 2851
Piscataqua River Valley, 1452
Pishel, Robert Gordon, 3105
Pitman house, Newport, R. I., 1530
Pittsburgh, Pa., 2469–80
Place, Charles A., 624, 998, 1143, 4191
Placzek, Adolf, 2013
Plaistow, N. H., 1444
Planning, city, 23, 64, 74, 104, 523, 643
Planning, city, Bethlehem, Pa., 2237
Planning, city, Tidewater colonies, 2532
Planning, city, Washington, D. C., 2576, 2578, 2579, 2607, 2608, 2625, 2631, 2637, 2646–48, 2650
Pleasant Hill, Ky., 1898, 2858
Plum Grove, Iowa City, Iowa, 3898
Plymouth, Mass., 1232–41
Podbury-Ives house, Stotham, Mass., 1336
Poe house, Richmond, Va., 3543
Poellot, Daniel E., 3757
Pohick Meeting House, Alexandria, Va., 284
Pohl, Frederick J., 1536
Polk, George W., 3238
Polley, G. Henry, 343
Pond, Fern Nance, 3795
Pontalba buildings, New Orleans, La., 2907, 2916
Poole, Martha Sprigg, 3055
Poole, S. Alicia, 3943
Poole house, New York City, 1953
Poor, Alfred Easton, 538, 863
Poore, Alfred, 1121
Pope, John Russell, 344
Poplar Forest, Bedford County, Va., 3423, 3424, 3426, 3427